La Vend

Anthony Trollope

Alpha Editions

This edition published in 2024

ISBN : 9789362921048

Design and Setting By
Alpha Editions
www.alphaedis.com
Email - info@alphaedis.com

Contents

VOLUME I

CHAPTER I.
THE POITEVINS.

The history of France in 1792 has been too fully written, and too generally read to leave the novelist any excuse for describing the state of Paris at the close of the summer of that year. It is known to every one that the palace of Louis XVI was sacked on the 10th of August. That he himself with his family took refuge in the National Assembly, and that he was taken thence to the prison of the Temple.

The doings on the fatal 10th of August, and the few following days had, however, various effects in Paris, all of which we do not clearly trace in history. We well know how the Mountain became powerful from that day; that from that day Marat ceased to shun the light, and Danton to curb the licence of his tongue that then, patriotism in France began to totter, and that, from that time, Paris ceased to be a fitting abode for aught that was virtuous, innocent, or high-minded; but the steady march of history cannot stop to let us see the various lights in which the inhabitants of Paris regarded the loss of a King, and the commencement of the first French Republic.

The Assembly, though it had not contemplated the dethronement of the King, acquiesced in it; and acted as it would have done, had the establishment of a republic been decreed by a majority of its members. The municipality had determined that the King should fall, and, of course, rejoiced in the success of its work; and history plainly marking the acquiescence of the Assembly, and the activity of the city powers, naturally passes over the various feelings excited in different circles in Paris, by the overthrow of the monarchy.

Up to that period there was still in Paris much that was high, noble, and delightful. The haute noblesse had generally left the country; but the haute noblesse did not comprise the better educated, or most social families in Paris. Never had there been more talent, more wit, or more beauty in Paris than at the commencement of 1792; never had literary acquirement been more fully appreciated in society, more absolutely necessary in those who were ambitious of social popularity.

There were many of this class in Paris who had hitherto watched the progress of the Revolution with a full reliance in the panacea it was to afford for human woes; many who had sympathized with the early demands of the Tiers État; who had rapturously applauded the Tennis Court oath; who had taken an enthusiastic part in the fête of the Champ de Mars; men who had taught themselves to believe that sin, and avarice, and selfishness were about to be banished from the world by the lights of philosophy; but whom the rancour of the Jacobins, and the furious licence of the city authorities had now robbed of their golden hopes. The dethronement of the King, totally severed many such from the revolutionary party. They found that their high aspirations had been in vain; that their trust in reason had been misplaced, and that the experiment to which they had committed themselves had failed; disgusted, broken-spirited, and betrayed they left the city in crowds, and with few exceptions, the intellectual circles were broken up.

A few of the immediate friends of the King, a few ladies and gentlemen, warmly devoted to the family of Louis XVI, remained in Paris. At the time when the King was first subjected to actual personal restraint, a few young noblemen and gentlemen had formed themselves into a private club, and held their sittings in the Rue Vivienne. Their object was to assist the King in the difficulties with which he was surrounded, and their immediate aim was to withdraw him from the metropolis; Louis' own oft-repeated indecision alone prevented them from being successful. These royalists were chiefly from the province of Poitou, and as their meetings gradually became known and talked of in Paris, they were called the Poitevins.

They had among them one or two members of the Assembly, but the club chiefly consisted of young noblemen attached to the Court, or of officers in the body-guard of the King; their object, at first, had been to maintain, undiminished, the power of the throne; but they had long since forgotten their solicitude for the King's power, in their anxiety for his safety and personal freedom.

The storming of the Tuilleries, and the imprisonment of Louis, completely destroyed their body as a club; but the energy of each separate member was raised to the highest pitch. The Poitevins no longer met in the Rue Vivienne, but they separated with a determination on the part of each individual royalist to use every effort to replace the King.

There were three young men in this club, who were destined to play a conspicuous part in the great effort about to be made, in a portion of France, for the restitution of the monarchy; their fathers had lived within a few miles of each other, and though of different ages, and very different dispositions, they had come to Paris together since the commencement of the revolution.

M. de Lescure was a married man, about twenty-seven years of age, of grave and studious habits, but nevertheless of an active temperament. He was humane, charitable, and benevolent: his strongest passion was the love of his fellow-creatures; his pure heart had glowed, at an early age, with unutterable longings for the benefits promised to the human race by the school of philosophy from which the revolution originated. Liberty and fraternity had been with him principles, to have realized which he would willingly have sacrificed his all; but at the commencement of the revolution he had seen with horror the successive encroachments of the lower classes, and from conscience had attached himself to the Crown. Hitherto he had been without opportunity of showing the courage for which he was afterwards so conspicuous; he did not even himself know that he was a brave man; before, however, his career was ended, he had displayed the chivalry of a Bayard, and performed the feats of a Duguescin. A perfect man, we are told, would be a monster; and a certain dry obstinacy of manner, rather than of purpose, preserved de Lescure from the monstrosity of perfection. Circumstances decreed that the latter years of his life should be spent among scenes of bloodshed; that he should be concerned in all the horrors of civil war; that instruments of death should be familiar to his hands, and the groans of the dying continually in his ears. But though the horrors of war were awfully familiar to him, the harshness of war never became so; he spilt no blood that he could spare, he took no life that he could save. The cruelty of his enemies was unable to stifle the humanity of his heart; even a soldier and a servant of the republic became his friend as soon as he was vanquished.

Two young friends had followed M. de Lescure to Paris—Henri de Larochejaquelin and Adolphe Denot. The former was the son of the Marquis de Larochejaquelin, and the heir of an extensive property in Poitou; M. de Lescure and he were cousins, and the strictest friendship had long existed between the families. Young Larochejaquelin was of a temperament very different from that of his friend: he was eager, impetuous, warm-tempered, and fond of society; but he had formed his principles on those of M. de Lescure. The love of his fellow-creatures was not with him the leading passion of his heart, as it was with the other; but humanity had early been instilled into him as the virtue most necessary to cultivate, and he consequently fully appreciated and endeavoured to imitate the philanthropy of his friend.

At the time alluded to, Henri de Larochejaquelin was not quite twenty years of age. He was a lieutenant in the body-guard immediately attached to the King's person, and called the "Garde du Roi." At any other period, he would hardly yet have finished his education, but the revolution gave a precocious manhood to the rising generation. Henri's father, moreover, was very old; he had not married till late in life; and the young Marquis, when he was only seventeen, had to take on himself the guardianship of his sister Agatha, and the management of the paternal property. The old man was unable to leave his chair, and though he still retained his senses, was well pleased to give up to the son of his old age the rights and privileges which in the course of nature would descend to him.

Without being absolutely handsome, young Larochejaquelin was of a very prepossessing appearance. He was tall and robust, well made, and active. Though he had not attained that breadth of shoulder, and expansion of chest, which a few years would probably have given him, he had the perfect use of his limbs, and was full of health and youthful energy; his eyes were bright, and of a clear blue colour; his hair was light, and his upper lip could already boast that ornament which the then age, and his own position made allowable. He was a favourite with all who knew him—more so even than his friend de Lescure; and it is saying much in his favour to declare that a year's residence amongst all that was beautiful and charming in Paris, had hitherto done but little to spoil him.

Adolphe Denot was an orphan, but also possessed of a fair property in the province of Poitou. He had, when very young, been left to the guardianship of the Marquis de La Rochejaquelin, and had at intervals, during his holidays, and after he had left school, spent much of his time at Durbellière, the family residence of the La Rochejaquelins. Henri had of course contracted a close friendship with him; but this arose more from the position in which they were placed together, than a similarity of disposition. They were, indeed, very unlike; Adolphe was somewhat older than the other, but he had neither his manliness of manner nor strength of character; he was more ambitious to be popular, without the same capacity of making himself so: he had as much romantic love of poetical generosity, without the same forgetfulness of self to enable him to emulate in practice the characters, which he admired in description; he had much veneration for poetic virtue, though but little strength to accomplish practical excellence. He had, on leaving school, proclaimed himself to be an ardent admirer of Rousseau; he had been a warm partizan of the revolution, and had displayed a most devoted enthusiasm to his country at the fête of the Champ de Mars. Latterly, however, the circles which he mostly frequented in Paris had voted strong revolutionary ardour to be mauvais ton; a kind of modulated royalism, or rather Louis Seizeism, had become fashionable; and Adolphe Denot was not the man to remain wilfully out of the fashion. On the 10th of August, he was a staunch supporter of the monarchy.

Adolphe Denot was a much handsomer man than his friend; his features were better formed, and more regular; he had beautifully white teeth, an almost feminine mouth, a straight Grecian nose, and delicately small hands and feet; but he was vain of his person, and ostentatious; fond of dress and of jewellery. He was, moreover, suspicious of neglect, and vindictive when neglected; querulous of others, and intolerant of reproof himself; exigeant among men, and more than politely flattering among women. He was not, however, without talent, and a kind of poetic fecundity of language, which occasionally made him brilliant in society; it was, however, generally speaking, those who knew him least who liked him best.

Larochejaquelin, however, was always true to him; he knew that he was an orphan, without brother, sister, or relatives, and with the devotion of a real friend, he overlooked all his faults, and greatly magnified his talents. For

Henri's sake, M. de Lescure tolerated him, and the three were therefore much together; they came from the same country; they belonged to the same club; they had the same political sympathies; and were looked upon as dear and stedfast friends.

On the 10th of August, the King left the Tuilleries, and took refuge in the National Assembly; during the greater part of the night he remained there with his family. Early on the following morning, he was removed, under a guard, to the Feuillants; and on the 12th it was decided that he should be confined in the prison of the Temple.

It was on the morning of the 12th, that the last meeting of the little club of the Poitevins took place.

They met with throbbing hearts and blank faces; they all felt that evil days had come that the Revolution which had been so petted and caressed by the best and fairest in France, had become a beast of prey, and that war, anarchy, and misrule were at hand.

They sat waiting on the morning of the 12th, till they should learn the decision of the Assembly with regard to the King. De Lescure was there calm and grave, but with much melancholy in his countenance.

Larochejaquelin was there. Hot and eager, whispering plans for rescuing the King, to which the less resolute hardly dared to listen. Charette, the Prince de Talmont, d'Autachamps, Fleuriot, and others, all of whom now detested the Revolution, though they could not but feel the danger of proclaiming themselves royalists.

"Denot will be here directly," said La Rochejaquelin; "he is at the Assembly—they are not apt to be very tedious in their decisions."

"Danton has openly declared," said Fleuriot, "that the armed sections shall remain in revolt, unless the Assembly decree the abolition of the monarchy."

"Lafayette," said the Prince, "is the only man now who could save the country—if Lafayette will move, he might still save the throne."

"He could do nothing," said d'Autachamps, "but add himself to the ruins—the regiments, to a man, would side with the populace."

"I don't know," said Larochejaquelin, "I don't think so. See how our Swiss fought—could any men be more true to their officers or their colours? and do you think there are not thousands in the French army as true, as brave as they? If Lafayette would raise his hand, I for one would join him."

"Wait, Henri, wait," said de Lescure, "wait till you know whether Lafayette and the army will really be wanting to save the King. If Roland be still firm, and Vergniaud true to his principles, they may still quell the fury of the Jacobins—the moderate party has still a large majority in the Assembly."

"Roland and Vergniaud are both true," said Fleuriot, "but you will find, de Lescure, that they can do nothing but yield or go—they must vanish out of the Assembly and become nothing—or else they must go with the people."

"The people! How I hate that phrase, in the sense in which it is now used," said Larochejaquelin. "A mob of blood-thirsty ruffians wishes to overturn the throne—but what evidence have we that the people wish it."

"The people, Henri, have been taught to wish it," said de Lescure.

"No, Charles, the people of France have not been taught to wish it—with all the teaching they have had, they do not wish it—have they shewn any favour to the new priests whom the Revolution has sent to them; do they love much the Commissioners, who from time to time, come among them with the orders of the Assembly. Do the people in the Bocage wish it?—do they wish it in the Marais, Charette?—do they wish it in Anjou and Brittany? Danton, Robespierre, and Tallien wish it—the mob of Paris wishes it—but the people of France does not wish to depose their King."

"But unfortunately," said d'Autachamps, "it is Danton, Robespierre, and the mob of Paris who have now the supreme power, and for a time will have their way—they who are wise will lie by till the storm has blown over."

"And are we to remain quiet while we are robbed of every thing which we esteem as holy?" said Larochejaquelin; "are we all to acquiesce in the brutality of such men as Danton, for fear the mob of Paris should be too strong for us?"

"I for one, will not!" said Charette.

"Nor I," said Larochejaquelin—"not while I have a sword to draw, and an arm to use it. You are silent, Charles—is a Republic so much to your mind, that you have not a word, or even a wish for your King?"

"You are too talkative, Henri," replied the other; "will it not be well to think a little first before we proclaim definitively what we mean to do? We do not even know as yet in what position Louis XVI. may find himself tomorrow— he may be more firmly seated on his throne than he has been at any time since the Three Estates first met at Versailles."

As he ceased speaking, the door opened, and Adolphe Denot entered, hot with walking fast, and with his whole dress disordered by pushing through the dense masses of the crowd.

"Speak, Adolphe," said Henri, "have they decreed—has it come to the vote?"

"Are they still sitting?" said Fleuriot; "Danton, I am sure would not have yielded so soon as this:—if the chamber be closed, he must have been victorious."

"The King," said Denot, pausing for breath, "the King is to be taken to the Temple!"

There was a momentary silence among them all—their worst fears had been realized—the brute force of Paris had been triumphant. The firmness of Roland, the eloquence of Vergniaud, the patriotism of Guadet had been of no avail. The King of France—the heir of so long a line of royalty—the King, who had discarded the vices of his predecessors, and proved himself the friend of the people, was to be incarcerated in the worst prison in Paris by the vote of that very Assembly which he had himself called into existence.

"He is to be confined in the Temple," continued Denot, "with the Queen and the two children. The populace are mad; they would kill him, if they could lay their hands on him."

"Where are your hopes now, Charles?" said Larochejaquelin. "Is it yet time for us to proclaim what we are—is it yet time for us to move? or are we to set still, until Danton enrolls us in his list of suspected persons?"

No one immediately answered the appeal of the hot young loyalist, and after a moment or two de Lescure spoke.

"Adolphe, did you hear the words of the decree?"

"Again and again," said Denot. "I was at the door of the Assembly, and the decree was known to the crowd the moment the votes had been taken."

"But did you hear the exact words?"

"That Louis and his family should be imprisoned in the Temple," answered Denot.

"Did they say the King, or did they call him by his name?" asked de Lescure again. "Did they decree that the King should be imprisoned, or Louis Capet?"

As he spoke, the door again opened, and another member, who had been among the crowd, entered the room.

"Gentlemen," said he, "allow me the honour to congratulate you. Yon do not know your own happiness. You are no longer the burdened slaves of an effete monarchy; you are now the vigorous children of a young Republic."

"Vive le Roi, quand même," said Larochejaquelin, standing up in the middle of the room. "I am glad they have so plainly declared themselves; we are driven now to do the same. Prince, now is the time to stand by our King.

Charette, your hand; our dreams must now be accomplished. You will doubt no longer, Charles. Prudence herself would now feel that we have no longer aught to wait for."

"No—we must delay no longer," said Adolphe Denot. "A King is to be saved; every hour of delay is an hour of treason, while the King is in the hands of his enemies."

"A fine sentiment, Denot," said d'Autachamps; "but how will you avoid the treason?—how do you purpose to rescue his Majesty?"

"With my sword," said Adolphe, turning round shortly. "Do you doubt my will?"

"We only doubt your power, Adolphe," said de Lescure. "We only fear you may not be able to raise the standard of revolt against the armed sections of all Paris, backed by a decree of the Assembly."

"I can at any rate die in the attempt," replied Denot. "I cannot draw the breath of life from the atmosphere of a Republic! I will not live by the permission of Messieurs Danton and Robespierre."

"Whatever we do," said Fleuriot, "the club must be given up. We are known to be friendly to the King, and we are too weak to stand our ground; indeed, we should only incur useless danger by meeting here."

"And waste the time which we may well employ in the provinces," said Charette.

"You are right, Charette," said Rochejaquelin, whom the wildness of his friend Denot had a little sobered. "You are quite right—Paris is no longer a place for us. I will go back to the Bocage; there, at least, I may own among my neighbours that I am not a republican; there, perhaps, I may make some effort for my King—here I can make none. You will not stay in Paris, Charles, to hear unwashed revolutionists clatter of Louis Capet?"

"No, Henri, I also will return home. Charette is right. We should but waste our time in Paris, and be in danger. We shall probably be in safety in Poitou."

"Perhaps not in safety," said Henri. "We may, I trust, soon be in action."

"How in action?" said Fleuriot. "What do you intend to do?"

"To follow any one who will lead me to assist in restoring the King to his throne," replied Henri. "Let us, at any rate, retire to our provinces; and be assured that the National Assembly will soon hear of us."

The club was broken up; the young friends met no more in the Rue Vivienne. Within a week from the 10th of August, the denizens of the municipality had searched the rooms for any relics which might be discovered there indicatory of a feeling inimical to the Republic; their residences also were searched, and there were orders at the barriers that they should not pass out; but the future Vendean leaders had too quickly appreciated the signs of the time; they had gone before the revolutionary tribunal had had time to form itself. They were gone, and their names for a season were forgotten in Paris; but Henri Rochejaquelin was right—before long, the National Assembly did hear of them; before twelve months had passed, they were more feared by the Republic, than the allied forces of England, Austria, and Prussia.

CHAPTER II.
ST. FLORENT.

Nothing occurred in the provinces, subsequently called La Vendée, during the autumn or winter of 1792 of sufficient notice to claim a place in history, but during that time the feelings which afterwards occasioned the revolt in that country, were every day becoming more ardent. The people obstinately refused to attend the churches to which the constitutional clergy had been appointed; indeed, these pastors had found it all but impossible to live in the parishes assigned to them; no one would take them as tenants; no servants would live with them; the bakers and grocers would not deal with them; the tailors would not make their clothes for them, nor the shoemakers shoes. During the week they were debarred from all worldly commerce, and on Sundays they performed their religious ceremonies between empty walls.

The banished priests, on the other hand, who were strictly forbidden to perform any of the sacerdotal duties, continued among the trees and rocks to collect their own congregations undiminished in number, and much more than ordinarily zealous, in their religious duties; and with the licence which such sylvan chapels were found to foster, denunciations against the Republic, and prayers for the speedy restoration of the monarchy, were mingled with the sacred observances.

The execution of Louis, in January, 1793, greatly increased the attachment which was now felt in this locality to his family. In Nantes and Angers, in Saumur, Thouars, and other towns in which the presence of Republican forces commanded the adhesion of the inhabitants this event was commemorated by illuminations, but this very show of joy at so cruel a murder, more than the murder itself, acerbated the feelings both of the gentry and the peasants. They were given to understand that those who wished well to their country were now expected to show some sign of gratitude for what the blessed revolution had done for them—that those who desired to stand well with the Republic should rejoice openly at their deliverance from thraldom. In fact, those who lived in large towns, and who would not illuminate, were to be marked men—marked as secret friends to the monarchy—as inveterate foes to the Republic—and they were told that they were to be treated accordingly. Men then began to congregate in numbers round the churches, and in the village squares, and to ask each other whether they had better not act as enemies, if they were to be considered as enemies; to complain of their increasing poverty and diminished comfort; and to long for the coming time, when the King should enjoy his own again.

The feeling with the country gentry was very generally the same as with the peasantry, though hitherto they had openly expressed no opposition to the ruling Government. They had, however, been always elected to those situations which the leaders of the revolution had wished the people to fill exclusively with persons from their own ranks. They were chosen as mayors in the small towns, and were always requested to act as officers in the corps of the National Guards, which were formed in this, as in every other district of France. On this account the peculiar ill-will of the Republican Government was directed against them. In France, at that time, political inactivity was an impossibility. Revolt against the Republic, or active participation in its measures, was the only choice left to those who did not choose to fly their country, and many of the seigneurs of Anjou and Poitou would not adopt the latter alternative.

In March, the Commissaries of the Republic entered these provinces to collect from that district, its portion towards the levy of three hundred thousand men which had been ordered by the Convention. This was an intolerable grievance—it was not to be borne, that so many of their youths should be forcibly dragged away to fight the battles of the Republic—battles in which they would rather that the Republic should be worsted. Besides, every one would lose a relative, a friend, or a lover; the decree affected every individual in the district. The peasants declared that they would not obey the orders of the Convention—that they would not fight the battles of the Republic.

This was the commencement of the revolt. The troops of the Republic were, of course, put in motion to assist the officers who were entrusted with the carrying out of the conscription. There were garrisons in Nantes, in Anjou, and in Saumur; and detachments from these places were sent into the smaller towns and villages, into every mayoralty, to enforce the collection of the levy, and to take off with them the victims of the conscription. Among other places, an attempt was made to carry out the new law at St. Florent, and at this place was made the first successful resistance, by an armed force, to the troops of the Convention.

St. Florent is a small town on the south bank of the Loire, in the province of Anjou, and at the northern extremity of that district, now so well known by the name of La Vendée. It boasted of a weekly market, a few granaries for the storing of corn, and four yearly fairs for the sale of cattle. Its population and trade, at the commencement of the war, was hardly sufficient to entitle it to the name of a town; but it had early acquired some celebrity as a place in which the Republic was known to be very unpopular, and in which the attachment of the people to the throne was peculiarly warm.

Here the work of the conscription was commenced in silence. The lists were filled, and the names were drawn. No opposition was shown to the employés in this portion of their unpopular work. Indeed, it appears that no organized system of opposition had been planned; but the first attempt that was made to collect the unfortunate recruits upon whom the lots had fallen, was the signal for a general revolt. The first name on the list was that of Peter Berrier; and had Peter Berrier intended to prove himself a good citizen and a willing soldier, he should, without further call, have attended that day at the temporary barracks which had been established in St. Florent. But he had not done so, and there was nothing wonderful or unusual in this; for on all occasions of the kind many of the conscripts had to be sought out, and brought forth from the bosoms of their families, to which they retired, with a bashful diffidence as to their own peculiar fitness for martial glory. But in this instance not one of the chosen warriors obeyed the summons of the Convention, by attending at the barracks of St. Florent. Not one of the three hundred thousand men was there; and it was soon apparent to the colonel in command of the detachment, that he had before him the unpleasant duty of collecting one by one, from their different hiding-places, the whole contingent which the town of St. Florent was bound to supply.

Peter Berrier was the first on the list, and as it was well known that he was an ostler at a little auberge in the middle of the square, a corporal and a couple of soldiers was despatched to the house of entertainment to capture him; and the trio soon found that they would not have far to search, for Peter was standing at the gate of the inn yard, and with him three or four of his acquaintance—men equally well-known in St. Florent.

There was a sturdy farmer there of the better sort—a man who not only held a farm near the town, but had a small shop within it, for the sale of seeds and tools for planting—his name was Foret—and it was said that no man in St. Florent was more anxious for the restoration of the King. There was the keeper of the auberge himself, who seemed but little inclined to find fault with his servant, for the contumacious manner in which he treated the commands of the Convention; and there was the well-known postillion of St. Florent, the crack of whose whip was so welcome from Angers to Nantes, the sound of whose cheery voice was so warmly greeted at every hostelrie between those towns. The name of Cathelineau was not then so well known as it was some six months afterwards, but even then Cathelineau, the postillion, was the most popular man in St. Florent. He was the merriest among the mirthful, the friend of every child, the playmate of every lass in the town; but he was the comforter of those poorer than himself, and the solace of the aged and afflicted. He was the friend of the banished priest, and the trusted messenger of the royalist seigneur; all classes adored him, save those who sided with the Republic, and by them he had long been looked on as an open and declared enemy. St. Florent was justly proud of its postillion; and now that evil days were come upon the little town, that their priests were banished, and these young men called for to swell the armies of the hated

Convention, many flocked to Cathelineau to ask from whence he expected deliverance from all their troubles.

It was well known that Peter Berrier was the first whom the Colonel's myrmidons would be sent to seize, and many eyes were resting on the group collected at the gateway of the auberge, as the corporal and the two soldiers, without their muskets, but with pistols at their belts, marched across from the little barracks to the spot where they were standing. At any rate, Cathelineau had not advised a retreat, for there stood Peter Berrier— prominent in the front of the group—a little pale to be sure, and perhaps rather uneasy in his attitude; but still evidently prepared to bear the brunt of that day's proceeding. He was not going to run away, or he would long since have started. He was not going to obey the orders of the Convention, or he would not have stood there so openly and firmly, waiting the approach of the corporal and the two soldiers. It was very evident that there was to be a row in St. Florent that day, and that the postillion approved of it.

As the military party drew near to the gate of the inn yard, the corporal opened a small roll of paper, which he held in his hand, and standing still about six paces distant from the spot where Peter was maintaining his ground, read or pretended to read, the following words from the piece of paper which he held in his hands:

"In the name of the French Republic, and by command of the Convention, you, Peter Berrier, having been duly, legally, and specially drawn, chosen, and selected by lot, to serve in the armies of the Republic for one year, from the date of your first bearing arms, or for so long as your services may be necessary to the security of the Republic, are hereby required and desired to join the detachment of the Republican army at present serving in St. Florent, without let, delay, or hindrance, and thereby show yourself a friend to your country, and a good citizen of the Republic."

The corporal pronounced this form of invitation in that tone of voice, which proved that it was very familiar to him, and that he was much in the habit of requesting good citizens to join the armies of the Republic for such time as their services might be necessary; and, having finished it, he rolled up the piece of paper, stuck it into his belt, as he might soon require the use of his hands, and, walking quite close up to the group, said—

"Come, Peter Berrier, you are not such a fool, I hope, as to intend giving us any trouble. Come along."

Peter looked first into the farmer's face; then to his master's; and, lastly, to the postillion's; and, seeing that they were all evidently firm in their resolve, he plucked up spirit, and replied.—"Why, Mr Corporal, I have no inclination just at present to go to fight for the Republic. You see I have no quarrel yet with my master here, M. Debedin, and he cannot well spare me. I am afraid, Mr Corporal, I must decline."

"That's nonsense, you know," growled the corporal; "you must come, you know; and as well first as last. I don't want to be uncivil to a comrade, and I'd be sorry to have to lay a hand on you."

"Then you'd better keep your hands off," said Cathelineau, "we quiet people in St. Florent don't bear handling well."

The corporal looked up at the postillion, but he soon saw that he wasn't joking.

"Take my word for it, my friend," continued Cathelineau, "Peter Berrier does not wish to be a soldier, and, if you force him to become one, it is not on the side of the Republic that he will be found fighting."

"We'll take chances for that," replied the corporal, not exactly understanding what the other meant; "at any rate, back without him we won't go; and if you're determined for a riot, Messieurs, why I'm sorry; but I can't help it," and, appealing to Peter as a last hope, he said, "Come, Berrier, will you come with us quietly, or must we three drag you across the square to the barracks."

"At any rate, Mr Corporal," said Peter, "I will not go with you quietly; as to the being dragged, I can say nothing about that yet."

The corporal looked round towards the barracks, as he felt that it was possible that he might want more assistance, and he saw that a body of men under arms was standing immediately in front of the building, and that a couple of the officers were with them. The corporal saw at a glance that they were ready for immediate action, if their services should be requisite. In fact, the colonel of the detachment well knew the feeling in the place with reference to the levies of the conscription. He was sure, from the fact of not a single man having attended at the barracks, as directed, that there existed some general determination to resist the demands of the Convention, and he had consequently closely watched the proceedings of the corporal.

"Take your answer, Mr Corporal," said Cathelineau: "had Peter Berrier intended to have joined you he would not have troubled you to come across the square to fetch him. In one word, he will not go with you; if as you say, you intend to drag him across the market-place, you will find that you have enough to do. Peter Berrier has many friends in St. Florent."

The corporal again looked round, and he saw that the men under arms now stretched from the front of the barracks, nearly into the square; but he also saw that the inhabitants of the town were standing clustering at all the doors, and that men were crowding towards the square from the different inlets. Four or five of the more respectable inhabitants had also joined the group in the gateway, from the hands of one of whom the postillion quietly took a stout ash stick. The corporal, however, was not a coward, and he saw that, if he intended to return with Peter Berrier, he should not delay his work with any further parley, so he took his pistol from his belt and cocked it, and, stepping quite close to Berrier, said,

"Come men—forward, and bring him off; one man to each shoulder," and he himself seized hold of the breast of Peter's coat with his left hand and pulled him forward a step or two.

Peter was a little afraid of the pistol, but still he resisted manfully: from the corporal's position, Cathelineau was unable to reach with his stick the arm which had laid hold of Berrier, but it descended heavily on the first soldier, who came to the corporal's assistance. The blow fell directly across the man's wrist, and his arm dropt powerless to his side. The corporal immediately released his hold of Peter's coat, and turning on Cathelineau raised his pistol and fired; the shot missed the postillion, but it struck M. Debedin, the keeper of the auberge, and wounded him severely in the jaw. He was taken at once into the house, and the report was instantaneously spread through the town, that M. Debedin had been shot dead by the soldiery.

The ash stick of the postillion was again raised, and this time the corporal's head was the sufferer; the man's shako protected his skull, which, if uncovered, would have probably been fractured; but he was half-stunned, at any rate stupified by the blow, and was pulled about and pushed from one to another by the crowd who had now collected in the archway, without making any further attempt to carry off his prisoner.

The other soldier, when he saw his two comrades struck, fired his pistol also, and wounded some other person in the crowd. He then attempted to make his escape back towards the barracks, but he was tripped up violently as he attempted to run, and fell on his face on the pavement. The unfortunate trio were finally made prisoners of; they were disarmed, their hands bound together, and then left under a strong guard in the cow-house attached to the auberge.

This skirmish, in which Berrier was so successfully rescued, occurred with greater rapidity than it has been recounted; for, as soon as the colonel heard the first shot fired, he ordered his men to advance in a trot across the square. It took some little time for him to give his orders to the lieutenants, and for the lieutenants to put the men into motion; but within five minutes from the time that the first shot was fired, about forty men had been commanded to halt in front of the hotel; they all had their muskets in their hands and their bayonets fixed, and as soon as they halted a portion of them were wheeled round, so that the whole body formed a square. By this time, however, the corporal and the two soldiers were out of sight, and so was also Peter Berrier, for Cathelineau considered that now as the man had withstood the first shock, and had resolutely and manfully refused to comply with the order of the Convention, it was better that he should be out of the way, and that the brunt of the battle should be borne by his friends. Peter was consequently placed in the cow-house with the captives, and had the gratification of acting as guard over the three first prisoners taken in the Vendean war.

Cathelineau and Foret, however, stood out prominently before the men who were collected before the auberge, and had already taken on themselves the dangerous honour of leading the revolt.

"Men of St. Florent," said the colonel addressing the crowd, "I am most reluctant to order the soldiers to fire upon the inhabitants of the town; but unless you at once restore the three men who were sent over here on duty, and give up the man, Peter Berrier, who has been drawn as a conscript, I will do so at once."

"Peter Berrier is a free man," said Foret, "and declines going with you; and as for your three soldiers, they have fired at and killed or wounded two inhabitants of the town—they at any rate shall be brought before the mayor, before they are given up."

"Sergeant," said the colonel, "take out six men and make prisoner that man; if a rescue be attempted, the soldiers shall at once fire on the people, and on your own heads be your own blood."

The sergeant and the six men instantly stepped out, but Foret was surrounded by a dense crowd of friends, and the soldiers found it utterly impossible to lay hold of him.

"Your pistols, sergeant; use your pistols," roared the colonel, as he himself drew one of his own from his holsters, and at the same time gave orders to the men in the ranks to present their pieces.

The sergeant followed by his six men, made a desperate dash into the crowd with the object of getting hold of Foret; but in spite of the butt-end of their pistols, with which the soldiers laid about them, they found themselves overpowered, and were barely able to make good their retreat to the main body of the detachment; at the same time, a volley of stones, brickbats and rough missiles of all kinds, descended on the soldiers from every side, for they were now nearly surrounded; a stone struck the Colonel's horse and made him rear: immediately afterwards, another stone struck himself on the side of the face, and nearly dismounted him.

"Fire," roared the Colonel, and the whole detachment fired at the same moment; the soldiers fronting the auberge could not fire into the mob directly before them, or they would have run the risk of killing their own comrades, who were still struggling there with the townspeople; and in this way, Cathelineau and Foret were saved, but the carnage all around them was horrid; the soldiers had fired point blank into the dense crowd, and not a bullet had fallen idle to the ground. A terrible scream followed the discharge of musketry; the dying and the wounded literally covered the space round the soldiers, but they were quickly dragged into the back ground, and their places filled by men who were evidently determined that they would not easily be conquered.

Another volley of stones was soon showered on the soldiers, and this was kept up with wonderful activity—the women and children supplied the men with the materials—the stones in the streets were at once picked up—old walls were pulled down—every article that would answer for a missile was brought into use; an iron pot, which had been flung with immense violence by the handle, struck the second officer in command in the face, and dashed his brains out. Immediately that either part of the square battalion was in any confusion, the people dashed in, and attempted to force the muskets from the hands of the soldiers; in some cases they were successful, and before the body had commenced a retreat, Foret and Cathelineau were both armed with a musket and bayonet.

The colonel now saw that he could not maintain his position where he was; he had not brought out with him the whole force of the garrison, though in all he had not above seventy or eighty men; but he had behind the barrack a gun of very large calibre, properly mounted, with all the necessary equipments and ready for service. Such a piece of artillery accompanied every detachment, and was kept in preparation for immediate use at every military station; it had already been ascertained that this afforded the readiest means of putting down revolt. He resolved, therefore, on retreating while he had the power for doing so, and gave the necessary orders to the men.

With great difficulty, but slowly and steadily, his men executed them: amidst showers of stones, and the now determined attack of the people the soldiers returned to the barracks, leaving one of their officers, and one other man dead in the crowd; many of them were severely wounded; few, if any, had escaped some bruise or cut. The people now conceived that they were going to take refuge in the barrack, and determined to drive them utterly out of the town; but, as soon as the soldiers had filed into the barrack yard, another murderous fire was discharged by those who had been left at the station. Then Cathelineau, who was still in front of the crowd, and who was now armed with the bayonet, which he had taken from the point of the musket, remembered the cannon, and he became for a moment pale as he thought of the dreadful slaughter which would take place, if the colonel were able to effect his purpose of playing it upon the town.

"The cannon!" whispered he to Foret, who was still at his side; "they will fall like leaves in autumn, if we don't prevent it."

"Have they it ready?" said Foret.

"Always," said the other, "they have nothing to do but wheel it into the street; and they are at it, you hear the noise of the wheels this moment. We must bear one discharge from it, and the next, if there be a second, shall fall upon the soldiers."

Others, beside Cathelineau, recognised the sound of the moving wheels— and, "the cannon, the cannon, they will fire the cannon on us," was heard from side to side among the crowd; but none attempted to run, not one of the whole mass attempted to fly, and when the barrack gates flew open, and the deadly mouth of the huge instrument was close upon them, they rushed upon it, determined at any rate, to preserve their houses, their wives, and their children from the awful destruction of a prolonged firing.

"They must have one shot at us," said a man in a trembling whisper to his neighbour. "God send it were over!" replied the other, as the gates of the barrack-yard were thrown back.

The greater number of the soldiers and the two officers who had returned with them, made good their retreat into the barracks, under the fire of their comrades, who had been left there. Some three or four had been pulled and hustled into the crowd, and their arms were quickly taken from them and they were sent back to the auberge as prisoners. The colonel, as soon as he found himself in his own quarters, gave immediate orders that the gun should be wheeled round to the barrack-yard gate, which had hitherto been kept closed, and that the moment the gates could be got open it should be fired on the crowd. These gates faced directly into the square, and the destruction caused by one shot would have been tremendous. The colonel, moreover, calculated that in the confusion he would have been able to reload. The gun, in its original position, was pointed on the town, but it was immediately seen, that without moving it, it could not be brought to bear upon the crowd congregated round the barracks.

The first attack of the crowd had been at the barrack door, through which the soldiers had retreated; but this was soon changed to the yard gates. The people, however, were unable to knock them down before the wheels of the cannon were heard, as they had been considerably checked by the fire of the reserved party. Both soldiers and towns-people were now anxious to face each other, and the gates soon fell inwards towards the military. Had the men at the gun had their wits about them they would have fired through the gates; but they did not, they waited till they fell inwards across the cannon's mouth, and in his confusion the artillery-sergeant even then hesitated before he put the light to the touch-hole.

He had never time to do more than hesitate. Cathelineau had been close up to the wooden gates, against which he was so closely pressed that he was hardly able to change his bayonet from his right to his left-hand, and to cock the pistol which he had taken from the corporal, who had commenced the day's work. However, he contrived to do so, and when the wood-work fell, he sprang forward, and though he stumbled over the fragments of the timber, he fired as he did so, and the artillery sergeant fell dead beside the cannon; the unextinguished light was immediately seized by his comrade, but he had not time to use it; it was knocked from his hand before it was well raised from the ground, and the harmless piece of cannon was soon entirely surrounded by crowds of the townspeople. They were not content with spiking it in such a way as to make it utterly impossible that it should be discharged; but they succeeded in turning it entirely round, so that the back of the carriage faced towards the town.

The soldiers still continued the fight within the barrack-yard, and from the barrack windows; but they were so completely mixed with the townspeople, that the officers were afraid to order the men to fire from the windows, least they should kill their own comrades. At last the colonel himself was taken prisoner; he was literally dragged out of one of the windows by the people, and soon afterwards the remainder of the troops gave up. One of the three officers and six men were killed; the rest were nearly all more or less wounded, and were all, without exception, made prisoners of war.

Cathelineau and Foret had been in front of the battle all through; but neither of them were wounded. It was to Foret that the colonel had given up his sword, after he had been dragged headforemost through a window, had had his head cut open with a brick-bat, and his sheath and sword-belt literally torn from his side. He had certainly not capitulated before he was obliged to do, and the people did not like him the worse for it.

And now the unarmed soldiery, maimed and lame, with broken heads and bloody faces, were led down in triumph into the square; and after them was brought the great trophy of the day, the cannon, with its awful mouth still turned away from the town. Cathelineau and Foret led the procession, the former still carrying his bayonet, for he had given up both the musket and pistols to some one else, and Foret armed with the Colonel's sword: they were fully recognized as the victorious leaders of the day.

At the bottom of the square they met a whole concourse of women, the wives and sisters of the champions—among whom the sister and sweetheart of Peter Berrier were conspicuous; they had come out to thank the townspeople for what they had done for them. With the women were two of the old curés of that and a neighbouring parish—pastors whom the decree of the Convention had banished from their own churches, but whom all the powers of the Convention had been unable to silence. To them this day's battle was a most acceptable sign of better days coming; they foresaw a succession of future victories on behalf of the people, which would surely end in the restoration of the Bourbons to the throne, and of the clergy to their churches. The curés shook hands warmly with those in the front ranks of the people, gave their blessing to Cathelineau and Foret, and then invited the people, with one accord, to give thanks to God for the great success which He had given them.

In one moment the whole crowd were on their knees in the market-place, while the two priests stood among them with their arms raised, uttering thanksgiving to the Lord for his mercy, and praying for the eternal welfare of those who had fallen in the affray. The soldiers of the republic found themselves standing alone as prisoners in the midst of the kneeling crowd; they looked awkward and confused enough, but they could not help themselves; they could not have escaped, even if they had been unanimous in attempting to do so; for they were unarmed, and the people knelt so closely round them, that they could hardly move. It was out of the question that they should also kneel, and join in the thanksgiving for having been so utterly beaten; so there they stood, their wounds stiffening and their blood running, till the priests had finished, and the people had risen.

And then another ceremony was performed; the priests were besought to come and bless the cannon, the first great trophy of the Royalist insurrection; and they did so. The cannon was a lucky cannon, a kind cannon, and a good cannon—a bon enfant, and worthy to be blessed; it had refused to pour forth its murderous fire against the inhabitants of a town that was so friendly to the King. It was decidedly a royalist cannon; it had very plainly declared the side it meant to take; nothing but miraculous interference on its own part could have prevented its having been discharged on he people, when it stood ready pointed on the town, with the torch absolutely glimmering at the touch-hole. It had been brought to St. Florent by republican soldiers, dragged by republican horses, and loaded with republican gunpowder; but it should never be used except in the service of the King, and against the enemies of the throne.

And so the priests blessed the cannon, and the people baptized it, and called it Marie-Jeanne, and the women brought out their little children, and sat them straddle-legged across it, whole rows of them at the same time, till the cannon looked like a huge bunch of grapes on which the fruit clustered thickly. By this time it was dark, and the people lighted huge bonfires through the town, and the children remained up, and as many as could cling on it still sat upon the cannon, and ropes were got and fastened to it, and all the girls of St. Florent dragged Marie-Jeanne round the town, and at last she was dragged into the yard of the auberge, in front of which the fight had commenced, and there she was left for the night, under a strong guard.

While these rejoicings were going on out of doors, Cathelineau and Forte, the two priests, and a few others—the wise men of the town—were collected together within the auberge, and were consulting as to their future proceedings.

"We have done much," said Cathelineau, "and I rejoice at it. Too much, a great deal, for us now to remain idle. We cannot go back. We are now the enemies of the Republic, and we must attack our enemies elsewhere, or they will attack and overwhelm us in our little town."

They then determined that Cathelineau, on the next morning, should address the people from the window of the market-place, and that afterwards he and Forte should go through the neighbouring country and implore the assistance of the people, of the gentry, the priests, the farmers, and the peasants, in opposing the hated levy of the Republican forces; but first they would go to the gentry, and the names of many were mentioned whom it was thought would be sure to join them. The first was that of Henri de Larochejaquelin, and the next that of his friend M. de Lescure. Who loved the people so well as they, and whom did the people love so truly? Yes, they would call on young Larochejaquelin and his friend to be their leaders.

Early on the morrow, the postillion addressed the people from the market-place. He did not seek to himself the honour of doing so, nor, when he was asked to come forward as the leader of the people, did he refuse to do so. He was not covetous of the honour, but he would not refuse the danger. During the whole of the combat every one had looked to him as to the leader. He had not constituted himself the people's general, he had not for a moment thought of assuming the position; but he as little thought of refusing the danger or the responsibility, when the duties of a general seemed, by the will of all, to fall to his lot.

"Friends," said he, addressing them from the market-house, "we have saved ourselves for a while from the grasp of the Republic. But for the battle of yesterday, every one here would have a brother, a son, or a cousin, now enrolled as a conscript in the army of the Convention. Many of yourselves would have been conscripts, and would have this morning waked to the loss of your liberty. We did much yesterday when we bound the hands of the soldiers; but we have much more to do than we have yet done. Already in Nantes and in Angers are they talking of what we yesterday performed. We shall doubtless have many friends in Nantes and Angers, but the Republic also has many friends in those towns, and the soldiers of the Republic are strong there. It will not be long before they hurry to St. Florent to avenge the disgrace of their comrades; and bitter will be their revenge if they take you unprepared. You have declared war against the Republic, and you must be prepared to fight it out to the end."

"We will, we will," shouted the people. "Down with the Republic—down with the Convention. Long live the King—our own King once again."

"Very well, my friends," continued Cathelineau, "so be it. We will fight it out then. We will combat with the Republic, sooner than be carried away from our wives, our children, and our sweethearts. We will fight for our own curés and our own churches; but our battle will be no holiday-work, it will be a different affair from that of yesterday. We must learn to carry arms, and to stand under them. You showed yesterday that you had courage—you must now show that you can join patience and perseverance to your courage."

"We will, Cathelineau, we will," shouted they "Tell us what we must do, Cathelineau, and we will do it.

"We must see," continued he, "who will be our friends and our allies. St. Florent cannot fight single-handed against the Republic. There are others in Anjou, and Poitou also, besides ourselves, who do not wish to leave their homes and their fields. There are noblemen and gentlemen, our friends and masters, who will lead you better than I can."

"No, no, Cathelineau is our general; we will follow no one but Cathelineau."

"You will, my friends, you will; but we need not quarrel about that. Forte and I, with Peter Berrier, will visit those who we think will join us; but you must at once prepare yourselves. You must arm yourselves. We will distribute the muskets of the soldiers as far as they will go. You must prepare yourselves. If we do not at once attack the Republicans elsewhere, they will soon overwhelm us in St. Florent. We will go to Cholet—the men of Cholet will surely second us—they are as fond of their sons and their brethren as we are. Cholet will join us, and Beaupréau, and Coron, and Torfou. We will go and ask them whether they prefer the Republic to their homes—whether the leaders of the Convention are dearer to them than their own lords— whether their new priests love them, as the old ones did? And I know what will be their answer."

He ceased speaking, and his audience crowded around him to shake hands with him, and to bless him; and before the sun was in the middle of the sky he had left St. Florent on his mission, in company with Forte and Peter Berrier.

CHAPTER III.
DURBELLIÈRE.

The château of Durbellière, the family seat of the Larochejacquelins, was situated in the very centre of the Bocage, between the small towns of Chatillon and Vihiers—in the province of Poitou, and about twelve leagues from St. Florent.

It was a large mansion, surrounded by extensive gardens, and a considerable domain. There were few residences of more importance as betokening greater wealth in the province of Poitou; but it was neither magnificent nor picturesque. The landlords of the country were not men of extensive property or expensive habits—they built no costly castles, and gave no sumptuous banquets; but they lived at home, on their incomes, and had always something to spare for the poorer of their neighbours. Farming was their business—the chase their amusement—loyalty their strongest passion, and the prosperity of their tenantry their chief ambition.

The château of Durbellière was a large square building, three stories high, with seven front windows to each of the upper stories, and three on each side of the large door on the ground floor. Eight stone steps of great width led up to the front door; but between the top step and the door there was a square flagged area of considerable space; and on the right hand, and on the left, two large whitewashed lions reclined on brick and mortar pedestals. An enormous range of kitchens, offices and cellars, ran under the whole house; the windows opened into a low area, or rather trench, which ran along the front and back of the house, and to which there were no rails or palings of any kind. The servants' door was at the side of the house, and the servants and people coming to them, to save themselves the trouble of walking round to this door, were in the habit of jumping into the area and entering the kitchen by the window. Doubtless some lady of the house, when the mansion was first built, had protested strongly against this unsightly practice; but habit had now accustomed the family to this mode of ingress and egress, and the servants of Durbèlliere consequently never used any other.

The back of the château was just the same as the front, the same windows, the same broad steps, the same pedestals and the same whitewashed lions, only the steps, instead of leading on to a large gravelled square, led into a trim garden. There were no windows, whatsoever, on one side of the house, and on the other only those necessary to light the huge staircase of the mansion.

The rooms were square, very large, and extremely lofty; the salon alone was carpetted, and none of them were papered, the drawing-room, the dining-room and the grand salon were ornamented with painted panels, which displayed light-coloured shepherds and shepherdesses in almost every possible attitude. In these rooms, also, there were highly ornamented stoves, which stood out about four feet from the wall, topped with marble slabs, on which were sculptured all the gods and demi-gods of the heathen mythology—that in the drawing-room exhibited Vulcan catching Mars and Venus in his marble net; and the unhappy position of the god of war was certainly calculated to read a useful lesson to any Parisian rover, who might attempt to disturb the domestic felicity of any family in the Bocage.

The house was not above a hundred yards from the high road, from which there were two entrances about two hundred yards apart. There were large wooden, gates at each, which were usually left open, but each of which was guarded by two white-washed lions—not quite so much at ease as those on the pedestals, for they were fixed a-top of pillars hardly broad enough to support them. But this doubtless only increased their watchfulness.

But the glory of the château was the large garden behind the house. It was completely enclosed by a very high wall, and, like the house, was nearly square in its proportions. It contained miles of walks, and each walk so like the others, that a stranger might wander there for a week without knowing that he had retraversed the same ground, were it not that he could not fail to recognize the quaint groups of figures which met him at every turn. A few of these were of stone, rudely sculptured, but by far the greater number were of painted wood, and, like the shepherds and shepherdesses in the drawing-room, displayed every action of rural life. You would suddenly come upon a rosy-coloured gentleman, with a gun to his shoulder, in the act of shooting game—then a girl with a basket of huge cabbages—an old man in a fit of the cholic; the same rosy gentleman violently kissing a violet-coloured young lady; and, at the next turn, you would find the violet-coloured young lady fast asleep upon a bank. You would meet a fat curé a dozen times in half-an-hour, and always well employed. He would be saying his prayers—drinking beer—blessing a young maiden, and cudgelling a mule that wouldn't stir a step for him, till the large yellow drops of sweat were falling from his face. It was inconceivable how so many painted figures, in such a variety of attitudes, could have been designed and executed; but there they were, the great glory of the old gardener, and the endless amusement of the peasants of the neighbourhood, who were allowed to walk there on the summer Sunday evenings.

The gardens of Durbellière were also wonderful in another respect. It was supposed to be impossible to consume, or even to gather, all the cherries which they produced in the early summer. The trees between the walks were all cherry-trees—old standard trees of a variety of sorts; but they all bore fruit of some description or another, some sweet and some bitter; some large, some small, and some perfectly diminutive; some black, some red, and some white. Every species of known cherry was in that garden in abundance; but even the gardener himself did not know the extent of the produce. Birds of all kinds flocked there in enormous numbers, and banqueted gloriously during the summer. No one disturbed them except the painted sportsman; and the song of the linnet and the thrush was heard all day, and that of the nightingale during the night.

The old Marquis de Larochejaquelin had been crossed in love early in life, and he had not recovered from his sorrow till he was above fifty, when he married, and outlived his young wife, who left him different children. Henri and Agatha were the only two now living with him. As has already been said, the old man was very infirm, and had lost the use of his limbs.

When the weather was cold or wet, he sat with his daughter, Agatha, near his bright wood fire, and watched her needle, or listened to her songs; but, if the sun appeared at all, he was dragged out in his garden chair among the birds and the painted figures, and was happy in spite of his infirmities.

He was most affectionate to his children, and indulgent to a fault. He was kind to every one, and, unless the birds were disturbed, the cherry-trees injured, or the figures upset, he was never angry even with a servant. Everybody loved and venerated the old Marquis, and even in his foibles, he was thoroughly respected. He had a vast collection of stuffed birds of every description, and the peasants round him were so anxious to gratify him by adding to his stock, that there began to be a doubt whether room in the château could be found for the presents which were continually brought. The upper story of the house had never been required by the family, and the rooms had not even been roofed or plastered. One great partition wall ran across the space, and the only ceiling was the bare high-pointed roof of the house. This place was called the granary, and was used for a drying ground. And here the superfluous birds were brought, much to the old man's grief, for he knew that he should never see them again; but he could not refuse them when they were given to him, and the room which he inhabited would conveniently hold no more.

The happiness of the last years of the old man's life was much disturbed by the events of the French revolution. He had been very anxious when he saw his young son join a club, which was sure to incur the ill-will of the ruling power in Paris; and yet he could not dissuade him from doing so; and, though he had rejoiced when his son returned to Poitou still safe, the imprisonment of the King had woefully afflicted him, and his death had nearly killed him. He had now expressed his opposition to the levies of a conscription with a degree of energy which had astonished his family. He knew the names and persons of every man and woman living on his estate, indeed, of every child above the age of ten; and, when he was told the names of those who were drawn as conscripts, he desired that they might all be told in his name that he hoped they would not obey.

Henri de Larochejacquelin has already been introduced to the reader. He returned to Poitou as soon as the Republic was proclaimed, together with de Lescure and Adolphe Denot. Adolphe had been staying a great portion of the winter at Durbellière, but he had since gone to his own place, and was now at Clisson, the seat of M. de Lescure.

Marie de Lescure, the sister of Henri's friend, was staying at Durbellière with Agatha Larochejaquelin; and her visit, which had been prolonged from before Christmas, had certainly not been made less agreeable by the fact of Henri's having been at home the whole time. She and Agatha were both pretty, but they were very different. Marie had dark hair, nearly black, very dark eyes, and a beautiful rich complexion; her skin was dark, but never sallow; her colour was not bright, but always clear and transparent; her hair curled naturally round her head, and the heavy curls fell upon her neck and shoulders; she was rather under the middle height, but the symmetry of her figure was so perfect, that no one would have called her too short. She had high animal spirits, and was always happy and good humoured; was very fond of amusement of every kind, and able to extract amusement out of everything. She was the great favourite of the old Marquis, not that he loved her so well as his own daughter, but her habits and manners suited him better than Agatha's; she could better sympathize with the old man's wishes and fancies; she would smooth the plumage of his birds for him; arrange and re-arrange his shells; feed his cats, his dogs, his tame deer, and his white peacock—for the old Marquis had live pets as well as dead favourites. Then she would sing merry little songs to him, and laugh at him, and quiz his painted figures, and help to wheel his chair, or pretend to do so.

She did all these things more readily than Agatha did, for her spirits were lighter. Not that Agatha was unhappy, or inattentive to her father; but she was quieter than Marie and of a more contemplative mood. She also had dark hair, but it was a dark brown, and she wore it braided close to her forehead. Her complexion was clear and bright, her forehead was white, and the colour in her cheeks, when she had colour there, was that of the clearest carnation. She was considerably taller than Marie, but her figure was exquisitely perfect, and her gait was that of a queen. She was the Rose of Poitou, the beauty and queen of the whole district. She was all but worshipped by the peasantry around her; if they admired her beauty much, they much more strongly appreciated her virtues, her charity, her considerate kindness, her want of selfishness, her devotion to her friends and neighbours, and lastly, her strong feeling of loyalty, her love for the king while he lived, and her passionate regret for him since he had perished on the scaffold. In this she inherited all the feelings of her father, and it was greatly her attachment to the throne and to the name of the King, which led to so high a pitch the enthusiasm of the peasantry in behalf of the royalists.

Many wishes, surmises and anticipations had arisen as to who was to carry off this rich prize; who should be the happy husband of Agatha Larochejaquelin; but her friends had hitherto been anxious in vain; she still went "in maiden meditation fancy free." Not that she was without professed admirers; but they had none of them yet touched her heart. Many thought that she would be the bride of her brother's friend, Adolphe Denot; for he was more at the château than any one else, was very handsome, and had a good property. Adolphe was moreover seen to be very attentive to Mademoiselle Agatha; and thrown so much with her as he was, how could he fail of being in love with her.

This belief much disturbed the comfort of Agatha's humble friends, for Adolphe Denot was not popular among them: there was a haughtiness in his manner to the poor, to which their own lords and masters had never accustomed them. He was supercilious and proud in his bearing towards them, and had none of the cheering, frank look and tone of their own dear young M. Henri. They need not, however, have been alarmed, for Agatha Larochejaquelin was not at all disposed to take Adolphe Denot as her lord; she was passionately attached to her brother, and for his sake she had been kind, attentive, nay, almost affectionate to his friend; she and Adolphe had been much together since they were children. He had been absent from Durbellière for about a year, during which time, he had ceased to be a boy, and on his return to the château had taken on himself the airs, if not the manners of a man. Agatha's manner to him was not altered, it was still friendly and affectionate, and Adolphe, with his usual vanity, misinterpreted it; he flattered himself that the beautiful girl loved him, and he soon persuaded himself that he was devotedly attached to her.

He had not yet positively declared his love, but Agatha felt from his manner that she had to expect a declaration, and she consequently altered her own; she became less familiar with him, she avoided all opportunities of being alone with him; she still called him by his Christian name, for she had always done so; she was still kind and attentive to him, for he was a guest in her father's house; but Adolphe felt that she was altered, and he became angry and moody; he thought that she was coquetting and that he was slighted; and without much notice to any one, he left the house.

Agatha was glad that he was gone; she wished to spare him the humiliation of a refusal; she understood his character well, and felt that the wound inflicted on his self-love, by being rejected, would be more painful to him than his actual disappointment; she knew that Adolphe would not die for love, but she also knew that he would not quietly bear the fancied slight of unreturned affection. If, by her conduct, she could induce him to change his own, to drop the lover, and be to her again simply her brother's friend, all might yet be well; but if he persevered and declared his love, she felt that there would be a quarrel, not only between him and her, but between him and Henri.

To tell the truth, Henri had rather fostered his friend's passion for Agatha. He had wished to see them married; and, though he had not exactly told his friend as much, he had said so much that both Agatha and Denot knew what his wishes were. This, of course, gave great encouragement to the lover, but it greatly grieved poor Agatha; and now that Adolphe was gone, she made up her mind to open her heart to her brother.

A day or two before the revolt of St. Florent, they were sitting together in the drawing-room; it was late in the evening, the old Marquis had retired for the night, and Marie de Lescure was engaged elsewhere, so that Agatha and her brother were left alone together. He was reading, but she was sitting gazing at the fire. She could hardly summon up courage to say, even to her dear brother, what she wished to say.

"Henri," she said at last, "does Adolphe return here from Fleury?" (Fleury was the name of Denot's house).

"I hope he will," said Henri; "but what makes you ask? the place is dull without him, isn't it?"

"Dull! you don't find Marie dull, do you, Henri?"

"Oh, Marie!" said he, laughing, "Marie amuses our father, and she charms me; but you might find the house dull, in spite of Marie—eh, Agatha?"

"Indeed no, Henri; the house was not dull even when you were in Paris, and Marie was at Clisson, and papa and I were alone together here; it was not my being dull made me ask whether Adolphe was to return."

"But you wouldn't be sorry that he should come back, Agatha? You don't want to banish poor Adolphe from Durbellière, I hope?"

"No," said Agatha, doubtfully, "no, I don't want to banish him—of course, Henri, I can't want to banish your friend from the house; but—"

"But what?" said Henri, now perceiving that his sister had something on her mind—something that she wished to say to him; "but what, dearest Agatha?"

"I don't want to banish him from the house, Henri; but I wish he would not return just at present; but you haven't answered my question—you haven't told me whether you expect him."

"I think he will return; but he did not himself say exactly when. I am sorry to hear what you say, Agatha—very sorry—I thought you and Adolphe were great friends. I was even a little jealous," added he, laughing, "at the close alliance between you, and I thought of getting up a little separate party of my own with Marie."

"Don't separate yourself from me, Henri!" said she; "don't let us be separated in anything, even in thought; not but that I should be delighted to see a dearer friendship between you and Marie, even than that between Marie and myself; but don't plan any separate alliance for me. I hope you have not been doing so—tell me, Henri, that you have not." And then she added, blushing deeply up to her pale forehead, "You have not proposed to Adolphe that I should be his wife?"

"No, Agatha, I have not proposed it to him; I should not have dreamt of doing so, without knowing that it would not be disagreeable to you."

"There's my own dear brother! My own Henri!" said she, going over to him, caressing him, and kissing his forehead.

"I will never make an offer of your hand to any one Agatha; you shall choose for yourself; I will never cause you sorrow in that way: but I will own, dearest, that I have wished you should marry Adolphe, and I have also fancied that you loved him."

"No, Henri, no, I do not love him—I can never love him—that is, as my husband. I do love him as your friend. I will continue to love him as such, as long as he remains your friend."

"I fancied also," continued he; "nay, I did more than fancy—I am sure he loves you—is it not so?"

"He has never told me so," said she, again blushing; "it is that he may not tell me so, that I now say that I hope he is not returning. Oh, Henri, my own dearest brother, do not let him come to Durbellière; prevent him in some way; go to him for a while; make some plan with him; and give me warning when he is coming, and I will be at Clisson with Marie."

"Will it not be better for both of you, Agatha, that you should understand each other? I know he loves you, though he has not told me so. You must tell him, kindly, that you cannot return his affection: you cannot always run away from him."

"He will forget me soon. He will, at any rate, forget his love, when he finds that I avoid his company; but, Henri, if he formally asks my hand, and is refused, that he will neither forget nor forgive."

"He must take his chance, dearest, like other men."

"But he isn't like other men, Henri. You know he is—he is rather impatient of refusal; he could not bear as well as some men any mortification to his pride."

"I trust he has too much real pride to feel himself disgraced, because he is not loved. I grieve for him, for I love him myself; and I know his affections are strong; but I think it is better he should know the truth at once, and it must be from your own lips. I cannot tell him you will not accept him before he himself makes the offer."

Agatha did not reply; she could not explain even to her brother all that she felt. She could not point out to him how very weak—how selfish his friend was. She could not tell him that his bosom friend would suffer ten times more from the wound to his pride in being rejected, than from the effects of disappointed love; but she rightly judged her lover's character. Adolphe Denot loved her as warmly as he was capable of loving ought but himself; but were she to die, his grief would be very short lived; he would not, however, endure to see that she preferred any one to himself.

"I am sorry for this, Agatha—very sorry," continued her brother; "I had fondly hoped to see you Adolphe's wife, but it is over now. I will never press you against your will."

"My own Henri—how good you are to your Agatha. I knew you would not torture me with a request that I should marry a man I did not love. I grieve that I interfere with your plans; but I will live with you, and be your old maid sister, and nurse and love your children, and they shall love their old maid aunt."

"There are other men, Agatha, besides Adolphe. Perhaps your next request will be a very different one; perhaps, then, you will be singing the praises of some admirer, and asking me to give him a brother's place in my heart."

"And when I ask it, you will do so; but Henri," and she put her hands upon his shoulder, as she stood close to his chair, "don't let Adolphe come here immediately."

"He must do so, dearest, now I think of it: we have other things to think of besides ladies' hearts, and other matters to plan besides wedding favours; the troops will be in Clisson on Monday next, to collect the conscripts. I have promised to be with de Lescure, and Adolphe is to meet me there; they are both then to come here. Not a man shall be taken who does not choose to go; and there are not many who wish to go from choice. There will be warm work in Poitou next week, Agatha; few of us then can think of love or marriage. You and Marie will be making sword-knots and embroidering flags; that will be your work. A harder task will soon follow it—that of dressing wounds and staunching blood. We shall have hot work, and more than plenty of it. May God send us well through it."

"Amen; with all my heart I say, amen," said Agatha; "but will these poor men resist the soldiers, Henri?"

"Indeed they will, Agatha."

"But can they? They have not arms, nor practice in the way of fighting—they have no leaders."

"We will take arms from our enemies. We will be apt scholars in fighting for our wives, and our sisters, and our houses. As for leaders, the man who is most fit shall lead the others."

"And you, Henri—merciful Heaven! what are you about to do—will you take up arms against the whole republic?"

"With God's blessing I will—against the whole republic."

"May the Lord, in his mercy, look on you and give you his assistance; and as your cause is just and holy, He will do so. Whatever women can do, we will do; you shall have our prayers for your success our tears for your reverses, and our praises for your courage; and when you require it, as some of you will too soon, our tenderest care in your sufferings." At this moment Marie de Lescure entered the room. "Marie," continued Agatha, "you will help to succour those who are wounded in fighting for their King?"

"Indeed, and indeed I will," said the bright-eyed girl, eagerly, "and regret only that I cannot do more; that I cannot myself be in the battle. But, M. Larochejaquelin, will the people rise? will there really be fighting? will Charles be there?"

"Indeed he will, Marie; the first among the foremost. Agatha asked me but now, who would be our leaders? Is there a man in the Bocage—aye, in all Poitou, who will not follow Charles de Lescure?"

"May the blessed Saviour watch over him and protect him," said Marie, shuddering.

"But tell me, Henri;" said Agatha, "where will it commence—where will they first resist the troops?"

"I cannot say exactly," said he, "in many places at once I hope. In St. Florent, they say, not a man will join; in Clisson and Torfou they begin on Monday. Charles, and I, and Adolphe will be in Clisson. Father Jerome has the whole lists; he says that in St. Laud's, in Echanbroignes, and Clisson, they are ready, to a man, to oppose the troops: he will go with me to Clisson on Sunday afternoon; on Monday, with God's will, we will be in the thick of it."

"And will Father Jerome be there, among the soldiers?" said Marie.

"Why not," said Henri, "will the peasants fight worse when they see their priest before them?"

"And if he should fall?"

"He will fall in the service of his God and his King; Father Jerome will be here himself tomorrow."

"The Curé of St Laud's," said Agatha, "is not the man to sit idle, when good work is to be done, but, oh! what awful times are these, when the priests themselves have to go out to fight for their altars and their crucifix."

"I will return home with you, M Larochejaquelin, when you go to Clisson," said Marie.

"And leave Agatha alone?" said Henri

"Don't mind me, Henri," said Agatha, "I shall be well here. Marie cannot leave Madame de Lescure alone, when her husband is, away and in such danger."

"You will soon have company here enough," said Henri. "De Lescure, and I, and Adolphe, and Heaven knows whom besides. Charette will be in arms, and d'Autachamps, the Prince de Talmont, and M. Bonchamps. At present their business is at a distance from us; but we shall probably be all brought together sooner or later, and they will all be welcome at Durbellière."

"They shall be welcome if they are friends of yours, and friends of the King; but come, Marie, it is late, let us go to bed; next week, perhaps, we shall be wanting rest, and unable to take it."

They met the next morning at breakfast, and the old Marquis was there also, and the priest, to whom they had alluded in their conversation on the preceding evening—Father Jerome, the Curé of St. Laud's—such at least had he been, and so was he still called, though his parish had been taken away from him, and his place filled by a constitutional pastor; that is, by a priest who had taken the oath to the Constitution, required by the National Assembly Father Jerome was banished from his church, and deprived of the small emoluments of his office; but he was not silenced, for he still continued to perform the ceremonies of his religion, sometimes in some gentleman's drawing-room, sometimes in a farmer's house, or a peasant's cottage, but oftener out in the open air, under the shadow of a spreading beech, on a rude altar hastily built for him with rocks and stones.

The church of St Laud's was perfectly deserted—not a single person would attend there to hear mass said by the strange priest—the peasants would as soon have been present at some infernal rite, avowedly celebrated in honour of the devil—and yet the Curé newly sent there was not a bad man But he was a constitutional priest, and that was enough to recommend him to the ill-will of the peasantry In peaceable and happy times, prior to the revolution, the Curé of St Laud's had been a remarkable person, he was a man of more activity, both of mind and body, than his brethren, he was more intimate with the gentry than the generality of clergymen in the neighbourhood, and at the same time more actively engaged in promoting the welfare of the poor. The country cures generally were men who knew little of the world and its ways—who were uneducated, save as regards their own profession—who had few ideas beyond their own duties and station, This was not so with Father Jerome; he had travelled and heard the ways of men in other countries; he had not read much but he had seen a good deal, and he was a man of quick apprehension—and above all a man of much energy. He had expressed great hostility to the revolution since its commencement; at a time when so few were hostile to it, he had foreseen that it would destroy the religion and the religious feeling of the country, and he had constantly besought his flock to remain true to their old customs. He was certainly a devout man in his own way, though he was somewhat unscrupulous in his devotions; the people were as superstitious as they were faithful, and he never hesitated in using their superstition to forward his own views. His whole anxiety was for their welfare; but he cherished their very faults, their ignorance and their follies, to enable himself to serve them in his own manner. He was unwilling that they should receive other education than that which they now had—he was jealous of any one's interfering with them but their landlord and himself. He would not own that any change: could better their condition, or that anything more was desirable for them than that they should live contented and obedient, and die faithful in hope.

Durbellière had not been in his parish, but he had always been peculiarly intimate with the family of the Larochejaquelins, and had warmly welcomed the return of Henri to the Bocage, at a time when so many of the nobility were leaving the country. They were now about to join hand and heart in saving the people from the horrors of the conscription, and though the Curé's nominal mission was to be purely spiritual, he was quite prepared to give temporal aid to his allies, should it at any time appear expedient to himself to do so.

Father Jerome was a tall, well-made, brawny man; his face was not exactly handsome, but it was bold and intellectual; his eye was bright and clear, and his forehead high and open—he was a man of immense muscular power and capable of great physical exertion—he was above forty-five years of age but still apparently in the prime of his strength. He wore a long rusty black, or rather grey curé's frock, which fell from his shoulders down to his heels, and was fastened round his body with a black belt—this garment was much the worse for wear, for Father Jerome had now been deprived of his income for some twelve months; but he was no whit ashamed of his threadbare coat, he rather gloried in it, and could not be induced by the liberal offers of his more wealthy friends to lay it aside.

Father Jerome greeted them all as he entered the breakfast-room. He was received with great kindness by the old Marquis, who pressed his hand and made him sit beside himself; he blessed the two young girls fervently, and nodded affectionately to Henri, whom he had seen on the preceding day. It was evident that the Curé of St. Laud's was quite at home at Durbellière.

"We have awful times coming on us now, Father Jerome," said Agatha.

"Not so, Mademoiselle," said the priest, "we have good times coming, we will have a King and our Church again, we poor cure will have our homes and our altars again; our own parishes and our old flocks."

"Come what, come may," said Henri, "we cannot be worse than the Convention would make us."

"But we firmly trust that by God's will and with God's aid, we will soon be rid of all our troubles," said the priest. "M le Marquis, we have your best wishes, I know; and your full approval. I hope we shall soon be able to lay our trophies at your feet."

"The approval of an old man like me is but of little avail; but you shall have my prayers. I would, however, that God had spared me from these days; it is grievous for me to see my son going out to fight against his own countrymen, at his own door-sill; it would be more grievous still, where he now to hesitate in doing so."

"No true son of Poitou hesitates now," said the enthusiastic priest. "I yesterday saw every conscript in the parish of St. Laud's, and not a single man hesitated—not one dreams of joining the republicans; and, moreover, there is not an able-bodied man who will not come forward to assist the conscripts in withstanding the soldiers; the women, too, Mademoiselle, are equally eager. Barère will find it difficult, I think, to raise a troop from Poitou."

"Will the conscripts from hence be required to join at Chatillon or at Cholet?" said the old man.

"Those from St. Laud's, at Chatillon," said Henri; "but the men will not leave their homes, they will know how to receive the soldiers if they come amongst them."

So saying, he got up and went out, and the priest followed him; they had much to do, and many things to arrange; to distribute arms and gunpowder, and make the most of their little means. It was not their present intention to lead the men from their homes, but they wished to prepare them to receive the republican troops, when they came into the country to enforce the collection of the republican levy.

CHAPTER IV.
CATHELINEAU.

The revolt of St. Florent took place on the day after that on which the priest had breakfasted at Durbellière, and the rumours of it went quickly through the country. As Cathelineau had said, the news was soon known in Nantes and Angers, and the commander of the republican troops determined most thoroughly to avenge the insolence and rebellion of the vain people of St. Florent. He was not, however, able to accomplish his threat on the instant, for he also was collecting conscripts in the neighbourhood of Nantes, and the peasantry had heard of the doings of St. Florent as well as the soldiers, and the men of Brittany seemed inclined to follow the example of the men of Anjou.

He had, therefore, for a time enough to occupy his own troops, without destroying the rebels of St. Florent—and it was well for St. Florent that it was so. Had he at once marched five hundred men, with four pieces of cannon against the town, he might have reduced the place to ashes, and taken a bloody revenge for their victory The men of St Florent would have had no means of opposing such a force, and the peasantry generally were not armed, the tactics of the royalists were not settled, and the revolt through the province was not general. The destruction of St Florent was postponed for a month, and at the expiration of that time, the troops of the republic had too much to do, to return to the little town where the war had commenced.

The rumour of what had been done at St. Florent, was also soon known in Coron, in Torfou, and in Clisson. The battle was fought on Thursday, and early on Saturday morning, M. de Lescure had heard some indistinct rumour of the occurrence; indistinct at least it seemed to him, for he could not believe that the success of the townspeople was so complete, as it was represented to him to be; he heard at the same time that the revolt had been headed by Cathelineau and Foret, and that as soon as the battle was over, they had started for Durbellière to engage the assistance of Henri Larochejaquelin. De Lescure, therefore, determined to go at once to Durbellière; and Adolphe Denot, who was with him, accompanied him.

They found Henri in the midst of his preparations, weighing out gunpowder with the assistance of the priest and the two girls. There was a large quarry on the Marquis' estate, and a considerable supply of gunpowder for blasting had been lately brought to Durbellière from Nantes, as it could not be purchased in the neighbouring towns. As the priest remarked, blasting powder was not the best, but it was good enough to treat republicans with— at any rate they could get no better, and it was lucky that they chanced to have that.

Charles de Lescure shuddered as he saw the dangerous employment on which his sister was engaged; but Henri's sister was doing the same thing, and he knew that dangerous times for all of them were coming. Adolphe was disgusted that Agatha's white hands should be employed in so vile a service, but he thought little of the danger to which she was exposed.

"You are well employed, ladies," said de Lescure, "but not an hour too soon. I am rejoiced to see you so well supplied, Henri; this is indeed a Godsend. Father Jerome, is this strictly canonical; gunpowder I fear is altogether a temporal affair."

"But rebellion and hell-fire are synonymous," said the priest, "and loyalty is the road to Paradise. I am strictly within my calling, M. de Lescure. Mademoiselle, these packets are too large. You are giving too good measure. Remember how many are the claimants for our bounty."

"You have, of course, all heard what occurred at St. Florent the day before yesterday," said de Lescure.

"Not a word," said Henri. "What happened there? we hear nothing here till a week after it is known in the towns."

They all left off what they were doing, and listened anxiously for M. de Lescure's tidings. "Good news, I trust," said the Curé, whose face showed a fearful degree of anxiety. "Good news, I trust in God; the men of St. Florent, I am sure, have not disgraced themselves."

"Indeed, they have not, Father Jerome. If the half of what I hear be true, they have already played a grand part. What I hear is this—not a conscript was to be seen at the barracks when they were summoned. Three or four soldiers were sent to commence the collection in the town, and they were at once taken prisoners by a party headed by Cathelineau, the postillion. The Colonel then turned out, and fired on the crowd; but he could not stand his ground before the people, who drove him back to the barracks; half his men were killed in retreating. The people then attacked the barracks, and regularly carried them by storm; took the cannon which was with the detachment, and made prisoners of every soldier that was not killed in the fray. If the half of it be true, St. Florent has made a fine beginning for us."

"Glorious fellows!" said Adolphe. "What would I not give to have been with them?"

"You will have plenty of opportunity, M. Denot," said the priest, who held Adolphe in great aversion.

"But, Charles, the carnage of the people must have been dreadful," said Henri; "they had nothing but their hands and nails to fight with, against the muskets and bayonets of the soldiers—against artillery even."

"The Lord supplied them with weapons, my son," said the priest, solemnly. "Cannot He, who has given them courage and good hearts to stand against the enemies of their country, also give them weapons to fight his battles?"

"They say, too, that by some miracle the cannon could not be got to fire on the town. They say it was loaded and ready, but that the powder would not ignite when the torch was put to it," said de Lescure.

"They say," added Denot, "that the Colonel himself repeatedly tried to fire it, but could not; and that when he found that Providence, interfered for the people, he laid down his sword, and gave himself up."

"The man who came to me from the town," continued de Lescure, "had a thousand wonderful stories. He says, that twenty times in the day Cathelineau stood, unharmed before the bayonets of the soldiers; that twenty times he was shot at, but it was impossible to wound him. They say that God has interfered for the protection of St. Florent."

"Most probable," said the priest, "most probable; for who, my children, shall attempt to judge the ways of God? Why should He not put out his right hand to assist his own?"

"And were there not many of the townspeople killed?" asked Agatha.

"We did not hear," replied de Lescure; "but the news of their triumph would travel faster than the account of their misfortunes; there could not but have been much bloodshed."

"After all," said Henri, "we do not know how much of this is true. We must not believe it all; it is too glorious to be true."

"Do not say so, M. Larochejaquelin," said the priest, "do not say so; we will do greater things than that with the assistance of God and the blessed Virgin; but we will not envy the men of St. Florent the honour they have won."

"You believe it all, then, Father Jerome," said Marie. "You believe that the republicans have been beaten."

"Every word, Mademoiselle, every word religiously. I should be a heathen else, or worse than that, a republican."

The group who were discussing the probability of the victory said to have been gained at St. Florent, were standing at the window of one of the front rooms of the château, which looked immediately on one of the whitewashed recumbent lions, and from it they could see the wooden gates, the lodge, and the paved road which ran from Chatillon to Vihiers in front of the château. As the priest finished speaking, three men rode through the gates, into the avenue, directly up to the house-door: one was tolerably well mounted on a large horse, the second was on a shaggy pony, and the third, who was rather behind the others, was seated on a mule of most unprepossessing appearance, whose sides he did not for a moment cease to lacerate with his heels, to enable himself to keep up with his companions.

"That is Foret, from St. Florent himself!" shouted the priest, rushing out towards the door, as soon as he saw the first horseman turn in at the gate; "a good man, and true as any living, and one who hates a skulking republican as he does the devil."

"And that is the postillion himself, on the pony!" shouted Henri, running after him. "I could swear to him, by his hat, among a thousand."

"Who is the man on the mule, Adolphe?" said de Lescure, remaining at the window. "By the bye," he added, turning to the two girls who remained with him, and who were trembling in every joint, at they knew not what, "I forgot, in my hurry, or rather I hadn't time as yet to tell Henri that I had heard that these men were coming here."

"Are those the very men who gained the victory at St. Florent?" asked Marie.

"So we heard," replied de Lescure, "and now, and not till now, I believe it; their coming here is strong confirmation; the Curé is right, it seems."

"And is that man the good postillion of whom the people talk?"

"He is—at least he is no longer a postillion. He will cease to be a postillion now; from henceforth he will be only a soldier."

The Curé and Larochejaquelin had rushed down the steps, and seized the hands of Foret and Cathelineau, as they got off their horses. It was soon evident to them that the noise of their deeds had gone before them. Foret at once returned the greeting of Father Jerome, for they had long known each other, and the difference between their stations was not so very great; but Cathelineau hardly knew how to accept, or how to refuse, the unwonted mark of friendship shewn him by a wealthy seigneur; it had not been his lot to shake hands with gentlemen, and he had no wish to step beyond his proper sphere, because he had been put prominently forward in the affair of St. Florent; but he had no help for it; before he knew where he was, Larochejaquelin had got him by the hand, and was dragging him into the salon of Durbellière. It appeared to the postillion that the room was full; there were ladies there too—young, beautiful, and modest—such as he was in the habit of seeing through the windows of the carriages which he drove; the old Marquis was there too now; the butler had just wheeled in his chair, and Cathelineau perceived that he was expected to join the group at once. A vista was opened for him up to the old man's chair; his eyes swam, and he hardly recollected the faces of the different people round him. He wished that he had waited at the gate, and sent in for M. Henri; he could have talked to him alone. Why had he ridden up so boldly to the château gate? He had never trembled, for a moment, during the hot work at St. Florent, but now he felt that circumstances could almost make him a coward.

On a sudden he remembered that his hat was still on his head, and he snatched his hand out of Henri's to remove it, and then, when it was off, he wanted to go back to the hall to put it down.

Henri saw his confusion, and, taking it from him, put it on a chair, and then they all shook hands with him. He first found his hand in that of the Marquis, and heard the old man bless him, and then the Priest blessed him, and then he felt the soft, sweet hands of those bright angels within his own horny palm; he heard them speaking to him, though he knew not what they said; and then he could restrain himself no longer, for tears forced themselves into his eyes, and, in the midst of them all, he cried like a child.

There was infection in his tears, for Agatha and Marie, when they saw them, cried too, and the eyes of some of the men also were not dry; they all knew what the feelings of the man were, and they fully sympathised with him. It was strange how little they said about St. Florent at first; the moment the men had been seen, they were most anxious for the tidings of what had been done; but now they all seemed satisfied as to the truth of what they had heard—there was no longer any doubt. The heroes of St. Florent were there, and, though neither of them had yet spoken a word about the battle which had been fought, the presence of the victors was sufficient evidence of the victory.

The Curé, however, and M. de Lescure soon took Foret apart, and learnt from him the details of what had been done, while the father and son, and the two girls, endeavoured to put the postillion at his ease in his new position.

Cathelineau was a very good-looking man, about thirty-five years of age; his hair was very dark, and curled in short, thick clusters; his whiskers were large and bushy, and met beneath his face; his upper lip was short, his mouth was beautifully formed, and there was a deep dimple on his chin; but the charm of his face was in the soft benignant expression of his eyes; he looked as though he loved his fellow-creatures—he looked as though he could not hear, unmoved, a tale of woe or oppression—of injuries inflicted on the weak, or of unfair advantages assumed by the strong. It was this which had made him so much beloved; and it was not only the expression of his countenance, but of his heart also.

"And were you not wounded, Cathelineau?" asked the old gentleman.

"No, M. le Marquis, thank God! I was not."

"Nor Foret?"

"No, M. le Marquis."

"But were there many wounded?" said Agatha.

"Ah! Mademoiselle, there were—many, very many!"

"I knew there must have been," said Marie, shuddering.

"We cannot have war without the horrors of war," said Henri. "It is better, is it not, Cathelineau, that some of us should fall, than that all of us should be slaves?"

"A thousand times, M. Larochejaquelin ten thousand times!" said he, with a return of that determined vigour with which he had addressed his fellow-townsmen the day before.

"Yes, you are right, ten thousand times better! and, Marie, you would not be your brother's sister if you did not think so," said Henri; "but you do think so, and so does Agatha, though she cries so fast."

"I am not crying, Henri," said Agatha, removing her handkerchief from her eyes, which belied her assertion; "but one cannot but think of all the misery which is coming on us: were there—were there any women wounded in the battle?"

"There were, Mademoiselle; but those who were so, never complained; and those who were killed will never have need to complain again."

"Were there women killed?"

"There were two, Mademoiselle; one a young girl; the other has left children to avenge her death."

"That is the worst of all," said Henri, shuddering. "Cathelineau, we must keep the women in the houses; our men will not fight if they see their wives and sweethearts bleeding beside them; such a sight would make me throw my sword away myself."

"It would make you throw away the scabbard, M. Larochejaquelin; but I fear we shall see enough of such sights," and then he blushed deeply, as he reflected that what he had said would frighten the fair girls sitting near him; "but I beg pardon, ladies—I—"

"Don't mind us, Cathelineau," said Agatha; "you will not frighten us; our brothers will fight by your side; and you will find that we are worthy of our brothers. Marie and I will take our chance without repining."

"And what is to come next, Cathelineau?" said Henri; "we have thrown down the gauntlet now, and we must be ready for all the consequences. You see, we were preparing for the same work," and he pointed to the open packets of gunpowder which were lying scattered on the table. "What are we to do now? we shall soon have swarms of republican soldiers upon us, and it will be well to be prepared. We look to you for counsel now, you know."

"Not so, M. Larochejaquelin; it was to seek council that I and Foret came hither; it was to throw ourselves at the feet of my Lord the Marquis, and at yours, and at those of M. de Lescure; and to implore you to join us, to fight with us, and to save us; to lead us against the republicans, and to help us to save our homes."

"They will, Cathelineau; they will, my excellent friend," said the old man. "Henri shall fight with you—he would not be my son else; and Charles de Lescure there will fight with you for his King as long as the breath is in his body. The Curé there—Father Jerome—will pray for you, and bless your arms; and I believe you'll find he'll fight for you too; the whole country are your friends."

"Yes," said Henri. "The whole province, down to the sea, will be with us. Charette is in the Marais ready to take up arms, the moment the collection of the conscripts is commenced, or before, if it be necessary. M. Bonchamps, who is now at Angers, will join us at once, and give us what we so much want—military skill. The Prince de Talmont is with us, M. Fleuriot, and M. d'Autachamps, every gentleman of standing in the country will help the good cause; my friend here, Adolphe Denot, will fight for us to the last drop of his blood."

Cathelineau bowed graciously, as he was in this way introduced by Larochejaquelin to his friend. Denot also bowed, but he did it anything but graciously: two things were disagreeable to him, he felt himself at the present moment to be in the back-ground, and the hero of the day, the fêted person, was no better than a postillion. When the rest of the party had all given their hands to Cathelineau he had remained behind, he did not like to put himself on an equality with such a person; he fancied even then his dignity was hurt by having to remain in his company.

"And what step shall we first take, M. Larochejaquelin?" said Cathelineau.

"What do you propose yourself?" said Henri.

"I think we should not wait for them to punish us for our first success. I think we should follow up our little victory, and attack the republicans, at Beauprieu, perhaps, or at Cholet; we should so teach our men to fight, teach them to garrison and protect their own towns, and then, perhaps, before very long, we might fly at higher game; we might endeavour to drive these wolves from their own strong places; from Angers perhaps, or Nantes, or better still, from Saumur."

"Why Saumur, especially," said Henri; "surely Nantes would be a better mark than Saumur; besides Saumur is a perfect fortress, walled on all sides, almost impregnable; whereas Nantes is not fortified at all. Saumur is reckoned the strongest town in the south of France; it is the only fortified town in Anjou, Poitou, Tourraine or Southern Britanny."

"That is just the reason, my friend," said Cathelineau, now reassured by his own enthusiasm, and by his intense anxiety on the subject, "that is the very reason why Saumur should be our aim. The republicans now fear nothing from us, and will take no more than ordinary precautions; if we should now attack other places, and commence our proceedings with some success, they would make Saumur utterly impregnable; and what could we do with such a place as that opposed to us on the borders of our country, and on the very road to Paris. But think what it would be in our favour; it commands the Loire, it commands the road from Paris, besides, it contains what we so much want, arms, ammunition, and artillery; it is from Saumur that the republican troops are supplied with gunpowder; believe me, Saumur should be our mark. I know it is difficult, there will be danger and difficulties enough, I know; but it is not impossible, and I believe it may be done," and then he looked round, and saw where he was, and that every one in the room was listening to him, and he added, "but I am too bold to say so much before my Lord the Marquis, and M. Larochejaquelin, and M. de Lescure, and the other gentlemen, whose opinions are so much better than my own."

"He is right, Henri," said de Lescure; "take my word, he is right. We will do it, my friend," and he put his hand on the postillion's shoulder. "We will be masters of Saumur, and you shall lead us there; we will help you to plant the King's standard on the citadel of the town."

Cathelineau was still sitting, and he looked up into de Lescure's face with thankful admiration. "Ah! M. de Lescure, with such guides as you, with such a heart, such courage as yours, no walls shall hinder us, no enemies prevent us."

"You shall have many such friends, Cathelineau," said he; "many as eager, and very many more useful."

"None more useful," said the postillion; "none could be more useful."

"No; none more useful," said the Marquis; "may you have many friends as good, and then you will succeed."

"Saumur let it be, then," said Henri. "I have no doubt you are right; and indeed I do not claim to be great in council; I only hope I may not be found backward in action."

"That you never, never will," said Agatha. "That he never will, Mademoiselle: a Larochejaquelin was never backward in the hour of need," said Cathelineau.

"They know how to flatter in St. Florent, my friend," said she smiling.

"If that be flattery, all the country flatters. I only speak as I hear others speaking; they say that beauty and courage were always to be found at Durbellière."

"Nay, Agatha; but is he not Bayard complete?" said Marie laughing. "I am sure we should be obliged; it is an age since we received a compliment here in the Bocage."

"The ladies are laughing at me," said Cathelineau, rising, "and it is time that I and my friend should cease to trouble you."

"But where would you go, Cathelineau?" said Henri.

"Back to St. Florent; we have gained our object; we can tell our townsmen that the gentlemen of Poitou will fight on their side."

"We will tell them so together, tomorrow by sunset," said Henri; "it is now late, you and Foret stay here tonight; not a word either of you, for your life. I command this garrison; do not you, Cathelineau, be the first to shew an example of disobedience. Father Jerome, lay hands on Foret, lest he fly. Why, my friend, have we so much time to spare, that we can afford to lose it in foolish ceremony? Have we not a thousand plans to mature—a thousand things to settle, which we must settle, and none but we, and which we must discuss together? Are there not here four, six of us, brothers in arms together? I count you one, Father Jerome; and are we not here with the benefit of our father's advice? When shall we all meet again, or when could we meet that our meeting would be more desirable? Well, go if you will, Cathelineau," added he, seeing that the postillion hesitated; "but every one here will tell you that you are wrong to do so."

"Stay, my friend," said the Marquis, who understood well the different feelings which perplexed the mind of the postillion; "stay, my friend, and take your supper with us; you have undertaken a great work, and have shewn yourself fit for it, do not let little things embarrass you. Agatha, darling, see that beds be got ready for our friends. Father Jerome also will remain here tonight, and Charles, and Adolphe; we may not have many merry suppers more, we will at any rate enjoy tonight."

"And Cathelineau," said Henri, "you will not, I trust, be less welcome in St. Florent tomorrow because I accompany you."

It was then decided that they should all remain there that night, that de Lescure and Adolphe should return with Marie to Clisson on the following morning, and that Henri and the priest should accompany Foret and the postillion to St. Florent, there to make the best arrangement within their power for the immediate protection of the place.

They were not very merry that evening, but they were by no means unhappy; as Henri had said they had much to talk of, and they spent an anxious evening, but each satisfied the other. Cathelineau felt himself to be in a new world, sitting down at table to eat with such companions as those around him. The sweet, kind face of Agatha disturbed him most. It almost unmanned him; he thought that it would be happiness enough for a life to be allowed to remain unseen where he might gaze on her. He felt that such beauty, such ineffable loveliness as hers could almost make him forget his country and his countrymen; and then he shuddered and turned his eyes away from her. But there she sat close to him: and she would speak to him, and ask him questions; she asked after his friends in St. Florent, after the women who were wounded, and she gave him money for the children who were made orphans; and then her hand touched his again, and he thought that he was asleep and dreaming.

Much of importance to their future plans was arranged that night, and such a council of war was probably never before assembled. The old man joined in their contemplated designs with as much energy as the youngest among them; the words rash and imprudent never once crossed his lips; nothing seemed rash to him that was to be undertaken for the restoration of the King. The priest took a very prominent part in it, and his word was certainly not for peace; he was the most urgent of the party for decided measures. De Lescure, Larochejaquelin, and Denot, argued, debated, and considered, as though war had always been their profession; but they all submitted, or were willing to submit, to Cathelineau; he had already commenced the war, and had been successful; he had already shewn the ready wit to contrive, and the bold hand to execute; his fitness to lead was acknowledged, and though two days since he was only a postillion, he was tacitly acknowledged by this little band of royalists, to be their leader.

And there too among these confederates sat Agatha and Marie, if not talking themselves, yet listening with almost breathless attention to the plans of the party; sharing their anxiety, promising their women's aid, enchanting them with their smiles, or encouraging them with their tears. Cathelineau had heard how knights of old, famed in song, had spent their lives among scenes of battle and danger, and all for the smiles of the lady of their love; and now he thought he understood it. He could do the same to be greeted with the smiles of Agatha Larochejaquelin, and he would not dream of any richer reward. She was as an angel to him, who had left her own bright place in heaven to illuminate the holy cause in which he had now engaged himself; under such protection he could not be other than successful.

When Foret and Cathelineau dismounted, and were taken into the house by Henri and the Curé, they left their steeds in the care of Peter Berrier; but Peter has not been left ever since leading them up and down in sight of the white-washed lions. The revolt of St. Florent had been heard of in the servants' hall as well as in the salon upstairs, and it was soon known that the heroes of the revolt were in the house, and that their horses were before the door. A couple of men and two or three boys soon hurried round, and Peter was relieved from his charge, and courteously led into the servants' hall by Momont, the grey-headed old butler and favourite servant of the Marquis, and Jacques Chapeau, the valet, groom, and confidential factotum of Larochejaquelin. Peter was soon encouraged to tell his tale, and to explain the mission which had brought him and his two companions to Durbellière, and under ordinary circumstances the having to tell so good a tale would have been a great joy to him; but at the present moment Peter was not quite satisfied with his own position; why was the postillion in the salon while he was in the kitchen? Peter usually was a modest man enough, and respectful to his superiors; the kitchen table in a nobleman's house would generally be an elysium to him; he had no idea that he was good enough to consort with Marquises and their daughters; but he did think himself equal to Cathelineau, the postillion, and as Cathelineau was in the salon, why should he be in the kitchen? He quite understood that Cathelineau was thus welcomed, thus raised from his ordinary position in consequence of what he had done at St. Florent, but why shouldn't he, Berrier, be welcomed, and raised also? He couldn't see that Cathelineau had done more than he had himself. He was the first man to resist; he had been the first hero, and yet he was left for half an hour to lead about a horse, an ass, and an old mule, as though he were still the ostler at an auberge, and then he was merely taken into the servants' hall, and asked to eat cold meat, while Cathelineau was brought into a grand room upstairs to talk to lords and ladies; this made Peter fidgety and uncomfortable; and when he heard, moreover, that Cathelineau was to sup upstairs at the same table with the Marquis and the ladies, all his pleasure in the revolt was destroyed, he had no taste for the wine before him, and he wished in his heart that he had joined the troops, and become a good republican. He could not bear the aristocratic foppery of that Cathelineau.

"And were you a conscript yourself, Peter Berrier?" said Jacques Chapeau.

"Of course I was," said Peter. "Why, haven't you heard what the revolt of St. Florent was about?"

"Well; we have heard something about it," said Momont; "but we didn't exactly hear your name mentioned."

"You couldn't have heard much of the truth then," said Berrier.

"We heard," said Chapeau, "how good Cathelineau began by taking three soldiers prisoners."

"I had twice more to do with those three prisoners than ever he had," said Peter.

"Well; we never heard that," said Momont.

"But we heard," said Chapeau, "how Cathelineau led a few of the townsmen against a whole regiment of soldiers, and scattered them through the town like chaff."

"Scattered them like chaff!" said Peter.

"And we heard," said Momont, "how he stormed the barracks, slaughtered all the soldiers, and dragged the Colonel with his own hand through the barrack window."

"Through the barrack window!" repeated Peter, with an air intended to throw discredit on the whole story.

"And we heard," said Gather's confidential maid, "how he laid his hand upon the cannon and charmed it, so that it would not go off, though the fiery torch was absolutely laid upon the gunpowder."

"That the cannon wouldn't go off though the torch was laid upon the gunpowder!" said Peter.

"And we heard," said the cook, "how all the girls in the town came and crowned him with bay leaves; and how the priest blessed him."

"And how the young made him their captain and their general," said the housekeeper.

"And how they christened him the Saviour of St. Florent," said the laundress.

"And gave him all the money in the town, and the biggest sword they could find," said the page.

"You heard all this, did you?" said Peter Berrier.

"Indeed we did," said Jacques Chapeau, "and a great deal more from M. de Lescure's own man, who went back to Clisson only an hour since, and who had it all from one who came direct from St. Florent."

"And you heard not a word of Peter Berrier?"

"Not a word, not a word," said they all at once.

"Then, friends, let me tell you, you have not heard much of the truth, although M. de Lescure's own man did see the man who came direct from St. Florent; I think I may say, without boasting, and I believe Monsieur the postillion upstairs will not be inclined to contradict me, that without me, there would have been no revolt."

"No revolt without you? No revolt without Peter Berrier? No revolt without M. Debedin's ostler?" said they one after another.

"No—no revolt without M. Debedin's ostler, Madame." The last question had been asked by the cook. "M. Debedin's ostler is as good, I suppose, as M. Gaspardieu's postillion."

"What, as good as Cathelineau?" asked Momont.

"As good as our good postillion!" shouted Chapeau.

"As good as the holy man who charmed the cannon!" said the confidential maid in a tone of angry amazement.

"Would all the girls in St. Florent crown you with bay leaves!" jeered the cook.

"Will they ever make you a great captain!" screamed the housekeeper.

"Or call you the Saviour of St. Florent!" added the laundress.

"Or trust you with all the money, I'd like to know!" suggested the page.

Peter Berrier felt that he was ill-used after all that he had gone through for his King and his country; he sat apart for the rest of the evening, and meditated whether he would go over to the republicans, and bring an army down upon Durbellière, or whether he would more nobly revenge himself by turning out a more enterprising royalist than even the postillion himself.

CHAPTER V.
DE LESCURE.

De Lescure with his sister returned on the following morning to Clisson; for so was his château called. Clisson is about two leagues south of the town of Brassiere, in the province of Poitou, and is situated in the southern part of the Bocage. M. de Lescure owned the château and a considerable territory around it. He was a man of large property in that country where the properties were all comparatively small, and was in other respects also by far the most influential person in the neighbourhood. He had married a lady with a large fortune, which gave him more means of assisting the poor than most of the gentlemen resident in the Bocage possessed. He took a deep interest in the welfare of those around him; he shared their joys, and sympathized with their grief, and he was consequently beloved, and almost adored.

He had now undertaken to join with his whole heart the insurgents against the Republic, and he was fully determined to do so; he had made up his mind that it was his duty to oppose measures which he thought destructive to the happiness of his countrymen, and to make an effort to re-establish the throne; but he did not bring to the work the sanguine hope of success, the absolute pleasure in the task which animated Larochejaquelin; nor yet the sacred enthusiastic chivalry of Cathelineau, who was firmly convinced of the truth of his cause, and believed that the justice of God would not allow the murderers of a King, and the blasphemers of his name to prevail against the arms of people who were both loyal and faithful.

De Lescure had studied and thought much; he was older than Larochejaquelin, much better educated than Cathelineau. He was as ardent in the cause as they were; why else had he undertaken it? but he understood better than they did the fearful chances which were against them: the odds against which they had to fight, the almost insuperable difficulties in their way. He knew that the peasantry around them would be brave and enthusiastic followers, but he also knew that it would be long before they were disciplined soldiers. He was sure that they would fight stoutly round their homes and their families; but he felt that it would be almost impossible to lead any body of them to a distance from their own fields. He foresaw also all the horrors into which they were about to plunge; horrors, of which an honourable death on the field of battle would be the least. The Republic had already shown the bitterness of their malice towards those who opposed them, and de Lescure knew what mercy it would shew to those of his party who fell into its power.

Besides, how could they hope for success against the arms of a whole nation supported by a despotic government. His friends talked sanguinely of aid from England, from Austria, and from Prussia; but he feared that that aid would come too late, after their houses were burnt, and their fields destroyed; after the best among them had fallen; after their children had been murdered; when the country should be depopulated, and nothing but the name of La Vendée left.

With all these fears around his heart, and yet with a firm determination to give himself entirely to the cause in which he was embarked, de Lescure rode home to tell his young wife, to whom he was but barely two years married, that he must not only leave her, and give up the life so congenial to both their tastes, which they had lately led; but that he was going to place himself in constant danger, and leave her and all he loved in danger also.

"You must be very good to Victoriana," he said to his sister; "you must be very good to each other, Marie, for you will both have much to bear."

"We will, we will," said Marie; "but you, Charles, you will be with us; at any rate not far from us."

"I may be near you, and yet not with you; or I may soon be placed beyond all human troubles. I would have you prepare yourself; of all the curses which can fall on a country, a civil war is the most cruel."

Madame de Lescure was the daughter of a nobleman of high rank; she had been celebrated as a beauty, and known to possess a great fortune; she had been feted and caressed in the world, but she had not been spoiled; she was possessed of much quiet sense; and though she was a woman of strong passions, she kept them under control. When her husband told her, therefore, that the quiet morning of their life was over, that they had now to wade through contest, bloodshed, and civil war, and that probably all their earthly bliss would be brought to a violent end before the country was again quiet, she neither screamed nor fainted; but she felt, what he intended that she should feel that she must, now, more entirely than ever, look for her happiness in some world beyond the present one.

"I know, Victorine," said he, when they were alone together in the evening, when not even his own dear sister Marie was there to mar the sacred sweetness of their conference, "I know that I am doing right, and that gives me strength to leave you, and our darling child. I know that I am about to do my duty; and you would not wish that I should remain here in safety, when my King and my country require my services."

"No, Charles; I would never wish that you should be disgraced in your own estimation. I could perfectly disregard what all others said of you, as long as you were satisfied with your own conduct; but I would not for any worldly happiness, that you should live a coward in your own esteem."

"My own, own Victorine," said he, "how right you are! What true happiness could we have ever had, if we attempted to enjoy it at the expense of our countrymen! Every man owes his life to his country; in happy, quiet times, that debt is best paid by the performance of homely quiet duties; but our great Father has not intended that lot for us."

"His will be done. He may yet turn away from us this misery. We may yet live, Charles, to look on these things as our dearest reminiscences."

"We may; but it is not the chance for which we should be best prepared. We are not to expect that God will raise his arm especially to vindicate our injuries; it would be all but blasphemous to ask Him to do so. We are but a link in the chain of events which His wisdom has designed. Should we wish that that chain should be broken for our purposes?"

"Surely not. I would not be so presumptuous as to name my own wishes in my prayers to the Creator."

"No; leave it to His wisdom to arrange our weal or woe in this world; satisfied with this, that He has promised us happiness in the world which is to come."

"I must leave you on Monday, dearest," continued he, after a pause, during which he sat with his wife's hand within his own.

"So soon, Charles!"

"Yes, dearest, on Monday. Henri, and Adolphe, and others, will be here on Sunday; and our different duties will commence immediately."

"And will yours keep you altogether away from Clisson?"

"Very nearly so; at any rate, I could not name the day or the week, when I might be with you. You and Marie will be all in all to each other now; do not let her droop and grow sad, Victorine."

"Nay, Charles, it is she should comfort me; she loves no dear husband. Marie dotes on you; but she can never feel for a brother, as I must feel for you."

"She is younger than you, Victorine, and has not your strength of mind."

"She has fewer cares to trouble her; but we will help each other; it will be much to me to have her with me in your absence. I know she is giving up much in returning to Clisson, and she does it solely for my sake."

"How! what is she giving up? Will she not be better in her own home than elsewhere in such times as these."

"She might choose to change her home, Charles; I had a happy, happy home, but I should not have been contented to remain there till now. I found that something more than my own old home was necessary to my happiness."

"You have made but a sad exchange, my love."

"Would I for all the world recall what I have done? Have I ever repented? Shall I ever repent? No; not though your body were brought breathless to your own hall door, would I exchange my right to mourn over it, for the lot of the happiest bride just stepping from the altar in all the pride of loveliness and rank?"

"My own true love. But tell me, what is this you mean about Marie. Surely she is not betrothed without my knowledge."

"Betrothed! Oh, no! Nor won, nor wooed, as far as I believe; but we women, Charles, see through each other's little secrets. I think she is not indifferent to Henri Larochejaquelin; and how should she be! How few she sees from whom to choose; and if all France were before her feet, how could she make a better choice than him."

"Poor Marie, from my heart I pity her; in any other times than these, how I would have gloried to have given Henri my sister; but now, these are no times to marry, or to give in marriage. Henri has stern, hard work to do, and he is bent on doing it; ay, and he will do it. No one will carry the standard of his King further into the ranks of the republicans than Henri Larochejaquelin."

"I know one, Charles, who will, at any rate, be beside him."

"But he is so full of glorious confidence—so certain of success. He will go to battle with the assured hope of victory. I shall fight expecting nothing but defeat."

"You are melancholy, tonight, my love: something ails you beyond your dread of the coming struggle."

"Can I be other than melancholy? I have no hope."

"No hope, Charles. Oh! do not say you have no hope."

"None in this world, Victorine. The Indian widow, when she throws herself on the burning pile, with a noble courage does what she has been taught to look upon as a sacred duty, but she cannot but dread the fire which is to consume her."

"You would not liken yourself to her?"

"Through the mercy of our blessed Saviour I am not so mistaken in my creed; but I am hardly less calamitous in my fate: but it is not the prospect of my own sufferings which disturb me; I at any rate may be assured of an honourable, even an enviable death. It is my anxiety for you—for our little one—and for dear Marie, which makes my spirit sad."

"God will temper the wind to the shorn lamb," said Madame de Lescure. "Our trials will not be harder than we can bear."

"God bless you for those words, dearest: there is comfort in them—real, true comfort. But remember them yourself Victorine; remember them when you will most want them. When great sorrow comes home to your bosom, as it will do; when affliction is heavy on you, when worldly comforts are leaving you, when enemies are around you, when the voices of cruel men are in your ears, and their cruel deeds before your eyes, then remember, my love, that God will temper the wind to the shorn lamb."

"I will, my own Charles, I will," said she, now kneeling at his feet, and burying her face in her hands upon his knees; "if I am called upon to bear these miseries, I will remember it."

"And look up, Victorine; look up, dearest. I would have you prepared for the worst. Listen to me now calmly, love, and then I need not harrow you with these thoughts again. It may be God's pleasure that I should outlive this war; but as, with His will, I am determined that I will never lay down my sword till the soldiers of the Republic are driven from the province, it is most improbable that I should do so. You must teach yourself, Victorine, to look for my death, as an event certain to occur, which any day may bring forth; and when the heavy news is brought to you, bear it as a Christian woman should bear the afflictions of this, world. I do not ask you not to weep for me, for that would be putting too violent a constraint upon your nature, but do not weep over much. Above all, Victorine, do not allow your sorrow to paralyse your actions. You will have to act then, not only for yourself, but for your child—for my daughter; and if you then give way to the violence of sorrow, who shall think and care for her?"

She laid her beautiful head upon his bosom, and wept, and promised, and prayed for him. And when he had finished what he felt he had to say, what he wished to say once, and but once, before he left her, he became more cheerful, and seemed to have more spirit for his work than he had hitherto shewn.

"And so," he said, after a while, "poor Marie is in love."

"Nay; I did not say she was in love-not in the deep depth of absolute love—but I think she is not indifferent to Henri: were she truly and earnestly in love, she would have told me so."

"Not indifferent to him, and yet not in love. Faith, Victorine, I know not the difference; but you women are such adepts in the science, that you have your degrees of comparison in it."

"Marie, then, has not yet reached the first degree, for hers is not even downright positive love; but I am sure she is fond of Henri's society; and now, poor girl, she must give it up—and probably for ever."

"As you said a while since, Victorine, how should she not like his society? I can fancy no man more fit to be the cynosure of a woman's eye than Larochejaquelin. He has that beauty which women love to look on: the bold bright eye, the open forehead, the frank, easy smile, and his face is only a faithful index to his heart; he is as frank as brave, and yet as tender-hearted as he looks to be; he is specially formed to love and to be loved."

"Poor Marie! I grieve that you brought her from Durbellière."

"Not so, Victorine; this is the place for Marie now; indeed, dear girl, she knew that well herself. The Marquis pressed her hard to stay, and I said nothing; but Marie insisted on coming home. I thought Henri looked somewhat more sombre than is his wont, as he was leading her down the steps: but he cannot, must not, think of love now, Victorine. La Vendée now wants all his energies."

"But you would not forbid him to love her, Charles?"

"I could forbid him nothing, for I love him as Joseph loved his younger brother Benjamin."

"And he will be here now backwards and forwards, will he not?"

"Probably he will—that is as circumstances may arise—he is, at any rate, as likely to be at Clisson as Durbellière."

"He will be more likely, Charles, take my word for it; you cannot prevent their meeting; you cannot hinder them from loving each other."

"Were the King upon his throne, it would be my greatest joy to give my sister to my friend, but now—it is the same for all of us—we must take the chance of these horrid times; and could they be taught to quench the warm feelings of their young hearts, it were well for both of them. The cold, callous disposition would escape much misery, which will weigh down to the grave the loving and the generous."

On the next morning, Madame de Lescure spoke to her sister-in-law on the same subject. She could not bring herself to look on things around her quite so darkly as her husband did. She could not think that there was no longer any hope in their once happy country for the young and the generous, the beautiful and the brave; of herself and her own lot, her thoughts were sombre enough. De Lescure had imbued her with that presentiment, which he himself felt so strongly, that he should perish in the conflict in which he was about to engage; but all would not surely be doomed to share her cup of sorrow. She loved Marie dearly, and she loved Henri, not only from what her husband so often said of him, but from what she knew of him herself; and she longed in her woman's heart that they should be happy together.

It was still March, but it was on a bright warm spring morning, that Madame de Lescure was walking with her sister-in-law in the gardens at Clisson. Marie was talking of her brother—of the part he was to take in the war—of the gallant Cathelineau, and of the events which were so quickly coming on them; but Madame de Lescure by degrees weaned her from the subject and brought her to that on which she wished to speak.

"M. Larochejaquelin will be much here as long as this fighting lasts and M. Denot: we shall have plenty of brave knights coming to and fro to lay their trophies at your feet."

"Poor M. Denot—his trophies if he gets any will be taken to Durbellière; and I fear me, when he offers them, they will not be welcomed. Agatha loves him not; she thinks he shares his adoration too equally between her and his looking-glass."

"I do not wonder at it; no one can deny that M. Denot is attractive, but he attracts without retaining; were I ever so much in want of lovers, I could not endure M. Denot's attentions for more than one evening at the utmost; but our other knight—our other preux chevalier, sans peur et sans reproche—at whose feet will he lay his trophies, Marie? who is to wreath a crown of bay leaves for his brow?"

"His countrywomen should all unite to do it, Victorine—for he is going out to battle for them all—every village girl, whose lover is still left to walk with her on the Sabbath evening—every young wife, who can still lay her baby in her husband's arms—every mother, who still rejoices in the smile of her stalwart son; they should all unite to wreath a crown for the brow of Henri Larochejaquelin."

"And so they shall, Marie; but there will be others also, whose valour will claim a token of admiration from the gratitude of their countrywomen; we will all do this for Henri and our other brave defenders; but if I know his character, the gratitude of many will not make him happy without the favour of one, and she will be the lady of his love; the remembrance of whose smiles will bear him scatheless through the din of the battle."

"I should be vain, Victorine, if I pretended to misunderstand your questions," said Marie; "but why you should mix my name with that of M. Larochejaquelin, without vanity I do not know."

"It does not offend you, Marie?"

"Offend me, dearest Victorine! how should I be offended with anything you could say?"

"But would it offend you to see Henri Larochejaquelin at your feet."

"Is there any girl in France who would have a right to be offended at seeing him there, if he came with a tale of true love?"

"You may be sure at least that Henri will never sully his lips with false vows," said Madame de Lescure.

"He has at any rate made no vows to me, Victorine, nor given me cause to suppose he ever will."

"But should he do so, Marie?"

"Now you ask me questions which you know it only becomes me to answer in one way."

"Why, Marie, I declare you and I have changed characters this morning. You are all sobriety when I make a poor attempt at joking with you. Were I, as usual, talking of my sober cares, you would be as giddy as a girl of fifteen, and talk to me of twenty lovers that you have."

"It is very different talking of twenty lovers, and of one."

"Then you own there is one lover in the case—eh, Marie?"

"Now you are crafty, Victorine, and try to trap me into confessions. You know I have no confession to make, or I should have made it long ago to you."

"I know, Marie, that Larochejaquelin is sad when you are not by, and that he has a word for no one else when you are present; but I know not whether that means love. I know also that your bright eyes brighten when they rest on him, and that your heart beats somewhat faster at the mention of his name; but I know not whether that means love."

"Victorine," said Marie, turning round upon her companion her beautiful face, on which two lustrous tears were shining, "Victorine, you are treating your poor sister unfairly. I know not that my eyes are turned oftener on him than on others; and when my heart would play the rebel within me, I always try to check it."

"Nay, Marie, dear Marie, I did but joke! You do not think I would accuse you of an unmaidenly partiality; if it grieves you we will not mention Henri's name again, though I remember when you did not spare me so easily; when Charles' name was always in my ear, when you swore that every dress I wore was his choice, that every flower I plucked was for his eye; and there had been no more then between Charles and me, than there has now between you and Henri; and yet you see what has become of it. You thought yourself wonderfully clever then, Marie; you were quite a prophetess then. Why should not I now foresee a little. Why should not I also be clever?"

"Well, Victorine, time will shew," said Marie, smiling through her tears; "but do not teach me to love him too dearly, till I know whether he will value my love. If he would prize it, I fear he might have it for the asking for; but I will not throw it at his feet, that he should keep it loosely for awhile, and then scorn it, and lay it by."

CHAPTER VI.
RECRUITING.

On the Monday following the meeting at Durbellière, Larochejaquelin, Denot, the Curé of St. Laud, Foret and Cathelineau joined M. de Lescure at Clisson, and on the day afterwards, the soldiers of the Republic, when attempting to collect the conscripts at a small town near Clisson, were resisted and treated as they had been at St. Florent. There was not quite so much of a battle, for the officer in command knew what was likely to occur, and not having received any reinforcement of troops, thought it advisable to give in early in the day, and capitulate with the honours of war. He was allowed to march his men out of the town, each man having stipulated that he would not again serve in any detachment sent into La Vendée for the collection of conscripts; but they were not allowed to take their arms with them, muskets, bayonets, and gunpowder being too valuable to the insurgents to be disregarded. So the soldiers marched unarmed to Nantes, and from thence returned, before two months were over, in spite of the promises they had given, and requited the mercy of the Vendeans with the most horrid cruelties.

The people were equally triumphant in many other towns. In Beauprieu, Coron, Châtillon, and other places, the collection of conscripts was opposed successfully, and generally speaking, without much bloodshed. In Coron, the military fired on the people, and killed three or four of them, but were ultimately driven out, In Beauprieu, they gave up their arms at once, and marched out of the place. In Châtillon, they attempted to defend the barracks, but they found, when too late, that they had not a single day's provisions; and as the townspeople also knew this, they were at no pains to besiege the stronghold of the soldiers. They knew that twenty-four hours would starve them out. As it was, the lieutenant in command gave up, half an hour after his usual dinner time.

These things all occurred within a week of the revolt at St. Florent. Beauprieu and Châtillon were carried on the Wednesday. Coron was victorious on the Thursday; and on the Friday following, a strong detachment of soldiers marched out of Cholet, of their own accord, without attempting to collect their portion of the levy, and crossed the river Loire, at the Pont de Cé, thus retreating from La Vendée.

These triumphs inspired the insurgents with high hopes of future victories; they gave them the prestige of success, made them confident in the hour of battle, and taught them by degrees to bear, undaunted, the fire of their enemies. The officers of the Republic were most injudicious in allowing their enemies to gather head as they did; had they brought a really formidable force of men, in one body, into the province of Anjou, immediately upon the revolt of St. Florent, they might doubtless have driven the Vendeans, who were then unarmed and undisciplined, back to their farms; but they affected to despise them, they neglected to take vigorous measures, till the whole country was in arms; and they then found that all the available force which they were enabled to collect, was insufficient to quell the spirit, or daunt the patriotism of the revolted provinces.

Towards the end of April, the first attempt was made by the Vendean chiefs to collect a body of men under arms, and to put them into motion, for the purpose of performing service at a distance from their own homes; and though considerable difficulty was felt in inducing them to follow the standards, their first attempts were successful. In the early part of May, they altogether succeeded in driving the soldiers out of Thouars. A few days later, they did the same at Fontenay, though here they met with a violent opposition, and much blood was shed. At these two latter places, the cannon which Cathelineau had taken in so gallant a manner at St. Florent, was brought into action, and quite supported its character as a staunch royalist. At Fontenay, with its aid, they took three or four other pieces of cannon, but none which they prized as they did Marie Jeanne. It was universally credited among the peasantry, that at Cathelineau's touch, this remarkable piece of artillery had positively refused to discharge itself against the Vendeans; and their leaders certainly were at no pains to disabuse them of a belief which contributed so strongly to their enthusiasm.

Some of the more astute among the people had certainly thought for a while that the cannon was a humbug, that it was useless either to royalist or to republican, in fact, that it would never go off at all. But these sceptics were cured of their infidelity at Thouars, when they saw the soldiers as well as the republicans of the town fall in heaps beneath the thunders of Marie Jeanne.

During April and the three weeks of May, Larochejaquelin and de Lescure, together with Cathelineau, Denot, and M. Bonchamps, were actively engaged in collecting and exhorting the people, planning what they should do, and preparing themselves to bear that burst of republican fury which they knew would, sooner or later, fall upon them.

Much of this time was spent at Clisson, as that place was centrically situated for their different manoeuvres; and there certainly appeared reason to suppose that Madame de Lescure was not altogether wrong in her surmises respecting Marie. Here also, at Clisson, Cathelinean frequently joined the party, and though he shewed by his language and demeanour that he had not forgotten that he was a postillion, he gradually acquired a confidence and ease of manner among his new associates, and displayed a mixture of intelligence and enthusiasm, which induced his confederates generally to acknowledge his voice as the first in their councils.

They were occasionally at Durbellière; but there Cathelineau was again abashed and confused. He could not calmly endure the quiet loveliness of Agatha's face, or the sweet music of her voice. He himself felt that his brain was not cool when there; that his mind was gradually teaching itself to dwell on subjects, which in his position would be awfully dangerous to him. He never owned to himself that he was in love with the fair angel, whom he considered as much above him as the skies are above the earth; but he would walk for hours through those eternal paths in the château garden, regardless of the figures, regardless of the various turns and twists he took, dreaming of the bliss of being beloved by such a woman as Agatha Larochejaquelin. He built for himself splendid castles in the air, in which he revelled day after day; and in these dreams he always endowed himself with that one gift which no talents, no courage, no success could give him—high birth and noble blood, for he strongly felt that without these, no one might look up to the goddess of his idolatry; it was his delight to imagine to himself with what ecstasy he would receive from her lips the only adequate reward of his patriotism; he would quicken his pace with joy as he dreamt that he heard her sweet voice bidding him to persevere, and then he would return to her after hard fighting, long doubtful but victorious battles, and lay at her feet honours worthy of her acceptance.

It can hardly be said that he himself was the hero of his own reveries; he was assured beyond the shadow of a doubt, that the proud happiness which he pictured to his imagination was as much beyond his own reach, as though his thoughts were turned on some celestial being. No, it was a creation of his brain, in which he dwelt awhile, till his own strong good sense reminded him that he had other work before him than the indulgence in such dreams, and he determined that he would be at Durbellière as little as was possible.

It was singular though, that he contrived, while his imagination was thus rambling, to mingle in his thoughts the actual and the ideal. The revolt of La Vendée, the struggle of his brother royalists for the restoration of their King; the annihilation of republicanism, and re-establishment of the old clergy, were still the subjects of his meditations; and the bold plans which his mind then suggested to him, were those which were afterwards put into effect.

He still insisted on attacking the strongly fortified citadel of Saumur, and after their success at Fontenay, the chiefs agreed at once to make arrangements for that great undertaking. The tenth of June was settled on as the day on which the attack should be commenced, and their utmost efforts in the mean time were to be employed in raising recruits, arming and drilling them, and collecting ammunition and stores of war sufficient for so serious an operation.

For this purpose Cathelineau returned for a while to St. Florent. M. Charette was requested to bring up all the men he could collect from the Marais, a part of La Vendée which lies close upon the sea. M. Bonchamps was invited to join them from Angers. De Lescure returned to Fontenay, to ask the assistance of those who had been so successful there against the republicans; while Henri Larochejaquelin, was left at home in the Bocage, to secure the services of every available man from every village.

He had two comrades with him in his recruiting party; and though they were of very different characters, they were almost equally serviceable. One was his friend and priest, the Curé of St. Laud, and the other was his servant, Jacques Chapeau. The Curé had no scrupulous compunction in using his sacerdotal authority as a priest, when the temporal influence of Larochejaquelin, as landlord, was insufficient to induce a countryman to leave his wife and home to seek honour under the walls of Saumur. The peasants were all willing to oppose the republican troops, should they come into their own neighbourhood to collect conscripts; they were ready to attack any town where republican soldiers were quartered, providing they were not required to go above a day's march from their own homes; but many objected to enrol themselves for any length of time, to bind themselves as it were to a soldier's trade, and to march under arms to perform service at a distance from their farms, which to them seemed considerable. With such men as these, and with their wives and sisters, Henri argued, and used his blandest eloquence, and was usually successful; but when he failed, the Curé was not slow in having recourse to the irresistable thunders of the church.

No one could have been fitter for the duties of a recruiting-sergeant than Jacques Chapeau; and to his great natural talents in that line, he added a patriotic zeal, which he copied from his master. No one could be more zealous in the service of the King, and for the glory of La Vendée, than was Jacques Chapeau. Jacques had been in Paris with his master, and finding that all his fellow-servants in the metropolis were admirers of the revolution, he had himself acquired a strong revolutionary tendency. His party in Paris had been the extreme Ultra-Democrats: he had been five or six times at the Jacobins, three or four times at the Cordeliers; he had learnt to look on a lamp-rope as the proper destination of an aristocrat, and considered himself equal to anybody, bu his master, and his master's friends. On Henri's return to La Vendée, he had imbued himself with a high tone of loyalty, without any difficulty or constraint on his feelings; indeed, he was probably unaware that he had changed his party: he had an appetite for strong politics, was devotedly attached to his master, and had no prudential misgivings whatsoever. He had already been present at one or two affairs in which his party had been victorious, and war seemed to him twice more exciting, twice more delightful than the French Opera, or even the Jacobin Clubs.

Jacques Chapeau was about five years older than his master, and was as active and well made a little Frenchman, as ever danced all night at a ball outside the barriers of Paris. He was a light-hearted and kind-hearted creature, although he always considered it necessary to have mortal enemies—horrid, blasphemous, blood-thirsty fellows, men devoid of feeling, without faith, hope, or charity, who would willingly slaughter women and children for the mere pleasure of doing so. Such, in Chapeau's imagination, were all his enemies—such had been the aristocrats during the time of his revolutionary fervour—such now were the republicans. Chapeau loved his own side truly and faithfully, without any admixture of self in his calculations, but I certainly cannot say for him that he was a good Christian, for all the clergymen in Anjou could not have taught him to love his enemies.

On a beautiful summer's morning, on the 2nd of June, this remarkable recruiting party rode from Durbellière to the little village of Echanbroignes; the distance was about four leagues, and their road lay, the whole way, through the sweet green leafy lanes of the Bocage. The aspect of this province is very singular, and in summer most refreshing. The country is divided into small farms, which are almost entirely occupied with pasture; the farms are again divided into small fields, and each field is surrounded by a belt of trees, growing out of high, green, flowering hedges. The face of the country is like a thickly wooded demesne, divided and subdivided into an infinity of little paddocks. The narrow lanes of the country, which are barely broad enough for the wheels of a carriage, and are seldom visited by such a vehicle, lie between thick, high hedges, which completely overshadow them; the wayfarer, therefore, never has before him that long, straight, tedious, unsightly line of road, which adds so greatly to the fatigue of travelling in an open country, and is so painful to the eye.

Through such a lane as this our party rode quickly and cheerily; quickly, for they had much work before them for that day; and cheerily, for they knew that the people among whom they were going would join them with enthusiasm. They were all well mounted, for they rode the best horses from the stables of Durbellière: the old Marquis would have blushed to have given less than the best to the service of his King.

Chapeau was peculiarly elated at the prospect of his day's work; but his joy was not wholly professional; for Jacques now accounted himself a soldier by profession. He had another reason for the more than ordinary gaiety with which he trotted on towards Echanbroignes. There was there a certain smith, named Michael Stein, who had two stalwart sons, whom Jacques burnt to enrol in his loyal band of warriors; this smith had also one daughter, Annot

Stein, who, in the eyes of Jacques Chapeau, combined every female charm; she was young and rosy; she had soft hair and bright eyes; she could dance all night, and was known to possess in her on right some mysterious little fortune, left to her by nobody knew what grandfather or grandmother, and amounting, so said report, to the comfortable sum of five hundred francs. When Chapeau had risen to some high military position, a field-marshal's baton, or the gold-laced cap of a serjeant-major, with whom could he share his honours better than with his dear little friend, Annot Stein? Jacques wanted her advice upon this subject, and he therefore rejoiced greatly that the path of duty was leading him this morning to Echanbroignes.

"We may be sure, Father Jerome," said Henri, "of those men from St. Michael?"

"Of every man. You will find there will not be a defaulter."

"God send it; one traitor makes many, as sheep follow each other through a hedge row."

"Do not fear them, my son. Father Francois has the list of them; he will have every man collected by daylight on the 7th, and he will come on with them himself as far as the cross-roads; they will there meet my own children from St. Laud."

"There were to be one hundred and seventy-five from St. Michael."

"Yes; and one hundred and forty from St. Laud; and thirty will have joined us from Petit Ange de Poitou before we reach the turn from St. Michael."

"And have you positively determined you will start with them from St. Laud's yourself, Father Jerome."

"With God's will, my son, I most assuredly shall do so; and from that to the walls of Saumur, they shall see before them my tattered Curé's frock, and the blessed symbol of their hope. I will carry the cross before them from the porch of the little church which shall once more be my own, till I plant it on the citadel of Saumur beside the standard of the King."

"Oh! if we had a few more Father Jeromes!" said Henri.

"There might perhaps be more soldiers in La Vendée than at present; but perhaps also there would be fewer Christians," said the priest. "May God forgive me if, in my zeal for my King, I am too remiss in His service."

They rode on a little way in silence, for Father Jerome felt a slight qualm of conscience at his warlike proceedings, and Henri did not like to interrupt his meditations; but the Curé soon recovered himself.

"I shall have a goodly assemblage of followers," said he, "before I reach Coron. Those from Echanbroignes will join us half-a-mile from the town. There will be above two hundred from Echanbroignes."

"Will there? So many as that, think you?"

"They will muster certainly not short of two hundred. Near seven hundred men will follow me into Coron on the evening of the 7th."

"They will find provisions there in plenty—meat, bread, and wine. They are not used to lie soft; they will not grumble at having clean straw to sleep on."

"They shall grumble at nothing, my friend; if your care can supply them with food, well; if not, we will find bread enough among the townsfolk. There is not a housewife in Coron, who would refuse me the contents of her larder."

"The bullocks are ready for the butcher's axe in the stalls at Durbellière, please your reverence," said Chapeau, who rode near enough to his master to take a part in the conversation as occasion offered. "And the stone wine-jars are ready corked. Momont saw to the latter part himself. May the saints direct that the drinking have not the same effect upon our friends that the corking had on Momont, or there will be many sick head-aches in Coron on the next morning."

"There will be too many of us for that, Jacques. Five hundred throats will dispose of much good wine, so as to do but little injury."

"That would be true, your reverence, were not some throats so much wider than others. You will always see that one porker half empties the trough before others have moistened their snouts in the mess."

"We will see to that, Jacques. We will appoint some temperate fellow butler, or rather some strong-fisted fellow, whose thick head much wine will not hurt; though he may swill himself he will not let others do so."

"If it were not displeasing to yourself and to M. Henri, I would undertake all that myself. Each man of the five hundred should have his own share of meat and drink at Coron, and the same again at Doué."

"Will not Jacques be with you?" said the priest, turning round to Henri. "What should bring him to Coron among my men?"

"He says he has friends here in Echanbroignes, and he has begged that he may be here with them on the evening of the 6th, so as to accompany them into Coron on the 7th. We shall all meet at Doué on the 8th."

"I was thinking, your reverence, if any here were loiterers, as there may be some, I fear; or if there should be any ill inclined to leave their homes, my example might encourage them. I have a liking for the village, and I should feel disgraced were a single able-bodied man to be found near it after the morning of the 7th."

"I trust they will not need any one to remind them of their promise, when they have once pledged themselves to the service of their King," said the priest. "However, you will be, doubtless, useful to me at Coron. But, Henri, what will you do without him?"

"Adolphe and I will be together, and will do well. We shall have an absolute barrack at Durbellière. We shall have above one hundred men in the house. Agatha and the women are at work night and day."

"You have the worst part of the whole affair—the ammunition."

"It is all packed and ready for the carts; a few days since the cellars were half-full of the lead and iron, which we have been casting; they are now, I trust, half-way to Saumur, under Foret's care."

"How many men has he with him?" asked the priest.

"He has all the men from Clisson, from St. Paul's and St. Briulph's— except a few of Charles' own tenants, who went on forward to join him at Doué, and who have our supply of flags with them, made in the château at Clisson. Madame de Lescure and poor Marie have worked their fingers to the bone."

"God bless them! God will bless them, for they are working in the spirit which he loves."

"Agatha and Annette, between them, have packed nearly every ounce of gunpowder," said Henri, who could not help boasting of his sister. "Night and day they have been handling it without regarding for a moment the destruction which the slightest accident might bring upon them."

"It is that spirit, my son, which will enable us to beat twice our own strength in numbers, and ten times our own strength in arms and discipline How many men has Foret with him?"

"Above six hundred. I do not know his exact numbers," said Henri.

"And you, yourself?"

"I shall muster a thousand strong, that is for a certainty; I believe I shall be nearer twelve thousand."

"Let me see—that will be, say two thousand five hundred from the Bocage."

"Oh! more than that your reverence," said Chapeau, "you are not counting M. de Lescure's men, who have gone on with the flags—or the men from Beauprieu who will follow M. d'Elbée, or the men from St. Florent, who will come down with Cathelineau."

"I don't count Beauprieu, or Cholet or St. Florent; there will be two thousand five hundred from our own country, out of three thousand three hundred male adults, that is three men, Henry, out of every four—they cannot at any rate say that the spirit of the people is not with us."

As the priest spoke, they rode into the street of the little village of Echanbroignes, and having stopped at the door of the Mayor's house, Henri and the Curé dismounted, and giving their horses up to Jacques, warmly greeted that worthy civic authority, who came out to meet them.

The appointment of a mayor in every village in France, had been enjoined at an early time in the revolution, and after the death of the King, these functionaries were, generally speaking, strong republicans; but the Vendeans in opposition to the spirit of the revolution, had persisted in electing the Seigneurs, wherever they could get a Seigneur to act as mayor; and, where this was not the case, some person in the immediate employment of the landlord was chosen. This was the case at Echanbroignes, where the agent or intendant of the proprietor was mayor. He expected the visit which was now paid to him, and having twenty times expressed his delight at the honour which was done him, he got his hat and accompanied his visitors to the door of the church, where with his own hands he commenced a violent assault on the bell-rope, which hung down in the middle of the porch.

He was ringing the tocsin, which was to call together the people of the village. They also very generally knew who was coming among them on that day, and the purpose for which they were corning; and at the first sound of the bell, all such as intended to shew themselves, came crowding on to the little space before the church; it was but few who remained at home, and they were mostly those to whom home at the present moment was peculiarly sweet; one or two swains newly married, or just about to be married; one or two fathers, who could hardly bring themselves in these dangerous times to leave their little prattling children, and one or two who were averse to lose the profits of their trade.

In spite of the speedy appearance of his townspeople, the Mayor persisted in his operations on the bell-rope until the perspiration ran down his face. He was sounding the tocsin, and he felt the importance of what he was doing. Every one knew that a tocsin bell to be duly rung, should be rung long and loud—not with a little merry jingle, such as befitted the announcement of a wedding, but in a manner to strike astonishment, if not alarm, into its hearers; and on this occasion great justice was done to the tocsin.

"That will do, M. Mayor; that will do, I think!" said the Curé, "it looks to me as though our friends were all here."

The Mayor gave an awful pull, the bell leapt wildly up, gave one loud concluding flourish, and then was quiet.

"Now, M. Mayor," said the Curé, "you have by heart the few words I gave you, have you not?"

"Indeed, Father Jerome, I have," said the Mayor, "and am not likely to forget them. Let me see—let me see. Now, my friends, will you be quiet a moment while I speak to you. Ambrose Corvelin, will you hold your noisy tongue awhile—perhaps M. de Larochejaquelin, I had better get up on the wall, they will hear me better?"

"Do, M. Mayor, do," said Henri; and the Mayor was lifted on to the low wall which ran round the churchyard, and roared out the following words, at the top of his voice:

"In the holy name of God, and by command of the King, this parish of Echanbroignes is invited to send as many men as possible to Saumur, to be there, or at any other such place in the neighbourhood as may be appointed, at three o'clock on the afternoon of the 9th of June. And may God defend the right. Amen!" And having said this, the Mayor jumped off the wall, and the crowd commenced shouting and cheering.

"Wait one moment, and hear me say a few words, my friends," said Henri, springing to the place which the Mayor had just left. "Most of you, I believe, know who I am."

"We do, M Henri," said they. "We do, M. Larochejaquelin. We all know who you are. We know that you are our friend."

"I am very glad you think so," continued he; "for you will know, that if I am your friend, I shall not deceive you. I have come here to ask you to share with me the honour and the danger of restoring his father's kingdom and his father's throne to the son of your murdered King. I have come here to ask you also to assist me and others, who are your friends, in protecting yourselves, your pastors, your houses, your wives and daughters, from the tyranny and cruelty of the republicans."

"We will!" shouted the crowd. "We will go at once. We will be at Saumur on Wednesday. We will follow M. Larochejaquelin wherever he would lead us."

"You all know Cathelineau," continued Henri; "you all know the good postillion of St. Florent?"

"We do, God bless him! we do. We all know the Saint of Anjou."

"Come and meet him, my friends, under the walls of Saumur; or rather, I should say, come and meet him within the walls of Saumur. Come and greet the noble fellows of St. Florent, who have set us so loyal an example. Come and meet the brave men of Fontenay, who trampled on the dirty tricolour, and drove out General Coustard from his covert, like a hunted fox. He is now at Saumur; we will turn him out from thence."

"We will! we will! We will hang up Coustard by the heels."

"We will strip him rather of his spurs and his epaulettes, of his sword and blue coat, and send him back to the Convention, that they may see what will become of the heroes, whom they send to seek for glory in La Vendée. Thanks, my friends; thanks for your kindness. I will lead you to no dangers which I will not share with you. You shall suffer no hardship of which I will not partake. I will look for no glory in which you shall not be my partners."

During the time that the Mayor had been giving his invitation to the people, and Henri had been speaking to them, Father Jerome had been busily employed with Jacques Chapeau over six or seven little lists which he held in his hand. These were lists of the names of able-bodied men, which had been drawn out by the Curé of the parish, and Jacques had already marked those of one or two whom he had found to be absent, and among them the names of Michael Stems' two stalwart sons. Father Jerome again handed the lists to Jacques, and as Henri descended from the wall, amid the greeting of the populace, he ascended it, and gave them a little clerical admonition.

"My children," said he, "it delights my heart to find that so few of you are absent from us this morning—from the whole parish there are but five, I believe, who have not readily come forward to proclaim their zeal for their God, their King, and their Church: those five, I doubt not, will be here when we proceed to check the names. Let it not be said that there was one recreant in Echanbroignes—one man afraid to answer when called for by his country. Is there danger in the bloody battle we have before us?—let us all share it, and it will be lighter. Is it a grievous thing for you to leave your wives and your children?—let no man presume to think that he will be happier than his neighbours, for that man shall assuredly be the most miserable. It is possible that some of you may leave your bodies beneath the walls of Saumur, be it so; will you complain because the Creator may require from some of you the life which he has given? Is it not enough for you to know, that he who falls fighting with this blessed symbol before his eyes, shall that night rest among the angels of Heaven?" and the Curé held up on high, above the people, a huge cross, which he had had brought to him out of the church. "God has blessed you, my children, in giving you the sacred privilege of fighting in His cause. You would indeed be weak—senseless as the brutes—unfeeling as the rocks—aye, impious as the republicans, had you not replied to the summons as you have done; but you have shown that you know your duty. I see, my children, that you are true Vendeans. I bless you now, and on tomorrow week, I will be among you before the walls of Saumur."

Having finished speaking, the priest also jumped off the wall, and again the people shouted and cheered. And now they went to work with the lists: Henri, the Mayor, and the Curé each took a pencil, and called the names of the different men, as they were written down. There was of course much delay in getting the men as they were called; but Chapeau had sworn in three or four assistants, and he and they dived in among the crowd, hurried this way and that, and shouted, screamed, and screeched with great effect. The lists were made out with some regard to the localities; the men from the lower end of the village were to go to Henri's side; those from the northern part to Father Jerome's table; and the inhabitants of the intermediate village were checked off by the Mayor. Chapeau and his friends were most diligent in marshalling them; to be sure, Jacques knew the names of but few of them; but he made them tell him whether they were villagers, northerns, or lower-end men; and though the men in many instances couldn't answer this themselves, the divisions were effected, the names of all were called over, those who were there were checked off and informed what was expected of them, and where and by whom arms would be supplied to them: and those who were not there became the unhappy victims of a black list.

Father Jerome, when he said that there were only five absent, was something but not much out in his reckoning: his object, however, had been to make the people think that he knew exactly who was there, and who was not there; and in this he was successful. During the calling of the lists, one or two stragglers dropped in who hoped to escape detection: respecting a few others, some good ground of excuse was alleged; but on this head the Curé was most severe: he would accept no plea but that of absolute downright sickness, and of this he required to have most ample testimony—even Henri sometimes pleaded for the people, but unsuccessfully. The Republic by their proscription would have decimated the men; the Curé of St. Laud insisted on taking them all.

The houses of those who had not presented themselves were to be visited, and the two first on the list were Jean and Peter Stein.

"Jean and Peter Stein," said Henri. "Why, Jacques, are they not friends of yours? are they not sons of Michael Stein, the smith?"

"Quiet, M. Henri; pray be quiet for a moment, and I will explain."

"Are they not strong, active lads," said the Curé, turning somewhat angrily on Chapeau, as though he were responsible for the principles of his friends.

"They are, they are, your reverence, fine strong active lads as you ever laid your eyes on."

"And they are afraid to carry a musket for their king?"

"Not a bit, Father Jerome, not a bit afraid; nor yet unwilling, M. Henri. I will explain it all; only let us be a little by ourselves."

"There is a mystery, Father Jerome," said Henri, "and Chapeau must have his own way in explaining it."

"Exactly, M. Henri; I will explain all." By this time he had got the priest and his master somewhat out of the crowd. "You see, M. Henri, there are not two young men in the Bocage more determined to fight for the good cause this moment, than Jean and Peter Stein."

"Why, Jacques, I do not see it yet, certainly."

"Oh! Sir, it's a fact; they are dying to have a musket in their hands. I pledge for them my word of honour," and Jacques laid his hand upon his heart. "You will find they are with me, your reverence, when I meet you at the cross-roads, within half a mile of Coron, on Monday morning. But, M. Henri, they have a father."

"Have a father!" said the Curé, "of course they have."

"You don't mean to tell me that Michael Stein, the smith, is a republican?"

"A republican!" said Jaques. "Oh! no, the heavens preserve us, he's nothing so bad as that, or his own son wouldn't remain under his roof another night, or his daughter either. No; Annot wouldn't remain with him another hour, were he twenty times her father, if he turned republican."

"Why does he prevent his sons joining the muster, then?" said Henri.

"He is very fond of money, M. Henri. Old Michael Stein is very fond of money; and every one in the country who owns a franc at all, is buying an old sword or a gun, or turning a reaping-hook into a sabre, or getting a long pike made with an axe at the end of it; so Michael Stein's smithy is turned into a perfect armoury, and he and his two sons are at work at the anvil morning, noon, and night: they made Annot blow the bellows this morning, till she looks for all the world like a tinker's wife."

"That alters the case," said Father Jerome; "they are doing good service, if they are making arms for our men; they are better employed than though they joined us themselves."

"Don't say so, Father Jerome," said Jacques, "pray don't say so, Jean and Peter would die were they not to be of the party at Saumur; but Michael is so passionate and so headstrong, and he swears they shall not go. Now go they will, and therefore I supplicate that my word may be taken, and that I may be saved the dishonour of hearing the names of my friends read out aloud with those of men who will disgrace their parish and their country."

The request of Jacques was granted, and the names of Jean and Peter Stein were erased from the top of the black list.

It was eight in the evening before the recruiting party had finished their work, and it was not yet noon when they rode into the little village. Henri and the Curé got their supper and slept at the Mayor's house, and even there they were not allowed to be quiet; some of those who were to be at Saumur, were continually calling for new instructions; one wanted to know what arms he was to carry, another what provisions he was to bring, a third was anxious to be a corporal, and a fourth and fifth begged that they might not be separated, as one was going to marry the sister of the other. None of these were turned away unanswered; the door of the Mayor's house was not closed for a moment, and Henri, to be enabled to eat his supper at all, was obliged to give his last military orders with a crust of bread in his hand, and his mouth full of meat.

As might be supposed, Jacques spent the evening with Annot Stein, at least it was his intention to have done so; but he had been so leading a person in the day's transactions that he also was besieged by the villagers, and was hardly able to whisper a word into his sweetheart's ear. There he sat, however, very busy and supremely happy in the smith's kitchen, with a pipe in his mouth and a bottle of wine before him. The old smith sat opposite to him, while the two young men stood among a lot of others round the little table, and Annot bustled in and out of the room, now going close enough up to her lover to enable him to pinch her elbow unseen by her father, and then leaning against the dresser, and listening to his military eloquence.

"And so, my friend," said Chapeau, "Jean and Peter are not to go to Saumur?"

"Not a foot, Chapeau," said the old man, "not a foot, Chapeau; let ye fight, we will make swords for you: is not that fair, neighbour?"

"I have nothing to say against it, M. Stein, not a word; only such fellows as they, they would surely get promoted."

"Oh, ay; you will all be sergeants, no doubt. I have nothing to say against that; only none of mine shall go waging wars in distant lands."

"Distant lands, say you! is not Saumur in Anjou? and is not Anjou within three miles of you, here where you are sitting?"

"May be so, M. Chapeau; but still, with your leave, I say Saumur is distant. Can you get there in one day from here?"

"Why no, not in one day."

"Nor in two?"

"Why, no again; though they might do it in two. They'll start from here Monday morning with light, and they'll reach Saumur on Wednesday in time to look about them, and learn what they have to do the next morning."

"That's three day's going, and three coming, and heaven only knows how many days there; and you don't call that distant! Who's to feed them all I'd like to know?"

"Feed them!" said Chapeau. "I wish you could see all the bullocks and the wine at Durbellière; they'll have rations like fighting-cocks. I only pray that too much good living make them not lazy."

"Were I a man," said Annot, as she put on the table a fresh bottle of wine, which she had just brought in from the little inn, "were I a man, as I would I were, I would go, whether or no."

"Would you, minx," said the father; "it's well for you that your petticoats keep you at home."

"Don't be too sure of her, Michael Stein," said Paul Rouel, the keeper of the inn; "she'll marry a soldier yet before the wars are over."

"Let her do as her mother did before her, and marry an honest tradesman; that is, if she can find one to take her."

"Find one!" said Annot, "if I can't get a husband without finding one, indeed, I'm sure I'll not fash myself with seeking: let him find me that wants me."

"And it won't be the first that finds you either, that'll be allowed to take to you, will it Annot?" said the innkeeper.

"That's as may be, Master Rouel," said Annot. "Those who ask no questions are seldom told many lies."

"I know Annot Stein loves a soldier in her heart," said another old man, who was sitting inside the large open chimney. "The girls think there is no trade like soldiering. I went for a soldier when I was young, and it was all to oblige Lolotte Gobelin; and what think ye, when I was gone, she got married to Jean Geldert, down at Petit Ange. There's nothing for the girls like soldiering."

"You give us great encouragement truly," said Jacques. "I hope our sweethearts will not all do as Lolotte did. You would not serve your lover so, when he was fighting for his King and country—would you, Annot?"

"I might, then, if I didn't like him," said she.

"She's no better than her neighbours, M. Chapeau," said one of her brothers. "There was young Boullin, the baker, at St. Paul's. Till we heard of these wars, Annot was as fond of him as could be. It was none but he then; but now, she will not as much as turn her head if she sees his white jacket."

"Hold thine unmannerly, loutish, stupid tongue, wilt thou, thou dolt," said Annot, deeply offended. "Boullin indeed! I danced with him last harvest-home; I know not why, unless for sheer good-nature; and now, forsooth, I am to have Boullin for ever thrust in my teeth. Bah! I hate a baker. I would as lieve take a butcher at once."

Jacques Chapean also was offended.

"I wonder, Jean Stein," said he, "that you know not better than to liken your sister to such as young Boullin—a very good young man in his way, I have no doubt. You should remember there is a difference in these things."

"I don't know," said Jean, "why a smith's daughter should not marry a baker's son; but I did not mean to vex Annot, and will say no more about him; only good bread is a very good thing to have in one's house."

"And a butcher is a good trade too," said the old man inside the chimney. "Jean Geldert, he that Lolotte Gobelin ran off with, he was a butcher."

CHAPTER VII.
SUNDAY IN THE BOCAGE.

The remainder of that week was spent by Henri and the Curé as actively and as successfully as the day in which they visited Echanbroignes. The numbers they enrolled exceeded their hopes, and they found among the people many more arms than they expected, though mostly of a very rude kind. The party separated on the Saturday night, with the understanding that they were to meet together at Done on the Tuesday evening, to proceed from thence to the attack of Saumur. Henri Larochejaquelin returned to Durbellière. The Curé of St. Laud went to his own parish, to perform mass among his own people on the following morning, and Jacques Chapeau, according to agreement, took up his quarters at the smith's house in Echanbroignes.

On the following morning, he and Annot, and most of the young men and women of the village walked over to St. Laud's to receive mass from Father Jerome, and to hear the discourse which he had promised to give respecting the duties of the people in the coming times.

The people, as in olden days, were crowded round the church about half-past ten o'clock; but the doors of the church were closed. The revolt in La Vendée had already gone far enough to prevent the possibility of the constitutional priests officiating in the churches to which they had been appointed by the National Assembly; but it had not yet gone far enough to enable the old nonjuring Cures to resume generally their own places in their own churches: the people, however, now crowded round the church of St. Laud's, till they should learn where on that day Father Jerome would perform mass.

The church of St. Laud's did not stand in any village, nor was it surrounded even by a cluster of cottages. It stood by itself on the side of a narrow little road, and was so completely surrounded by beech and flowering ash trees, that a stranger would not know that he was in the neighbourhood of a place of worship till it was immediately in front of him. Opposite to the door of the church and on the other side of the road, was a cross erected on a little mound; and at its foot a Capuchin monk in his arse brown frock, with his hood thrown back, and his eyes turned to heaven, was always kneeling: the effigy at least of one was doing so, for it was a painted wooden monk that was so perpetually at his prayers.

The church itself was small, but it boasted of a pretty grey tower; and on each side of the door of the church were two works of art, much celebrated in the neighbourhood. On the left side, beneath the window, a large niche was grated in with thick, rusty iron bars. It occupied the whole extent from the portico to the corner of the church, and from the ground to the window;

and, within the bars, six monster demons—spirits of the unrepentent dead, the forms of wretches who had died without owning the name of their Saviour, were withering in the torments of hell-fire; awful indeed was the appearance of these figures; they were larger than human, and twisted into every variety of contortion which it was conceived possible that agony could assume. Their eyes were made to protrude from their faces, their fiery tongues were hanging from their scorched lips; the hairs of each demon stood on end and looked like agonized snakes; they were of various hideous colours; one was a dingy blue; another a horrid dirty yellow, as though perpetual jaundice were his punishment; another was a foul unhealthy green; a fourth was of a brick-dust colour; a fifth was fiery red, and he was leaping high as though to escape the flame; but in vain, for a huge blue flake of fire had caught him by the leg, and bound him fast; his fiery red hands were closed upon the bars, his tortured face was pressed against them, and his screeching mouth was stretched wide open so as to display two awful rows of red-hot teeth; the sixth a jet black devil, cowered in a corner and grinned, as though even there he had some pleasure in the misery of his companions.

The space occupied on the other side was much larger, for it was carried up so far as to darken a great portion of the window. That on the left represented the misery of hell—torment without hope. That on the right contained two tableaus: the lower one was purgatory, here four recumbent figures lay in the four corners, uncomfortably enough; for the bed of each figure was six sharp spikes, each of which perforated the occupier of it. But yet these dead men were not horrible to look at as those six other wretches; their eyes were turned on a round aperture above, the edge of which was all gilt and shining, for the glory of heaven shone into it. This aperture entered into paradise. Through the aperture the imaginative artist had made a spirit to be passing—his head and shoulders were in paradise; these were also gilt and glorious, and on his shoulders two little seraphims were fixing wings; his nether parts below the aperture, were still brown and dingy, as were the four recumbent spirits who rested on their gridirons till the time should come that they also should be passed through.

Above the aperture was to be seen paradise in all its blazon of glory, numberless little golden-headen cherubims encircled a throne, on which was seated the beneficent majesty of Heaven. From the towers and roofs projected numerous brazen-mouthed instruments, which welcomed into everlasting joy the purified spirit which was ascending from purgatory.

Thus were paradise, purgatory and pandemonium represented at St. Laud's, and abominable as such representations now appear to be, they had, to a certain extent, a salutary effect with the people who were in the habit of looking at them. That they were absolute accurate representations of the places represented, they never for a moment presumed to doubt; and if the joys of heaven, as displayed there, were not of much avail in adding to the zeal of the faithful, the horrors of hell were certainly most efficacious in frightening the people into compliance with the rules laid down for them, and in preventing them from neglecting their priests and religious duties.

The people were crowded round the church; some were kneeling with the wooden monk at the foot of the cross, and some round the bars of purgatory. Others were prostrated before the six condemned demons, and some sat by the road-side, on the roots of the trees, telling their beads. Many men were talking of the state of the times, and of the wars to come; some were foretelling misery and desolation, and others were speaking of the happy days about to return, when their King and their priests should have their own, and La Vendée should be the most honoured province in France.

They made a pretty scene, waiting there beneath the shade till their priest should come to lead them to some rural chapel. The bright colours worn by the women in their Sunday clothes, and the picturesque forms of the men, in their huge broad-brimmed flapping hats, harmonized well with the thick green foliage around them. They shewed no sign of impatience, they were quite content to wait there, and pray, or gossip, or make love to each other, till such time as Father Jerome should please to come; they had no idea that their time was badly spent in waiting for so good a man.

At any rate he came before they were tired, and with him came a man who was a stranger to them all, except to Jacques Chapeau. This man was but little, if anything, better dressed than themselves; he looked like one of their own farmers of the better days; certainly from his dress and manner he had no pretensions to be called a gentleman, and yet he walked and talked with Father Jerome as though he were his equal.

"God bless you, my children, God bless you," said the Curé, in answer to the various greetings he received from his flock. "Follow me, my children, and we will worship God beneath the canopy of his holy throne," and then turning to the stranger, he added: "the next time you visit me at St. Laud's, M. d'Elbée, we shall, I doubt not, have our church again. I could now desire the people to force the doors for me, and no one would dare to hinder them; but I have been thrust from my altar and pulpit by a self-constituted vain authority—but yet by authority; and I will not resume them till I do so by the order of the King or of his servants."

"I reverence the house of God," replied M. d'Elbée, "because his spirit has sanctified it; but walls and pillars are not necessary to my worship; a cross beneath a rock is as perfect a church to them who have the will to worship, as though they had above them the towers of Notre Dame, or the dome of St. Peter's."

"You are right, my son; it is the heart that God regards; and where that is in earnest, his mercy will dispense with the outward symbols of our religion; but still it is our especial duty to preserve to his use everything which the piety of former ages has sanctified; to part willingly with nothing which appertains in any way to His church. The best we have is too little for His glory. It should be our greatest honour to give to Him; it is through His great mercy that He receives our unworthy offerings. Come, my children, follow me; our altar is prepared above."

The priest led the way through a little shaded path at the back of the church; behind a farmhouse and up a slight acclivity, on the side of which the rocks in different places appeared through the green turf, and the crowd followed him at a respectful distance.

"And who is that with Father Jerome—who is the stranger, M. Chapeau?" said one and another of them, crowding round Jacques—for it soon got abroad among them, that Jacques Chapeau had seen the stranger in some of his former military movements in La Vendée. Chapeau was walking beside his mistress, and was not at all sorry of the opportunity of shewing off.

"Who is he, indeed?" said Jacques. "Can it be that none of you know M. d'Elbée?"

"D'Elbée!—d'Elbée!—indeed; no, then, I never heard the name till this moment," said one.

"Nor I," said another; "but he must be a good man, or Father Jerome would not walk with him just before performing mass."

"You are right there, Jean," said Jacques, "M. d'Elbée is a good man; he has as much religion as though he were a priest himself."

"And he must be a thorough royalist," said another, "or Father Jerome wouldn't walk with him at all."

"You are right, too, my friend; M. d'Elbée is a great royalist. He is the especial friend of our good Cathelineau."

"The friend of Cathelineau and of Father Jerome," said a fourth, "then I am sure M. d'Elbée must be something out of the common way."

"You are right again, he is very much out of the common way, he is one of our great generals," said Chapeau.

"One of our great generals, is he," said two or three at once. "I knew he was going to Saumur," said Jean, "or Father Jerome wouldn't have walked so peaceable with him, great as he may be."

"But if he is a great general," said Annot, "why has he no lace upon his coat; why doesn't he wear a sword and look smart like M. Larochejaquelin? At any rate he is a very shabby general."

"He has a terrible long nose too," said another girl. "And he has not a morsel of starch in his shirt ruffles, I declare," said a third, who officiated as laundress to the Mayor of Echanbroignes.

"I'm sure the republicans will never be afraid of such a general as he is. You are joking with us now, Jacques. I am sure he is not a general; he is more like a grocer from Nantes."

"And is not Cathelineau like a postilion?" said Jacques, "and I hope you will allow he is a great soldier. You know nothing of these things yet, Annot. M. Larochejaquelin is so smart because he is a young nobleman; not because he is a general."

"And is not M. d'Elbée a nobleman?" said one of the girls.

"Not a bit of it," said Chapeau.

"Well, I think the generals should all be noblemen; I declare," said the laundress, "M. Larochejaquelin did look so nice last Wednesday, when he was getting off his horse."

"That is all; but Cathelineau," said Annot, "he is the finest fellow of them all. I'd sooner have Cathelinean for my lover, than the Duc de Chartres, and he's the king's cousin."

"You are a foolish girl, Annot," said Chapeau. "You might as well want the picture of St. John out of the church window down yonder, and take that for your lover, as Cathelineau. Don't you know he's the Saint of Anjou?"

"He might marry a wife, and have a house full of children, for all that; that's the difference between being a saint and a priest; there's no harm in being in love with a saint, and I am very much in love with Cathelineau."

"Why, you little ninny, you never saw him," said Chapean.

"No matter," said Annot; "ninny, or no ninny, I'll go where I'm like to see him; and I'm sure I'll never bear the sight of another man afterwards; the dear, good, sweet Cathelineau, with his curly hair, and fine whiskers, and black bright eyes; he's better than all the noblemen: I declare I dreamed of him these last two nights."

Chapeau left the side of his mistress, muttering something about stupid foolish chits of girls, and continued his description of M. d'Elbée to the men.

"Indeed he is a very great general. I don't know very well where he came from, but I believe somewhere down in the Marais, from his being such a friend of M. Charette; but he has been fighting against the republicans this long time, even before Cathelineau began, I believe, though I don't exactly know where. I know he was made a prisoner in Paris, and nearly killed there by some of those bloody-minded rebels; then he escaped, and he was at the siege of Machecoult, and got honourably wounded, and was left for dead: and then he was at Thouars—no, not at Thouars; we heard he was coming, but he didn't come; but he was at Fontenay, and that's where I first saw him. M. Bonchamps brought him in and introduced him to M. de Lescure, and our M. Larochejaquelin, and I was astonished to see how much they made of him, for he was dressed just as he is now, and had no sword or anything. Well, as soon as he came in they all went to work talking, and settling how Fontenay was to be attacked, for though its a little place, and not walled and fortified like Saumur, we had a deal of trouble with it; but before a word was spoken, M. d'Elbée stood up and said, 'Brethren,' said he, 'let us ask the assistance of our Saviour:' so down they went on their knees, and he said an awful long prayer, for all the world like a priest. And then again before we fired a shot, he bade all the soldiers kneel down, and down we went, the republicans firing at us all the time. The soldiers call him Old Providence, for they say he talks a deal about Providence when he is fighting."

"You may be sure that's what makes Father Jerome so fond of him," said Jean. "I knew he was a good man."

"And he was a desperate fellow to fight afterwards," continued Chapeau. "But he walked into the thick of the fighting just as he is now."

"But he had a sword, or a gun, or a spear?" said Jean.

"Neither the one or the other; he was just as he is this minute, giving orders, and directing some of the men there who knew him well. Presently, he said to a young gentleman who was near him: 'Lend me that sword a moment, will you?' and he took it out of his hands, and made a rush through the gate of Fontenay, and I saw no more of him that day."

"Why did you not rush after him, then, M. Chapeau?"

"Rush after him! Why, you simpleton; do you think in wars like that every man is to rush just where he pleases; you'll soon be taught the difference. M. d'Elbée was a general, and might go where he liked; but I was a corporal under M. Henri, with ten men under me. We had to remain where we were, and cut off the republicans, if they showed their noses at a point in the street which we covered; it's only the generals that go rushing about in that way. But here we are at Father Jerome's altar. Well; I'm very hot. I'm sure its nearly half a league up here from the church."

They had now come to a rude altar, constructed on a piece of rock, in front of which was a small space of green turf: the whole spot was closely surrounded by beech and ash-trees; so closely, indeed, that the sun hardly made its way into it, and the rocks around it rising up through the grass afforded ample accommodation for the people. In a moment, they were on their knees on the grass; some almost immediately before the altar; others kneeling against the rocks; others again with their heads and hands resting against the trunk of a huge beech-tree.

Hither had been brought the necessary appurtenances for the performance of mass. A small, but beautifully white cloth was spread upon a flat portion of the rock; bread was there, and a small quantum of wine; a little patina and a humble chalice. M. d'Elbée took his place among the crowd before the altar, and Father Jerome, having dressed himself in his robes, performed, with a fine, full, sonorous voice, the morning service of his church. When so occupied, he had no longer the look of the banished priest: his sacred vestments had not shared the decay which had fallen on his ordinary clothes. No bishop rising from his throne to bless the congregation assembled in his cathedral, could assume more dignity, or inspire more solemnity than the Curé of St. Laud, as he performed mass at his sylvan altar in La Vendée.

After mass was finished, the priest gave them an extempore discourse on the necessity of their absolutely submitting themselves to their teachers, spiritual masters, and pastors; and before he had finished, he turned their attention to the especial necessity of their obeying the leaders, now among them, in carrying on the war against the Republic, and as he concluded, he said:

"I rejoice at all times, my children, that you are an obedient and a docile people, content to accept the word of God from those whom he has sent to teach it to you—that you are not a stiff-necked generation, prone to follow your own vain conceits, or foolish enough to conceive that your little earthly knowledge can be superior to the wisdom which comes from above, as others are. I have always rejoiced at this, my children, for in it I have seen hope for you, when I could see none for others; but now also I rejoice greatly to see that you unite the courage of men to the docility of babes. Hitherto your lot has been that of peace, and if you have not enjoyed riches, you have at any rate been contented: another destiny is before you now—peace and content have left the country, and have been followed by robbery, confusion, and war. My children, you must, for a while, give over your accustomed peaceful duties; your hands—your hearts—all your energy, and all your courage, are required by God for his own purposes—yes, required by that Creator who gave you strength and energy—who gave you the power and the will to do great deeds for His holy name.

"His enemies are in the land: impious wretches—who do not hesitate to wage war against His throne—are endeavouring to destroy all that is good, and all that is holy in France. Do you not know, my children, that they have murdered your King?—and that they have imprisoned your Queen, and her son, who is now your King? Would you be content to remain quiet in your homes, while your King is lying in a prison, in hourly danger of death? They have excluded you from your churches, they have caused God's holy houses to be closed; they have sent among you teachers who can only lead you astray—whose teaching can only bring you to the gates of hell. The enemies of the Lord are around you; and you are now required to take arms in your hands, to go out against them, and if needs be to give your blood—nay your life for your country, your King, and your Church.

"I greatly rejoice, my children, that you are an obedient people; I know that you will now do your utmost, and I know that you will succeed. The Lord will not desert His people when they combat for His glory, when they faithfully turn to Him for victory. You have been taught how He chose the Israelites as an especial people—how He loved and favoured them: as long as they were faithful and obedient He never deserted them. They conquered hosts ten times their numbers—they were victorious against armed warriors, and mighty giants. The Lord blinded their enemies so that they saw not; He blunted their weapons; He paralyzed their courage; chariots and horses did not avail them; nor strong walls, nor mighty men of battle. The Lord loved the Israelites, and as long as they were faithful and obedient, they prevailed against all their enemies.

"You, my children, are now God's people; if you are truly faithful, you shall assuredly prevail; if you go out to battle firmly, absolutely, entirely trusting in the strength of His right hand—that right hand, that Almighty arm shall be on your side. And who then shall stand against you?—though tens, and hundreds of thousands swarm around you, they shall yield before you—they shall fall before you as the giant Goliath fell before the shepherd David.

"Be not afraid, therefore, my children: we will go together; we will remember that every man who falls on our side in this holy war, falls as he is doing Christ's service, and that his death is to be envied, for it is a passport into Heaven. We will remember this in the hour of battle, when our enemies are before us, when death is staring us in the face, and remembering it, we shall not be afraid. If we die fighting truly in this cause, our immortal souls will be wafted off to paradise— to everlasting joy: if we live, it will be to receive, here in our own dear fields, the thanks of a grateful King, to feel that we have done our duty as Christians and as men, and to hear our children bless the days, when the courage of La Vendée restored the honour of France."

Father Jerome's exhortation had a strong effect upon the people; he knew and calculated their strength and their weakness—they were brave and credulous, and when he finished speaking, there was hardly one there who in the least doubted that the event of the war would be entirely successful:

they felt that they were a chosen people, set apart for a good work—that glory and victory awaited them in the contest, and especially that they were about to fight under the immediate protection of the Almighty.

As soon as the service was over, they all left the little sylvan chapel by different paths, and in different directions; some went back to the church, some went off across the fields, some took a short cut to the road, but they all returned home without delay. Every man was to set out early on the morrow for the rendezvous, and the women were preparing to shed their tears and say their last farewell to their lovers, brothers, and husbands, before they started on so great an enterprise. They had all been gay enough during the morning—they became a little melancholy on their return home, but before the evening was far advanced, nothing was to be heard but sobs and vows, kisses and blessings.

Jacques Chapeau returned to Echanbroignes with the party of villagers who had gone from thence to hear Father Jerome, but he did not attach himself expressly to Annot, indeed he said not a word to her on the way, but addressed the benefit of his conversation to his male friends generally; to tell the truth, he was something offended at the warm admiration which his sweetheart had expressed for Cathelineau. He wasn't exactly jealous of the postillion, for Annot had never seen him, and couldn't, therefore, really love him; but he felt that she ought not to have talked about another man's eyes and whiskers, even though that other man was a saint and a general. It was heartless, too, of Annot to say such things at such a time, just as he was going to leave her, on the eve of battle, and when he had left his own master, and all the glorious confusion and good living in—at Durbellière, merely that he might spend his last quiet day in her company.

It was base of her to say that she had dreamed twice of Cathelineau; and she was punished for it, for she had to walk home almost unnoticed. At first she was very angry, and kicked up the dust with her Sunday shoes in fine style; but before long her heart softened, and she watched anxiously for some word or look from Jacques on which she might base an attempt at a reconciliation. Jacques knew what she was about, and would not even look at her: he went on talking with Jean and Peter and the others, about the wars, and republicans and royalists, as though poor Annot Stein had not been there at all. From the chapel of St. Laud to the village of Echanbroignes, he did not speak a word to her, and when the four entered the old smith's house, poor Annot was bursting with anger, and melting with love; she could not settle with herself whether he hated Chapeau or loved him most; she felt that she would have liked to poison him, only she knew that she could not live without him.

She hurried into her little sleeping place, and had a long debate with herself whether she should instantly go to bed and pray that Jacques might be killed at Saumur, or whether she should array herself in all her charms, and literally dazzle her lover into fondness and obedience by her beauty and graces— after many tears the latter alternative was decided on.

It was a lovely summer evening, and at about eight o'clock hardly a person in the whole village was to be found within doors; the elderly were sitting smoking at their doors, husbands were saying a thousand last words to their weeping wives, young men were sharpening their swords, and preparing their little kit for the morrow's march, and the girls were helping them; but everything was done in the open air. Jean and Peter Stein were secretly preparing for a stolen march to Saumur; for their father was still inexorable, and they were determined not to be left behind when all the world was fighting for glory. Old Michael was smoking at his ease, and Jacques was standing talking to him, wondering in his heart whether Annot could be really angry with him, when that young lady reappeared in the kitchen.

"Where have you been, Annot?" said Michael Stein, "you didn't get your supper, yet child."

"I was sick with the heat, father; walking home from St. Laud's."

"I would not have you sick tonight, Annot, and our friends leaving us before sun-rise tomorrow. Here is M. Chapeau complaining you are a bad hostess."

"M. Chapeau has enough to think of tonight, without my teasing him," said Annot; "great soldiers like him have not time to talk to silly girls. I will walk across the green to Dame Rouel's, father; I shall be back before sunset."

And Annot went out across the green, at the corner of which stood the smith's forge. Jacques Chapeau was not slow to follow her, and Dame Rouel did not see much of either of them that evening.

"Annot," said Jacques, calling to his sweetheart, who perseveringly looked straight before her, determined not to know that she was followed. "Annot, stop awhile. You are not in such a hurry, are you, to see Dame Rouel?"

"Ah, M. Chapeau, is that you?—in a hurry to see Dame Rouel. No—I'm in no particular hurry."

"Will you take a turn down to the mill, then, Annot? Heaven knows when you and I may walk to the old mill again; it may be long enough before I see Echanbroignes again."

Annot made no answer, but she turned into the little path which led through the fields to the mill.

"I suppose it may," said she, determined, if possible, that the amende should be made by Jacques and not by herself.

"I see you are indifferent about that," said Jacques, with a soft and sentimental look, which nearly melted Annot; "well, when you hear of my death, you will sometimes think of me, will you not?"

"Oh, I will, M. Chapeau! Of course I'll think of you, and of all my friends."

Jacques walked on a few minutes or two in silence, cutting off the heads of the blue-bells with his little cane. "I am not different to you then from any one else, eh, Annot?" said he.

"How different, M. Chapeau?"

"You will think as much of young Boullin, the baker?"

"I don't like young Boullin, the baker, and I don't thank you for mentioning his name one bit."

"Well! people say you are very partial to young Boullin."

"People lie—they always do; everybody tries to tease and plague me now. You and Jean, and father, and that old fool, Rouel, are all alike," and Annot gave symptoms of hysterical tears.

Jacques was again silent for awhile, but he had commenced walking very near to his companion, and she did not appear to resent it. After a while he said: "You are not glad that I'm going, Annot?"

"You would not have me sorry that you are going to fight with all the other brave men, would you?"

"Is that all I am to get from you, after all? is that all the regard you have for me? very well, Annot—it is well at any rate we should understand each other. They were right, I find, when they told me that you were such a coquette, you would have a dozen lovers at the same time."

"And they were right, I find, when they told me you were too fond of yourself ever to love any girl truly."

"Oh, Annot! and is it come to this? I'm sorry I ever came to Echanbroignes. I'm sorry I ever saw you."

"And if you are, M. Chapeau, I'm sure I'm sorry enough I ever saw you;" and Annot again increased the distance between her and her lover.

They walked on from hence in silence till they came to the little mill, and each stood gazing on the stream, which ran gurgling down beneath the ash and willow-trees, which dipped their boughs in its waters.

"How kind you were, the last time we were here together," said Jacques; "how kind and generous you were then; you are very different now."

"And you are very different, too, M. Chapeau; much more different than I am; it's all your own fault; you choose to give yourself airs, and I won't put up with it, and I believe we may as well part."

"Give myself airs! No; but it's you give yourself airs, and say things which cut me to the heart—things which I can't bear; and, therefore, perhaps, we may as well part;" and Jacques assumed a most melancholy aspect, as he added, "So, good bye, Annot; there's my hand. I wouldn't, at any rate, part anything but friends after all."

"Good bye," said poor Annot, putting out her hand to her lover, and sobbing violently. "Good bye; I'm sure I never thought it would come to this. I'm sure I gave up everybody and everything for your sake."

"Well; and didn't I give up everybody, too. Haven't I come all the way over here week after week, when people wondered what made me leave Durbellière so much; and wasn't it all for love of you? Oh, Annot! Annot!" and even the manly dignity of M. Chapeau succumbed to tears.

"It's no good talking," said she, greatly softened; "for you can't have loved me, and treated me as you did this day, letting me walk all alone from St. Laud, without so much as a word or a look; and that before all the people: and I that went merely to walk back with you. Oh! I could have died on the roadside to find myself treated in such a way."

"And what must I have felt to hear you talking as you did before them all? Do you think I felt nothing?"

"Talking, Jacques; what talk?"

"Why; saying that you loved Cathelineau better than any one. That he was the only man you admired; that you dreamed of him always, and I don't know how much more about his eyes and whiskers."

"Why now, Jacques; you don't mean to be jealous?"

"Jealous; no I'm not jealous."

"Jealous of a man you know I never saw," said Annot, smiling through her tears.

"Jealous. No, I tell you I'm not jealous; but still, one doesn't like to hear one's mistress talking of another man's eyes, and whiskers, and those sort of things; no man would like it, Annot; though I care about it as little myself as any man."

"But don't you know Cathelineau is a saint, Jacques?"

"Oh! but you said saints might marry, and have a lot of children, and so they may."

"But I never saw Cathelineau, Jacques," and she put her hand upon his arm.

"And you are not in love with him, Annot?"

"How can I be in love with a man I never put eyes on?"

"And you won't say again, that you'd like to have him for a lover?"

"That was only my little joke, Jacques. Surely, a girl may joke sometimes."

"And you do love me, don't you?" and Jacques now got very close to his mistress.

"Ah! but why did you let me walk home all the way by myself? You know I love you dearly; but you must beg my pardon for that, before I'll ever tell you so again."

And Jacques did beg her pardon in a manner of his own twenty times, sitting by the gurgling mill-stream, and to tell the truth Annot seemed well pleased with the way in which he did it; and then when the fountain of her love was opened, and the sluice gate of her displeasure removed, she told him how she would pray for him till he came back safe from the wars; how she would never speak a word to mortal man in the way of courting, till he came back to make her his wife; how she would grieve, should he be wounded; how she would die, should he be killed in battle: and then she gave him a little charm, which she had worked for him, and put it round his neck, and told him she had taken it with her to St. Laud, to give it him there beneath the cross, only he had gone away from her, so that she couldn't do so: and then Jacques begged pardon again and again in his own queer way; and then, having sat there by the mill-stream till the last red streak of sunlight was gone, they returned home to the village, and Annot told her father that Dame Rouel had been so very pressing, she had made them stay there to eat bread and cheese. And so Annot, at last, went to bed without her supper, and dreamed not of Cathelineau, but of her own lover, Jacques Chapeau.

CHAPTER VIII.
AGATHA LAROCHEJAQUELIN.

As Chapeau had said, great preparations were made at Durbellière for the coming campaign. The old Marquis had joined with his son in furnishing everything which their limited means would admit of, for the wants of the royalists. Durbellière had become quite a depôt; the large granaries at the top of the house were no longer empty; they were stored with sacks of meal, with pikes and muskets, and with shoes for the soldiers. Agatha's own room looked like an apartment in a hospital; it was filled with lint, salves, and ointments, to give ease to those whom the wars should send home wounded; all the contents of the cellars were sacrificed; wine, beer, and brandy, were alike given up to aid the spirits of the combatants; the cattle were drawn in from the farms, and kept round the house in out-houses and barns, ready to be slaughtered, as occasion might require, an abattoir was formed in the stable yard, and a butcher kept in regular employment; a huge oven was built in an outhouse attached to the stables, and here bakers, from neighbouring parishes, were continually kept at work: they neither expected, or received wages; they, and all the others employed got their meals in the large kitchen of the château, and were content to give their work to the cause without fee or reward. Provisions, cattle, and implements, were also sent from M. de Lescure's house to Durbellière, as it was considered to be more central, and as it was supposed that there were still some republicans in the neighbourhood of Bressuire, whereas, it was well known that there were none in the rural districts; the more respectable of the farmers also, and other country gentlemen sent something; and oxen, sheep, and loads of meal; jars of oil, and casks of wine were coming in during the whole week before the siege of Saumur, and the same horses took them out again in the shape of bread, meat, and rations, to the different points where they would be required.

As soon as M. de Lescure had left home, on his recruiting service in the south of La Vendée, the ladies of his house went over to Durbellière, to remain there till Henri Larochejaquelin should start for Saumur, and give their aid to Agatha in all her work. Adolphe Denot was also there: he, too, had been diligently employed in collecting the different sinews of wars; and as far as his own means went had certainly not begrudged them. There was still an unhappy air of dissatisfaction about him, which was not to be observed with any one else: his position did not content his vanity; the people did not talk of him as they did of Cathelineau, and Henri Larochejaquelin; he heard nothing of La Vendée relying on his efforts; the names of various men were mentioned as trustworthy leaders, but his own was never among them. De Lescure, Charette, d'Elbée, Stofflet, were all talked of; and what had they done more than he had; or what, indeed, so much: the two latter were men of low origin, who had merely shown courage in the time of need: indeed, what more had Cathelineau done; whereas, he had never failed in courage, and had given, moreover, his money, and his property; yet he felt that he was looked on as a nobody. Jacques Chapeau was almost of more importance.

And then, again, his love for Agatha tormented him. He had thought to pique her by a show of indifference himself, but he found that this plan did not answer: it was evident, even to him, that Agatha was not vexed by his silence, his altered demeanour, and sudden departure. He had miscalculated her character, and now found that he must use other means to rouse the affection in her heart, without which he felt, at present, that he could not live happily. He thought that she could not have seen with indifference the efforts he was making in the cause which she loved so well; and he determined to throw himself at her feet before he started for Saumur, and implore her to give him a place in her affections, while her heart was softened by the emotions, which the departure of so many of her friends, on the eve of battle, would occasion.

Agatha had had but little conversation with him since his last arrival at Durbellière, but still she felt that he was about to propose to her. She shunned him as much as she could; she scrupulously avoided the opportunity which he anxiously sought; she never allowed herself to be alone with him; but she was nevertheless sure the evil hour would come; she saw it in his eye as they sat together at their meals—she heard it in the tones of his voice every time he spoke. She knew from his manner that he was preparing himself for the interview, and she also knew that he would not submit tamely to the only answer she could bring herself to give him.

"Marie," said she to her cousin, on the Saturday evening, "I am in the greatest distress, pray help me, dearest. I am sure you know what ails me."

"In distress, Agatha, and wanting help from me!—you that are wont to help all the world yourself! But I know, from your face, you are only half in earnest."

"Indeed, and indeed, I never was much more so. I never was more truly in want of council. Can you not guess what my sorrow is?"

"Not unless it is, that you have a lover too much?—or perhaps you find the baker's yeast runs short?"

"Ah, Marie, will you always joke when I am serious!"

"Well then, Agatha, now I am serious—is it that you have a lover too much?"

"Can any trouble be more grievous?"

"Oh, dear, yes! ten times worse. My case is ten times worse: and alas, alas! there is no cure for that."

"Your case, Marie?"

"Yes, my case, Agatha—a lover too few!"

"Ah, Marie, do not joke with me tonight. I want your common sense, and not your wit, just now. Be a good, dear girl, and tell me what I shall say to him. I know he will not go to Saumur before—before he has proposed to me."

"Then, in the name of common sense, dear Agatha, tell him the truth, whatever it may be."

"You know I do not—cannot love him."

"Nay, I know nothing. You have not said yet who 'him' is—but I own I can give a guess. I suppose poor Adolphe Denot is the man you cannot love? Poor Adolphe! he must be told so, that is all."

"But how shall I tell him, Marie? He is so unlike other men. Henri is his friend, and yet he has never spoken to him about me, nor to my father. If he would ask my hand from Henri, as another would, Henri would talk to him, and explain to him that it could not be-that my heart is too much occupied with other cares, to care for loving or being loved."

"That means, Agatha, till the right lover comes."

"No, Marie; but till these wars are over. Not that I could ever love Adolphe Denot; but now, at present, methinks love should be banished from the country, and not allowed to return till the King is on his throne again."

"Well, Agatha, I don't know. That would be somewhat hard upon us poor girls, whose lovers are more to our taste, than M. Denot is to yours. I know not that our knights will fight the worse for a few stray smiles, though the times be so frightful."

"Do you smile on yours then, Marie; and I will smile to see you happy. But tell me, dearest, what shall I say to Adolphe? You would not have me give him hope, when I feel I can never love him?"

"God forbid!—why should you? But has he never spoken to Henri on the subject, or to the Marquis?"

"Never a word. I'm sure he never spoke of it to my father, and Henri told me that he had never said a word to him."

"Then you have spoken to your brother on the subject? And what did he say?"

"He said just what a dear, good brother should have said. He said he was sorry for his friend, but that on no account whatever would he sacrifice his sister's happiness."

"M. Larochejaquelin always does just what he ought to do. He is as good and kind to you as Charles is to me."

"Henri and I are so nearly of an age; we were always companions together. I do not think any lover will be agreeable to me as long as he is with me."

"But if he should take a love of his own, Agatha? It won't do, you know, for sisters to monopolize their brothers; or what shall we spinsters do?"

"He shall bring his love here, and she shall be my own sister. If he makes the choice I think he will, I shall not have to open a new place in my heart for her, shall I, Marie?"

"Nay, I know not. Now it is you that wander from the subject."

"And it is cruel in you to bring me back to it. If he proposes to me tomorrow, Marie, what shall I say to him?"

"Keep out of his way tomorrow. He goes on Monday morning."

"It is very well to say, 'Keep out of his way;' but if he formally demands an interview, I cannot refuse it."

"If he formally desires an interview, do you give him a formal reception: if he formally offers you his hand, do you formally decline the honour."

"I would it were you, Marie, that he loved."

"A thousand thanks to you, Mademoiselle Larochejaquelin. I appreciate your generosity, but really I have no vacancy for M. Denot, just at present."

"Ah! but you would reject him with so much more ease, than I can do it."

"Practice, my dear, is everything: this time you may feel a little awkward, but you will find you will dispose of your second lover without much difficulty, and you will give his congé to your third with as much ease, as though you were merely dismissing a disobedient kitchen-maid."

"I cannot bear to give pain; and Adolphe will be pained; his self-love will be wounded at the idea of being rejected."

"Then spare his self-love, and accept him."

"No; that I will not do."

"Then wound his self-love, and reject him."

"Would I could do the one without the other; would I could persuade him I was not worthy of him."

"Nay, do not attempt that; that will be direct encouragement."

"I will tell him that I am averse to marriage; in truth, that will be no falsehood. I do not think that my heart is capable of more love than it feels at present."

"That may be true now, Agatha; but suppose your heart should enlarge before the autumn, at the touch of some gallant wizard—take my advice, dear girl, make no rash promises."

"I will tell him that I cannot think of love till the King is on the throne once more."

"If you say so, he will promise valiantly to restore His Majesty, and then to return to you to look for his reward. Shall I tell you, Agatha, what I should say?"

"Do, dearest Marie: tell me in sober earnest; and if there be ought of sobriety mixed with your wit, I will take your advice."

"I would say to him thus: 'M. Denot,' or 'Adolphe,' just as your custom is to address him—but mind, mark you, make him speak out firmly and formally first, that your answer may be equally firm and formal. 'M. Denot, you have paid me the greatest honour which a gentleman can pay a lady, and I am most grateful for the good opinion which you have expressed. I should be ungrateful were I to leave you for one moment in doubt as to my real sentiments: I cannot love you as I ought to love my husband. I hope you will never doubt my true friendship for you; but more than sincere friendship I cannot give you.' There, Agatha, not a word more, nor a word less than that; sit quite straight on your chair, as though you were nailed to it; do not look to the right or to the left; do not frown or smile."

"There will not be the least danger of my smiling, Marie."

"But do not frown neither; fancy that you are the district judge, giving sentence on a knotty piece of law; show neither sentiment, pride, nor anger. Be quite cold, inflexible and determined; and, above all things, do not move from your seat; and I think you will find your lover will take his answer: but if he do not—repeat it all over again, with a little more emphasis, and rather slower than before. If it be necessary, you may repeat it a third time, or indeed till he goes away, but never vary the words. He must be a most determined man if he requires the third dose. I never heard of but one who wasn't satisfied with the second, and he was an Irishman."

"If I could only insist on his sitting still and silent to hear me make my formidable speech, your advice might be very good."

"That, my dear, is your own strong point: if he attempts to interrupt you, hear what he says, and then begin again. By the time you have got to your 'real sentiments,' I doubt not he will be in his tantrums: but do you not get into tantrums too, or else you are as good as lost; let nothing tempt you to put in an unpremeditated word; one word might be fatal; but, above all, do not move; nothing but an awful degree of calm on your part will frighten him into quiescence: if you once but move, you will find M. Denot at your feet, and your hand pressed to his lips. You might as well have surrendered at once, if anything like that occur."

"Well, Marie, let what will happen, at any rate I will not surrender, as you call it. As to sitting like the district judge, and pronouncing sentence on my lover as you advise—I fear I lack the nerve for it."

Agatha was quite right in her forebodings. Adolphe Denot had firmly made up his mind to learn his fate before he started for Saumur, and immediately on rising from breakfast, he whispered to Agatha that he wished to speak to her alone for a moment. In her despair she proposed that he should wait till after mass, and Adolphe consented; but during the whole morning she felt how weak she had been in postponing the evil hour; she had a thousand last things to do for her brother, a thousand last words to say to him; but she was fit neither to do nor to say anything; even her prayers were disturbed; in spite of herself her thoughts clung to the interview which she had to go through.

Since the constitutional priests had been sent into the country, and the old Curés silenced, a little temporary chapel had been fitted up in the château at Durbellière, and here the former parish priest officiated every Sunday; the peasants of the parish of St. Aubin were allowed to come to this little chapel; at first a few only had attended, but the number had increased by degrees, and at the time when the revolt commenced, the greater portion of the pastor's old flock crowded into or round the château every Sunday; so that the Sabbath morning at Durbellière was rather a noisy time. This was especially the case on the 6th of June, as the people had so much to talk about, and most of the men wished to see either the old or the young master, and most of the women wanted to speak to one of the ladies; by degrees, however, the château was cleared, and Agatha with a trembling heart retreated to her own little sitting-room upstairs to keep her appointment with Adolphe Denot.

She had not been long there, when Adolphe knocked at the door: he had been there scores of times before, and had never knocked; but, although he was going to propose to make Agatha his wife, he felt that he could no longer treat her, with his accustomed familiarity.

He entered the room and found Agatha seated; so far she had taken her friend's advice; she was very pale, but still she looked calm and dignified, and was certainly much less confused than her lover.

"Agatha," said he, having walked up to the fire-place, and leaning with his arm upon the mantle-piece, "Agatha, tomorrow I start for Saumur."

He was dressed very point-de-vice; the frills of his shirt were most accurately starched; his long black hair was most scrupulously brushed; his hands were most delicately white; his boots most brilliantly polished; he appeared more fit to adorn the salon of an ambassador, than to take a place as a warrior beneath the walls of a besieged town. Adolphe was always particular in his dress, but he now exceeded himself; and he appeared to be the more singular in this respect at Durbellière just at present, as the whole of the party except himself women included, had forgotten or laid aside, as unimportant, the usual cares of the toilet.

"You, at any rate, go in good company, Adolphe," said Agatha, attempting to smile. "May you all be successful, and return as heroes—heroes, indeed, you are already; but may you gather fresh laurels at Saumur. I am sure you will. I, for one, am not in the least despondent."

"Yes, Agatha, I shall go to Saumur, determined at any rate not to lose there any little honour I may yet have won. If I cannot place the white flag of La Vendée on the citadel of Saumur, I will at any rate fall in attempting it."

"I am very sure, that if you fail, it will not be for lack of courage, or of resolution. You and Henri, and M. de Lescure and our good friend Cathelineau, have taught us to expect victory as the sure result of your attempts."

"Ah! Agatha, one word from your lips, such as I long to hear, would make me feel that I could chain victory to my sword, and rush into the midst of battle panoplied against every harm."

"Your duty to your King should be your best assurance of victory; your trust in your Saviour, your panoply against harm; if these did not avail you, as I know they do, the vain word of a woman would be of little service."

"You speak coldly, Agatha, and you look coldly on me. I trust your feelings are not cold also."

"I should have hoped that many years of very intimate acquaintance between us, of friendship commenced in childhood, and now cemented by common sympathies and common dangers, would have made you aware that my feelings are not cold towards you."

"Oh no! not cold in the ordinary sense. You wish me well, I doubt not, and your kind heart would grieve, if you heard that I had fallen beneath the swords of the republicans; but you would do the same for Cathelineau or M. de Bonchamps. If I cannot wake a warmer interest in your heart than that, I should prefer that you should forget me altogether."

Agatha began to fear that at this rate the interview would have no end. If Adolphe remained with his arm on the marble slab, and his head on one side, making sentimental speeches, till she should give him encouragement to fall at her feet, it certainly would not be ended by bed-time. She, therefore, summoned all her courage, and said,

"When you asked me to meet you here, your purpose was not to reproach me with coldness—was it Adolphe? Perhaps it will be better for both of us that this interview should terminate now. We shall part friends, dear friends; and I will rejoice at your triumphs, when you are victorious; and will lament at your reverses, should you be unlucky. I shall do the same for my own dear Henri, and I know that you two will not be separated. There is my hand," she added, thinking that he appeared to hesitate; "and now let us go down to our friends, who are expecting us."

"Are you so soon weary of hearing the few words I wish to say to you?" said Adolphe, who had taken her hand, and who seemed inclined to keep it.

"No, I am not weary. I will hear anything you wish to say." And Agatha having withdrawn her hand, sat down, and again found herself in a position to take advantage of Marie's good advice.

Adolphe remained silent for a minute or two, with his head supported on his hand, and gazing on the lady of his love with a look that was intended to fascinate her. Agatha sat perfectly still; she was evidently mindful of the lesson she had received: at last, Adolphe started up from his position, walked a step or two into the middle of the room, thrust his right hand into his bosom; and said abruptly, "Agatha, this is child's play; we are deceiving each other; we are deceiving ourselves; we would appear to be calm when there is no calm within us."

"Do not say we. I am not deceiving myself; I trust I am not deceiving you."

"And is your heart really so tranquil?" said he. "Does that fair bosom control no emotion? Is that lovely face, so exquisitely pale, a true index of the spirit within? Oh! Agatha! it cannot be; while my own heart is so torn with love; while I feel my own pulses beat so strongly; while my own brain burns so fiercely, I cannot believe that your bosom is a stranger to all emotion! Some passion akin to humanity must make you feel that you are not all divine! Speak, Agatha; if that lovely form has within it ought that partakes of the weakness of a woman, tell me, that at some future time you will accept the love I offer you; tell me, that I may live in hope. Oh, Agatha! bid me not despair," and M. Denot in bodily reality fell prostrate at her feet.

When Agatha had gone up to her room, she had prepared herself for a most disagreeable interview, but she had not expected anything so really dreadful as this. Adolphe had not contented himself with kneeling at her feet on one knee, and keeping his head erect in the method usual in such cases; but he had gone down upon both knees, had thrown his head upon her feet, and was now embracing her shoes and stockings in a very vehement manner; her legs were literally caught in a trap; she couldn't move them; and Adolphe was sobbing so loudly that it was difficult to make him hear anything.

"Adolphe, Adolphe, get up!" she almost screamed, "this is ridiculous in the extreme; if you will not get up, I must really call for some one. I cannot allow you to remain there!"

"Oh, Agatha, Agatha!" sobbed Adolphe.

"Nonsense, Adolphe," said Agatha. "Are you a man, to lie grovelling on the floor like that? Rise up, or you will lose my esteem for ever, if that be of any value to you."

"Give me one gleam of hope, and I will rise," said he, still remaining on his knees, but now looking up into her face; "tell me not to despair, and I will then accomplish any feat of manhood. Give me one look of comfort, and I will again be the warrior ready for the battle; it is you only who can give me back my courage; it is you only who can restore to me the privilege of standing erect before all mankind."

"I can tell you nothing, Adolphe, but this—that, if you continue on your knees, I shall despise you; if you will rise, I will give you at any rate a reasonable answer."

"Despise me, Agatha! no, you cannot despise me; the unutterable burning love of a true heart is not despicable; the character which I bear before mankind is not despicable. Man is not despicable when he kneels before the object which he worships; and, Agatha, with all my heart, I worship you!"

"Now you are profane as well as contemptible, and I shall leave you," and she walked towards the door.

"Stay then," said he, "stay, and I will rise," and, suiting the action to the word, he got up. "Now speak to me in earnest, Agatha; and, since you will have it so, I also, if possible, will be calm. Speak to me; but, unless you would have the misery of a disturbed spirit on your conscience, bid me not despair!"

"Is that your calmness, Adolphe?"

"Can a man, rushing towards the brink of a precipice, be calm? Can a man be calm on the verge of the grave? I love you, Agatha, with a true and holy love; but still with a love fierce and untameable. You reviled me when I said I worshipped you, but I adore the ground you tread on, and the air you breathe. I would shed my last drop of blood to bring you ease; but I could not live and see you give that fair hand to another. My joy would be to remain ever as your slave; but then the heart that beats beneath your bosom must be my own. Agatha, I await your answer; one word from your lips can transport me to paradise!"

"If I am to understand that you are asking me for love—for a warmer love than that which always accompanies true friendship—I am obliged to say that I cannot give it you." Adolphe remained standing in the middle of the room, with his hand still fixed in his bosom, and with a look intended to represent both thunder and lightning. He had really thought that the little scene which he had gone through, very much to his own satisfaction, would have a strong effect on Agatha, and he was somewhat staggered by the cool and positive tone of her reply. "It grieves me that I should give you pain," she continued, "if my answer does pain you; but I should never forgive myself, were I not to speak the truth to you plainly, and at once."

"And do you mean that for your final, and only answer to me?"

"Certainly, my only answer; for I can give you no other. I know you will be too kind, too sensible, to make it necessary that I should repeat it."

"This is dreadful," said Denot, putting his hand to his brow, "this is very dreadful!" and he commenced pacing up and down the room.

"Come," said she, good naturedly, "let us go down—let us forget this little episode—you have so much of happiness, and of glory before you, that I should grieve to see you mar your career by a hopeless passion. Take the true advice of a devoted friend," and she put her hand kindly on his arm, "let us both forget this morning's scene—let us only remember our childhood's friendship; think, Adolphe, how much you have to do for your King and your country, and do hot damp your glorious exertion by fostering a silly passion. Am not I the same to you as a sister? Wait till these wars are over, and then I will gather flowers for you to present to some mistress who shall truly love you."

"No, Agatha, the flowers you gather for me shall never leave my own bosom. If it be the myrtle, I will wear it with joy to my dying day, next my heart: if it is to be a cyprus branch, it shall soon be laid with me in the tomb."

"You will think less sadly in a short time," said Agatha; "your spirits will recover their proper tone amid the excitement of battle. We had better part now, Adolphe;" and she essayed to leave the room, but he was now leaning against the door, and did not seem inclined to let her depart so easily.

"You will not, I hope, begrudge me a few moments," said he, speaking between his teeth.

"You may reject me with scorn, but you can hardly refuse me the courtesy which any gentleman would have a right to expect from your hands."

"You know that I will refuse you nothing which, either in courtesy or kindness, I can do for you," said she, again sitting down. He, however, seeing her once more seated, did not appear much inclined to conclude what he had to say to her, for he continued walking up and down the room, in a rather disturbed manner; "but you should remember," she added, "how soon Henri is going to leave me, and how much we have all to think and to talk of."

"I see my presence is unwelcome, and it shall not trouble you long. I would soon rid your eyes of my hated form, but I must first say a few words, though my throat be choked with speaking them. My passion for you is no idle boyish love; it has grown with my growth, and matured itself with my manhood. I cannot now say to myself that it shall cease to be. I cannot restore calmness to my heart or rest to my bosom. My love is a fire which cannot now be quenched; it must be nourished, or it will destroy the heart which is unable to restrain it. Think, Agatha, of all the misery you are inflicting; think also of the celestial joy one word of yours is capable of giving."

"I have said before that I grieve to pain you; but I cannot speak a falsehood. Were it to save us both from instant death, I could not say that I love you in the sense you mean."

"Oh, Agatha! I do not ask you to love me—that is not to love me now; if you will only say that your heart is not for ever closed against my prayers, I will leave you contented."

"I can say nothing which would give you any hope of that which can never happen."

"And that is all I am to expect from you in return for as true a love as man ever bore to woman?"

"I cannot make you the return you wish. I can give you no other answer."

"Well, Agatha, so be it. You shall find now that I can be calm, when my unalterable resolve requires it. You shall find that I am a man; at any rate, you shall not again have to tell me that I am despicable," and he curled his upper lip, and showed his teeth in a very ferocious manner. "You shall never repeat that word in regard to Adolphe Denot. Should kind fortune favour my now dearest wish, you will soon hear that my bones are whitening under the walls of Saumur. You will hear that your des-pi-ca-ble lover," and he hissed out the offending word, syllable by syllable, between his closed teeth, "has perished in his attempt to be the first to place the white flag of La Vendée above the tri-colour. If some friendly bullet will send me to my quiet home, Adolphe Denot shall trouble you no longer," and as he spoke the last few words, he softened his voice, and re-assumed his sentimental look; but he did not remain long in his quiet mood, for he again became furious, as he added: "But if fortune should deny me this boon, if I cannot find the death I go to seek, I swear by your own surpassing beauty, by your glorious unequalled form, that I will not live without you. Death shall be welcome to me," and he raised his hands to heaven, and then dashed them against his breast. "Oh! how dearly welcome! Yes, heroic death upon the battlefield shall calm this beating heart—shall quell these agonized pangs. Yes, Agatha, if fortune be but kind, death, cold death, shall soon relieve us both; shall leave you free to bestow upon a colder suitor the prize you have refused to my hot, impatient love; but if," (and here he glanced very wildly round him), "my prayers are not heard, if after Saumur's field, life be still left within my body's sanctuary, I will return to seize you as my own, though hosts in armour try to stop my way. I will not live without you. I will not endure to see another man aspire to the hand which has been refused to me. Adieu, Agatha, adieu! I trust we shall meet no more; in thinking of me, at any rate, your memory shall not call me despicable," and he rushed out of the door and down stairs, without waiting to hear whether Agatha intended making any answer to this poetical expression of his fixed resolution.

In the commencement of his final harangue, Agatha had determined to hear him quietly to the end; but she had not expected anything so very mad as the exhibition he made. However, she sat quietly through the whole of it, and was glad that she was spared the necessity of a reply.

Nothing more was seen of Adolphe Denot that night. Henri asked his sister whether she had seen him, and she told him that he had made a declaration of love to her, and had expressed himself ill-satisfied with the only answer she had been able to give him. She did not tell her brother how like a demoniac his friend had behaved. To Marie she was more explicit; to her she repeated as nearly as possible the whole scene as it had occurred; and although Agatha was almost weeping with sorrow, there was so much that was ludicrous in the affair, that Marie could not keep herself from laughing.

"He will trouble you no more," said she. "You will find that he will not return to Durbellière to carry you off through the armed hosts. He will go to England or emigrate; and in a few years' time, when you meet him again, you will find him settled down, and as quiet as his neighbours. He is like new-made wine, my dear—he only wants age."

On the following morning, by break of day, the party left Durbellière, and Adolphe Denot joined his friend on the gravelled ring before the house; and Agatha, who had been with her brother in his room, looking from the widow saw her unmanageable lover mount his horse in a quiet, decent way, like the rest of the party.

CHAPTER IX.
LE MOUCHOIR ROUGE.

Nothing interfered to oppose the advance of the royalist troops towards Saumur. At Coron, as had been proposed, Larochejaquelin and Denot joined Father Jerome; and Cathelineau also, and M. d'Elbée joined them there. Every house in the town was open to them, and the provisions, which by the care of M. de Larochejaquelin had been sent there, were almost unneeded. If there was any remnant of republican feeling in Coron, at any rate it did not dare to shew itself. The road which the royalists intended to take ran from Cholet, through Coron, Vihiers, and Doué, to Saumur. The republicans, who were now in great force at Saumur, under Generals Coustard and Quetineau, had sent small parties of soldiers into the town of Vihiers and Doué, the inhabitants of which were mostly republican. Before the arrival of M. de Larochejaquelin, the blues, as the republican troops were called by the Vendeans, had been driven out of Vihiers by a party of royalists under the direction of Stofflet, who had raised himself to distinction soon after the commencement of the revolt. This man was a gamekeeper in the employment of an emigrant nobleman, and though he was a rough, harsh, uneducated, quarrelsome man, nevertheless, by his zeal and courage, he had acquired great influence among the people, and was now at the head of a numerous, and, for La Vendée, well-armed body of men.

Our friends accordingly found the road open for them as far as Doué. After their junction with Stofflet, their army amounted to about 7,500 men; and at Done they were to meet M. Bonchamps and M. de Lescure, who, it was supposed, would bring with them as many more. They marched out of Vihiers early on the Tuesday morning, having remained there only about a couple of hours, and before nightfall they saw the spire of Doué church. They then rested, intending to force their way into the town early on the following morning; but they had barely commenced their preparations for the evening, when a party of royalists came out to them from the town, inviting them in. M. de Lescure and M. Bonchamps were already there. The republican soldiers had been attacked and utterly routed; most of them were now prisoners in the town; those who had escaped had retreated to Saumur, and even they had left their arms behind them.

All this good fortune greatly inspirited the Vendeans. The men talked with the utmost certainty of what they would do when they were masters of Saumur. Cathelineau had brought with him the celebrated cannon of St. Florent, 'Marie Jeanne,' and she now stood in the market place of Done, covered with ribbons and flowers. Many of the men had never hitherto seen this wonderful piece of artillery, and they hastened to look at it. 'Marie Jeanne' that night was patted, kissed, and caressed by thousands. Cathelineau was equally the object of their admiration; every peasant who had not yet seen him, hurried to gaze on him; and after his arrival in Doué, he was two hours employed in a military operation, hitherto undertaken, I believe, by no other general: he was endeavouring to shake hands with every man in the army. Chapeau here was again of great use, for he stood at Cathelineau's elbow, and hurried the men away as soon as they touched his hand. But for this precaution, the work could never have been done; and as it was, some of the men were discontented, and declared their intention of returning home, for Cathelineau was called away before he had completed his task: he was obliged to go to the Town Hall to attend a council that was held there of the different Vendean chiefs.

The arms which they had taken in Vihiers and Doué, were of the greatest use to them; in both places they had found a cannon; they had taken nine or ten from Fontenay, and others from Thouars. Most of the men among them now had muskets, and they were able to take to Saumur with them twenty-four pieces of heavy artillery. What could the infamous blues expect to do against a force so numerous, so well armed, and so well officered!

That evening a council of war was held by the different chiefs of the Vendeans in the Town Hall of Doué. Lescure, Larochejaquelin, Cathelineau, d'Elbée, and Stofflet were there. M. Bonchamps, who had been very severely wounded at Fontenay, but who had insisted on being carried along with his own men, was brought in on a litter. Father Jerome was there, and another priest who had come with M. Bonchamps. There were a couple of old royalist noblemen, not sufficiently active to take a part in the actual fighting, but sufficiently zealous in the cause to leave their homes for the purpose of giving the young commanders the benefit of their experience. Foret also, Cathelineau's friend, was present, and Adolphe Denot: indeed many others, from time to time, crowded into the room, for the door was not well kept, nor were the councils of the generals in any way a secret. Jacques Chapeau, as a matter of course, managed to make his way into the room, and took upon himself the duties of doorkeeper.

The Mayor's arm-chair stood at the head of the table, as the leaders dropped into the room one after another, but no one appeared willing to occupy it. Hitherto there had been no chief among the Vendeans; this was the first meeting which had been held with anything approaching to the solemnity of a general assembly, and it occurred to each of them that whoever should then seat himself in the Mayor's chair, would be assuming that he was the chief leader of the revolt.

"Come, M. de Lescure," said Stofflet, "we have much to do, and but little time; let us make the most of it: do you take the President's seat. Gentlemen, I am sure we could have no better President than M. de Lescure?"

They all agreed, with the exception of the chosen leader. "By no means," said he. "I was the last here who joined the cause, and I certainly will not place myself first among those who have led the way in the work we have taken up. No; here is the man who shall be our President." And as he spoke he caught hold of Cathelineau, who was immediately behind him, and absolutely forced him into the chair.

"Indeed, indeed, M. de Lescure—" said Cathelineau, endeavouring to extricate himself from the seat; but both his voice and his exertions were stopped, for three or four of them united to hold him where he was, and declared that he should be the President for the evening.

"Indeed, and indeed you will not stir," said Henri, who stood behind his chair, and placed his hands heavily on the postillion's shoulders.

"It was you that brought us here," said de Lescure, "and you must not now avoid the responsibility."

"Ah! M. de Lescure," said he, "there are so many more fitting than me."

"Not one in all La Vendée," said M. Bonchamps: "sit where you are, Cathelineau."

"You must do it, Cathelineau;" whispered his friend Foret; "the peasants would not endure to see any man put above you."

"Cathelineau will not shrink from the burden which the Lord has called upon him to bear," said Father Jerome.

"Providence," said d'Elbée, "has summoned the good Cathelineau to this high duty; he will not, I am sure, oppose its decrees."

And thus Cathelineau found himself seated in the Mayor's chair at the head of the table, whilst the highest noblemen and gentry of the country took their places around it, and from that moment Cathelineau became the General-in-Chief of the Vendeans.

Each leader then gave in the numbers of the men who had come with him, and it was found that the army consisted of above fifteen thousand men. Lists were then made out of the arms and accoutrements which they possessed, and the men in a rude way were drafted into regiments under the command of the leaders who had brought them. There was a small body of cavalry equipped in most various manners, and mounted on horses, which resembled anything rather than a regular squadron of troopers: these were under the immediate command of Henri Larochejaquelin.

"Gentlemen," said Cathelineau, "we have, you know, three different attacks to make, three positions to carry, before we can be masters of Saumur."

"Yes," said Bonchamps, "there in the camp at Varin on the right, and the redoubts of Bournan on the left; the fortifications of the town itself lie between them, and a little to the rear of both."

"Exactly, M. Bonchamps; the town itself, I take, is the easiest task of the three; but as we are situated it must be the last."

"I think you will find that Varin is their strongest point," said de Lescure.

"M. de Lescure is right," said Cathelineau. "We shall find them very strong in their camp. I had with me, yesterday, two men from Saumur; they knew nothing of General Quetineau's intentions, but they had seen detachments of men constantly going to and fro between Saumur and the camp; they calculate that we shall think that the weaker side."

"Bournan is right on our way," said Bonchamps; "but the ground lies so advantageously for them, that they will cut us to pieces if we attempt to push our way up the hill against the heavy artillery they will have there."

"M. Bonchamps is quite right there," said Cathelineau. "I think we should not attack Bournan, till we can do so from the side of the town. I think Bournan should not be our first object; but nevertheless, we must be prepared to meet at Varin the great body of the army; we must drive them from thence back into the town."

"Yes," said Henri, "and follow them in, as we are driving them. The sight of their comrades in disorder will itself conquer the men in the citadel; it is always so with the blues."

"We must remember, Henri," said de Lescure, "these are not conscripts, nor yet merely the Marsellaise, we have to deal with: the men who fought at Jemappes and at Valmy are here; the old cuirassiers of the French army."

"They are cowards, Charles," said Henri, "or they would not have deserted their King."

"They are good soldiers, nevertheless," said Bonchamps. "I have fought among them, and know it."

"They are the better worth our fighting then," said Henri.

"Providence can give us the victory over tried veterans as well as over untried conscripts; it were a sin to doubt it," said M. d'Elbée.

"That would be a good subject for a sermon to the soldiers, but a bad argument in a council chamber," said Bonchamps. "We shall find the cuirassiers tough fellows to deal with."

"We must take our enemies as we find them," said Cathelineau; "but if you will allow me, gentlemen, and as you have placed me here, I will tell you what I would propose?'

"Do, Cathelineau, do!" said Henri; "let us have one plan, and then make the best we can of it; we can at any rate do our duty like men."

"I think we should leave this early tomorrow morning, and move across the country as though we were going to Montreuil; we shall so come on the Montreuil road about a league from Saumur, and not very far, that is about half a league, from the camp at Varin."

"And then, Cathelineau, will you attack the camp tomorrow evening?" said de Lescure.

"I think not, M. de Lescure; but I would make a feint to do so, and I would thus keep the republicans on the alert all night; a small body of our men may, I think, in that way fatigue the masses of the republicans in the camp—we might harass them the whole night, which will be dark from eleven till near three; and then with the earliest sunrise our real attack should be made."

"Bravo, Cathelineau!" said Henri; "and then fall on them when they are in want of sleep."

"Yes," said de Lescure, "and they will have learnt to think that our attacks in that quarter are only feints."

"Such may be our good luck, M. de Lescure; at any rate, if you think of nothing better, we may try it."

It was thus decided, and arranged that Larochejquelin should, on the following evening, leave the main body of the army with all the mounted men belonging to it, and advance near enough to the camp at Varin to allow of his being seen and heard by the republicans, and that he should almost immediately retreat: that a body of infantry should then move on, and take up a position near to the camp, which should also return after a while, and that as soon as darkness had come on, a third advance should be made by a larger body of men, who should, if possible, approach within musket shot o the trenches, and endeavour to throw the republicans into disorder. At four o'clock in the morning, the real attack was to be made by the combined Vendean forces, of which Cathelineau was to lead the centre, de Lescure the left, consisting of the men brought by himself and Larochejaquelin from the centre of the Bocage; and d'Elbée the right, which was formed of men chiefly brought by M. Bonchamps from the province of Anjou. M. Bonchamps was himself too ill from the effects of his wounds to accompany the army beyond Doué.

Early on the following morning the whole army, with the exception of the men left with Foret, defiled out of Doué, and crossed over to the Montreuil road, dragging with them their cannons, baggage-waggons, and ammunition; their movements were not made with very great order, nor with much celerity; but, about six o'clock in the evening, on the 10th of June, Cathelineau took up his position about a league from Saumur. They got possession of one or two farm-houses, and were not long in making their arrangements for the night; the men were accustomed to sleep out in the open air since the war commenced, and were well content to remain in clusters round the cannons and the waggons.

At eight o'clock, Larochejaquelin had his little troop of cavalry ready mounted, and started with them for the camp of Varin. As he and his companions dashed along through the waggons and by the cannons the peasants who were preparing to lay down for the night, and who knew nothing of the plans of their Generals, rose up one after another wondering.

"There goes 'le Mouchoir Rouge,'" said one, alluding to Henri's costume; for when in action he always wore a red handkerchief round his waist, and another round his neck.

"Yes; that is 'le Mouchoir Rouge,'" said another, "he is off for Saumur; the horsemen are already starting for Saumur."

"Come, then; they shall not go alone," said another. "We will start for Saumur. We will not lie here while others are in the battle."

These were men from the neighbourhood of Durbellière, who were now placed under the orders of M. de Lescure; but who conceived that, as their lord and master was gone before them, it must be their duty to follow. The word was passed from one to another, and the whole body of them was soon in motion. It must be remembered that they were, in no respect, similar to disciplined troops; they had received no military instruction, and did not therefore, know, that they were doing wrong in following their own master; they were in receipt of no pay; amenable to no authority, and consequently afraid of no penalties; their only idea was to do the best they could for the cause, to fight with courage and perseverance, and to trust to God for the result: it was not, therefore, wondering that, in the present instance, they so completely mistook their duty.

Cathelineau's men, who were intended to form the centre of the attack on the next morning, were placed just to the right of the road, but their baggage and cannons had not been moved from it; in fact, they were nearly mixed with M. de Lescure's men; whereas M. d'Elbée's portion of the army was removed a good deal further to the right, and was placed immediately on the banks of the river Thoué. The camp at Varin, which was to be attacked, was situated between the river and the road to Saumur. In Cathelineau's division there were some few who understood the plan which had been decided on, and some others who knew that they should not move without orders, and they did what they could to prevent their companions from joining the rush made by M. de Lescure's party; but their efforts were nearly in vain. Every man learnt in the confusion that the attack was to be made on Saumur that night, and no man wished to be left behind.

"Come friends, let us follow 'le Mouchoir Rouge;' he never meant, I am sure, to leave us here," said the spokesman of one party.

"The Saint of Angers is on before us," said the others; "he would let no man see the enemy before himself. The good Cathelineau is gone to Saumur, let us follow him!"

In this way they soon learnt to believe that both Cathelineau and Larochejaquelin were on before them, and they were not long in hurrying after them. Within twenty minutes, about six thousand men started off without a leader or any defined object, to besiege the walls of Saumur; they did not even know that a vast entrenched encampment of the enemy's troops lay directly in their way. The men had, most of them, muskets with three or four rounds of powder and ball each; many of them also had bayonets. They were better armed than they had hitherto ever been, and they consequently conceived themselves invincible. Cathelineau's men, however, would not stir without 'Marie Jeanne,' and that devoted, hard-worked cannon was seized by scores, and hurried off with them towards Saumur.

De Lescure and Cathelineau were together in a farm-house, within five hundred yards of the place where the baggage had been left, and within half a mile of the most distant of the men who had thus taken upon themselves to march, or rather to rush, away without orders; and some of those who still had their senses about them, soon let their Generals know what was going forward.

They were seated together, planning the attack for the next morning. Denot was with Larochejaquelin, and d'Elbée and Stofflet were together with the detachment on the banks of the river: they were, therefore, alone when Father Jerome rushed into the room.

"The men are off, M. de Lescure," said he: "do you not hear them? For Heaven's sake go down to them, Cathelineau; some one has told them that you and Larochejaquelin were gone to Saumur; and they are all preparing to follow you."

"Heaven and earth!" said de Lescure, "they will be destroyed."

"Unless you stop them they will," said Father Jerome, "they will all fall upon the camp just as the republicans are under arms, and prepared to receive them. Hurry, Cathelineau; you alone can stop them."

Cathelineau without uttering a word, seized his sword, and rushed out of the room without his cap; and followed by M. de Lescure, hurried through the farm-yard, leapt a little gate, and got upon the road a few yards from the place where the waggons had been left. The whole place was in the utmost confusion: the men were hurrying to and fro, hardly knowing what they were doing or going to do: the most ardent of them were already a quarter of a mile advanced on the road to Saumur; others were still following them; those who knew that they should have stayed quiet during the night, were in the utmost distress; they did not know whether to support their comrades, or to remain where they were.

"'What ails them, Peter?" said Cathelineau, catching hold of the arm of a man who had followed him from St. Florent, "if they advance they will be destroyed at Varin;" and as he spoke, he leapt upon the top of one of the waggons laden with provisions, which had come from Durbellière.

It was a beautiful warm evening in June, and the air was heavy with the sweet scent of the flowering hedges; it was now nearly nine o'clock, and the sun had set; but the whole western horizon was gorgeous with the crimson streaks which accompanied its setting. Standing in the waggon, Cathelineau could see the crowds of hurrying royalists rushing along the road, wherever the thick foliage of trees was sufficiently broken to leave any portion of it visible, and he could hear the eager hum of their voices both near him and at a distance.

"No power on earth could bring them back," said he. "Now, Peter, run to the stable for your life; my horse is there and M. de Lescure's—bring them both. They are both saddled. Run my friend; a moment lost now will cost a hundred lives."

It was Peter Berrier to whom he spoke, and in spite of his evil treatment at Durbellière, Peter ran for the horses, as though he was running for the King's crown.

"It is impossible to stop them," said Cathelineau, still standing on the waggon, and speaking to de Lescure, whom he had outran. "All La Vendée could not stop them; but we may head them, M. de Lescure, and lead them on; we must attack the camp tonight."

"Our loss will be terrible if we do," said de Lescure.

"It will, it will be terrible, and we shall be repulsed; but that will be better than letting them rush into positive destruction. In an hour's time they will be between the camp, the town, and the heights of Bournan, and nothing then could save them."

"Let us go, then," said de Lescure; "but will you not send to d'Elbée?"

"Yes; but do not desire him to follow us. In two hours time he will have enough to do to cover our retreat."

"We shall, at any rate, have the darkness in our favour," said de Lescure.

"We shall; but we have two dreadful hours of light before that time comes: here are our horses—let us mount; there is nothing for us now but a hard ride, a good drubbing—and then, the best face we can put upon it tomorrow."

Orders were then given to Peter Berrier to make the best of his way across to M. d'Elbée, and to explain to him what had occurred, and bid him keep his men in reserve under arms, and as near to the waggons as he could. "And be sure," said Catheineau, "be sure, Peter, to make him understand, that he is at once to leave the river and come across to the road, to keep his men, you know, immediately close to the waggons."

"I understand," said Peter, "I understand," and he at once started off on his important errand.

"It is a bad messenger, I fear," said Cathelineau; "but we have no better; indeed we are lucky even to find him."

"I wonder," said Peter Berrier to himself, as he ran across the fields, "I wonder whether they'll make nothing of this job, too, as they did of that day at St. Florent. I suppose they will; some men haven't the luck ever to be thought much of."

Notwithstanding his gloomy presentiments, Peter made the best of his way to M. d'Elbée, and having found him, told him how the men had started by themselves for Saumur; how de Lescure and Cathelineau had followed them; how they intended to attack the camp at Varin that night, and he ended by saying, "And you, M. d'Elbe—"

"Of course we must follow them," said d'Elbée.

"Not a foot," said Peter; "that is just why they sent me, instead of any common messenger; that I might explain it all to you properly. You are not to stir a foot after them; but are to remain here, just where you are, till they return."

"That is impossible," said d'Elbée. "What good on earth can I do, remaining here?"

"Why, Cathelineau will know where to find you, when he wants you."

"You are mistaken, Peter Berrier," said d'Elbée. "You must be mistaken. Perhaps he meant that I should go over to the road, to cover their retreat. God knows they will want some one to do so."

"That is just it," said Peter. "They mean to retreat down the river, and you are to remain just where you are."

As might be expected, M. d'Elbée was completely puzzled, and he sent off three or four men, to endeavour to get fresh orders, either from Cathelineau or from de Lescure; and while waiting to receive them, he kept his useless position by the river side.

In the mean time, Cathelineau and de Lescure had hurried off, at the top of their horses' speed, to endeavour to head the column of madmen who were rushing towards almost certain destruction. They will, at any rate, meet Larochejaquelin on his return, and he will stop them. This thought occurred to both of them, but neither of them spoke; indeed, they were moving too quickly, and with too much trouble to be able to speak. There object now was not to stop the men who thronged the roads; they only wanted to head them before they came to the portion of the road which passed close by the trenches of the camp at Varin.

They were so far successful, that they found themselves nearly at the head of the column by the time they came within sight of the great banks which the royalists had thrown up. It was still light enough for them to see the arms of the republican troops, and they were near enough to the camp to hear the movements of the men within it, in spite of the increasing noise of their own troops.

"They are ready to receive us," said de Lescure to himself, "and a warm reception they are likely to give us."

He now separated himself from Cathelineau, and galloped before the trenches to an open space where Larochejaquelin had stationed himself with the cavalry. Henri had completely surprised the sentinels on duty in the camps; he and about twenty others had dismounted, had shot four or five sentries at their post, and had again retreated to their horses before the republicans were able to return his fire. But what was his surprise on preparing to remount his horse, to hear the rush of his own men coming along the road, and to see the cloud of dust which enveloped them. Henri tried to speak to them, and to learn what new plan brought them there; but the foremost men were too much out of breath to speak to him: however, they shouted and hurraed at seeing him, and slackened their pace a little. They were then almost within musket shot of the republicans, and the balls from the trenches began to drop very near them. Henri was still in an agony of suspense, not knowing what to do or to propose, when de Lescure emerged from out of the cloud of dust, and galloped up to him.

"What on earth has brought you here, Charles?" said Henri. "Why have the men come on in this way? Every man within the camp will have a musket in his hand in five minutes time."

"It is too late now to help it," said de Lescure; "if we both live over this night, I will explain it to you. Cathelineau is behind there; we must lead the men to the attack; he will be in the trenches immediately."

"Lead on," said Henri, jumping off his horse, "or rather I will go first; but stop, the men must have five minutes to get their breath; they are all choked with running. Come, my men," said he, turning to the crowds who were clustering round them, "we will disturb the dreams of these republicans; the blues are not fond of fighting by night, but if they are asleep I think we will soon wake them," and accompanied by his friend, he rushed down into the trenches, and the men followed him by hundreds, covered with dust, choked with thirst, breathless with their long run, and utterly ignorant what they were going to do, or how they were to find an entrance into the camp.

At the same moment, Cathelineau leapt into the trench at the point nearest to the road by which he had come, and his men followed him enthusiastically, shouting at the top of their voices "Vive le roi!" "A bas la république." Hitherto they had been successful in every effort they had made. The republican troops had fled from every point which had been attacked; the Vendeans had, as yet, met no disasters, and they thought themselves, by the special favour of the Almighty, invincible when fighting against the enemies of the King.

The camp at Varin was not a regularly fortified position; but it was surrounded by a deep trench, with steep earth-works thrown up inside it. These were high enough to afford great protection to those within, and steep enough to offer a considerable obstacle to any attacking party: but the earth was still soft, and the foremost among the Vendeans were not long in finding themselves within the entrenchment; but when there they met a terribly hot reception.

The feigned attack made by Larochejaquelin had just served to warn the republicans, and by the time the real attack was made, every man was under arms. As de Lescure had said, the old soldiers of Valmy and of Jemappes were there. Men accustomed to arms, who well knew the smell of powder, and who were prepared to contest every inch of ground before they gave it up. These men, too, wore defensive armour, and the Vendeans, unaccustomed to meet enemies so well prepared, were dismayed, when they perceived that their enemies did not as usual give way before them.

The slaughter in the trenches was tremendous: the first attack had been made with great spirit, and about four hundred of the Vendeans were in the camp before the murderous fire of the republicans commenced, among these were de Lescure, Larochejaquelin, and Cathelineau; and they made their way even to the centre of the camp; but those who had not made a portion of the first assault, fell back by twenties and thirties under the fire of the republicans; twice Larochejaquelin returned and nearly cleared the top of the trenches, in order to make way for the men below to come up; but they were frightened and intimidated; their powder was all gone, and they perceived that their first attempt had failed; their friends and comrades were falling on every side of them; and, after a while, they retreated from the trenches beyond reach of musket shot. Cathelineau had expected that this would be the case, and though he had been one of the first within the camp, he was prepared to leave it again as soon as he could make the men, who were with him, understand that it was necessary they should do so. It was now dusk, and the uncertain light favoured his intention.

"'Where is your master?" said he to Jacques, whom he chanced to find close to him; "tell him to lead his men down the trenches again, back to the road, at once, at once; beg him to be the first to leap down himself; they will not go unless he leads them."

Jacques did as he was bid, and Larochejaquelin led the men back to the trenches.

"Come, my friends," said he, "we have given them enough for tonight—we have broken their sleep; come, we will visit them again tomorrow." And he dashed through a body of republicans who were now firing from the trenches, and about one hundred of his own men followed him.

The republicans had stuck huge pine-wood torches into the green sods a-top of the trenches, which gave a ghastly glaring light immediately in their own vicinity, though they did not relieve the darkness at a few paces distant. As Henri rushed through them, some of the soldiers observed his peculiar costume and hallaoed out, "fire upon the red scarf," (tirez sur le mouchoir rouge,) but the confusion was too great to allow of this friendly piece of advice being followed, or else the musketeers were bad marksmen, for Henri went safely through the trench, though many of his men were wounded in following him.

Cathelineau's men soon followed, as did also Cathelineau himself; the last man who leapt into the trenches was de Lescure; but he also got safely through them—not above twenty-five or thirty of those who had forced their way into the camp, fell; but above three hundred of those who had only attempted it, were left dead or wounded in the trenches. And now the retreat commenced, and Cathelineau found it impossible to accomplish it with anything like order; the three leaders endeavoured to make the men conceive that they had been entirely successful in all which it had been thought desirable to accomplish, but they had seen too much bloodshed to be deceived—they were completely dismayed and disheartened, and returned back towards Montreuil, almost quicker than they had come.

The men had brought 'Marie Jeanne' with them; but in the species of attack which they had made, the cannon was not of the slightest use; it had not been once discharged. A great effort was now made to take it back with them, but the attempt was unsuccessful: they had not dragged it above five hundred yards, when they heard that the republicans were following them; and then, as every man was obliged to think of himself, poor 'Marie Jeanne' was left to her fate.

It was soon evident to Cathelineau and de Lescure, that they were pursued; but the night was dark, and they calculated that M. d'Elbée's men would be drawn up at the waggons; it was more than probable that they would then be able, not only to stop the pursuit, but to avenge themselves on their pursuers. What then was their surprise on reaching the waggons, to find them utterly deserted—there was not a single man with them.

This was a great aggravation to the misery of their predicament. They had no resource but to fly on to Montreuil, which was still above two leagues distant from them; and should the republican troops persevere in the pursuit, their loss upon the road would be terrific. The darkness was their only friend, and on they went towards Montreuil.

The republican soldiers were stopped by the waggons and cannons; it was then as dark as a night in June ever is; it was well known also that the Republic had no friends in Montreull; the troops had been driven from the place by M. de Lescure, on his road to Doué, and the royalists would be able to make a very strong stand in the streets of the town; the pursuit was, therefore, given up, and the blues returned to the camp at Varin, with all the artillery and the baggage belonging to the royalists.

M. d'Elbée remained all the while in his position by the river; he heard the firing—he also heard the confused noise of the retreat, but he felt that it was impossible for him, at that hour of night, to take any steps without knowing what had been done, or what he had better do: at about four in the morning, he learnt exactly what had occurred, and then he rejoined Cathelineau at Montreuil.

The Vendeans, during the night, lost every cannon they possessed; all their baggage, consisting of provisions, wearing apparel, and ammunition; they lost also about five hundred men, in killed, wounded and prisoners; but all this was not of so much injury as the loss of the prestige of victory. The peasants had conceived themselves invincible, and they were struck with consternation to find they were liable to repulse and defeat. Early on the following morning, another council of war was held, but the spirits and hopes of the Generals had been greatly damped.

CHAPTER X.
THE BISHOP OF AGRA.

On this occasion the meeting of the leaders was kept strictly secret; none were admitted but those who were known to be the chosen chiefs of the Vendeans; it consisted of Cathelineau, de Lescure, Larochejaquelin, d'Elbée, Stofflet, and Father Jerome. They had been closeted together about an hour and a half, when Father Jerome left the room, and rode off towards Thouars, on the best horse which could be found for him; no one seemed to know where or for what he was going, though much anxiety was expressed on the subject. Those who knew him, were well aware that he was not about to desert the cause in its first reverse. In the meantime, the Generals tried to reassure the men. Cathelineau explained to them that they had brought on themselves the evils which they now suffered by their absurd attempt to act without orders; and de Lescure and Larochejaquelin endeavoured to rouse their energies by pointing out to them the necessity of recovering their favourite cannon.

"Ah! M. Henri," said one of the men from Durbellière, "how can we get her again when we have lost our guns, and have got no powder?"

"How!" said Henri, "with your sticks and your hands, my friends—as your neighbours in St. Florent took her, at first, from the blues; we all think much of the men of St. Florent, because it was they first took 'Marie Jeanne;' let us be the men who rescue her from these traitors, and these people will think much of us."

About two o'clock in the day a closed carriage was driven into Montreuil very fast, by the road from Thouars; the blinds were kept so completely down, that no one could see who was within it; it was driven up to the door of the house in which the council had been held; the doors of the carriage and of the house were opened, and two persons alighted and ran into the house so quickly that their persons could hardly be recognized, even by those who were looking at them.

"That last is Father Jerome, at any rate," said a townsman.

"Who on earth had he with him?" said another; "he must be some giant," said a third, "did you see how he stooped going into the door."

"A giant, stupid;" said a fourth, "how could a giant get out of such a carriage as that; besides, where could Father Jerome find giants in these days."

"Well, I don't know," said the other, "but I am sure he was eight feet high; didn't you see his back as he ran into the house."

Soon after the mysterious entry into the house, Henri left it, and went out to the fields beyond the town, where most of the men were still resting after the long fatigue of the night; much discontentment had been expressed by them, and many had already declared their intention of returning home. Every measure had been taken to comfort them; they had been supplied with provisions and tobacco from the town, and every effort had been used to renew their hopes and courage. Cathelineau had passed the greater portion of the morning among them, going from one quarter to another, assuring the men that their loss was most trifling, that their future victory was certain—it was nearly in vain; they declared that they could do nothing without 'Marie Jeanne.'

Henri now went among them, and as he did so, Jacques Chapeau proceeded through the town, imploring all the men who were in it, to go out and join the rest of the army, as a holy man had been sent direct from Rome by the Pope, to tell the people of La Vendée what it was their duty to do.

Henri did not say quite so much as this, but he told the men that a friend of theirs—a bishop of the Church—one especially appointed by the King before he died, to provide for the spiritual comfort of his poor people in the west of France, was now among them, and would soon address them. He directed them to stay where they were till this man of God should be among them, and he besought them strictly to follow any advice which he might give them.

Every one in the town flocked out to the army—men, women and children were soon in the fields, and the report was spread abroad through them all, that the mysterious carriage which had rattled through the streets of Montreuil, had brought to that favoured town a holy bishop, sent expressly by their father the Pope to give good advice to his dear children in La Vendée.

About four o'clock in the afternoon the stranger walked among them. Father Jerome walked on his right hand, and Cathelineau on his left. M. de Lescure followed immediately behind them. He was a very tall man—nearly seven feet high; and his peculiar costume added in appearance to his real height— he was dressed in the gorgeous robes of a bishop of the Church of Rome as he would appear at the altar of his cathedral when about to celebrate high mass; he had his mitre on his head and his crozier in his hand; and as he walked through the crowd, the men and women everywhere kneeled down and bowed their heads to the earth; the people were delighted to have so holy a man among them—to see a bishop in La Vendée. The bells were all rung, and every sign of joy was shewn; the peasants were already beginning to forget their defeat of the previous night.

As he walked through the kneeling crowd, he stood still a moment or two, from time to time, and blessed the people; his voice was full and deep, but very musical; his face was supremely handsome, but devoid of all traces of passion. As he lifted his hands to heaven, and implored the Almighty to protect the righteous arms of his poor children in La Vendée, he certainly looked every inch a bishop; the peasants congregated round him, and kissed his garments—if they could even touch the shoes on his feet, they thought themselves happy.

It took the little procession two hours to move in this way through the whole of the army, during which time the bishop's companions did not speak a word; they merely moved on, with their eyes turned towards the ground. At length they reached a temporary altar, standing on a platform raised five steps above the ground, which had been erected under the care of M. d'Elbe since the arrival of the bishop in Montreuil. Here were collected M. d'Elbée, Stofflet, Larochejaquelin, Adolphe Denot, and the other principal leaders of the army, and as the little procession drew near, they knelt upon the top step of the platform, and Cathelineau, de Lescure and Father Jerome knelt with them. The bishop then blessed them each separately, commencing with Cathelineau; he placed his crozier on the altar, and putting both his hands on the head of the kneeling General, he said in a loud and solemn voice:

"May the Lord bless you, my son! may he enable you to direct the arms of his faithful people, so as to show forth His glory, and magnify His name; may he help your endeavours to restore to a suffering people their Church and their King; may His dear Son preserve you in danger, comfort you in affliction, be near you in the hour of death, and reward you in heaven." He then went round to them all, and blessed them each, though in a somewhat shorter form; and, at last, standing on the top step, in the front of the whole army, so that every one could see him, he uttered a general benediction on the people, and a prayer for their success; and while he did so, boys dressed in surplices made their way through the crowd, swinging censers filled with burning frankincense, and loading the air with that peculiar scent, which always fills the mind with devotional ideas.

As soon as this was over, and the people had risen from their knees, Cathelineau spoke to them, and told them that the Bishop of Agra had been especially appointed by their King to watch over and protect their spiritual interest; that Monseigneur had heard with great grief of the misfortune which had happened to them the preceding evening, and that he would now tell them how, with God's assistance, they might hope in future to avoid such calamities.

The bishop then addressed them, and said:

"My children, I rejoice that Providence has given me the privilege of seeing so many of you collected here today. You have been brought together for a great and holy purpose; the enemies of the Almighty God are in your country—enemies who can never prevail to the breath of one hair against His omnipotence; but who may, and who will prevail to the destruction of your families here, and the perdition of your souls hereafter, if you fail in performing the duties which are before you. You are now called, my children—called especially from on high, to deliver your land from these enemies; to go out to the battle, and to fight in God's name, till you have restored the King to his throne, and your pastors to their churches; and I rejoice to learn that you have so readily undertaken the task which is before you. Till yesterday your success was most wonderful; your career has been glorious. You unhesitatingly obeyed the leaders who commanded you, and they led you from one victory to another: but yesterday you were beaten back—yesterday evening, for the first time, you found your enemy too strong for you; they did not fall beneath your bullets; they did not feel your swords! Why was this, my children? Why was it that on yesterday evening the protecting hand of heaven was withdrawn from you?" Here the bishop paused in his address, as though expecting a reply, and then, after waiting a minute, during which the whole army remained in most perfect quiet, answered the question himself "Because, my children, you yesterday followed no accustomed leader; you obeyed no order; you went out to the battle with self-proud hearts, and a vain confidence in yourselves, rather than in the Almighty. It is not by such efforts as that, that the chosen soldiers of La Vendée can expect to conquer the enemies of France. You were vain in your own conceits; you trusted in your own strength; you were puffed up with worldly glory: and your strength has proved weakness, and your glory has been turned to disgrace. I trust, my children, you will not require another such a lesson; I trust you will not again forget your God and your Saviour, as you did on yesterday evening. Tomorrow morning the General, under whom the hand of Providence has placed you, the good Cathelineau, shall again lead you against your enemies; and, if you confidently trust in God for the result, he shall assuredly lead you to victory."

The bishop then again blessed the army, and walked off the field, surrounded by the different leaders of the army, and left the town without being again seen by the multitude.

The effect which this singular visit had upon the people was almost miraculous. Their faith was so perfect, that it never occurred to them to doubt the truth of anything which fell from consecrated lips. The word of a priest with them was never doubted, but the promises of a bishop were assurances direct from heaven: they would consider it gross impiety to have any doubt of victory, when victory had been promised them by so holy a man as he who had just addressed them. After the Bishop of Agra had left the town, Larochejaquelin and de Lescure went through the army, talking to the men, and they found them eager to renew the attack on the camp of Varin. Though Varin was nearly three leagues from them, and though they had been up nearly the whole previous night, they would willingly have returned to the attack that evening, had they been allowed to do so.

This was not considered expedient: but it was resolved that the attack on the camp should be renewed as early as possible on the following morning, as it was considered that the republicans would not expect so quick a return of an army which had been completely routed; and might, therefore, to a certain extent, be taken by surprise.

"We must run fast, friends," said Chapeau to his allies from Durbellière and Echanbroignes, "for the first men who reach Varin, will retake 'Marie Jeanne;' we will have a share in her, as well as the men of St. Florent."

With sunrise the next morning, the army was again on the move towards Saumur: it was arranged that Cathelineau, de Lescure, Denot, and Larochejaquelin should lead the men through the trenches and into the camp; and that d'Elbe should remain on the road, prepared, if necessary, to second the attack, but ready should the first attempt be successful, to fall on the republicans as they retreated from the camp to the town, and, if possible, to follow them within the walls. Stofflet was to lead a division of fifteen hundred men past the camp, between the heights of Bournan and the town, so as to intercept the republicans, should they attempt from that position, to relieve their comrades when retreating from the camp. There was a bridge over the Thoué, close to the town of Saumur, called the bridge of Fouchard. This bridge was between Bournan and the town, as also between the camp and the town, and the possession of this bridge would be of great advantage to the royalist army. Stofflet was charged to obtain this advantage, if he did not find that the cannons from the town prevented him.

About four o'clock the army was on the move from Montreuil, and by eight they were again in front of the camp at Varin; the portion of the road which they had passed in such confusion the night but one before, and where they had left their cannon and their waggons, was now stripped of all signs of the encampment, which had been made there, nothing but the deep ruts, made by the cannon wheels, were to be seen; everything which they had brought with them, the trophies of all their victories, the white flags which the ladies of La Vende had worked for them; the provisions, the wine and meat, which the kindness of their landlords had sent with them, were all gone—were in the hands of the republicans; these reflections served to rouse the anger of the peasants, and made them determined to get back what they had lost, though they pulled down the walls of Saumur with their nails.

At a few moments after eight, the attack commenced; the first assault was headed by Cathelineau, who rushed into the trenches, accompanied by the Curé of St. Laud. Father Jerome held a large crucifix in his hands, and as he followed Cathelineau, he lifted it high above his head, to encourage the men who were about to make the assault; hundreds of them were on the verge of the trench as he did so; others were following them closely; they were already within fire of the republican batteries, the balls from which were falling among them; but, regardless of the firing, they all fell on their knees, with their faces towards the earth, as soon as they saw the crucifix in the hands of their priest; and there, on the very field of battle, offered up a prayer that they might that day be victorious.

"They will be cut down like grass, simpletons that they are," said Stofflet; "besides, the first moment is everything; two hundred should by this time have been within the camp."

"Let them alone," said M. d'Elbée, "they are quite right as they are; they will not fight the worse for saying their prayers."

As he finished speaking, the men rose again, and rushed against the earth-work.

Their attempt of the preceding evening had had one good effect—it had taught the peasants that those who hesitated were in five times more imminent danger than those who at once got into the trench; and that the men climbing up the embankment, or at the top of it, were not nearly so liable to be struck, as the men at the bottom of the trench, or as those beyond it; they therefore eagerly stuck their hands and feet into the earth, and made the best of their way into the encampment.

It had been expected by the republicans that the next attack of the royalists would probably be made at Bournan, and they had consequently moved most of the cuirassiers from Varin to strengthen that important place; the men left in the encampment, consisted chiefly of those tribes of republicans who were enrolled into the French army under the name of Marseillaise—men who were as ferocious in the hour of victory, as they were prone to fly at the first suspicion of defeat—men who delighted in bloodshed, but who preferred finding their victims ready bound for the slaughter. It was the abject cowardice of these troops, which gave so wonderful a career of success to the Vendeans; it was their diabolical cruelty which has made the sufferings of the royalists more notorious even than their bravery.

De Lescure, Larochejaquelin, and Adolphe Denot led their men further along the road to the point at which Henri had been standing when he first saw the crowd of royalists coming towards him on the former evening, and from thence they also got into the encampment. As has been said, they had no powder; the men who commenced the assault were armed with muskets and bayonets, but the greater number of the assailants had no bayonets at all, and many of them nothing but sticks; still they forced their way into the centre of the camp; here a very strong opposition was made to them; the republicans were so well armed, that the royalists were unable to disperse them when any number of them made a stand together; when they moved from their ground, however, the Vendeans uniformly succeeded in driving them before them.

Cathelineau's men also made their way through the camp, and there Cathelineau and Larochejaquelin met each other.

"Well done, my friend; well done," said Henri, seizing the postillion by the hand, "this is a glorious meeting; the blues are beaten; we have only now to drive them into the river."

"Or into the road," said Jacques, who as usual was close to his master, "when once there, M. d'Elbée will not be long in handing them over to providence."

"Once more, my children, once more," said the priest, "drive them out, drive them out, vive le roi quand même!" and as he spoke, he brandished the crucifix over his head like a tomahawk; the sacred symbol was covered with gore, which appeared to have come from the head of some unfortunate republican.

"Ah, my friends!" hallaoed Cathelineau, advancing on before the others, "look—look there; there is our 'Marie Jeanne;' hurry then, hurry;" and there, immediately before them, was their own sacred trophy; their favourite cannon: they wanted no further incentive; the men who had followed Larochejaquelin, and the men of St. Florent who had come with Cathelineau, saw it at the same time, and vieing with each other, rushed onwards to gain the prize.

The republicans were amazed at the impetuosity of their enemies, and at last fled before them; when once these newly-levied troops were turned, their officers found it impossible to recover them; it was then sauve qui peut, and the devil take the hindmost. The passage from the camp towards the town was still open; no attack having been made from that quarter; and through the wooden gate, which had been erected there, the valiant Marseillaise rushed out as quick as their legs could carry them; the officers of the Vendeans offered quarter to all who would throw down their arms, and many of them did so, but most of them attempted to gain the town; they knew that if once they could cross the bridge at Fouchard they would be within the protection afforded by the castle guns—but not one of them reached the bridge.

M. d'Elbée had found that he could not himself take the position which had been pointed out to him, as, had he done so, his men would have been cut to pieces by the cannons from the castle, but he effectually prevented any one else from doing so; not thirty men from the whole encampment got into the town of Saumur, and those who did so, made their way through the river Thoué.

The success of the Vendeans, as far as it went, was most complete; they recovered their baggage and their cannons—above all, their favourite 'Marie Jeanne;' they took more prisoners than they knew how to keep; they armed themselves again, and again acquired unmeasured confidence in their own invincibility; they wanted immediately to be led out to attack the walls of Saumur, but Cathelineau and de Lescure knew that this would be running into useless danger. They had now once more plenty of ammunition; they had artillery, and were in a position to bombard the town; they would at any rate make a breech in the walls before they attempted to enter the streets; it was therefore decided that they would that evening remain where they were, and commence the attack on the citadel itself with daylight on the following morning.

"It grieved me to think," said Jacques Chapeau, as he pulled the huge baskets down from the carts, from which the republicans had not yet had time to move them, "it grieved my very heart to think, M. Henri, that this good wine from the cellars of Durbellière should have gone down republican throats; the thoughts of it lay heavy on my heart last night, so that I could not sleep. Thank heaven, I am spared that disgrace."

It was with the utmost difficulty that Cathelineau and de Lescure were able to get sentries to remain at the necessary positions during the night; the peasants had gained the battle, and were determined to enjoy themselves that evening; they would be ready they said to fight again, when the sun rose the next morning. The officers themselves had to act as sentinels; and after having been the first during the day to rush into every danger, and after having led the attack and the pursuit, and having then arranged the operations for the morrow, they had to remain on the watch during the night, lest the camp should be sacrificed by an attack from the republican forces, stationed at Bournan, or in the town—such is the lot of those who take upon themselves the management of men, without any power to ensure obedience to their orders.

VOLUME II.

CHAPTER I.
SAUMUR.

In the next three days the Vendeans bombarded the town, and during that time fired against it everything they could cram into their cannons, in the shape of warlike missiles; and they did not do so in vain, for the walls, in portions, began to give way and to crumble into the moat, which ran round the town, and communicated with the river Loire on each side of it. The town is built on the Loire, and between the Loire and the Thoué. After passing over the latter river at the bridge of Fouchard, the road in a few yards came to the draw-bridge over the moat; and from the close vicinity of the two rivers, no difficulty was found in keeping the moat supplied with water in the driest weather. About a mile below the town, the Thoue runs into the Loire.

Cathelineau found the men very impatient during the bombardment; they did not now dream of going home till the work was over, and Saumur taken; but they were very anxious to make a dash at the walls of the town; they could not understand why they should not clamber into the citadel, as they had done, over the green sods into the camp at Varin. On the fourth morning they were destined to have their wish. A temporary bridge over the Thoué had been made near Varin, over which a great portion of the cannon had been taken to a point near the Loire, from which the royalists had been able to do great damage to the walls; they had succeeded in making a complete breach of some yards, through which an easy entrance might be made, were it not for the moat; much of the rubbish from the walls had fallen into it, so as considerably to lessen the breadth; but there was still about twenty feet of water to be passed, and it was impossible, under the immediate guns of the castle, to contrive anything in the shape of a bridge.

Notwithstanding the difficulties of the place, it was decided that Larochejaquelin should take two hundred of his men and endeavour to make his way through the water, and while he was doing this, de Lescure was to force his passage over the bridge at Fouchard, and if possible, carry the gate of the town; in doing this he would pass under the heights of Bournan, and to this point M. d'Elbée was to accompany him with the great bulk of the army, so as to secure his flank from any attack from the republican force, which still retained their position there, and which had hitherto kept up an intercourse with the town across the bridge of Fouchard.

At five o'clock the greater portion of the army left the camp with d'Elbée and de Lescure. When they came within two furlongs of the bridge, the army separated, the chief body remaining with M. d'Elbée and the remainder going on with M. de Lescure towards the town. The road turns a little before it reaches the bridge over the Thoué, and up to this point, the Vendeans, in their progress, were tolerably protected from the guns of the town; but immediately they turned upon the bridge, they became exposed to a tremendous fire. The men at once perceived this and hesitated to cross the river; two of the foremost of their men fell as they put their feet upon the bridge.

De Lescure had marched from the camp at the head of his men. Father Jerome was on his right hand, and Stofflet and Adolphe Denot at his left. Henri had asked his friend to accompany him in the attack which he was to make near the river, but Adolphe had excused himself, alleging that he had a great dislike to the water, and that he would in preference accompany Charles de Lescure. Henri had not thought much about it, and certainly had imputed no blame to his friend, as there would be full as much scope for gallantry with his cousin as with himself. When de Lescure saw that his men hesitated, he said, "Come my men, forward with 'Marie Jeanne,' we will soon pick their locks for them," and rushed on the bridge alone; seeing that no one followed him he returned, and said to Denot:

"We must shew them an example, Adolphe; we will run to the other side of the bridge and return; after that, they will follow us."

De Lescure did not in the least doubt the courage of his friend, and again ran on to the bridge. Stofflet and Father Jerome immediately followed him, but Adolphe Denot did not stir. He was armed with a heavy sabre, and when de Lescure spoke to him, he raised his arm as though attempting to follow him, but the effort was too much for him, his whole body shook, his face turned crimson, and he remained standing where he was. As soon as de Lescure found that Adolphe did not follow him, he immediately came back, and taking him by the arm, shook him slightly, and whispered in his ear:

"Adolphe, what ails you? remember yourself, this is not the time to be asleep," but still Denot did not follow him; he again raised his arm, he put out his foot to spring forward, but he found he could not do it; he slunk back, and leant against the wall at the corner of the bridge, as though he were fainting.

De Lescure could not wait a moment longer. He would have risked anything but his own reputation to save that of his friend; but his brave companions were still on the bridge, and there he returned for the third time; his cap was shot away, his boot was cut, his clothes were pierced in different places, but still he was not himself wounded.

"See, my friends," said he aloud to the men behind him, "the blues do not know how to fire," and he pointed to his shoulder, from which, as he spoke, a ball had cut the epaulette.

He then crossed completely over the bridge, together with Stofflet and the priest; the people with one tremendous rush followed him, and Adolphe Denot was carried along with the crowd.

As soon as they found themselves immediately beneath the walls of the town, they were not exposed to so murderous a fire as they had been on the bridge itself, but still the work was hot enough. 'Marie Jeanne' had been carried across with them, and was soon brought into play; they had still enough ammunition left to enable their favourite to show her puissance in battering against the chief gates of Saumur. The men made various attempts to get into the town, but they were not successful, though the gates were shattered to pieces, and the passage was almost free; the republican troops within were too strong, and their firing too hot. At last the blues made a sortie from the town, and drove the Vendeans back towards the bridge; M. de Lescure still kept his place in the front, and was endeavouring to encourage his men to recover their position, when a ball struck his arm and broke it, and he fell with his knee upon the ground. As soon as the peasants saw him fall, and found that he was wounded, they wanted to take him in their arms, and carry him at once back across the bridge, but he would not allow them.

"What ails you, friends?" said he; "did you never never see a man stumble before? Come, the passage is free; now at length we will quench our thirst in Saumur," and taking his sword in his left hand, he again attempted to make good his ground.

M. d'Elbée had seen the Vendeans retreating back towards the bridge, and knowing that victory with them must be now or never (for it would have been impossible to have induced the peasants to remain longer from their homes, had they been repulsed), he determined to quit his post and to second de Lescure at the bridge. The firing from the town had ceased, for the republicans and royalists were so mixed together, that the men on the walls would have been as likely to kill their friends as their enemies; and as the first company, fatigued, discouraged and overpowered, were beginning to give way, d'Elbée, with about two thousand men, pushed across the bridge, and the whole mass of the contending forces, blues and Vendeans together, were hurried back through the gateway into the town; and de Lescure, as he entered it, found that it was already in the hands of his own party—the white flag was at that moment rising above the tricolour on the ramparts.

Adolphe Denot was one of the first of the Vendeans who entered the town through the gate. This shewed no great merit in him, for, as has been said, the men who had made the first attack, and the republicans who opposed it, were carried into the town by the impulse of the men behind them; but still he had endeavoured to do what he could to efface the ineffable disgrace which he felt must now attach to him in the opinion of M. de Lescure. As they were making their way up the principal street, still striking down the republicans wherever they continued to make resistance, but more often giving quarter, and promising protection, de Lescure with a pistol held by the barrel in his left hand, and with his right arm hastily tied up in the red handkerchief taken from a peasant's neck, said to the man who was next to him, but whom he did not at the moment perceive to be Denot:

"Look at Larochejaquelin, the gallant fellow; look at the red scarf on the castle wall. I could swear to him among a thousand."

"Yes," said Adolphe, unwilling not to reply when spoken to, and yet ashamed to speak to de Lescure, "yes, that is Henri. I wish I were with him."

"Oh, that is you, is it?" said de Lescure, just turning to look at him, and then hurrying away. But before he had moved on five paces, he returned, and putting his pistol into his girdle, gave Adolphe his left hand, and whispered to him:

"No one shall ever hear of it, Adolphe," said he, "and I will forget it. Think of your Saviour in such moments, Adolphe, and your heart will not fail you again."

The tears came into Denot's eyes as de Lescure left him. He felt that he must be despised; he felt grateful for the promise which had been given him, and yet he felt a kind of hatred for the man to whom he had afforded an opportunity of forgiving him. He felt that he never could like de Lescure again, never be happy in his company; he knew that de Lescure would religiously keep his word, that he would never mention to human being that horrid passage at the bridge; but he knew also that it could never be forgotten. Adolphe Denot was not absolutely a coward; he had not bragged that he would do anything which he knew it was contrary to his nature to do, when he told Agatha that he would be the first to place the white flag on the citadel of Saumur: he felt then all the aspirations of a brave man; he felt a desire even to hurry into the thick of the battle; but he had not the assured, sustained courage to support him in the moment of extreme danger. As de Lescure said, his heart failed him.

We must now return to Henri Larochejaquelin. He had taken with him two hundred of the best men from the parishes of St. Aubin, St. Laud and Echanbroignes; four or five officers accompanied him, among whom was a young lad, just fourteen years of age; his name was Arthur Mondyon, and he was a cadet from a noble family in Poitou; in the army he had at first been always called Le Petit Chevalier. His family had all emigrated, and he had been left at school in Paris; but on the breaking out of the wars he had run away from school, had forged himself a false passport into La Vendée, and declared his determination of fighting for his King. De Lescure had tried much to persuade him to stay at Clisson, but in vain; he had afterwards been attached to a garrison that was kept in the town of Chatillon, as he would then be in comparative safety; but the little Chevalier had a will of his own; he would not remain within walls while fighting was going on, and he had insisted on accompanying Larochejaquelin to Saumur. He was now installed as Henri's aide-de-camp.

Jacques Chapeau also accompanied the party who were to make their way into the town through the water. The men were all armed with muskets and bayonets, but their muskets were not loaded, nor did they carry any powder with them; it would have been useless in the attack they were about to make, and was much wanted elsewhere.

Henri was at his post about the time at which de Lescure was preparing to cross the bridge at Fouchard. It was an awful looking place at which ha had to make his entrance there was certainly a considerable breach in the wall, and the fragments of it had fallen into the fosse, so as to lessen its width; but, nevertheless, there was full twenty feet of running water to cross, which had more the appearance of a branch of the river Loire, than of a moat round a town.

Henri saw that his men looked a little alarmed at what they had to go through; he had a light straw hat on his head, and taking it off, he threw it into the water, a little above the point he had to pass, and as the running water carried it down he said:

"Whoever gives me that on the other side will be my friend for life." And as he spoke he himself leapt into the water, and swam across.

Jacques made a plunge for the hat: had it been in the middle of the Loire he would have gone after it under similar circumstances, though he couldn't swim a stroke; he did not go near the hat however, but went head over heels into the water; the impetus carried him through, and he was the second to scramble upon the broken mortar on the other side. The Chevalier was more active; he leapt in and seized the hat as it was going down the stream, and swimming like a young duck, brought it back to its owner.

"Ah! Chevalier," said Henri, reproaching him playfully, and helping him up out of the water, "you have robbed some poor fellow of a chance; you, you know, cannot be more my friend, than you already are."

The men quickly followed: they all got a ducking; some few lost their arms, one or two were slightly wounded by their comrades, but none of them were drowned. Henri soon made his way over the ruins into the town, and carried everything before him. The greater part of the garrison of the town were endeavouring to repulse the attack made by de Lescure; others had retired into the castle, in which the republican General thought that he might still hold out against the Vendeans. Many were already escaping out of the town by the bridge over the Loire, and throwing down their arms, were hurrying along the road to Tours.

It was in this manner, and almost without opposition, that Larochejaquelin found himself, together with his brave followers, in the middle of Saumur; their own success astonished them; hardly a shot was fired at them in their passage; they went through the town without losing a man; the republican soldiers whom they did see threw down their arms and fled; the very sight of the Vendeans in the centre of the town overwhelmed them with panic. The appearance of Henri's troop was very singular; every man wore round his neck and round his waist a red cotton handkerchief; this costume had been adopted to preserve Larochejaquelin from the especial danger of being made the butt of republican marksmen. There was now no especial mouchoir rouge among them. They certainly had a frightful appearance, as they hurried through the streets with their bayonets fixed, dripping with mud and water, and conspicuous with their red necks and red waists; at least so thought the republicans, for they offered very little opposition to them.

Henri had just time to see that his friends had entered the town by the gate on the Doué road, but he did not wait to speak to them. The republican soldiers were escaping from the town in the opposite direction, and he could not resist the temptation of following them. He was at the head of his men, just passing over the Loire by a wooden bridge, called the bridge of the Green Cross, and having possessed himself of a sword in his passage through the town, was making good use of it, when a dragoon turned suddenly round, and fired a pistol almost in his face: near as the man was to him, in his hurry he missed him, and the bullet merely grazed Henri's cheek, without even raising the skin. "Ah, bungler," said Henri, raising his sword, "you are no good for either King or nation," and he struck the unfortunate man dead at his feet.

Not only the soldiers, but the inhabitants of the town were escaping by hundreds over the bridge, and Henri saw that if he pursued them farther, he must, sooner or later, find himself surrounded and overpowered by numbers; he returned, therefore, and destroyed the bridge, so as to prevent the return of the soldiers who had fled in their first panic, and also to prevent any more of the inhabitants from leaving their homes.

"God has certainly fought on our side today," said he to one of his Mends: "with barely two hundred men, all dripping like drowned rats, we have made our way, almost without opposition, through the town, and thousands of soldiers are even yet flying before us."

"Ah! M. Henri," said the little Chevalier, "it is a great honour to fight for one's King; one fears nothing then: a single royalist should always drive before him ten republicans."

Henri now returned and joined de Lescure, who was in possession of the town, though the citadel was still in the hands of General Quetineau, who held the command of the garrison. It was not till the cousins had embraced each other, that Henri saw that de Lescure was wounded.

"Yes," said de Lescure, "I have at length acquired the privilege of shedding my blood in the cause; but it is only a broken arm; Victorine will have a little trouble with me when I return to Clisson."

"And Adolphe, my brave Adolphe, you are wounded, too?" said Henri.

Denot muttered something, and turned away; he did not dare to look his friends in the face.

"He envies me my honour," said de Lescure; "but it might have been his chance as well as mine, for he was not two feet from me when I was wounded." This was true, for de Lescure had been struck after Denot had crossed the bridge with the other men.

A flag of truce was now sent out by General Quetineau to the royalists, with a proposal that he would give up the castle, and lay down his arms, on being allowed to march out with all his men, and take the road to Angers; but this proposition was not acceded to.

"No!" said de Lescure to the General's messenger: "tell M. Quetineau that the Vendeans cannot accede to those terms—we cannot allow his soldiers to march to Angers, and to return within a week to inflict new cruelties on our poor peasants. M. Quetineau must surrender without any terms: the practices of our army must be his only guarantee, that his men will not be massacred in cold blood, as the unfortunate royalists are massacred when they fall into the hands of the republicans."

The republicans were not in a condition to insist upon anything; as M. de Lescure had said, the practices of the Vendeans were a guarantee that no blood would be unnecessarily shed, and relying on this assurance alone, M. Quetineau surrendered the castle and gave up his sword. De Lescure took possession of it till he should be able to hand it over to his General, and the Vendeans found themselves complete masters of Saumur.

There was, however, still a very strong detachment of republican troops on the heights of Bournan, who were watched on one side by Foret and his detachment, and on the other by a portion of M. d'Elbée's army. These men had done some execution, as they covered with their cannon a portion of the road over which the Vendeans had passed, but they had taken no active part whatever in the engagement. What made this the more singular, was that the garrison at Bournan was composed of the very best soldiers of the French republican army. They were under the command of General Coustard, who kept his position during the whole attack, inactive and unmolested; had he attacked M. d'Elbée's army in the rear, when that officer advanced to support de Lescure's division, the Vendeans would probably have been destroyed between the two republican armies. Whether the two Generals of the Convention misunderstood each other, or whether the soldiers at Bournan were unwilling to rout the royalists, it is impossible to say; but they remained at Bournan till the night, and then leaving their post during the darkness, made good their retreat to Angers.

As soon as the white flag was seen on the walls of Saumur, Cathelineau left the position which he had held, and entered the town. It was greatly in opposition to his own wishes that he had been induced to remain at a distance from the absolute attack, and now he felt almost ashamed of himself as the officers and men crowded round him to congratulate him on the victory which he had gained.

"No, M. de Lescure," he said, as that officer tendered him General Quetineau's sword, "no, I will never take it from him who has won it with so much constancy and valour. I must own I envy you your good fortune, but I will not rob you of the fruits of your exertions."

"But Cathelineau," said the other, "you are our General, the customs of war require—"

"The customs of war are all changed," replied Cathelineau, "when such as you and M. de Larochejaquelin make yourselves second to a poor postillion; at any rate," he added, pressing between his own, the left hand of M. de Lescure, which still held the sword, "if I am to be the commander, I must be obeyed. M. de Lescure will not set a bad example when I tell him to keep General Quetineau's sword."

"And you, General Quetineau," said Cathelineau, "what are your wishes— your own personal wishes I mean? I have not forgotten that you alone of the republican leaders have shewn mercy to the poor royalists, when they were in your power; you at any rate shall not say that the Vendean brigands do not know how to requite kind services." Cathelineau alluded to the name which the republicans had given to the royalists at the commencement of the war.

"It little matters to me," said Quetineau, "what becomes of me; were you to give me unconditional liberty, I should go to Paris—and the Convention would accuse me of betraying my trust, and I should become another victim of the guillotine."

"Of the guillotine!" said Henri; "why, what bloody monsters are those you serve they send you soldiers who know nothing but how to run; do they expect that with such troops as these you should be victorious, when opposed to men who are individually striving for everything that is dear to them?"

"The Convention," said Quetineau, "would ensure success by punishing defeat. You will find in the end that they are politic; there will, however, be many victims, and I am fated to be one of them."

"Stay with us, General Quetineau," said de Lescure, "join our forces, and here you will find that honesty and courage are respected. You cannot, you do not approve of the tyranny of the Convention. We know each other of old, and I know that in joining the army, you never intended to serve under a Republic. You cannot say that in your heart you are a republican."

"Did I wish to shew myself a royalist, it would not now become me to proclaim myself one," answered Quetineau. "I entered the army of the King, but I have chosen to remain a soldier of the Republic. Whatever may be my feelings, adversity shall not make me false to the colours I have carried; besides, gentlemen, if I escaped the anger of the Convention myself, I have a wife in Paris, whose life would be made to satisfy it; under such circumstances, I presume you would not counsel me to become a royalist."

This was an argument which it was impossible to answer. General Quetineau accepted the present of his liberty, and soon as he was free, he returned to Paris; he was immediately sent to the revolutionary tribunal and tried for his life; and as he himself had predicted, was guillotined by the Convention for the cowardice of the troops, whom he had been called upon to take under his command. In the old days of Greece, when the Kings sinned, the people suffered for it: this law was reversed under the first French Republic; when the soldiers ran away, the Generals were beheaded.

The joy of the Vendeans, when they found themselves masters of Saumur, knew no bounds, but they were grotesque rather than unruly in their demonstrations; they plundered nothing from the poor people, or even from the shopkeepers; the money that was found in the republican chest was divided among them, but as this consisted almost entirely of assignats, it was of but little value. The shopkeepers were surprised at the liberality of their enemies and conquerors, who were willing to dispose of these assignats for anything they would fetch—a little wine, or a few ounces of tobacco; whereas, their own friends, the republicans, had insisted that they should be taken at their nominal value as money, for all goods exposed for sale.

An enormous poplar had been planted by the towns-people in the centre of the marketplace, which they called the tree of liberty. This was now a doomed tree. On the evening of the day in which they took the town, the royalist peasants went in procession, and with many cheers hewed it to the ground; it was then treated with every possible contumely—it was chopped, and hacked, and barked; it was kicked, and cuffed, and spat upon; the branches were cut off, and on the bare top was placed a large tattered cap of liberty; the Vendean marksmen then turned out, and fired at the cap till it was cut to pieces; after that, all the papers and books, which had belonged to the municipality, every document which could be found in the Town-hall, were brought into the square, and piled around the roots of the tree; and then the whole was set on fire—and tree, papers, and cap of liberty, were consumed together.

On the next morning, considerable difficulty was experienced in disposing of the prisoners there were about two thousand in the town, and the Vendeans knew that they had no means of keeping them, nor did they wish to be at the great expense of feeding them; it was contrary to their inclination, their practice, and their consciences, to kill them in cold blood: and they knew from experience, that if they gave them their liberty, the same men would return within a fortnight, newly-armed, to carry on the war against their liberators, in spite of any oaths they might take to the contrary.

"I'll tell you what we will do, M. Henri," said Chapeau, speaking to his master, "we will put a mark upon them, so that if we catch them again, we may know them; and then I do think it would be all right to hang them; or perhaps for the second time we might cut off their ears, and hang them the third time."

"But how would you mark them, Jacques; men are not like cattle that you can brand them."

"I will tell you what," said the little Chevalier, "shave them all like pigs; they cannot all buy wigs, and we shall know them by their bald sconces."

"That is the very thing, M. Arthur," said Chapeau delighted, "we will shave their heads as clear as the palm of my hand. I am an excellent barber myself; and I will even get a dozen or two assistants; hair shall be cheap in Saumur tomorrow; though I fear soap and razors will be scarce."

Chapeau was so delighted with the proposal that he at once hurried away to carry it into execution; and Arthur, though he felt that his dignity as an officer would be somewhat compromised, could not resist the boyish temptation to follow him and see the fun.

He and Chapeau were not long in raising an efficient corps of barbers and assistant barbers; and few of the shopkeepers, when called upon, thought it advisable to refuse the loan of a razor and a shaving dish. They established themselves in the large room of the Town-hall, and had the prisoners brought in by a score at a time; vehemently did the men plead for their hair, and loud did they swear that if allowed to escape free, they would never again carry arms against the Vendeans; but neither their oaths or their prayers were of any avail, nor yet the bribes which were offered by those who had ought to give; the order to sit down was given imperatively, and if not immediately obeyed, the command was somewhat roughly enforced.

They were shaved by twenty at a time, and while one lot was being operated on, another twenty, who were next destined to fill the chairs, were kept standing against the wall. The long hair was first cut off with scissors, and then the head and whiskers were closely shaved. The first candidates for the soap-dish were very unruly under the operation, but they only got their ears snipped and their skin chipped, and had to return to their prisons with their polls all bloody as well as bald. Those who looked on, took a lesson from the folly of their comrades, and most of them remained quiet. The manoeuvres of the men however were very different during the process; some took it with good humour, and endeavoured to laugh as their locks were falling; some sat still as death; others looked fierce and warlike; some were even moved to tears; some fought, and kicked and scratched, and at last had to be corded to their seats. One unfortunate went down upon his knees, and implored Chapeau by the memory of his mistress, if ever he had been in love, by his regard for his wife, if he chanced to be married, not to shave his head. He was engaged to be married, he said, to a young girl at Angers, who had many lovers; she had preferred him for the beauty of his hair: if he returned back bald, he knew that he would be rejected. Chapeau for a time was moved, but the patriot and the royalist triumphed over the man, and Jacques, turning away his face on which a tear was gleaming, with a wave of his hand motioned the young man to the chair.

Insult was added to injury, for the Chevalier stood at the door with a brush, and a large jar of red paint, and as each man went out of the room, Arthur made a huge cross upon his bare pate. The poor wretches in their attempt to rub it off, merely converted the cross into a red patch, and as they were made to walk across the market-place with their bald red heads, they gave rise to shouts of laughter, not only from the royalists, but from the inhabitants of the town.

For three days the shaving went on, and as the men became experienced from practice, it was conducted with wonderful rapidity. At last, the prisoners were all deprived of their hair, and set at liberty—a temporary bridge was thrown across the Loire, near the Green Cross, and the men were allowed to march over. As soon as they found themselves on the other side of the Loire, they were free.

"Come, my bald pates, come my knights of the ruddy scalp," said Jacques, standing at the corner of the bridge as they passed over, "away with you to the Convention; and if your friends like your appearance, send them to Saumur, and they shall be shaved close, and the barber shall ask for no fee; but remember, if you return again yourselves, your ears will be the next sacrifice you will be called on to make for your country."

CHAPTER II.
COUNCIL OF WAR.

The taking of the fortified town of Saumur, and the total dispersion of the large army which had been collected there by the Republic, was an enterprise of much greater magnitude than anything which had previously been undertaken by the Vendeans: it gave them great advantages, it supplied them plentifully with arms, ammunition and clothes for their soldiers, and greatly inspirited the peasants; but it made the Convention feel that it had no contemptible enemy to deal with in La Vendée, and that the best soldiers of France would be required to crush the loyalty which inspired the peasants of Anjou and Poitou.

The Vendean leaders felt that their responsibilities were greatly increased, and that very much depended on the decision to which they might now come as regarded their further operations. A general council of war was accordingly held in Saumur, at which the matter was debated among them. Twelve of the Vendeans were admitted to this consultation, and all others were strictly excluded; they were Cathelineau, Bonchamps, who though badly wounded, had caused himself to be brought thither from Doué, de Lescure, who had remained in action for eight hours after his arm was broken, and had consequently suffered much from it, Larochejaquein, d'Elbée, Stofflet, Adolphe Denot, Father Jerome, Foret, M. Donnessan, Lescure's father-in-law, Marigny, and the Prince de Talmont.

The first question was the selection of a chief officer. Cathelineau had been named before the battle of Saumur; but, as he himself alleged, his command was to last only during that siege; he had been, he said, selected for a special purpose, which purpose, by the grace of God, was accomplished, and he was now ready to resign his commission into the hands of those who had given it to him.

"I am not so foolish," said he, "as to suppose that I am qualified to take the command in the war which we have now to carry on. No; one privilege I beg to exercise on retiring from my command. I will name a successor; let any one who pleases name another; we will then put it to the vote, and let him who has most votes be our General."

"So be it," said Henri. "Nothing can be better."

"I name M. de Lescure," said Cathelineau. "Some of us are beloved by the people, but are not educated; others are highly educated, but are not yet known to the peasants. We are all, I am sure, brave men: but M. de Lescure is beloved by all; his knowledge fits him for his high position, and his cool, constant, determined courage, no man who has seen him in the hour of battle will doubt. I name M. de Lescure."

De Lescure was about to rise, when Henri put his hand upon his friends arm, and said:

"Let me speak, Charles. We all know that what Cathelineau has said of my cousin is no more than the truth. Be still, Charles: when I have spoken you can then say what you please, but I am sure you will agree with me. Nevertheless, I will not give my vote that he be our chief General. Cathelineau has desired that any one differing from him should name another, and that the question should then be put to the vote. I differ from him, and, therefore, I name another. I name the good Cathelineau, the Saint of Anjou."

"Now let us vote," said the Prince de Talmont. "Come, Bonchamps, do you begin."

"I never heard of deposing a Commander-in-Chief in consequence of a complete victory," said Bonchamps. "The Convention murders their Generals when they are defeated, but even the Convention rewards them for victory. I vote for Cathelineau."

"And you, Foret," said the Prince.

"I say Cathelineau," said Foret: "the peasants generally would be disappointed to see any put above him."

"I certainly vote for Cathelineau," said Father Jerome, who came next.

"We should be offending our Creator," said M. d'Elbée, "were we to reject the great and good Commander, whom His gracious providence has sent us. I vote for Cathelineau."

"And you, M. Denot," said the Prince. Adolphe Denot especially disliked Cathelineau: he was jealous of his reputation and popularity: he could not bear to feel himself in any way under the control of a man so much his inferior in rank; he fancied, moreover, that Cathelineau regarded Agatha Larochejaquelin; he had been quick enough to perceive that the ineffable grace and beauty of his mistress had filled the heart of the poor postillion with admiration, and he feared that his own rejection had been caused by some mutual feeling in Agatha's breast, which future events might warm into love. Adolphe, therefore, hated Cathelineau, and would have delighted, had he dared to do so, to express his disapprobation of the choice; but, after pausing for a few moments, he found that he did not dare; so he merely said:

"Oh, Cathelineau, of course. When you are all resolved, what's the use of voting about it?"

"To show that we all are resolved," said de Lescure; "to make Cathelineau understand that it is positively his duty to take the position we wish him to fill."

And so, one after another, they all recorded their votes that Cathelineau should be the Commander-in-Chief of the Vendean army; and they all declared that they would, without reserve, obey any military orders, which he might give them.

"Well, gentlemen," said he, again seating himself at the head of the table, "I should pay but a bad compliment to your understanding, were I any further to insist on my own unworthiness. I will not, at any rate, be wanting in zeal for the good cause, and I will trust to Him who directs us all, for assistance in the difficult duties which you have imposed on me."

They then debated on the all-important question of what should be their next movement, and on this subject there was much difference of opinion. Bonchamps was again asked to speak first, and he advised that they should at once proceed to Paris.

"We can do nothing," said he, "while the present Convention sits in Paris; it has but one head, but it has ten thousand bloody hands. There can be no peace, no rest in France, while Danton, Robespierre and Barrère are omnipotent. Let us at once start for Paris: Brittany will join us, and parts of Normandy; the Southerns will follow us; the men of Bordeaux and of the Gironde: have not their own orators, the leaders of the Revolution, been murdered in their seats, because they were not willing that all France should become one Golgotha? Lyons, even, and Marseilles, are now sick of the monsters who have crawled forth from the haunts of the Jacobins to depopulate the country, and annihilate humanity. There is now but a small faction, even in Paris, to whom the restoration of order would not be acceptable. The intensity of their cruelty is the only strength of the governing faction; the extent of their abominations alone makes them terrible. Hundreds will fly from one Indian snake, so potent is its venom, so sure to inflict death: but let one brave man set his heel upon its head, and the noxious animal is destroyed for ever: so it is with the party who now rules the Convention. Now that we have with us the all-powerful prestige of victory, let us march at once to Paris; hundreds will join us on the way, and what force can at the moment be collected to stop us? Let us proceed at once to Paris, and proclaim at the door of the Convention, in the gardens of the Tuilleries, in the Place Louis Quinze, where our sainted monarch so nobly shed his blood, that France again submits herself to her King."

"Would that we could!" said de Lescure; "would that the spirit of revolution was yet sufficiently quenched in France to allow us to follow your advice; but there is much, very much to be done before a royalist army can march from La Vendée to Paris; unthought of sufferings to be endured, the blood of thousands to be sacrificed, before France will own that she has been wrong in the experiment she has made. We must fight our battles by inches, and be satisfied, if, when dying, we can think that we have left to our children a probability of final victory. Normandy and the Gironde may be unwilling to submit to the Jacobin leaders, but they are as yet as warmly attached to the Republic as Paris itself. And, Bonchamps, you little know the dispositions and character of the men, who at our bidding have left their homes and come to Saumur, if you think that at our bidding they will march to Paris; they are even now burning to return home, to recount to their wives and children what they have done.

"Not half the number that came to Saumur would leave the town with us on the road to Paris; and before we could reach Tours, the army would have melted away from us like snow from a mountain top, when the sun begins to shine. It is here, in our own locality, that we should endeavour to extend our influence. In Southern Brittany the people, I believe, are with us, but the towns are full of the troops of the Republic. Let us drive them out of Angers, Ancenis, and Nantes, as we have driven them from Saumur. Let us force them from the banks of the Loire, and become masters of the coast of Southern Brittany. Then we may expect men and money from England. Then we may fairly hope for such foreign aid as may enable us to face the Republic; but at present, if we march to Paris, we march to certain destruction."

"M. de Lescure is right," said Stofflet, "our men would not go far from their homes; we must remember that they are not paid, nor have we the means of paying them; if we had English gold, we might perhaps make our way to Paris."

"Our men are not so mercenary, Stofflet," said Bonchamps, "I do not think they have shewn any great desire for plunder."

"No," said Stofflet, "but they must live; if they are to have neither pay nor plunder, how are they to get to Paris?"

"I agree with you, Bonchamps," said Henri, "come what, come may, I would make a dash at Paris; we shall be cut to pieces here, while we are waiting for English aid; some of the men would follow us—most of them I believe; where we meet with friends, they will give us provisions; where we find enemies, we will take them, and pay the owners in republican assignats; they would get no other payment in the market-towns. I am sorry to disagree with you, Charles, but my voice is for Paris."

"And mine also, certainly," said Adolphe, "let our career be short, at any rate let it be glorious; let us march to Paris and strike terror into the tyrants of the Convention."

"It is difficult to strike terror into tyrants," said de Lescure quickly, "when the number of their supporters is ten times greater than that of their opponents."

"Well, Cathelineau," said Bonchamps, "what do you say? it is for you to settle the question between us; are we to go forward to Paris, or march back to Nantes?"

"I would wish to hear what others say; for myself, I fear that M. de Lescure is right. I fear the peasants would not follow us so far from their own homes. What does the Prince de Talmont say?"

"I will have no voice in the matter," said the Prince. "I have joined you but lately, and as yet am only fit to follow where others lead."

"And you, M. d'Elbée?" said Cathelineau.

"I hardly know how to speak," said d'Elbée, "where the subject is so important."

"M. d'Elbée is not wont to be so modest," said Stofflet; "does he not trust that Providence will inspire him with wisdom, when he opens his mouth to give his opinion?"

"Certainly, Stofflet; I trust in that all-seeing eye, at which you are so willing to scoff; but I do not expect that I am to be allowed to see further into futurity than another; however, if I am to express an opinion, I think we should endeavour to march on Paris; if we find that the men desert us, and that others do not join our standards, we must return."

"And how are we to return," said de Lescure, "and to whom? think you that we can collect another army in La Vendée, when one has deserted us on the road? will the peasants again trust in us, after they have once left us? Never If the army dissolves itself in despair, you will never be able to establish it again."

"Who talks of despair, Charles?" said Henri, "you did not despair when you were thundering against the gates of Saumur with four republicans to one royalist opposed to you; why should you despair now; or why should the army despair; I believe they would go anywhere at the command of their priests, and with the hope of restoring the King to his throne."

The question was then put to the vote. De Lescure and four others, voted for attacking Nantes. Bonchamps, and five others, declared for proceeding at once to Paris, with the view of arresting the present leaders of the

Convention. Cathelineau was then called on to express his opinion, which would of course be decisive.

"I think M. de Lescure is right," said he, "I think we are not in a position to advance to Paris. I have not the heart to ask the men to follow me into a strange country, so far from their own homes."

The numbers were now equally divided, but as Cathelineau was the Commander-in-Chief, his voice turned the scale; and the expedition to Paris was postponed.

"So be it," said Bonchamps; "let us prepare then for Nantes; it is not fortified like Saumur, but the troops there are very numerous."

It was then decided that Cathelineau should name six lieutenants under him, to take command of the different districts from which the army was collected, and to which the men would be sure to return; and also appoint an officer in command of the artillery, and another in command of the cavalry. Cathelineau would have willingly dispensed with the task of selecting his officers—a work in which he could hardly fail to give offence to some, and in which he might probably give entire satisfaction to none; but it was to be done, and he felt that it was useless for him to shrink from it.

"M. Bonchamps," said he, "will of course take the command of the men of Anjou, and M. de Lescure of those from the southern parts of the Bocage, and they will assist me, I hope, in selecting the others. It is very difficult to select, where so many are fit."

"Rather say," said Henri, laughing, "where so many are equally unfit. Why, Bonchamps and Marigny are the only soldiers by profession we have among us."

"You'll all be soldiers shortly," said Father Jerome. "You are at any rate going the right way to learn the trade."

"Marigny of course will take the artillery," said Bonchamps. "We are very lucky in having so good an artillery officer among us."

"There is no one, at any rate, to dispute your claim, Marigny," said de Lescure.

"So he's president over 'Marie Jeanne' and the gunpowder," said Henri; "that's settled, isn't it Cathelineau?"

"Unless M. Marigny refuses," said Cathelineau.

"I am not modest enough for that, General," said Marigny. "Do you furnish me with guns, and I'll fight them. Do you collect the gunpowder, and I'll consume it."

"And the Prince de Talmont will take the cavalry?" said Cathelineau.

"No, indeed," said the Prince. "I will not interfere with Henri Larochejaquelin."

"Henri Larochejaquelin is much obliged to you, Prince," said Henri, "but he is not ambitious of making a fool of himself; nor does he wish to be made a fool of. Moreover, Henri Larochejaquelin does not wish to quarrel with an old friend like you, Prince; but he might be tempted to do so, if you take any liberties with his name."

"But, Cathelineau," said the Prince, "Henri has been at the head of the cavalry all through."

"Don't set a bad example, Prince," said de Lescure. "Let every man coincide with Cathelineau's directions without a word; so shall we be spared the ill effects of over modesty, and of too much assurance."

"Besides," said Cathelineau, "M. Larochejaquelin will be much wanted elsewhere. As a matter of course, he will be the leader of all the parishes round Chatillon; I doubt if the men would follow any one else."

"Dear Cathelineau," said Henri, "if you will take my advice, you will not make leaders of us youngsters at all. Adolphe and I will be well contented to be hussars for awhile. Let these grey-headed seniors be our leaders," and he pointed to d'Elbée whose hair was grizzled.

Henri had seen that the spirit of jealousy was already rising in Adolphe Denot's face. No allusion had been made to his services; his advice had never been asked in the council; there was no probability that he would be named as one of the leaders; he had hardly spoken a word since they had assembled in the council-room. Henri, though his own heart was a stranger to the jealousy and dread of neglect which tormented Adolphe, sympathised with, and felt for his friend; and he thought that if they were both together excluded from command at his request, the blow would be less keenly felt. They were the two youngest in the room, and their youth was a good reason why they should not be named; but Henri was the younger of the two, and he knew that if he were selected as one of the chiefs, Adolphe would be miserable at finding himself left out.

De Lescure, however, would not allow of this. He had promised that he would not disgrace Denot, by telling of the cowardice he had shewn at the Bridge of Fouchard, and he was determined to keep his word; but he would not allow his cousin, his pupil, his bosom friend, the man whom he loved with the affection of a brother and a father, to sink himself to the same level as a coward.

"How absurd is this!" said he, angrily. "I wonder, Henri, that you should be the first to create such foolish difficulties, when our very existence depends on perfect unanimity. In proportion as our means of enforcing obedience is slender, should our resolution be firm, implicitly to obey the directions of those who are selected as our leaders. We have made Cathelineau our General, and desired him to select his officers, and when he selects you as one, you object. If you object from a proper modesty, it argues that those who accept, shew an improper degree of assurance. You should think of these things, Henri."

"I resign myself to my dignity, and am dumb," said Henri laughing. "Go on, Cathelineau, and if the men you name, say but one word, one syllable against your choice—I'll slay them."

Cathelineau knew that all his difficulty still lay before him; those whom he had already chosen would as a matter of course be among the number; but who were to be the other three?

"M. Donnissan," said be, in a whisper to de Lescure, who was sitting next to him. "I do not know what his wishes might be."

"My father-in-law feels himself too old," answered de Lescure; "d'Elbée would be a much fitter person; he is thought so much of at Beauprieu."

"And the other two?" asked Cathelineau.

"Name one yourself, and ask Bonchamps to name the other."

"M. d'Elbée," said Cathelineau, aloud, "you will not, I am sure, refuse to take your portion of our labours."

"You will find," whispered Stofflet to his neighbour, "that as Providence has called upon him, he will be willing enough."

"I will do my best," said d'Elbée "as I am called upon; and may the Lord direct me, that I may fight His battle so as to do honour to His name."

"I think I will name Stofflet," said Cathelineau, consulting with Bonchamps and de Lescure; "he is a brave man, and though rude in his manner, he will make perhaps the best soldier among us; already the men obey him almost more implicitly than any one."

"Do—do!" said Bonchamps; "you cannot do better."

"I think you will be right to do so," said de Lescure, "though I do not like the man; but the peasants know him, and he is one of themselves. Yesterday morning I had ample proof of his courage. As you say, he is a brave man and a good soldier."

Stofflet was then informed that he had been named, and though he muttered some expressions as to his own want of the necessary qualifications, he was evidently well pleased that the choice had fallen on him.

And now the last of the lot was to be chosen. As the two last names had been mentioned, Denot's brow had grown blacker and blacker. Henri Larochejaquelin, during the whole proceeding, had been walking about the room, sitting now in one place, and now in another. At the present moment, he was sitting next to Adolphe, who, when Stofflet's name was mentioned, whispered to him, but almost audibly:

"Gracious heaven! Stofflet!—the whole affair is becoming discreditable. How can any gentleman serve under such a man as that?"

"You think too much of rank, Adolphe," said Henri; "we should entirely forget all distinctions of person now; unless we do so we can never succeed."

"But do you think we are more likely to set the King upon his throne, by making such a brute as that a General? I wonder whom our Commander-in-Chief will choose next—Foret, I suppose."

After having again consulted for some time, Bonchamps said to Cathelineau: "I do not think you can do better than name Adolphe Denot."

This was said in a low voice, but Adolphe's ears were not slow to catch his own name, and he was once more happy. Though he was named last, he would be equal with the others.

"Not so," said de Lescure, who had no idea that Denot had overheard the mention of his name, "Adolphe is not yet sufficiently known to the people; besides we have hitherto forgotten one, who though absent, we must not forget—one who was the first in the field against the Republic, who is already at the head of an army, and who has on various occasions shown himself capable to lead an army. We must not forget Charette."

The last words were spoken out loud, and though they were eagerly responded to by every one else, they fell with a heavy sound on Adolphe Denot's ear. To know that he was excluded after he had been named, to feel that he had been proposed merely to be rejected; it was more than he could bear; and as soon as Cathelineau had formally announced the name of M. Charette as one of their leaders, he started abruptly from his chair and said:

"Oh, of course, gentlemen, if you prefer Charette, so be it! He, doubtless will be better able to assist your endeavours than I should; but you might have spared me the mortification of putting my name on your list of officers, merely to scratch it off again."

"What matters it, Adolphe," said Larochejaquelin, blushing for his friend, "will you not share my command? Will not your word be as influential in the parishes of Chatillon as my own?"

"I sincerely beg your pardon, M. Denot," said Cathelineau, "if I have hurt your feelings, but you are as much aware as we are that we should be very wrong to neglect the merits of M. Charette; his achievements claim from us this distinction, and his power and influence would probably be lost to La Vendée, if we did not now incorporate his army with ours."

"I have nothing further to say," said Denot. "I must own I do not altogether admire the selection which has been made; but I have nothing further to say on the subject."

"I am sorry, Adolphe, that you have said so much," said de Lescure.

"You would have been apt to say more yourself if you had been passed over," said Adolphe, forgetting in his passion how he had disgraced himself before de Lescure at the bridge of Fouchard.

"I fear you misunderstand the purpose, which has collected here in Saumur so many men in arms," said he. "I fear that you think the peasants of our country have turned themselves into soldiers, that we might become generals, and play at being great men. Indeed, such is not the case; if personal ambition has brought you here, you had better leave us. We have come here to fight, and very probably to die for our King and our religion; and, being called upon to act as leaders, we must bear a heavier share of the burden, and undergo greater perils than others; but we seek no especial dignity, we look for no other pre-eminence, than that of suffering more than others. I fear these are not the feelings that influence you."

"My feelings, Sir, are as pure as your own!" said Denot.

"If so," said Father Jerome, "you had better teach us all to think so, by taking care that your conduct is also as pure as M. de Lescure's."

"Oh, Father Jerome, do not anger him," said Henri. "Come with me, Adolphe, and we will quietly talk over this; they don't exactly understand what you mean yet."

"But they shall understand what I mean," said Denot, whose anger was now beyond control, "and they shall know that I will not remain here to be rebuked by a priest, who has thrust himself into affairs with which he has no concern; or to make myself subservient to men who are not fit to be my equals. I will not deign to be a common soldier, when such a man as Stofflet is made an officer."

And he got up from the chair in which he had again seated himself, and stalked out of the room.

"He has at any rate proved to us," said Bonchamps, "that I was wrong to nominate him, and that you were right not to accept the nomination."

"I grieve that he should be vexed with me," said Stofflet; "but I did not seek to put myself above him."

"Time and experience will make him wise," said de Lescure: "let us pity his folly and forgive it."

The council was then broken up, and the different officers went each to perform his own duties. When Denot left the room, Henri immediately followed him.

"Adolphe," said he, as he overtook him in the market-place, "Adolphe, indeed you are wrong, no one meant to show you any indignity."

"And have you also followed me to tell me I am wrong—of course I am wrong—I am wrong because I will not submit, as you and Charles do, to ignorant boors like Stofflet and Cathelineau, because—"

"Like Cathelineau! why, Adolphe, you are mad," said Henri, "why you yourself voted that Cathelineau should be our General."

"Voted! Why, Henri, what a child you are! Do you call that voting when all was arranged beforehand? You are blind, I tell you. You will vote next, I suppose, that your great General's valour shall de rewarded with your sister's hand!"

"My sister's hand! what is it you are speaking of?"

"Yes, Agatha's hand! think you that when you make a General of such as him, that his ambition will rest there? if you are content to be lieutenant to a postillion, I presume you will feel yourself honoured by a nearer connexion with him."

"Denot, you are raving mad! Cathelineau looking for my sister's hand?"

"Yes, Agatha's hand, the postillion looking for your sister's hand; and, Sir, you will find that I am not mad. Before long, Cathelineau will look for Agatha's hand: her heart he has already," and without waiting for any further answer, he hurried away.

"He must be raving mad," said Henri, "unlucky in love, and thwarted in ambition, he is unable to bear his griefs like a man. What a phantasy has jealousy created in his brain But Agatha was right; a man who could speak of her, even in his madness, as he has now spoken, was not worthy of her. Cathelineau! were he ten times lower than a postillion by birth, he would still be twenty times made noble by achievements and by character, and yet I would not wish—but nonsense! he thinks no more of wedding Agatha than I of Diana."

CHAPTER III.
RETURN TO DURBELLIÈRE.

When Adolphe Denot left his friend Henri in the street of Saumur, and ran off from him, Henri was so completely astonished by his parting words, so utterly dumb-founded by what he said respecting Agatha, that he made no attempt to follow him, but returned after awhile to the house, in which he, Charles and Adolphe were lodging, and as he walked slowly through the streets, he continued saying to himself, "Poor fellow, he is mad! he is certainly raving mad!"

From that time, no tidings whatsoever were heard of Denot. He had never returned to his lodging, nor been seen anywhere, except in the stable, in which his horse had been put to stand—he had himself saddled his horse, and taken him from the stall, and from that moment nothing further could be learnt of him in Saumur. De Lescure and Henri made the most minute inquiries—but in vain; had he destroyed himself, or hid himself in the town, his horse would certainly have been found; it was surmised that he had started for Paris on some mad speculation; and though his friends deeply grieved at his misconduct, his absence, when they had so much to do and to think of was in itself, felt as a relief.

After remaining about a week in Saumur, the army was disbanded—or rather disbanded itself, for every effort was made, to keep together as great a body of men as possible. An attempt was made to garrison the town; and for this purpose, the leaders undertook to pay about one thousand men, at a certain rate per day, for their services, while they remained under arms in Saumur, but the idea, after a very short time, was abandoned; the men would not stay away from their homes, and in spite of the comforts which were procured for them, and the pay which was promised, the garrison very quickly dissolved.

Cathelineau succeeded in taking back with him to St. Florent, nearly all the men who had accompanied him; his next object was the attack of Nantes, and as St. Florent is between Saumur and that town, his men were able to return to their homes, without going much out of their direct way. He marched through the town of Angers on his return, and took possession of the stores which he found there, the republican garrison having fled as soon as they heard of his approach; many of Bonchamps' men accompanied him, and some of those who had come to Saumur with de Lescure and Henri Larochejaquelin, young men who had no wives or families, and who literally preferred the excitement of the campaign, to their ordinary home employments; all such men joined Cathelineau's army, but by far the greater number of the peasants of the Bocage returned with de Lescure and Larochejaquelin.

Charette had been invited to assist Cathelineau in his attack on Nantes, and he had promised to do so; de Lescure found it absolutely necessary to go home, on account of his wound, and Larochejaquelin went with him. They had already heard that the Convention had determined to invade La Vendée on every side with an overwhelming force, and it was necessary to protect the Southern portion of the province; this duty was allotted to our two friends, and they therefore returned home from Saumur, without expecting to enjoy for any length of time the fruits of their recent victory.

A litter was formed for de Lescure, for at present he found it impossible to bear the motion of riding, and Henri, the little Chevalier, Father Jerome and Chapeau, accompanied him on horseback. Many of the peasants had started from Saumur, before their party, and the whole road from that town through Dou and Vihiers to Durbellière, was thronged with crowds of these successful warriors, returning to their families, anxious to tell to their wives and sweethearts the feats they had accomplished.

They were within a league of Durbellière, and had reached a point where a cross-road led from the one they were on to the village of Echanbroignes, and at this place many of the cortege, which was now pretty numerous, turned off towards their own homes.

"M. Henri," said Chapeau, riding up to his master, from among two or three peasants, who had been walking for some time by his horse's side, and anxiously talking to him, "M. Henri?"

"Well, Jacques; what is it now?" said Henri.

"I have a favour to ask of Monsieur."

"A favour, Chapeau; I suppose you want to go to Echanbroignes already, to tell Michael Stein's pretty daughter, of all the gallant things you did at Saumur."

"Not till I have waited on you and M. de Lescure to the château. Momont would be dying if he had not some one to give him a true account of what has been done, and I do not know that any one could give him a much better history of it, than myself—of course not meaning such as you and M. de Lescure, who saw more of the fighting than any one else; but then you know, M. Henri, you will have too much to do, and too much to say to the Marquis, and to Mademoiselle, to be talking to an old man like Momont."

"Never fear, Chapeau. You shall have Momont's ears all to yourself; but what is it you do want?"

"Why, nothing myself exactly, M. Henri; but there are two men from Echanbroignes here, who wish you to allow them to go on to Durbellière, and stay a day or two there: they are two of our men, M. Henri; two of the red scarfs."

"Two of the red scarfs!" said Henri.

"Yes, M. Henri, two of the men who went through the water, and took the town; we call ourselves red scarfs, just to distinguish ourselves from the rest of the army: your honour is a red scarf that is the chief of the red scarfs; and we expect to be especially under your honour's protection."

"I am a red scarf, Henri;" said the little Chevalier. "There are just two hundred of us, and we mean to be the most dare-devil set in the whole army; won't we make the cowardly blues afraid of the Durbellière red scarfs!"

"And who are the two men, Jacques?" said Henri.

"Jean and Peter Stein," said Jacques: "you see, M. Henri, they ran away to the battle, just in direct opposition to old Michael's positive orders. You and the Curé must remember how I pledged my honour that they should be at Saumur, and so they were: but Michael Stein is an awful black man to deal with when his back is up: he thinks no more of giving a clout with his hammer, than another man does of a rap with his five knuckles."

"But his sons are brave fellows," said the little Chevalier, "and dashed into the water among the very first. Michael Stein can't but be proud that his two sons should be both red scarfs: if so, he must be a republican."

"He is no republican, Chevalier," said Chapeau, "that's quite certain, nor yet any of the family; but he is a very black man, and when once angered, not easy to be smoothed down again; and if M. Henri will allow Jean and Peter to come on to Durbellière, I can, perhaps, manage to go back with them on Sunday, and Michael Stein will mind me more than he will them: I can knock into his thick head better than they can do, the high honour which has befallen the lads, in their chancing to have been among the red scarfs."

"Well, Chapeau, let them come," said Henri. "No man that followed me gallantly into Saumur, shall be refused admittance when he wishes to follow me into Durbellière."

"We were cool enough, weren't we, Henri, when we marched into the town?" said the Chevalier.

"We'll have a more comfortable reception at the old château," said Henri; "at any rate, we'll have no more cold water. I must say, Arthur, I thought the water of that moat had a peculiarly nasty taste."

They were not long in reaching the château, and Henri soon found himself in his sister's arms. A confused account, first of the utter defeat of the Vendeans at Varin, and then of their complete victory at Saumur, had reached Durbellière; and though the former account had made them as miserable, as the latter had made them happy, neither one nor the other was entirely believed. De Lescure had sent an express to Clisson immediately after the taking of the town, and Madame de Lescure had sent from Clisson to Durbellière; but still it was delightful to have the good news corroborated by the conquerors themselves, and Agatha was supremely happy.

"My own dear, darling Henri," she said, clinging round his neck, "my own brave, gallant brother, and were you not wounded at all—are you sure you are not wounded?"

"Not a touch, not a scratch, Agatha, as deep as you might give me with your bodkin."

"Thank God! I thank Him with all my heart and soul: and I know you were the first everywhere. Charles wrote but a word or too to Victorine, but he said you were the very first to set your foot in Saumur."

"A mere accident, Agatha; while Charles had all the fighting—the real hard, up hill, hand to 'hand work—I and a few others walked into Saumur, or rather we swam in, and took possession of the town. The Chevalier here was beside me, and was over the breach as soon as I was."

"My brave young Arthur!" said Agatha, in her enthusiasm, kissing the forehead of the blushing Chevalier, "you have won your spurs like a knight and a hero; you shall be my knight and my hero. And I will give you my glove to wear in your cap. But, tell me Arthur, why have you and Henri, those red handkerchiefs tied round your waist? Chapeau has one too, and those other men, below there."

"That's our uniform," said Arthur. "We are all red scarfs; all the men who clambered into Saumur through the water, are to wear red scarfs till the war is over; and they are to be seen in the front, at every battle, seige and skirmish. Mind, Agatha, when you see a red scarf, that he is one of Henri Larochejaquelin's own body-guard; and when you see a bald pate, it belongs to a skulking republican."

"Are the republicans all bald then?" said Agatha.

"We shaved all we caught at Saumur, at any rate. We did not leave a hair upon one of them," said Arthur, rejoicing. "The red scarfs are fine barbers, when a republican wants shaving."

"Is Charles badly wounded?" asked Agatha.

"His arm is broken, and he remained in action for eight hours after receiving the wound, so that it was difficult to set; but now it is doing well," said Henri.

"I should have offered him my services before this: at any rate I will do so now; but Henri I have a thousand things to say to you; do not expect to go to bed tonight, till you have told me everything just as it happened," and Agatha hurried away, to give her sweet woman's aid to her wounded cousin, while Henri went into his father's room.

"Welcome, my hero! welcome, my gallant boy!" said the old man, almost rising from his chair, cripple as he was, in his anxiety to seize the hand of his beloved son.

"I have come home, safe, father," said Henri, "to lay my sword at your feet."

"You must not leave it there long, Henri, I fear, you must not leave it there long; these traitors are going to devour us alive; to surround us with their troops and burn us out of house and home; they will annihilate the people they say, destroy the towns, and root out the very trees and hedges. We shall see, Henri—we shall see. So they made a bad fight of it at Saumur?"

"They had two men to one against us, besides the advantage of position, discipline and arms, and yet they marched the best part of their troops off in the night without striking a blow."

"Thanks be to the Lord, we will have our King again; we will have our dear King once more, thanks be to the Almighty," said the old man, eager with joy. "And they fled, did they, without striking a blow!"

"Some of them did, father; but some fought well enough; it was desperate sharp work when poor Charles was wounded."

"God bless him! God bless him! I didn't doubt it was sharp work; but even with valour, or without valour, what could sedition and perjury avail against truth and loyalty! they were two to one; they had stone walls and deep rivers to protect them; they had arms and powder, and steel cuirasses; they had disciplined troops and all the appanages of war, and yet they were scattered like chaff; driven from their high walls and deep moats, by a few half-armed peasants; and why? why have our batons been more deadly than their swords? because we have had truth and loyalty on our side. Why have our stuff jackets prevailed against their steel armour; because they covered honest hearts that were fighting honestly for their King. His Majesty shall enjoy his own again, my boy. Vive le Roi! Vive le Roi!"

"I trust he may, father; but, as you say, we shall have some hard work to do first. Cathelineau and Charette will be before Nantes in a week's time. I should have been with them had we not heard that a strong body of republican troops is to be stationed at Parthenay. They say that Santerre is to command a party of Marseillaise, commissioned to exterminate the Vendeans."

"What, Santerre, the brewer of the Faubourgs?"

"The same, Danton's friend, he who used to be so loud at the Cordeliers; and Westerman is to assist him," said Henri.

"Worse again, Henri, worse again; was it not he who headed the rebels on the tenth of August, when our sainted King was driven from his home?"

"Yes, the same Westerman is now to drive us from our homes; or rather to burn us, our homes, and all together—such at least is the task allotted to him."

"God help our babes and our women!" said the old Marquis shuddering, "if they fall into the clutches of Santerre, and that other still blacker demon!"

"Do not fear, father; have we not shewn that we are men? Santerre will find that he has better soldiers to meet than any he brings with him."

"Fear, Henri! no, for myself I fear nothing. What injury can they do to an old man like me? I do not even fear for my own children; if their lives are required in the King's service, they know how to part with them in perfect confidence of eternal happiness hereafter; but, Henri, I do feel for our poor people; they are now full of joy and enthusiasm, for they are warm from victory, and the grief of the few, who are weeping for their relatives, is lost in the joy of the multitude. But this cannot always be so, we cannot expect continual victory, and even victory itself, when so often repeated, will bring death and desolation into every parish and into every family."

"I trust, father, the war will not be prolonged so distantly as you seem to think; the forces of Austria, England and Prussia already surround the frontiers of France; and we have every reason to hope that friendly troops from Britain will soon land on our own coast. I trust the autumn will find La Vendée crowned with glory, but once more at peace."

"God send it, my son!" said the Marquis.

"I do not doubt the glory—but I do doubt the peace."

"We cannot go back now, father," said Henri.

"Nor would I have you do so; we have a duty to do, and though it be painful we must do it. 'God will temper the wind to the shorn lamb,' and give us strength to bear our sufferings; but my heart shudders, when I am told that the Republic has let loose those wolves of Paris to shed the blood of our poor people."

The prospect of a prolonged civil war, of continued strife, and increased bloodshed, somewhat damped the joy with which the victory at Saumur was discussed in the aristocratic portion of the château; but no such gloomy notions were allowed to interfere with the triumph which reigned in the kitchen. Here victory was clothed in robes all couleur de rose, and it appeared that La Vendée, so happy in many other respects, was chiefly blessed in being surrounded by republicans whom she could conquer, and in having enemies who gave her the means of acquiring glory.

"And our own young master was the first royalist who put his foot in Saumur?" asked Momont, who had already received the information he required four or five times, and on each occasion had drunk Henri's health in about half-a-pint of wine.

"Indeed he was," said Chapeau, "the very first. You don't think he'd have let any one go before him."

"Here's his health then, and God bless him!" said Momont. "It was I first showed him how to fire a pistol; and very keen he was at taking to gunpowder."

"Indeed, and indeed he was," said the housekeeper. "When he was no more than twelve years old, not nigh as big as the little Chevalier, he let off the big blunderbuss in my bed-room, and I on my knees at prayers the while. God bless his sweet face, I always knew he'd make a great soldier."

"And don't you remember," said the laundress, "how he blew up Mademoiselle Agatha, making her sit on a milk-pan turned over, with a whole heap of gunpowder stuffed underneath, and she only six or seven years old?"

"Did he though," said the page, "blow up Mademoiselle Agatha?"

"Indeed he did, and blew every scrap of hair off her head and eyebrows. It's no wonder he's such a great general."

"And the Chevalier was second, wasn't he?" said the cook.

"Dear little darling fellow!" said the confidential maid; "and to think of him going to the wars with guns and swords and pistols! If anything had happened to him I should have cried my eyes out."

"And was the Chevalier the first to follow M. Henri into the town?" asked the page, who was a year older than Arthur Mondyon, and consequently felt himself somewhat disgraced at not having been at Saumur.

"Why," said Jacques, with a look which was intended to shew how unwilling he was to speak of himself, "I can't exactly say the Chevalier was the first to follow M. Henri, but if he wasn't the second, he was certainly the third who entered Saumur."

"Who then was the second?" said one or two at the same time.

"Why, I shouldn't have said anything about it, only you ask me so very particularly," said Jacques, "but I believe I was second myself; but Jean Stein can tell you everything; you weren't backward yourself Jean, there were not more than three or four of them before you and Peter."

"I don't know about that," said Jean, "but we all did the best we could, I believe."

"And was Chapeau really second?" said Momont, who was becoming jealous of the distinction likely to be paid to his junior fellow-servant. "You don't mean to say he went in before all the other gentlemen?"

"Gentlemen, indeed!" said Chapeau. "What an idea you have of taking a town by storm, if you think men are to stand back to make room for gentlemen, as though a party were going into dinner."

"But tell us now, Jean Stein," continued Momont, "was Chapeau really second?"

"Well then," said Jean, "he was certainly second into the water, but he was so long under it, I doubt whether he was second out—he certainly did get a regular good ducking did Chapeau. Why, you came out feet uppermost, Chapeau."

"Feet uppermost!" shouted Momont, "and is that your idea of storming a town, to go into it feet uppermost?"

"But do you really mean to say that you were absolutely wet through when you took Saumur?" said the laundress.

"Indeed we were," answered Chapeau, "wringing wet, every man of us."

"Lawks! how uncomfortable," said the cook. "And M. Henri, was he wet too?"

"Wet, to be sure he was wet as water could make him."

"And the little Chevalier, did he get himself wet?" said the confidential maid, "poor little fellow! it was like to give him his death of cold."

"But, Chapeau, tell me truly now: did you kill any of those bloody republicans with your own hand?" asked the housekeeper.

"Kill them," said Chapeau, "to be sure, I killed them when we were fighting."

"And how many, Chapeau; how many did you positively kill dead, you know?" said the confidential maid.

"What nonsense you do talk!" answered he, with a great air of military knowledge, "as if a man in battle knows when he kills and when he doesn't. You're not able to look about you in that sort of way in the middle of the smoke and noise and confusion."

"You don't mean to tell me you ever kill a man without knowing it!" said the housekeeper.

"You don't understand what a battle is at all," answered Chapeau, determined to communicate a little of his experience on the matter. "One hasn't time to look about one to see anything. Now supposing you had been with us at the taking of Saumur."

"Oh, the Lord forbid!" said the housekeeper. "I'd sooner be in my grave any day, than go to one of those horrid bloody battles."

"Or you, Momont; supposing you'd been there?"

"Maybe I might have done as much as another, old as I look," replied the butler.

"I'm sure you'd have done well, Momont. I'm sure you'd have done very well," endeavouring to conciliate him into listening; "but supposing you had been there, or at the camp of Varin—we'll say Varin, for after all, we had more fighting there than at Saumur. Supposing you were one of the attacking party; you find yourself close wedged in between your two comrades right opposite the trenches; you have a loaded musket in your hand, with a bayonet fixed to it, and you have five or six rounds of cartridges in your belt; you know that you are to do your best, or rather your worst with what you've got. Well, your commander gives the word of attack. We'll suppose it's the good Cathelineau. 'Friends,' he will say; 'dear friends; now is the time to prove ourselves men; now is the moment to prove that we love our King; we will soon shew the republicans that a few sods of turf are no obstacles in the way of Vendean royalists,' and then the gallant fellow rushes into the trenches; two thousand brave men follow him, shouting 'Vive le Roi!' and you, Momont, are one of the first. All of a sudden, as you are just in motion, prepared for your first spring, a sharp cutting gush of air passes close to your face, and nearly blinds you; you feel that you can hardly breathe, but you hear a groan, and a stumble; your next neighbour and three men behind him have been sent into eternity by a cannon-ball from the enemy. Do you think then that the man who fired the cannon knows, or cares who he has killed? Well, on you go; had you not been in a crowd, the enemy's fire, maybe, might have frightened you; but good company makes men brave: on you go, and throw yourself into the trench. You find a more active man than yourself just above you; he is already nearly at the top of the bank, his feet are stuck in the sods above your head; he is about to spring upon the rampart, when the bayonet of a republican passes through his breast, and he falls at your feet, or perhaps upon your head. You feel your heart shudder, and your blood runs cold, but it is no time for pausing now; you could not return if you would, neither can you remain where you are: up you go, grasping your musket in one hand and digging the other into the loose sods. Your eyes and mouth are crammed with dust, your face is bespattered with your comrade's blood, your ears are full of strange noises; your very nature changes within you; the smell of gunpowder and of carnage makes you feel like a beast of prey. You do not think any longer of the friends who have fallen beside you; you only long to grapple with the enemy who are before you."

"Oh, mercy me! how very shocking!" said the housekeeper. "Pray don't go on Chapeau; pray don't, or I shall have such horrid dreams."

"Oh! but you must go on, Chapeau," said the confidential maid, "I could never bear that you should leave off; it is very horrid, surely; but as Mademoiselle says, we must learn to look at blood and wounds now, and hear of them, too."

"Do pray tell us the rest," said the page, who sat listening intently with his mouth wide open. "I do so like it; pray tell us what Momont did after he became a beast of prey?"

Chapeau was supremely happy; he felt that his military experience and his descriptive talents were duly appreciated, and he continued:

"Well, you are now in the camp, on the enemy's ground, and you have to fight every inch, till you drive them out of it; six or seven of your comrades are close to you, and you all press on, still grasping your muskets and pushing your bayonets before you: the enemy make a rush to drive you back again; on they come against you, by twenties and by thirties; those who are behind, push forward those who are in front, and suddenly you find a heavy dragging weight upon your hands, and again you hear the moans of a dying man close to you—almost in your arms. A republican soldier has fallen on your bayonet. The struggles of the wounded man nearly overpower you; you twist and turn and wrench, and drag your musket to and fro, but it is no use; the weapon is jammed between his ribs; you have not space nor time to extricate it; you are obliged to leave it, and on you go unarmed, stumbling over the body of your fallen enemy. Whether the man dies or lives, whether his wound be mortal or no, you will never hear. And so you advance, till gradually you begin to feel, rather than to see, that the blues are retreating from you. You hear unarmed men asking for quarter, begging for their lives, and the sound of entreaty again softens your heart; you think of sparing life, instead of taking it; you embrace your friends as you meet them here and there; you laugh and sing as you feel that you have done your best and have conquered; and when you once more become sufficiently calm to be aware what you are yourself doing, you find that you have a sword in your hand, or a huge pistol; you know not from whom you took them, or where you got them, or in what manner you have used them. How can a man say then, whom he has killed in battle, or whether he has killed any man? I do not recollect that I ever fired a shot at Varin myself, and yet my musket was discharged and the pan was up. I will not say that I ever killed a man; but I will say that I never struck a man who asked for mercy, or fired a shot even on a republican, who had thrown down his arms."

Henri's voice was now heard in the hall, loudly calling for Jacques, and away he ran to join his master, as he finished his history.

"It makes my blood run cold," said the housekeeper, "to think of such horrid things."

"Chapeau describes it very well, though," said the confidential maid; "I'm sure he has seen it all himself. I'm sure he's a brave fellow."

"It's not always those who talk the most that are the bravest," said Momont.

Henri and his sister sat talking that night for a long time, after the other inhabitants of the château were in bed, and though they had so many subjects of interest to discuss, their conversation was chiefly respecting Adolphe Denot.

"I cannot guess what has become of him," said Henri; "I made every possible inquiry, short of that which might seem to compromise his character. I do not think he can have returned to the Bocage, or we should have heard of him."

"He must have gone to Fleury," said Agatha. "I am sure you will not find that he is at his own house."

"Impossible, my love; we must have heard of him on the way; had he gone round by Montrenil, he must still have passed over the bridge of Fouchard, and we should have heard of him there."

"He must have ridden over in the night; you see he so evidently wanted to conceal from you where he was going."

"My own impression is, that he is gone to Paris," said Henri; "but let him have gone where he may, of one thing I am sure; he was not in his right senses when he left the council-room, nor yet when he was speaking to me in the street; poor Adolphe! I pity him with all my heart. I can feel how miserable he must be."

"Why should he be miserable, Henri? The truth is, you mistake his character. I do not wish to make you think ill of your friend; but Adolphe is one of those men whom adversity will improve. You and our father have rather spoilt him between you; he is too proud, too apt to think that everything should bend to his wishes: he has yet to learn that in this world he must endure to have his dearest wishes thwarted; and till adversity has taught him that, his feelings will not be manly, nor his conduct sensible."

"Poor fellow!" said Henri, "if adversity will teach him, he is likely to get his lesson now. Did he part quietly with you, Agatha, on the day before we started to Saumur?"

"Anything but quietly," said she. "I would not tell you all he said, for on the eve of a battle in which you were to fight side by side, I did not wish to make you angry with your friend and companion: but had a raging madman, just escaped from his keepers, come to offer me his hand, his conduct could not have been worse than Adolphe Denot's."

"Was he violent with you, Agatha?"

"He did not offer to strike me, nor yet to touch me, if you mean that: but he threatened me; and that in such awful sounding, and yet ridiculous language, that you would hardly know whether to laugh or to be angry if I could repeat it."

"What did he say, Agatha?"

"Say! it would be impossible for me to tell you; he swung his arms like a country actor in a village barn, and declared that if he were not killed at Saumur, he would carry me away in spite of all that my friends could do to hinder him."

"Poor fellow! poor Adolphe!" said Henri.

"You are not sorry I refused him? You would, indeed, have had to say, poor Agatha! had I done otherwise."

"I am not sorry that you refused him, but I am sorry you could not love him."

"Why you say yourself he is mad: would you wish me to love a madman?"

"It is love that has made him mad. Adolphe is not like other men; his passions are stronger; his feelings more acute; his regrets more poignant."

"He should control his passions as other men must do," said Agatha: "all men who do not, are madmen." She remained silent for a few moments, and then added, "you are right in saying that love has made him mad; but it is the meanest of all love that has done so—it is self-love."

"I think you are too hard upon him, Agatha; but it is over now, and cannot be helped."

"What did he say to you, Henri, when he left you in Saurnur?"

"His name had been mentioned you know in the council as one of the leaders: Bonchamps, I believe, proposed it; but Charles objected, and named Charette in his place, and Cathelineau and the rest agreed to it. This angered Adolphe, and no wonder, for he is ambitious, and impatient of neglect. I wish they would have let him been named instead of me, but they would not, and when the list was finished, he was not on it. He got up and said something; I hardly know what, but he complained of Stofflet being one of the Generals; and then Charles rebuked him, and Adolphe in a passion left the room."

"And you followed him?" asked Agatha.

"Yes, I followed him; but he was like a raging madman. I don't know how it was; but instead of complaining about the Generals, he began complaining about you. I don't know exactly whether I ought to tell you what he said— indeed I had not intended to have done so."

"Nay, Henri; now you have raised my woman's curiosity, and you positively must tell me."

"I hardly know how to tell you," said Henri, "for I really forget how he said it. I don't know on earth how he introduced your name at all; but he ended in accusing you of having a more favoured lover."

Agatha blushed slightly as she answered:

"He has no right whatever to ask the question; nor if I have a favoured lover, should it be any ground of complaint to him. But to you, Henri, if you wish a promise from me on the subject, I will readily and willingly promise, that I will receive no man's love, and, far as I can master my own heart, I will myself entertain no passion without your sanction: and you, dear brother, you shall make me a return for my confidence; you shall ask me to marry no man whom I cannot love."

"Don't for a moment think, dearest, that what he said, made me uneasy as regarded you: but whom do you think he selected for you—of whom do you think he is jealous?"

"I cannot attempt to guess a madman's thoughts, Henri."

"I will tell you then," said he; "but you will be shocked as well as surprised. He is jealous of Cathelineau!"

"Cathelineau?" said Agatha, blushing now much more deeply than she had done before.

"Yes, Cathelineau, the postillion."

"No, not Cathelineau the postillion; but Cathelineau the Saint of Anjou, and the hero of St. Florent, and of Saumur. He at any rate has linked my name with that of a man worthy of a woman's love."

"Worthy, Agatha, had his birth and early years been different from what they were."

"Worthy as he is of any woman's love," said Agatha. "Great deeds and noble conduct make birth of no avail, to give either honour or disgrace."

"But, Agatha, surely you would not wed Cathelineau, were he to ask you?"

"Why should you ask that question, Henri?" said she: "are the words which Adolphe Denot has uttered in his wild insanity of such weight, as to make you regard as possible such an event? Have I not told you I would wed no one without your sanction? Do you not know that Cathelineau has never spoken to me but the coldest words of most distant respect? Do you not know that his heart and soul are intent on other things than woman's love? I, too, feel that this is not the time for love. While I live in continual dread that those I most value may fall in battle; while I fear that every messenger who comes to me in your absence, may have some fatal news to tell, I do not wish to take upon me a fresh burden of affection. Am I not best as I am, Henri, at present?" And she put her arm affectionately through his. "When the wars are over, and the King is on his throne, you shall bring me home a lover; some brave friend of your's who has proved himself a gallant knight."

"I would have him be a gallant knight, certainly," said Henri, "but he should also be a worthy gentleman."

"And is not Cathelineau a worthy gentleman?" forgetting in her enthusiasm that she was taking the cause of one who was being spoken of as her lover. "Oh, indeed he is; if valour, honesty, and honour, if trust in God, and forgetfulness of self, if humanity and generosity constitute a gentleman, then is Cathelineau the prince of gentlemen: but do not, pray do not mistake me, Henri: a lover of scenery admires the tops of distant mountains, and gazes on their snowy peaks with a pleasure almost amounting to awe; but no one seeks to build his house on the summit: so do I admire the virtues, the devotion, the courage of Cathelineau; but my admiration is mixed with no love which would make me wish to join my lot with his. I only say, that despite his birth and former low condition, he is worthy of any woman's love."

Henri did not quite like his sister's enthusiasm, though he hardly knew why it displeased him. He had thought of Cathelineau only as a soldier and a General, and had found nothing in him that he did not approve of; but he felt that he could not welcome him as his darling sister's husband; "if Adolphe should have prophesied rightly," said he, to himself as he went from his sister's room to his own chamber, "but no! whatever her feelings may be, she is too good to do anything that would displease me."

CHAPTER IV.
MICHAEL STEIN.

On the Sunday morning, after Henri's return to Durbellière, Jacques Chapeau, with Jean and Peter Stein, left the château very early, and started for Echanbroignes. Word had been sent to the old smith by some of the neighbours, who had been at Saumur, that his two sons were safe and sound, and that they had behaved well at the siege, and a message at the same time reached Annot, informing her that Jacques meant to spend his next Sunday at the village; the party was therefore expected, and great preparations were made for a fête at Echanbroignes. The heroes of that place considered that they had somewhat celebrated themselves; in the first place, on final inquiry, it appeared, that not one person from the village, who was at all able to go to Saumur, had neglected to do so. In the next place, many of the villagers were among the number of the red scarfs, and they claimed to themselves the privilege of being considered peculiarly valiant and particularly loyal; and lastly, though many of them had gone to Saumur, without arms, every man on his return had a musket with him, which the old men and women regarded as absolute trophies, taken by each man individually from some awful rebel whom he had slain in single combat. There were to be great rejoicings, therefore, at Echanbroignes, which were postponed for the arrival of Chapeau and the two Stems.

The old smith was very angry at his sons' behaviour. As Chapeau had said, he was a very black man, and when he was angered, it wasn't easy to smooth him; the operation, however, was attempted by some of his neighbours, and though they were not altogether successful, they succeeded in making the old man a little proud of his family.

"Yes, Paul Rouel;" he said to the village innkeeper, who was an ancient crony of his, "it's very well to talk of King and Church; but if King and Church are to teach sons to fly against their fathers, we may, I think, have a little too much of them; didn't I again and again tell the boys not to go?"

"But, Michael Stein, how could you expect them to stay here, with a score of old men like us, and a number of women and girls, when every young fellow in the parish had gone to the wars? besides, they say, they did gallantly at the wars, and gained great honour and glory."

"Gained a great fiddle-stick," said the smith.

"But, Michael Stein," said another old friend, named Gobelin, "you wouldn't have your children disgraced, would you? think how sheepish they would have looked, hiding themselves in the smithy here, when all the other young men were parading round the green with the guns and swords they have taken from the rebels, and the women and girls all admiring them. Why, neighbour, not a girl in the parish would have spoken to them."

"Girls spoken to them, indeed! I tell you, Gobelin, in the times now coming, any girl will be ready enough to speak to a young man that has a house over his head, and a five-franc piece in his pocket. No, neighbour Gobelin; I gave my boys a good trade, and desired them to stick to it; they have chosen instead to go for soldiers, and for soldiers they may go. They don't come into my smithy again, that's all."

"You don't mean you won't speak to the lads, and after their fighting so bravely and all!" said Paul Rouel, in a voice of horror.

"I didn't say I wouldn't speak to them, Rouel," said the father, "I am as fond of my sons as another man; and as they were resolved to disobey my commands, and to go fighting, why I'll not say but I'm glad they didn't disgrace themselves. I'd have been sorry to hear that they'd run away, or been the last to face the enemy; but they had no right to go, when there was work for them to do at home; they are welcome now to come and take the best I can give them, till their new trade calls them away again, and then they'll be welcome to go soldiering again; not a hammer shall they raise on my anvil, not a blast shall they blow in my smithy, not an ounce of iron shall they turn in my furnace."

"You'll think better of these things after a day or two, neighbour," said Gobelin.

"When I think once about a thing, Gobelin, I'm not much given to think again. But I tell you, I wish the boys no harm; let them be soldiers now, and I pray God they may be good soldiers; only, if I save a little money by hard work, I won't have them spend it among their comrades in strong drink; it'll be all the better for Annot, when I die, that's all."

In this resolution he remained fixed, and in this frame of mind he received his truant sons on their return to Echanbroignes on the Sunday morning. They entered the village together with Chapeau, about nine in the morning, having been met about a mile from the town, by four or five friends, who escorted them back. Annot was not there, for she was very busy at home, preparing breakfast for her brothers and lover. She at any rate was determined that the prodigal sons should be received with a fatted calf.

Chapeau marched up through the village at the head of the little procession to bear the brunt of the father's anger, as his station in life, and standing in the army made him feel superior even to the fury of old Michael Stein. As they approached the door of the smith's house, they saw him sitting in the little porch with a pipe in his mouth, for Michael was never found without one or two implements; he had always either his hammer or his pipe in lull activity.

"Welcome back to Echanbroignes, M. Chapeau, welcome back," said the old man. "I am heartily glad to see so brave a soldier in my poor cabin!" and he gave his hand to Jacques.

"And here be two other brave soldiers, Michael Stein, who, I hope, are also welcome to Echanbroignes; and this I will say, any father in Poitou might be proud to own them for his Sons: for gallanter fellows there are not in the whole army of La Vendée, and that is saying a long word."

There was a little crowd round the smith's house, and in spite of his unmilitary predilections, he could not help feeling proud at the public testimony that was paid to his sons' merits: he showed this by the tear that stood in his eye, as he said:

"They are welcome too, M. Chapeau; they are very welcome too. I am glad to see ye, safe and sound from the wars, lads. I am glad to see thee, Jean: I am glad to see thee, Peter," and he gave a hand to each of the two young men, who were delighted with their unexpected kind reception. "And this I will say before the neighbours here, as ye would go to the wars, and make soldiers of yourselves, I am well pleased to hear ye behaved yourselves like gallant brave men should do. I'd sooner that your friends should have had to tell me that ye were both stiff and cold, than that ye should have returned yourselves with shamed faces to own that ye had disgraced the trade ye have chosen to take up with."

"Bravo! Bravo!" said Chapeau, "I am glad in my heart, Michael Stein, to hear you speak so kindly to the lads; and so will M. Henri be glad to hear it, for they are two of his own especial troop—they are two of the gallant red scarfs, who swam into Saumur with their muskets tucked under their arms."

"But understand me, boys," continued the smith, still speaking so that the neighbours standing round could hear him. "I am right glad to see both of you, as I am to see M. Chapeau, or any other gallant friend who is kind enough to visit me and Annot. But mind, it is as visitors I receive you; in a few days, doubtless, you must go away to the wars again; till then ye shall have the best I can give, both to eat and to drink. Ye shall have your own way, and never be asked to do a turn of work. Ye shall have gay holyday times, and holyday fare, and anything the old man can do, and anything the old man can give to make you merry, he will do, and he will give, because you have come back gallantly, and have not brought dishonour to the roost where ye were hatched—but more than this I will not agree to. Ye would not abide at home, as I desired, and this therefore is no longer a home for you; ye would not be content to be forgers of weapons, but ye must e'en use them too, and ye have had your way. Now, lads, I must have my way; and for the rest of the time I must have it alone. This is no longer your home, lads, and I am no longer your master. Ye would be soldiers when I did not wish it; now let ye be soldiers, and I'm the less sorry for it, as it seems like that you'll prove good soldiers. And now, Peter and Jean, you're welcome both of you. Jacques Chapeau you are most heartily welcome—come Annot, let the lads have a swinging breakfast, for I know these soldiers fight not well unless they be fed well," and so finishing his speech, he led the way into the cottage.

The three men were too well pleased with their reception to grumble at the smith's mode of expressing his feeling. Jean and Peter were delighted to find that they were to be entertained with the best their father could afford, instead of with black looks and hard words, and that the only punishment to be immediately inflicted on them, was that they were to do no work; the party, therefore, entered the cottage tolerably well pleased with each other.

It is not to be supposed that Annot remained in the back-ground during the whole of her father's oration. She had come out of the cottage, and kissed her two brothers, and shaken hands with her lover; she then returned in again, and Chapeau had followed her, and as the two were left alone together, for a minute or two, I think it very probable that she kissed him also; but I cannot speak positively on this point.

Then they all sat down to breakfast, and Paul Rouel and old Gobelin, who had contrived to be of the party, were greatly surprised to hear and to see how civil Michael was to his sons. He pressed them to eat of the very best, as he did to Chapeau, and talked to them about the war, listened to all their tales, and had altogether lost the domineering authoritative tone of voice, with which he usually addressed his own family; it was only in talking to Annot that he was the same hot-tempered old man as ever. The two young men themselves were hardly at their ease; but they eat their breakfast, and made the best they could of it.

"Smothered fire burns longest, neighbour Gobelin," said Rouel, as he left the house. "Take my word, Michael will never forgive those two boys of his the longest day he has to live."

After breakfast, Michael Stein and his whole party went to mass, as did all the soldier peasants, who had returned from Saumur; and the old Curé of the parish, who had now recovered possession of his own church, with much solemnity returned thanks to God for the great victory which the Vendeans had gained, and sung a requiem for the souls of the royalists who had fallen in the battle. When they left the church, the peasants all formed themselves into a procession, the girls going first, and the men following them; and in this manner they paraded round the green, carrying a huge white flag, which had been embroidered in the village, and which bore in its centre, in conspicuous letters of gold, those three words, the loyal Shibboleth of La Vendée, "Vive le Roi!"

This flag they fixed on a pole erected in the centre of the green, and then they set to work to amuse themselves with twenty different games. The games, however, did not flourish—the men were too eager to talk of what they had done, and the girls were too willing to listen—they divided themselves into fifty little parties, in which fifty different accounts were given of the taking of Saumur, and in each party three or four different warriors were named as having been the most conspicuous heroes of the siege. Each narrator had some especially esteemed leader or chief, who in his eyes greatly exceeded the other leaders, and the prodigious feats of valour performed by this favoured warrior was the first and most wonderful subject of discourse. Then, but at a modest distance, as regards the glory of the achievements related, each peasant told what he had done himself; two or three probably made out their little history together, and told of each other's valour: that homely and somewhat vulgar Scotch proverb, "you scratch my back, and I'll scratch yours," was certainly unknown to them, but nevertheless they fully recognized the wise principle of mutual accommodation which that proverb teaches.

"It's no use talking, but there isn't one of them able to hold a candle to our M. Henri—is there, Louis? that is, for a downright thundering attack."

This was said by Jean Stein to two or three of the village girls, by whom he was looked on as a great hero, in consequence of his having gone to the war in spite of his father's commands, as well as on account of Chapeau's honourable testimony in his favour; and the man referred to, was one Louis Bourdin, who, as well as Jean, had been of the party who followed Henri through the moat.

"That there is not, Jean; that is, for positive standup fighting; not one. And we ought to know, for we have seen most of 'em. There's Cathelineau is a very good man at leading on the men."

"Oh, yes!" said Jean, "Cathelineau is a fine fellow too, and a very holy man; but somehow I don't think he's quite so forward as M. Henri. M. Henri is always the first."

"But doesn't he get dreadfully knocked about by the guns and bullets?" asked one of the girls.

"He doesn't matter that a pinch of snuff," said Louis.

"No, not a pinch of snuff," said Jean. "Do you mind, Louis, how he leapt off his horse, and dashed through the trenches, that first night at Varin? wasn't it beautiful?"

"You may say that, Jean," answered Louis; "it was beautiful. And what a night that was—you were along with him, Jean, and so was Chapeau. M. Henri was up first, I can swear to that; but it would puzzle any one to say who was second."

"Yourself Louis, was as quick as any one—I marked you well. Indeed then, said I to myself, if all our men are as forward as Louis Bourdin, the village will have a great name before the war is over."

"But tell me truly now, Louis Bourdin," said a little girl, who was listening intently all the time, "when you went up into that place, were there real soldiers in armour, with guns and cannon firing at you all the time?"

"Truly then there were, Lolotte, hundreds of them," said Bourdin.

"Well, that is horrible!" said the girls all at once.

"And do you remember, Jean," continued Bourdin, "when M. Henri dashed down again, how the traitor rebels hallooed out, 'Fire upon the red scarf!' Well, I did think it was all up with him then. You were close to him, Jean; nearer than I am to Lolotte now."

"And that's quite near enough," said Lolotte, giving him a push.

"Why I'm sure I was doing nothing; I was only wanting to show you. Jean Stein there, was, as I was saying, quite close to M. Henri; and as they leapt out of the camp together, twenty voices roared out at once, 'Fire upon the red scarf! fire upon the red scarf!' Oh! that was a fearful evening; it was dark then, and the light of the smoking, glaring torches made it five times more horrible. I thought we were as good as dead men then. I'm sure I for one can't guess how we ever got out alive."

"And yet, M. Henri wasn't wounded," said Jean; "well it was wonderful. After all, General d'Elbée must be right; Providence must give a shake to a rebel's arm, just as he's firing, so as to send his bullet anywhere but where it's meant to go."

"Yes," said Bourdin, "and it directs the shot of a royalist right into a rebel's heart."

"Well, if that be so," said Lolotte, "I'm sure I for one wouldn't like to fight on the rebel's side. They must be wonderful brave men to hold out at all, when Providence goes against them in that way."

"But they don't hold out, girl," said Jean, "they always run away; how they did run, Bourdin, when M. Henri led us into the town, through the broken wall; well, I believe they all thought at that time, the devil himself was coming for them out of the moat."

"Only think, girls, three or four thousand men running away as fast as their feet could carry them, from two hundred fellows, who hadn't a charge of dry powder among them, and who were all themselves dripping wet through; well that was fine."

Jacques Chapeau and Annot Stein had not joined any of these parties; they had disappeared soon after mass, and were not heard of for three or four hours afterwards; they took a long ramble by themselves, down by the mill-stream, and far beyond the mill; sitting down, every now and then among the willows, and then getting up and strolling on a bit further; they did not, this day, waste their time in foolish quarrels and fond reconciliations; but discoursed together, sundry serious matters of important business, as becomes people to do, when they think of arranging a partnership concern, from which each intends to get a comfortable means of living for the remainder of his or her life; upon the whole, they had but very few subjects of difference, and by their return to the smith's house at supper-time, they had fully agreed that no further time ought to be lost, in establishing a firm under the name of Jacques and Annot Chapeau and Co. The Co. being left to come afterwards or not, as God might please.

After supper was over, Annot had no difficulty in inducing her brothers to leave the house, and thus the coast was left clear for Jacques to ask the father's consent to his intended marriage. Neither he nor Annot expected much difficulty in persuading Michael to accept of so promising a son-in-law; but they were both determined that if they could not marry with his consent, they would do so without it. So Chapeau lighted his pipe, and sat himself down opposite the smith, and Annot retired to her own little sleeping chamber, where she might conveniently hear what her father and lover said to each other, respecting her intended nuptials.

"Well, Michael Stein, my old friend," said Jacques; "these are glorious times, are they not? The rebels beaten hollow, till they haven't a face to shew for themselves, and the King coming to La Vendée, to enjoy his own again; it will be a fine thing to see the King riding into the village of Echanbroignes to thank the gallant peasants, with his own mouth, for what they have done for him!"

"Yes, M. Chapeau! those will be fine times when they come; pray God you, and other young fellows like you, may live to see them; an old fellow like me has little chance of such happiness."

"And why not, my friend? what is to make those days so far off? I tell you, Michael Stein, the rebels were dead beaten at Saumur; they are scattered like chaff; their very best soldiers are altogether hors de combat; the war is as good as over. We may have to make a little trip or two, just to receive the English, who are coming to help us; we may have to go and meet them on the coast; or perhaps to Parthenay, to ask M. Santerre what he wants in that part of the world; but that is all, literally all; I tell you the rebels are clean beaten."

"I only wonder then, M. Chapeau, why you want the English to come and help you, if, as you say, you have conquered all the republicans yourselves?"

"Just to pay their respects to the King, and, perhaps, to lend us a hand in driving those Jacobins out of Paris—that's all. Till that's done the King is to live at Saumur."

"To live at Saumur, is he?"

"That's what those say who know most about it, and you know I'm in the way to know what's really going forward. He's to hold his court at Saumur, and Henri Larochejaquelin is to be commandant of the town, and have the command of all the forces there. I tell you, Michael Stein, we, that wear the red scarfs, will not be the worse off then."

"I hope not; in truth, M. Chapeau, I hope not; though they do say that they be not wise who put their trust in princes."

"Princes!" said Jacques, "I am not talking of princes, I am talking of the King himself, God bless him!"

"Well, perhaps, that does make a difference; and I say, God bless him too, with all my heart."

"I suppose you've heard, Michael Stein, that our young General, M. Henri, is going to be married?"

"Is he then?" said Michael. "No, truly, I did not hear a word of such a matter; to some grand lady of the court, I suppose?"

"No, but to his own beautiful young cousin, Mademoiselle de Lescure, the sister of our other General, you know."

"Well, may they be happy, both of them; I mind their fathers well; the old Marquis is still alive, but greatly ailing they tell me. I have much to be thankful for, and I do thank the Lord!" and as he spoke, Michael Stein crossed himself. "Now, I'm as old in a manner as the Marquis himself and yet you see I can still make the big hammer clink on the anvil."

"Indeed you can, Michael, and better too than many a young fellow. But, as we were saying, here is M. Henri going to be married, and his lady will surely be wanting some nice, tidy, handy, good-looking, smart young woman to be about her, more as a sort of a companion, you know, than a servant; in the same way, you mind, as I am now to M. Henri: now, wouldn't that be a nice berth for your daughter, Annot Stein?"

As Chapeau described the nice, tidy, smart, pretty young woman, that the future Madame de Larochejaquelin would be sure to require, Annot smoothed down her little apron with both her hands, gave a complaisant glance at her own neat little feet, and her bright holiday shoes, and then listened eagerly for her father's answer.

"I am sure, M. Chapeau, that Annot Stein is very thankful for your good wishes," said he, "and so is her father, very thankful; but she has not court-breeding enough for that sort of work; she has never learnt to speak smooth, and say pretty little flattering sayings, such as ladies like to hear. Nor when Madame would be out of sorts and ruffled, as great ladies will be sometimes, would she know how to say the right word just at the right time; and then Annot has too much of her father's rough blood, and if Madame scolded at all, it's ten chances to one, but she would scold again, and that, you know, wouldn't do. No, M. Chapeau, Annot had better remain as she is, and keep her father's house, till she marries some honest tradesman, like myself, when these deadly wars be over."

"Well, but my dear friend," said Chapeau, "I had another little proposition I wanted to make, which would fit in so well with what I suggested; and I can assure you Madame Henri, that is Mademoiselle de Lescure as she is now, you know, is the softest, sweetest-tempered creature living—she wouldn't quarrel with any one, much less with such a little angel as your daughter."

"I'm sure," said Michael, making a low bow to his guest, and pressing the handle of his pipe to his breast. "I'm sure my daughter will be very thankful for the great interest you take respecting her."

"But as I was saying, you know, about this other little proposition of mine?"

"Well, M. Chapeau, I'm listening with all my ears, and very thankful for your kind friendship."

"You see," said Jacques, "M. Henri is going to change his condition; we've both been young fellows together; we've had our amusements and our pleasures like other young men, and, maybe, been as fortunate as most. Well, my friend, M. Henri is going to settle down, and marry the girl of his heart, whom he loves better than all the world; and what can I do better than follow his example? The truth is, I mean to settle down too, Michael Stein."

"Well," said Michael, scratching his head, and listening for the remainder of Chapeau's little proposition.

"And I want to marry the girl of my heart, whom I love better than all the world, and her name is Annot Stein, and there's an end of it; and now you know all about it."

Annot's heart beat quickly as she heard him make the last important declaration; and beautifully she thought he made it. When Chapeau called her a little angel, she swore to herself that he was the dearest fellow that ever lived and when he finished by protesting that she was the girl of his heart, and that he loved her better than all the world, she longed to run out and throw her arms about his neck.

Michael Stein took a long pull at his pipe, and blew out a huge cloud of tobacco before he made any answer, and then he said:

"M. Chapeau, I am sensible how great an honour you propose to do me and my poor daughter; but I am not a proud man, no one can say that Michael Stein was ever proud or ambitious; my only wish is to see my little girl married to a decent hard-working fellow, like her father."

"Well, ain't I a hard-working fellow?"

"Let me look at your hands, M. Chapeau; the inside of your hands. No, you are not a hard-working fellow; your hand is as soft as a lady's."

"What signifies my hand? I shan't make a worse husband, shall I, because my hand is not as horny as your own."

"No, but a hard-fisted fellow is the only man that will suit my daughter."

"But, Michael Stein, she herself thinks—"

"Who ever heard of asking a girl what she thinks herself? Of course she'd sooner be a fine lady, and spend her time walking about a big chateau than be milking cows and minding goats."

"But won't she be earning her living and her wages honestly?"

"Wages! I don't like those sort of wages, M. Chapeau. I don't mean to say anything uncivil, and I hope you won't take it amiss, but there are two trades I don't fancy for my children: the one is that of a soldier, the other that of a great man's servant."

"Gracious me, Michael Stein! why I'm both," said Chapeau, rather offended.

"I beg your pardon again and again, and I really mean no offence: clown as I am, I hope I know better than to say anything to hurt my own guest in my own house."

Chapeau assured him he was not offended, and begged to know why the old man objected to see his children become soldiers or servants.

"They've no liberty," said Michael, "though they usually take a deal too much licence. They never are allowed to call their time their own, though they often misuse the time that ought to belong to other people."

For a long time Chapeau combatted such arguments as these, but without avail; the smith declared that now, as his two sons had become soldiers, it would break his heart if his daughter also were to marry one. He assured Jacques, with tears running down his rough cheeks, that he could not bring himself to give his daughter his blessing, if she left his house without his leave to marry a soldier. He declared that he also loved her better than all the world, and that he could not bear to part with her; and his tears and kindly words had such an effect upon Annot, that she could not restrain herself: she burst into tears herself and running out of her little room, threw herself into her father's arms.

"Get up, thou simpleton; get up, thou little fool," said he. "Why, Annot, what ails thee?"

"Oh, father! dear father!" said she.

"Get up then, Annot, and I'll speak to thee. I never saw thee in this way before."

"Oh, father!" she said, sobbing violently, "do you love your poor daughter so very, very much?"

"Love you, Annot! why yes, I do love you. If you'll be a good girl, that is, I will love you."

"I will be a good girl, dear father; indeed I'll be a good girl; at any rate I'll try. But then——" and she stood up, and commenced wiping her eyes with her little apron.

"Well, what then, Annot?" said the smith.

"But then——I wouldn't anger you, father, for all the world; indeed I wouldn't, for you always are so good to me, and I know I don't deserve it," and poor Annot continued sobbing and rubbing her eyes with her apron.

"Nonsense, girl, nonsense!" said Michael; "I don't find any fault with you. Don't think of getting yourself married till these wars be over, that's all," and he kissed her forehead, and patted her cheek as though all the difficulty were over.

"But, father——?" continued Annot, with her apron still to her face.

"Well, child, what is it? By the blessed mass, M. Chapeau, I don't know what the girl's crying for."

"Do you love your own little Annot so very, very much?" said she, and she put her soft arm round his rough neck, and placed her cheek quite close to his.

"There, Annot; why what nonsense, girl! Don't you know I love you? didn't you hear me say so this minute? Leave off, will you, you little slut! why, what will M. Chapeau think of us? Well, I declare she's crying still!"

"But if you really, really love me, father—"

"Bother the girl! she knows I love her better than anything else; God forgive me."

"If you really love me," repeated Annot, nestling her head in her father's bosom, "you must, you must, you must—do something that I'll ask you, father."

"And what is it, child? I doubt much it's nonsense."

"You must love Jacques Chapeau too, father," and having uttered these important words, Annot clung fast to her father's arms, as if she feared he was going to throw her off, and sobbed and cried as though her heart were breaking.

The battle between the contending factions, namely, the father on one side, and the daughter with her lover on the other, was prolonged for a considerable time, but the success was altogether with Annot. Chapeau would have had no chance himself against the hard, dry, common sense of the smith; but Annot made her appearance just at the right moment, before the father had irrevocably pledged himself, and the old man was obliged to succumb; he couldn't bring himself to refuse his daughter when she was lying on his bosom and appealing to his love; so at last he gave way entirely, and promised that he would love Jacques Chapeau also; and then Chapeau, he also cried; and, I shudder as I write it, he also kissed the tough, bronzed, old wiry smith, and promised that he would be a good husband and son-in-law.

As soon as Annot had got her wish, and had heard Jacques received as her betrothed husband, she also was wonderfully dutiful and affectionate. She declared that she didn't want to be married till the wars were nearly over, and the country was a little more quiet; that she would never go away and leave her father altogether, and that if ever she did go and live at Durbellière, she would certainly make an agreement with her master and mistress that she should be allowed to walk over to eat her dinner with her father every Sunday.

As soon as the smith found himself completely conquered, he resigned himself to his fate, and became exceedingly happy and good-humoured. He shook Chapeau's hand fifty times, till he had nearly squeezed it off. He sent to the inn for two bottles of the very best wine that was to be had; he made Annot prepare a second supper, and that not of simple bread and cheese, but of poached eggs and fried bacon, and then he did all that he possibly could to make Chapeau tipsy, and in the attempt he got very drunk himself, and so the day ended happily for them all.

CHAPTER V.
THE HOSPITAL OF ST. LAURENT.

De Lescure only remained three days at Durbellière, and then started again for his own house at Clisson, and Henri accompanied him. They had both been occupied during these three days in making such accommodation as was in their power for the sick and wounded, who were brought back into the Bocage in considerable numbers from Saumur. The safe and sound and whole of limb travelled faster than those who had lost arms and legs in the trenches at Varin, or who had received cuts and slashes and broken ribs at the bridge of Fouchard, and therefore the good news was first received in the Bocage; but those miserable accompaniments of victory, low tumbrils, laden with groaning sufferers lying on straw, slowly moving carts, every motion of which opened anew the wounds of their wretched occupants, and every species of vehicle as could be collected through the country, crammed with the wounded and the dying, and some even with the dead, were not long in following the triumphal return of the victorious peasants.

A kind of hospital was immediately opened at a little town called St. Laurent sur Sèvre, about two leagues from Durbellière, at which a convent of sisters of mercy had long been established. De Lescure and Larochejaquelin between them supplied the means, and the sisters of the establishment cheerfully gave their time, their skill, and tenderest attention to assuage the miseries of their suffering countrymen. Agatha knew the superior of the convent well, and assisted in all the necessary preparations. She was there when the hospital was first opened, and for a long time afterwards visited it once or twice a week, on which occasions she stayed for the night in the convent; had it not been that she could not bring herself to leave her father, she would have remained there altogether, as long as the war continued to supply the little wards with suffering patients. They were seldom, or rather never, empty as long as the Vendeans kept their position in the country, the sick and the wounded were nursed with the tenderest care at St. Laurent. The sisters who had commenced the task never remitted their zeal, nor did Agatha Larochejaquelin. The wards were by degrees increased in number, the building was enlarged, surgical skill was procured, every necessary for a hospital was obtained, whatever might be the cost, and whatever the risk; till at last, in spite of the difficulties which had to be encountered, the dangers which surrounded them, the slenderness of their means, and the always increasing number of their patients, the hospital of St. Laurent might have rivalled the cleanliness, care, and comfort of the Hotel Dieu in its present perfection.

As soon as the first arrangements for the commencement of this hospital had been made, de Lescure and Henri went to Clisson. It may easily be supposed that de Lescure was anxious to see his wife, and that she was more than anxious to see him. Henri also was not sorry to hear the praises of his valour sung by the sweet lips of Marie. He stayed one short happy week at Clisson, basking in the smiles of beauty, and they were the last hours of tranquillity that any of the party were destined to enjoy for many a long sad day. De Lescure's recovery was neither slow nor painful, and before the week was over, he was able to sit out on the lawn before the château, with one arm in a sling, and the other round his wife's waist, watching the setting of the sun, and listening to the thrushes and nightingales. Every now and again he would talk of the future battles to be fought, and of the enemies to be conquered, and of the dangers to be encountered; but he did not speak so sadly of the prospects of his party as he did when he had only just determined to take up arms with the Vendeans. The taking of Thouars, and Fontenay, of Montreuil, and Saumur, had inspired even him, and almost taught him to believe that La Vendée would be ultimately successful in re-establishing the throne.

De Lescure was delighted to see what he thought was a growing attachment between his sister and his friend. Had he had the power of choosing a husband for Marie out of all France, he would have chosen Henri Larochejaquelin: he loved him already as he could only love a brother, and he knew that he had all those qualities which would most tend to make a woman happy.

"Oh, if these wars were but over," said he to his wife, "how I would rejoice to give her to him, he is such a brave and gallant fellow—but as tender-hearted and kind as he is brave!"

"These weary, weary wars!" said Madame de Lescure, with a sigh, "would they were over: would, with all my heart, they had never been begun. How well does the devil do his work on earth, when he is able to drive the purest, the most high-minded, the best of God's creatures to war and bloodshed as the only means of securing to themselves the liberty of worshipping their Saviour and honouring their King!"

Henri himself, however, had not considered the propriety of waiting until the wars were over before he took a wife for himself, or at any rate before he asked the consent of the lady's friends: for the day before he left Clisson, he determined to speak to Charles on the subject; though he had long known Marie so well, and had now been staying a week in the house, he had never yet told her that he loved her. It was the custom of the age and the country for a lover first to consult the friends of the young lady, and though the peculiar circumstances of his position might have emboldened Henri to dispense with such a practice, he was the last man in the world to take advantage of his situation.

"Charles," said he, the evening before his departure, as he stood close to the garden seat, on which his cousin was sitting, and amused himself with pitching stones into the river, which ran beneath the lawn at Clisson. "Charles, I shall be off tomorrow; I almost envy you the broken arm which keeps you here."

"It won't keep me long now, Henri," said he; "I shall be at Chatillon in a week's time, unless you and d'Elbée have moved to Parthenay before that. Cathelineau will by that time be master of Nantes, that is, if he is ever to be master of it."

"Don't doubt it, Charles. I do not the least: think of all Charette's army. I would wager my sword to a case-dagger, that Nantes is in his hands this minute."

"We cannot always have the luck we had at Saumur, Henri?"

"No," said Henri, "nor can we always have a de Lescure to knock down for us the gates of the republicans."

"Nor yet a Larochejaquelin to force his way through the breach," said the other.

"Now we are even," said Henri, laughing; "but really, without joking, I feel confident that the white flag is floating at this moment on the castle at Nantes; but it is not of that, Charles, that I wish to speak now. You have always been an elder brother to me. We have always been like brothers, have we not?"

"Thank God, we have, Henri! and I do not think it likely that we shall ever be more distant to each other."

"No, that I'm sure we never shall. You are too good either to quarrel yourself, or to let me quarrel with you; but though we never can be more distant, we may yet be more near to each other. You know what I mean, Charles?"

"I believe I do," said de Lescure; "but why do you not speak out? You are not likely, I think, to say or to propose anything that we shall not approve of—that is, Victorine and I."

"God bless you both!" said Henri. "You are too kind to me; but can you consent to give me your own dear favourite sister—your sweet Marie? You know what I mean in saying that I would be nearer to you."

De Lescure was in the act of answering his cousin, when the quick fall of a horse's foot was heard in the avenue close to the house, and then there was a sudden pause as the brute was pulled up violently in the yard of the château, and the eager voices of domestics answering the rapid questions of the man who had alighted.

Interested as the two friends were in their conversation, the times were too full of important matters to allow of their remaining quiet, after having heard such tokens of a hurried messenger. Larochejaqnelin ran off to the yard of the château, and de Lescure followed him as quickly as his wounded arm would allow.

Henri had hardly got off the lawn, when he met a couple of servants coming from the yard, and between them a man booted, spurred, and armed, covered with dust and spattered with foam, whom he at once recognized as Foret, the friend and townsman of Cathelineau.

"What news, Foret, what news?" said Henri, rushing up to him, and seizing him by the hand. "Pray God you bring with you good tidings."

"The worst news that ever weighed heavy on a poor man's tongue, M. Henri," said Foret, sorrowfully.

"Cathelineau is not dead?" said Henri, but the tone of his inquiry shewed plainly how much he feared what the reply would be.

"He was not dead," answered Foret, "when I left him five leagues on this side Nantes, but he had not many days to live."

The two had turned back over the lawn, and now met de Lescure, as he hastened to join them.

"Cathelineau," said Henri, "is mortally wounded! Victory will have been bought too dear at such a price; but I know not yet even whether the Vendeans have been victorious."

"They have not—they have not," said Foret. "How could they be victorious when their great General had fallen?"

"Mortally wounded! Oh, Foret, you are indeed a messenger of evil," said de Lescure, giving him his hand.

"Yes, mortally wounded," said Foret. "I fear before this he may have ceased to breathe. I left him, gentlemen, a few leagues this side Nantes, and at his own request hurried on to tell you these sad tidings. Oh, M. de Lescure, our cause has had a heavy blow at Nantes, and yet at one time we had almost beaten them; but when the peasants saw Cathelineau fall, they would fight no longer."

"Where is he?" said Henri, "that is if he still lives."

"I crossed the river with him," answered Foret, "and brought him on as far as Remouille. He wished to be carried to the hospital you have opened at St.

Laurent, and unless he has died since I left him, he is there now. I hurried on by Montacué and Tiffauges to St. Laurent; and there, M. Henri, I saw Mademoiselle Agatha, and told her what had happened. If there be an angel upon earth she is one! When I told her that the good Cathelineau was dying, every shade of colour left her beautiful cheek; she became as pale as marble, and crossed her hands upon her bosom; she spoke to me not a word, nor did I look for reply, for I knew that in her heart she was praying that his soul might be taken up to heaven."

Henri at that moment remembered the enthusiastic declaration of his sister, that Cathelineau, despite his birth, was worthy of any woman's love, and he did not begrudge her the only means which now remained to her of proving her devotion to the character she had admired.

"I told her," continued Foret, "that if he lived so long, Cathelineau would reach the hospital on the following day, and then I hurried on to you. She told me I should find you here. It was then dark, but I reached Chatillon that night, for they sent a guide with me from St. Laurent. I left Chatillon again at the break of day, and have not lost much time in arriving here."

"No, indeed, Foret; and surely you must need rest and refreshment," said de Lescure. "Come into the château, and you shall have both."

"But tell us, Foret, of this reverse at Nantes," said Henri. "I will at once start for St. Laurent; I will, if possible, see Cathelineau before he dies; but let me know before I go to him how it has come to pass that victory has at last escaped him."

"Victory did not escape him," said Foret: "he was victorious to the last— victorious till he fell. You know, gentlemen, it had been arranged that Nantes should be attacked at the same moment by Charette from the southern banks of the Loire, and by Cathelineau from the northern, but this we were not able to accomplish. Charette was at his post, and entered the town gallantly over the Pont Rousseau, but we were unable to be there at the appointed time. For ten hours we were detained by a detachment of the blues at the little town of Nort, and though we carried it at last, without losing many of our men, the loss of the precious hours was very grievous. We pushed on to Nantes, however, without losing another minute, and though we found the rebels ready to receive us, they could not hold their ground against us at all. We drove them from the town in every direction. We were already in the chief square of Nantes, assured of our victory, and leading our men to one last attack, when a musket ball struck Cathelineau on the arm, and passing through the flesh entered his breast. He was on foot, in front of the brave peasants whom he was leading, and they all saw him fall. Oh, M. de Lescure, if you had heard the groan, the long wail of grief, which his poor followers from St. Florent uttered, when they saw their sainted leader fall before them, your ears would never forget the sound. We raised him up between us, and carried him back to a part of the town which was in our hands, and from thence over the Pont Rousseau to Pirmil, where I left him for a while, and returned to the town, but I could not get the peasants to follow me again—that is, his peasants; and he was too weak to speak to them himself. It was not till two hours after that he was able to speak a word."

"And you lost all the advantage you had gained?" asked de Lescure.

"We might still have been successful, for the blues would always rather run than fight when they have the choice, but the Prince de Talmont, in his eagerness, headed the fugitive rebels who were making for Savenay, and drove them back into the town; when there, they had no choice but to fight; indeed, their numbers were so much greater than our own, that they surrounded us. Our hearts were nearly broken, and our arms were weak; it ended in our retreating to Pirmil, and leaving the town in the hands of the republicans."

"How truly spoke that General who said, 'build a bridge of gold for a flying enemy!'" said de Lescure.

"And is Cathelineau's wound so surely mortal?" asked Henri.

"The surgeon who examined him in Pirmil said so; indeed, Cathelineau never doubted it himself. He told me, as soon as he could speak, that he should never live to see the Republic at an end. 'But,' added he, 'you, Foret, and others will; and it delights me to think that I have given my life to so good a cause.'"

Henri's horse was now ready, and he made no longer delay than to say adieu to his hostess, and to speak one or two last words to his cousin Marie, and then he made the best of his way to Chatillon and St. Laurent, hoping once more to see Cathelineau before he died. All his spurring and his hurrying was in vain.

A few hours before Henri could reach the hospital, the Saint of Anjou had breathed his last, and Agatha Larochejaquelin had soothed his dying moments.

As Foret had related, Agatha, on hearing of Cathelineau's wound, had turned deadly pale. It was not love that made her feel that the world was darkened by his fall; that from henceforward nothing to her could be bright and cheerful; at least not such love as that which usually warms a woman's heart, for Agatha had never hoped, or even wished to be more to Cathelineau than an admiring friend; nor yet was it grief for the loss of services which she knew were invaluable to the cause she had so warmly espoused. These two feelings were blended together in her breast. She had taught herself to look to Cathelineau as the future saviour of her country; she loved his virtue, his patriotism, and his valour; and her heart was capable of no other love while that existed in it so strongly. The idea of looking on Cathelineau as a lover, of seeing him kneeling at her feet, or listening to him while he whispered sweet praises of her beauty, had never occurred to her; had she dreamed it possible that he could do so, half her admiration of him would have vanished. No, there was nothing earthly, nothing mundane in Agatha's love, for though she did love the fallen hero of La Vendée, the patriot postillion of St. Florent, she did not shed a tear when she heard that he was dragging his wounded body to St. Laurent, that he might have the comfort of her tender care in his last moments; her hand did not shake as she wrote a line to her father to say that she could not leave the hospital that evening, or probably the next; nor did she for one half hour neglect the duties which her less distinguished patients required her to perform; but still she felt her heart was cold within her, and that if God had so willed it, she could, without regret, take her place in the grave beside the stricken idol of her admiration, who had fallen at Nantes while fighting for his God and his King.

Early on the morning after Foret's departure for Clisson, the litter which bore the wounded chief reached the hospital, and Agatha's arm assisted him from the door-step to the death-bed, which she had prepared for him. Agatha's feelings towards him have been imperfectly described; but what were his feelings towards her? What was the nature of the mysterious love, which no kind words had ever encouraged, which no look had ever declared, which he had hardly dared to acknowledge to his own heart, and which had yet induced the wounded man to make so painful a journey, to travel over twenty long, long leagues, that he might once more see the glorious face which had filled his breast with such an unutterable passion? Not for a moment had he ever dreamt that Agatha regarded him differently than she did the many others who had taken up arms in the service of their country. His name he knew must be familiar to her ears, for chance had made it prominent in the struggle; but beyond that, it had never occurred to his humble mind that Agatha Larochejaquelin had given one thought to the postillion of St. Florent. For some time, Cathelineau had been unable to define to himself the passion which he felt, but had gradually become aware that he loved Agatha passionately, incurably, and hopelessly. Her image had been present to him continually; it had been with him in the dead of night, and in the heat of day; in the hour of battle, and at the council-table; in the agony of defeat, and in the triumph of victory. When he found himself falling in the square at Nantes, and all visible objects seemed to swim before his eyes, still he saw Agatha's beautiful pale face, and then she seemed to smile kindly on him, and to bid him hope. As soon as his senses returned to him, he was made conscious that he was dying, and then he felt that he should die more happily if he could see once more the fair angel, who had illuminated and yet troubled the last few days of his existence.

Cathelineau had heard that Agatha had taken under her own kind care the hospital at St. Laurent, but he had not expected that she would be on the step to meet him as he was lifted out of his litter; but hers was the first face he saw on learning that his painful journey was at an end. His wound had been pronounced to be inevitably mortal, and he had been told that he might possibly live for two or three days, but that in all probability his sufferings would not be protracted so long. The fatal bullet had passed through his arm into his breast, had perforated his lungs, and there, within the vitals of his body, the deadly missile was still hidden. At some moments, his agony was extreme, but at others, he was nearly free from pain; and as his life grew nearer to its close, his intervals of ease became longer, and the periods of his suffering were shortened. He had confessed, and received absolution and the sacrament of his church at Remouille; and when he reached St. Laurent, nothing was left for him but to die.

He tried to thank her, as Agatha assisted him to the little chamber which she had prepared for him; but his own feelings, and his exertions in moving were at first too much for him. The power of speech, however, soon returned to him, and he said:

"How can I thank you, Mademoiselle, what am I to say to thank you for such care as this?"

"You are not to thank us at all," said Agatha, (there was one of the sisters of mercy with her in the room). "We are only doing what little women can do for the cause, for which you have done so much."

Again he essayed to speak, but the sister stopped him with a kind yet authoritative motion of her hand, and bade him rest tranquil a while, and so he did. Sometimes Agatha sat by the window, and watched his bed, and at others, she stole quietly out of the room to see her other patients, and then she would return again, and take her place by the window; and as long as she remained in the room, so that he could look upon her face, Cathelineau felt that he was happy.

He had been at St. Laurent some few hours, and was aware that his precious moments were fast ebbing. He hardly knew what it was that he longed to say, but yet he felt that he could not die in peace without expressing to the fair creature who sat beside him the gratitude he felt for her tender care. Poor Cathelineau! he did not dream how difficult he would find it to limit gratitude to its proper terms, when the heart from which he spoke felt so much more than gratitude!

"Ah, Mademoiselle!" he began, but she interrupted him.

"Hush, hush, Cathelineau!" she said. "Did you not hear sister Anna say that you should not speak."

"What avails it now for me to be silent?" said he. "I know, Mademoiselle, that I am dying, and, believe me, I do not fear to die. Your kind care can make my last few hours tranquil and easy, but it cannot much prolong them. Let me have the pleasure of telling you that I appreciate your kindness, and that I give you in return all that a dying man can give—my prayers."

"And I will pray for you, Cathelineau," said Agatha. "But will not every Vendean pray for the hero who first led them to victory, who first raised his hand against the Republic?"

"How precious are the praises of such as you!" said he. "Pray for me and for your other poor countrymen who have fallen in this contest; such prayers as yours will assuredly find entrance into heaven."

He then again laid tranquil for a while, but his spirit was not quiet within him; he felt that there was that which he longed to say before he died, and that the only moments in which the power of speaking would be left to him were fast passing from him.

"Do not bid me be silent," he said; "did I not know that no earthly power could prolong my life, I would do nothing to defeat the object of my kind nurses; but as it is, a few moments' speech are of value to me, but an extra hour or so of torpid life can avail me nothing. Ah, Mademoiselle, though I cannot but rejoice to see our cause assisted by the nobility and excellence of the country, though I know that the angelic aid of such as thou art—"

"Stop, stop," said Agatha, interrupting him, "if you will speak, at any rate do not flatter; your last words are too precious to be wasted in such idleness."

"It does not seem to be flattery in me to praise you, Mademoiselle; heaven knows that I do not wish to flatter; but my rude tongue knows not how to express what my heart feels. I would say, that valuable as is your aid to our poor peasants, I almost regret to see you embarked in a cause which will bathe the country in blood, and which, unless speedily victorious, will bring death and desolation on the noble spirits who have given to it all their energies and all their courage."

"Do you think so badly, Cathelineau, of the hopes of the royalists?"

"If we could make one great and glorious effort," said he, and his eyes shone as brightly as ever while he spoke; "if we could concentrate all our forces, and fill them with the zeal which, at different times, they all have shewn, we might still place the King upon his throne, and the white flag might still wave for ages from our churches, as a monument of the courage of La Vendée. But if, as I fear, the war become one of detached efforts, despite the wisdom of de Lescure, the skill of Bonchamps, the piety of d'Elbée, the gallant enthusiasm of Larochejaquelin, and the devoted courage of them all, the Republic by degrees will devour their armies, will consume their strength, will desolate the country, and put to the sword even their wives and children: neither high nobility, nor illustrious worth, nor surpassing beauty will shield the inhabitants of this devoted country from the brutality of the conquerors, who have abjured religion, and proclaimed that blood alone can satisfy their appetites."

"Surely God will not allow his enemies to prevail," said Agatha.

"God's ways are inscrutable," answered Cathelineau, "and his paths are not plain to mortal eyes; but it is not the less our duty to struggle on to do those things which appear to us to be acceptable to Him. But should these sad days come, should atheism and the love of blood stride without control through our villages; if it be doomed that our houses are to be burnt and our women to be slaughtered, why should all remain to be a prey to our enemies? Ah, Mademoiselle leave this devoted country for a while, take your sweet cousin with you; bid M. de Lescure send away his young wife: it is enough that men should have to fight with demons; men can fight and die, and suffer comparatively but little, but female beauty and female worth will be made to suffer ten thousand deaths from the ruthless atrocities of republican foes."

Agatha shuddered at the picture which Cathelineau's words conjured up, but her undaunted courage was not shaken.

"God will temper the wind to the shorn lamb," said she. "Neither I, nor Marie will leave our brothers, nor will Madame de Lescure leave her husband; it is little we can do to hasten victory, but we can lessen suffering and administer comfort, when comfort is most required. Had you, Cathelineau, loved some woman above all others, and been loved by her; had you had with you in your struggle some dear sister, or perhaps still dearer wife, would you have asked her to go from you, that you might have battled on, and struggled, and at last have died alone?"

"By God's dear love, I would," said he, raising himself, as he spoke, upon his bed. "My most earnest prayer to her should have been to leave me."

"And when she refused to do so; when she also swore by God's dear love, that she would stay with you till the last; as she would have done, Cathelineau, if she loved you as—as you should have been loved; would you then have refused the comfort her love so longed to give you?"

"I know not then what I would have done," said he, after lying with his eyes closed for a few moments without answering. "I have never known such love. Our women love their husbands and their brothers, but it is only angels love with such a love as that."

"Such is the love a man deserves who gives his all for his King and his country. If our husbands, and our brothers, and our dear friends, Cathelineau, are brave and noble, we will endeavour to imitate them; as long as there is an abiding-place for them in the country, there are duties for us. If God vouchsafed to spare you your life a while, that you might live to be the instrument of restoring His worship, do you think that I would run from your bedside, because I heard that the rebels were near you? Oh, Cathelineau! you do not know the passive courage of a woman's heart."

Cathelineau listened to her with all his ears, and gazed on her with all his eyes, as she spoke to him. It seemed to him as though another world had opened to his view even before his death; as though paradise could give him no holier bliss than to gaze on that face, and to listen to that voice.

"I never knew what a woman was till now," said he; "and how much better is it that I should die this moment, with your image before me, than return to a world, such as mine has been, where all henceforward would be distasteful to me."

"Should you live, Cathelineau, you would live to be honoured and valued. If it be God's pleasure that you should die, your memory will be honoured—and loved," said Agatha.

He did not answer her for a while, but lay still, with his eyes fixed upon her, as she sat with her elbow leaning on the window. Oh! what an unspeakable joy it was to him to hear such heavenly words spoken by her, whom he had almost worshipped; and yet her presence and her words turned his thoughts back from heaven to the earth which he had all but left. Could she really have loved him had it been his lot to survive these wars? Could she really have descended from her high pinnacle of state and fortune to bless so lowly a creature as him with her beauty and her excellence? As these thoughts passed through his brain, he began for the first time to long for life, to think that the promised blessings of heaven hardly compensated for those which he was forced to leave on earth; but his mind was under too strong control to be allowed to wander long upon such reflections. He soon recovered his wayward thoughts, and remembered that his one remaining earthly duty was to die.

"It is God's will that I should die," said he at last, "and I feel that He will soon release me from all worldly cares and sufferings; but you, Mademoiselle, have made the last moments of my life happy," and again he was silent for a minute or two, while he strove to find both courage and words to express that which he wished to say. "How different have been the last few weeks of my existence since first I was allowed to look upon your face!" A faint blush suffused Agatha's brow as Cathelineau spoke. "Yes, Mademoiselle," he continued, "I know you will forgive, when coming from a dying man, words which would have been insane had they been spoken at any other time—my life has been wholly different since that day when your brother led me, unwilling as I was, into your presence at Durbellière. Since that time I have had no other thought than of you; it was you who gave me courage in battle, and, more wonderful than that, enabled me to speak aloud, and with authority among those who were all so infinitely my superiors. It was your beauty that softened my rough heart, your spirit that made me dauntless, your influence that raised me up so high. I have not dared to love you as love is usually described, for they say that love without hope makes the heart miserable, and my thoughts of you have made me more blessed than I ever was before, and yet I hoped for nothing; but I have adored you as I hardly dared to adore anything that was only human. I hardly know why I should have had myself carried hither to tell you this, but I felt that I should die more easily, when I had confessed to you the liberty which my thoughts had taken with your image."

As he continued speaking, Agatha had risen from her seat, and she was now kneeling at the foot of his bed, hiding her face between her hands, and the tears were streaming fast down her cheeks.

"Tell me, Mademoiselle, that you forgive me," said he, "tell me that you pardon my love, and above all, pardon me for speaking of it. I have now but a few hours' breath, and in them I feel that I shall be but feeble; but tell me that you forgive me, and, though dying, I shall be happy."

Agatha was too agitated to speak for a time, but she stretched her hand out to him, and he grasped it in his own as forcibly as his strength would allow.

"I know that you have pardoned my boldness," said he. "May God bless you, and protect you in the dangers which are coming."

"May He bless you also, Cathelineau—dear Cathelineau," said Agatha, still sobbing. "May He bless you, and receive you into His glory, and seat you among His angels, and make you blessed and happy in His presence for ever and ever through eternity." And she drew herself nearer to him, and kissed the hand which she still held within her own, and bathed it with her tears, and pressed it again and again to her bosom. "The memory of the words you have spoken to me shall be dearer to me than the love of man, shall be more precious to me than any homage a living prince could lay at my feet—to remember that Cathelineau has loved me—that the sainted Cathelineau has held my image in his heart, shall be love enough for Agatha Larochejaquelin."

Cathelineau lingered on for the whole of that day, and the greater portion of the night. Agatha did not leave his bed-side for a moment, but sat during most of the time still holding his hand in hers. He spoke no farther respecting the singular passion he had nursed in his heart, nor did she allude to it; but when he spoke at all, he felt that he was speaking to a dear, and tried, and valued friend, and he spoke, therefore, without hesitation and without reserve. He desired her to give various messages from him to the Vendean chiefs, but especially to de Lescure, to whom he said he looked with most hope for a successful issue to the struggle. He begged that they might be told that his last breath was spent in advising that they should make one great, combined, and final effort for the total overthrow of republicanism in France, and not fritter away their strength in prolonged contests with an enemy so infinitely their superior in numbers. Agatha promised faithfully to be a true messenger of these last injunctions, and then she saw the Vendean chief expire in perfect tranquillity, happy in an assured hope of everlasting joy.

He died about three in the morning, and before five, Henri Larochejaquelin arrived at St. Laurent from Clisson. He had ridden hard through the previous day and the entire night, with the hope of once more seeing the leader, whom he had followed with so much devotion, and valued so truly; but he was too late.

He caught his sister in his arms as he ran up the hospital stairs. "Where is he?" said he; "is he still alive? Is there any hope?"

"There is no hope for us," answered Agatha; "but there is perfect certainty for him. The good Cathelineau has restored his spirit to Him who gave it to avenge His glory."

CHAPTER VI.
COMMISSIONERS OF THE REPUBLIC.

The taking Saumur frightened the Convention much more than any of the previous victories of the Vendeans. The republicans lost a vast quantity of military stores, arms, gunpowder, cannons, and soldiers' clothing; and, which was much worse than the loss itself these treasures had fallen into the hands of an enemy, whose chief weakness consisted in the want of such articles. The royalists since the beginning of the revolt had always shewn courage and determination in action; but they had never before been collected in such numbers, or combated with forces so fully prepared for resistance, as those whom they had so signally conquered at Saumur. The Convention began to be aware that some strong effort would be necessary to quell the spirit of the Vendeans. France at the time was surrounded by hostile troops. At the moment in which the republicans were flying from the royalists at Saumur, the soldiers of the Convention were marching out of Valenciennes, that fortified city having been taken by the united arms of Austria and England. Condé also had fallen, and on the Rhine, the French troops who had occupied Mayence with so much triumph, were again on the point of being driven from it by the Prussians.

The Committee of Public Safety, then the repository of the supreme power in Paris, was aware that unless the loyalty of La Vendée was utterly exterminated, the royalists of that district would sooner or later join themselves to the allies, and become the nucleus of an overpowering aristocratic party in France. There were at the time thousands, and tens and hundreds of thousands in France who would gladly have welcomed the extinction of the fearful Republic which domineered over them, had not every man feared to express his opinion. The Republic had declared, that opposition to its behests, in deed, or in word, or even in thought, as far as thoughts could be surmised, should be punished with death; and by adhering to the purport of this horrid decree, the voice of a nation returning to its senses was subdued. Men feared to rise against the incubus which oppressed them, lest others more cowardly than themselves should not join them; and the Committee of Public Safety felt that their prolonged existence depended on their being able to perpetuate this fear. It determined, therefore, to strike terror into the nation by exhibiting a fearful example in La Vendée. After full consideration, the Committee absolutely resolved to exterminate the inhabitants of the country—utterly to destroy them all, men, women, and children—to burn every town, every village, and every house—to put an end to all life in the doomed district, and to sweep from the face of the country man, beast, and vegetable. The land was to be left without proprietors, without a population, and without produce; it was to be converted into a huge Golgotha, a burial-place for every thing that had life within it; and then, when utterly purged by fire and massacre, it was to be given up to new colonists, good children of the Republic, who should enjoy the fertility of a land soaked with the blood of its former inhabitants. Such was the deliberate resolution of the Committee of Public Safety, and no time was lost in commencing the work of destruction.

Barrère, one of the members of the Committee, undertook to see the work put in a proper train, and for this purpose he left Paris for the scene of action. Westerman and Santerre accompanied him, and to them was committed the task of accomplishing the wishes of the Committee. There was already a republican army in La Vendée, under the command of General Biron, but the troops of which it was composed were chiefly raw levies, recruits lately collected by the conscription, without discipline, and, in a great degree, without courage; but the men who were now brought to carry on the war, were the best soldiers whom France could supply. Westerman brought with him a legion of German mercenaries, on whom he could rely for the perpetration of any atrocity, and Santerre was at the head of the seven thousand men, whom the allied army had permitted to march out of Valenciennes, and to return to Paris.

It was in the beginning of July that this worthy triumvirate met at Angers, on their road to La Vendée. Cathelineau had driven the republican garrison out of this town immediately after the victory at Saumur, but the royalists made no attempt to keep possession of it, and the troops who had evacuated it at their approach, returned to it almost immediately. It was now thronged with republican soldiers of all denominations, who exercised every species of tyranny over the townspeople. Food, drink, forage, clothes, and even luxuries were demanded, and taken in the name of the Convention from every shop, and the slightest resistance to these requisitions, was punished as treason to the Republic. The Vendeans, in possession of the same town only a fortnight before, had injured no one, had taken nothing without paying for it, aid had done everything to prevent the presence of their army being felt as a curse; and yet Angers was a noted republican town; it had shown no favours to the royalists, and received with open arms the messengers of the Convention. Such was the way in which the republicans rewarded their friends, and the royalists avenged themselves on their enemies.

One hot July evening, five men were seated in a parlour of the Mayor's house in Angers, but the poor Mayor himself was not allowed, nor probably did he wish, to be one of the party. Glasses were on the table before them, and the empty bottles, which were there also, showed, that however important the subjects might be which they were discussing, they still considered that some degree of self-indulgence was compatible with their duties. The air of the room was heavy with tobacco smoke, and one or two of the number still had cigars between their lips. They were all armed, though two of them were not in uniform, and the manner in which they had their arms disposed, showed that they did not quite conceive themselves to be in security in these their convivial moments. The men were Barrère, Westerman, and Santerre, and two of the republican Generals, Chouardin and Bourbotte.

Westerman and the two latter were in uniform, and the fact of their having arms, was only in keeping with their general appearance: but the other two were in plain clothes, and their pistols, which were lying among the glasses on the table, and the huge swords which stood upright against their chairs, gave a hideous aspect to the party, and made them look as though they were suspicious of each other.

Barrère alone had no sword. His hand was constantly playing with a little double-barrelled pistol, which he continually cocked and uncocked, the fellow of which lay immediately before him. He was a tall, well built, handsome man, about thirty years of age, with straight black hair, brushed upright from his forehead; his countenance gave the idea of eagerness and impetuosity, rather than cruelty or brutality. He was, however, essentially egotistical and insincere; he was republican, not from conviction, but from prudential motives; he adhered to the throne a while, and deserted it only when he saw that it was tottering; for a time he belonged to the moderate party in the Republic, and voted with the Girondists; he gradually joined the Jacobins, as he saw that they were triumphing over their rivals, and afterwards was one of those who handed over the leaders of the Reign of Terror to the guillotine, and assisted in denouncing Robespierre and St. Just. He was one of the very few who managed to outlive the Revolution, which he did for nearly half a century.

His face was hardly to be termed prepossessing, but it certainly did not denote the ruthless ferocity which the nature of the task he had undertaken would require, and which he exercised in its accomplishment. Nature had not formed him to be a monster gloating in blood; the Republic had altered the disposition which nature had given him, and he learnt among those with whom he had associated, to delight in the work which they required at his hands. Before the Reign of Terror was over, he had become one of those who most loudly called for more blood, while blood was running in torrents on every side; it was he who demanded the murder of the Queen, when even Robespierre was willing to save her. It was he who declared in the Convention that the dead were the only enemies who never returned; and yet this same man lived to publish a pamphlet, in which he advocated the doctrine, that under no circumstances could one human being be justified in taking the life of another.

He was dressed in a blue dress-coat, which in spite of the heat of the weather, was buttoned close round his body; he was rather a dandy in his costume, for his tightly-fitted breeches were made to show the form of his well-formed leg, and his cravat was without a wrinkle. Before the Revolution, Barrère had been a wealthy aristocrat.

Santerre, who sat next to him, was in every respect unlike the ci-devant nobleman. He was a large, rough, burly man, about forty years of age; his brown hair was long and uncombed, his face was coarse and hot, and the perspiration was even now running down it, though drinking and smoking was at present his hardest work; his lips were thick and sensual, and his face was surrounded by huge whiskers, which made him look uncouth and savage; his cravat was thrown off, and his shirt was open at the neck, so as to show his brown throat and brawny chest; a huge horse pistol lay before him close to his glass, and a still huger sword stood up against his chair. He was drinking hard and talking loudly, and was evidently quite at ease with his company; he was as completely at home in the Mayor's parlour at Angers, as when rushing into the Tuilleries at the head of his fellow citizens from the faubourg St. Antoine.

Santerre was of Flemish descent, and by trade a brewer. He was possessed of considerable wealth, which he freely spent among the poor, while famine pressed sore upon them; he was consequently loved, followed, and obeyed. He was the King of the Faubourgs; and though the most ruthless in his animosity to the royalists, he was not altogether a bad man, neither was he by nature absolutely cruel. He had adopted the Revolution from a belief that the great mass of the people would be better off in the world without kings, nobility, or aristocrats; and having made himself firm in this belief, he used to the utmost his coarse, huge, burly power in upsetting these encumbrances on the nation. His love of liberty had become a fanaticism. He had gone with the current, and he had no fine feelings to be distressed at the horrid work which he had to do, no humanity to be shocked; but he was not one of those who delighted in bloodshed and revelled in the tortures which he inflicted on others. He had been low in the world's esteem, and the Revolution had raised him to a degree of eminence; this gratified his ambition, and made him a ready tool in the hands of those who knew how to use his well-known popularity, his wealth, his coarse courage and great physical powers.

Westerman sat at the window a little away from the others. He was a man of indomitable courage and undying perseverance. He was a German, who had been banished from Prussia, and having entered the French army as a private soldier had gradually risen to be an officer. A short time before the storming of the Tuilleries he had foreseen that the democratic party was prevailing, and he had joined it. Danton and Santerre had discovered and appreciated his courage and energy, and he soon found himself a leader of the people. It was he who directed the movements of the populace on the 10th of August, when the Tuilleries was sacked, and the Swiss guards were massacred on the steps of the King's palace. Since that time Westerman had been a successful soldier in the republican army, not that he was by any means a vehement democrat: his object had been military success, and that only. He had neither political theories or political ambition. Chance had thrown him in the way of the Republic, and he had become a republican. He was then attached to the army of Dumourier as aide-de-camp to that General, and was in the confidence of him and of Danton, at the moment that Dumourier was endeavouring to hand over the armies of the Republic to the power of Prussia and of Austria. He again, however, was wise in time. Dumourier calculated too entirely on the affection of the army to himself and failed; but before he failed, Westerman had left him. He was now again a trustworthy servant of the Republic, and as such was sent to assist in the fearful work which the tyranny of the democrats required.

His unnatural ruthlessness and prompt obedience were of no avail to him. Soon after his return from the western provinces he perished under the guillotine.

"And so the good Cathelineau is dead," said Santerre. "The invincible, the invulnerable, the saint! ha, ha! What sweet names these dear friends of ours have given themselves."

"Yes," said General Bourbotte; "the messenger who told me had come direct from their hospital; Cathelineau breathed his last the day before yesterday at St. Laurent."

"Let us drink to his health, gentlemen; his spiritual health," said Santerre; "and to his safe journey;" and the brewer raised his glass to his lips, and drank the toast which he had proposed.

"Bon voyage, my dear Cathelineau," said Bourbotte, following his example.

"Cathelineau was a brave man," said Chouardin. "I am glad he died of his wounds; I should have been sorry that so gallant a fellow should have had to submit his neck to the sharp embraces of Mademoiselle Guillotine."

"That is hardly a patriotic sentiment, citizen General," said Barrère. "Gallantry on the part of an insurgent royalist is an inspiration of the devil, sent to induce man to perpetuate the degradation and misery of his fellow-men. Such gallantry, or rather such frenzy, should give rise to anything but admiration in the breast of a patriot."

"My fidelity to the Republic will not be doubted, I believe," said Chouardin, "because, as a soldier, I admire high courage when I find it in a soldier."

"If your fidelity be unimpeachable, your utility will be much questioned, if you wish to spare a royalist because he is a brave man," said Barrère. "By the same argument, I presume, you would refrain from knocking an adder on the head, because he rose boldly in your path."

"Who talked of sparing?" said Chouardin. "I only said that I would sooner that a brave enemy should die in battle than be handled by an executioner. Talk as you will, you cannot disgrace such a man as Cathelineau."

"Cannot I, indeed, citizen General?" said Westerman, rising from his seat and coming into the middle of the room. "I do then utterly despise, scorn, and abominate him, and all such as him. I can conceive nothing in human form more deplorably low, more pitiably degraded, than such a poor subservient slave as he was."

"There, Westerman, you are grossly wrong," said Santerre. "Your cowardly Marquis, run-fling from the throne which he pretends to reverence, but does not dare to protect; whose grand robes and courtly language alone have made him great; who has not heart enough even to love the gay puppets who have always surrounded him, or courage enough to fight for the unholy wealth he has amassed: this man I say is contemptible. Such creatures are as noxious vermin, whom one loathes, and loathing them destroys. You no less destroy the tiger, who ravages the green fields which your labour has adorned; who laps the blood of your flocks, and threatens the life of your children and servants, but you do not despise the tiger; you keep his hide, as a monument of your victory over a brave and powerful enemy. Cathelineau was the tiger, who was destroying, before it had ripened, the precious fruit of the Revolution."

"The tiger is a noble beast," said Westerman. "He is hungry, and he seeks his prey; he is satisfied, and he lays down and sleeps; but Cathelineau was a mean jackal, who strove for others, not for himself. I can understand the factious enmity of the born aristocrat, who is now called upon to give up the titles, dignities, and so-called honours, which, though stolen from the people, he has been taught to look upon as his right. He contends for a palpable possession which his hand has grasped, which he has tasted and long enjoyed. I know that he is a robber and a spoiler of the poor; I know, in short, that he is an aristocrat, and as such I would have him annihilated, abolished from the face of the earth. I would that the aristocrats of France had but one neck, that with a grasp of my own hand, I might at once choke out their pernicious breath," and the republican laid upon the table his huge hand, and tightly clenched his fingers as though he held between them the imaginary throat of the aristocracy of France; "but," continued he, "much as I hate a gentleman, ten times more strongly do I hate, despise, and abhor the subservient crew of spiritless slaves who uphold the power of the masters,

- 197 -

who domineer over them, who will not accept the sweet gift of liberty, who are kicked, and trodden on, and spat upon, and will not turn again; who will not rise against their tyrants, even when the means of doing so are brought to their hands; who willingly, nay, enthusiastically, lay their necks in the dust, that their fellow-creatures may put their feet upon them. Of such was this Cathelineau, and of such I understand are most of those who hound on these wretched peasants to sure destruction. For them I have no pity, and with them I have no sympathy. They have not the spirit of men, and I would rejoice that the dogs should lick their blood from off the walls, and that birds of prey should consume their flesh."

"Westerman is right," said Barrère; "they are mean curs, these Vendeans, and like curs they must be destroyed; the earth must be rid of men who know not how to take possession of their property in that earth which nature has given them. Believe me, citizen General, that any sympathy with such a reptile as Cathelineau is not compatible with the feeling which should animate the heart of a true republican, intending honestly and zealously to do the work of the Republic."

General Chouardin made no reply to the rebuke which these words conveyed; he did not dare to do so; he did not dare to repeat the opinion that there was anything admirable in the courage of a royalist. Much less than had now been said had before this been deemed sufficient to mark as a victim for the revolutionary tribunal some servant of the Republic, and few wished to experience the tender mercies of Fouquier Tinville, the public accuser. Even Santerre was silenced; despite his popularity, his well-known devotion to the cause, his hatred of the aristocrats, and his aversion to royalty, so horridly displayed at the execution of the King, even he felt that it might not be safe for him to urge that the memory of Cathelineau was not despicable.

"His death must have much weakened them," said Bourbotte. "I know them well, the miscreants! I doubt if they will follow any other leader, that is, in great numbers. The fools looked on this man as a kind of god; they now find that their god is dead. I doubt whether there is another leader among them, who can induce them to leave their parishes."

"If they won't come to us," said Barrère, "we must go to them; they have gone too far now to recede. Whether they return to their homes, or again take up arms, matters little; they must all be destroyed, for blood alone can establish the Republic on a basis which can never be overturned."

"The name of a royalist shall be as horrible in men's ears as that of a parricide," said Santerre.

"But what will you do if you find no army to oppose you?" said Bourbotte. "You cannot well fight without an enemy."

"Never fear," said Westerman, "your muskets shall not grow rusty for want of use. We will go from parish to parish, and leave behind us dead corpses, and burning houses."

"You will not ask soldiers to do the work of executioners?" said Bourbotte.

"I expect the soldiers to do the work of the Convention," said Barrère; "and I also expect the officers to do the same: these are not times in which a man can be chary as to the work which he does."

"We must not leave a royalist alive in the west of France," said Westerman. "You may be assured, Generals, that our soldiers will obey us, however slow yours may be to obey you."

"Perhaps so," said Bourbotte; "my men have not yet been taught to massacre unarmed crowds."

"It is difficult to know what they have been taught," said Westerman. "Whenever they have encountered a few peasants with clubs in their hands, your doughty heroes have invariably ran away."

Westerman as he spoke, stood leaning on the back of a chair, and Bourbotte also rose as he answered him.

"I have yet to learn," aid he, "that you yourself ever were able to make good soldiers out of country clowns in less than a month's time. When you have done so, then you may speak to me on the subject without impertinence."

"I give you my word, citizen General," answered Westerman, "I shall say to you, then and now, whatever I, in the performance of my duty, may think fits and if you deem me impertinent, you may settle that point with the Convention, or, if you prefer it, with myself."

"Westerman, you are unfair to General Bourbotte," said Santerre; "he has said nothing which need offend you."

"It is the General that is offended, not I," said Westerman; "I only beg that he may not talk mawkish nonsense, and tell us that his fellows are too valiant, and too noble to put to the sword unarmed royalists, when everybody knows they are good for nothing else, and that they would run and scatter from the fire of a few muskets, like a lot of plovers from a volley of stones."

"I grant you," said Bourbotte, "that my soldiers are men and not monsters. They are, as yet, French peasants, not German cut-throats."

"Now, by Heaven, Bourbotte," said the Prussian, "you shall swallow that word," and he seized a pistol from off the table. "German cut-throat! and that from you who have no other qualities of a soldier than what are to be found in a light pair of heels. You shall, at any rate, have to deal with one German, whether he be a cut-throat or not."

"In any way you please," said Bourbotte, "that is, in any open or honest way." And as he spoke, he stepped back one step, and took his sword out of the scabbard.

The pistol which Westerman had taken from the table belonged to Santerre, and when he saw it in the hand of his friend, he leapt up and seized hold of the German's arm.

"Are you mad Westerman," said he; "do you wish to fight here in the Mayor's house? I tell you, you were wrong, in taunting him as you did; sit quiet till I make peace between you."

"Taunting him! now, by Heaven, that is good. I will leave it to Barrère to say who first taunted the other. Nonsense, Santerre, leave hold of me I say: you do not think I am going to murder the man, do you?"

General Chouardin also got up and put himself between the two armed men. "Put up your sword, Bourbotte," whispered he, leading him off to the further window of the room; "you are no match for him here: if Barrère chooses he will have you recalled to Paris, and your neck will then not be worth a month's purchase."

"Gentlemen," said Barrère, "this will never do. You can neither of you serve the nation well if you persist in quarrelling between yourselves. General Bourbotte, you should apologize to our friend Westerman for the insult which you offered to his countrymen."

"My country is the country of my adoption," said Westerman. "I ceased to be a German when I took up the arms of France; but my soldiers are my children, and an insult to them is an injury to myself."

"If your anger can wait till the revolt in La Vendée has been quelled," said Chouardin, "my friend Bourbotte will be ready enough to satisfy your wishes as a citizen. Barrère truly says, this is no time for private quarrels."

"So be it," said Westerman. "Let General Bourbotte remember that he owes me an apology or redress."

"You shall have any redress, which any arms you may be pleased to name can give you," said Bourbotte.

"By my honour then, you are two fools," said Santerre; "two egregious fools, if you cannot at once forget the angry words which you each have used. Have your own way, however, so long as you do not fight here."

As the brewer was yet speaking, a servant knocked at the door, and said that a young man wished to say a few words to citizen Santerre on especial business, and on the service of the Republic.

"On the service of the Republic?" said Santerre. "Show him in here then; I have no official secrets from my colleagues."

The servant, however, stated that the young man would not make his appearance in the room where the party were sitting, and he declared he would go away if he could not see Santerre alone. The republican at length yielded, and followed the servant into a small sitting-room, where he found our friend, Adolphe Denot.

CHAPTER VII.
BATTLE OF AMAILLOU.

It will be remembered that Adolphe Denot left the council-room of the royalist leaders at Saumur in anger; and that, after a few words with Henri Larochejaquelin, departed no one knew whither, or for what purpose. On leaving Henri in the street, he had himself no fixed resolve as to his future conduct; he was only determined no longer to remain leagued with men, among whom he felt himself to be disgraced. De Lescure had seen him hesitate in the hour of danger, and had encouraged him in vain; he knew that after this he could never again bear to meet the calm grey eye of his friend's cousin; he had not only been not selected as one of the Generals, but he had even been rejected, and that by the very man who had seen his cowardice. His love, moreover, had been refused by Agatha, and he deemed this refusal an injury which demanded vengeance from his hands; from the moment in which he left her room in Durbellière, schemes had floated across his half-bewildered brain for the accomplishment of his object. He still loved Agatha, though his love was, as it were, mingled with hatred; he still wished to possess her, but he did not care how disagreeable, how horrible to herself might be the means by which he accomplished his object. He entertained ideas of seizing upon her person, taking her from Durbellière, and marrying her during the confusion which the Revolution had caused in the country. At first he had no distinct idea of treachery towards the royalists with whom he had sided; though vague thoughts of bringing the soldiers of the Convention to Durbellière, in the dead of night, had at different times entered his mind, he had never reduced such thoughs to a palpable plan, nor had he ever endeavoured to excuse to himself the iniquity of such a scheme, as a man does when he resolves to sacrifice his honour and his honesty to his passions.

It was in the council-room at Saumur that he first felt a desire to betray the friends of his life; it was in the moment of his hot anger, after leaving it, that he determined to put into effect the plan which he had already conceived; it was then that insane ambition and selfish love prompted him to forget every feeling which he had hitherto recognized as honourable, and to commit himself to a deed which would make it impossible that he should ever be reconciled with the companions of his youth. He had no presentiment that he should ever rise to honour or distinction in the army of the Republic; he never even thought of what his future life would be: revenge was his object, and the sweet delight of proving to Agatha Larochejaquelin that he was able to carry out the bold threats, which he knew that she had scorned and derided.

It would be too much to say that Adolphe Denot was insane, for that would imply that he was not responsible for his own actions; but there certainly lacked something in his brain or mind, which is necessary to perfect sanity. He was no fool; he had read, enjoyed, and perhaps written poetry; he was, for the times, well educated; he could talk fluently, and, occasionally, even persuasively; he understood rapidly, and perceived correctly, the arguments and motives of others; but he could not regulate his conduct, either from the lessons he had learnt from books, or from the doings or misdoings of those around him. He wished to be popular, powerful and distinguished, but he was utterly ignorant of the means by which men gain the affection, respect, and admiration of their fellow-men; he possessed talent without judgment, and ambition without principle. As a precocious boy, he had been too much admired; he had assumed at an early age the duty of a man, and had at once been found miserably wanting.

On leaving Henri in the streets of Saumur, he went to his lodging, took with him what money he had, got upon his horse, and rode out of the town by the temporary bridge which had been put up for the transit of the shaved prisoners. He had wandered about the country for three weeks, remaining sometimes in one place, and sometimes in another, endeavouring to mature his plans; and hearing of the arrival of Santerre in Augers, had come thither to offer his services to the republicans, in the invasion which he understood they contemplated making into the Bocage.

His appearance was not very attractive when first he introduced himself to the republican, for he was lean with anxiety and worn with care; his eyes were restless and bloodshot, and his limbs trembled beneath him. Santerre was not a man who much regarded externals; but, as he afterwards said, "he did not much like the hang-dog look of the royalist cur."

Denot, in an awkward way, got through his story; he had been one of the insurgent Vendeans, he said, but he now wished to serve the Republic. He was intimately acquainted with the royalist leaders, especially the two most popular of them, de Lescure and Larochejaquelin. He knew and was willing to betray their plans. He would accompany Santerre to the residences of these Vendean Generals, and undertake to give them, their families, and possessions, into the power of the republicans, and for these services he asked but one favour; that he should be present at the contemplated burning of Durbellière, and be allowed to save the life of one female who resided there. He represented that his animosity arose entirely from the rejection of his love, and that his only object was to carry off the sister of the Vendean chief from the burning ashes of her father's château.

"Are you aware, young man," said Santerre, with something of generosity in the warning which he gave—a generosity probably inspired by the wine he had drunk: "are you aware, that should I agree to your proposal, every other member of her family will be put to death before your eyes —her brother, her old father, and every pestilent royalist we may find about the place?"

"I suppose they will," said Denot moodily. "At any rate, they deserve no protection at my hands."

"You have probably eaten their bread and drank their wine. You say, indeed, you have lived long in this rambling château, and have fought side by side with this hot-headed young brigand. Bethink you, my friend, you are angry now, but it may turn your stomach, when you are cool, to see the blood of those you know so well running like water; besides, you are taking but an unlikely road to the heart of the girl you say you love. No one has heard your plot but myself: I advise you to abandon it; if you do so, I will forget that I have heard it. You are angry now; go home and sleep on it."

"Sleep on it! I have slept on it these three weeks. No, I did not come to you till I was fully resolved. As for these people, I owe them nothing; they have scorned and rejected me; and as for the girl's heart, it is not that I seek now. Let me gain her person, and her heart will follow. A woman soon learns to love him whom she is forced to obey."

"Well, be it as you will," said Santerre. "It is all a matter of taste; only remember, that before I accede to your proposal, I must consult with my colleagues in the next room, and that when once I have spoken to them it will be too late for me to go back."

Denot declared that he had formed his resolution after mature consideration, and that he was ready and willing to carry through the work he had proposed for himself; and Santerre, without making any further objection, rejoined his friends in the next room, and explained to them the offer which had been made to him. Barrère at first opposed any treaty with Denot. He recommended that the young man should be kept as a prisoner, and at once handed over to the revolutionary tribunal.

"What good can he do us?" said he; "we can find our way to this Durbellière without his assistance; let him and the girl he wishes to kidnap pay the penalty of their crimes against the Republic. She is, I suppose, one of those modern Joans of Arc, who inspire the flagging spirits of these peasants. Should she have beauty enough to make her worth preserving, let her be the prize of some true republican. As for him, let him stretch his neck beneath the guillotine."

Barrère, however, was overruled. The Generals who were with him knew too well the nature of the country they were about to invade, not to appreciate the value of such a guide as they might find in Denot: a guide, who not only knew the nature of the country they had to traverse, and the position of the places they wished to attack, but who was also intimate with the insurgent chiefs, acquainted with their persons and their plans, and who would probably disclose, under proper management, every secret of the revolt. It was accordingly agreed that his offer should be accepted, and he was introduced by Santerre to his four confederates.

"Sit down, my friend," said Barrère, "sit down. Our colleague here informs us that you are sick of these mawkish royalists, and are willing to serve the Republic. Is it so, young man?"

"I have told M. Santerre—" said Denot. "Citizen Santerre, if you please," said Barrère; "or General Santerre, if you like it better. Monsieur and Monseigneur are a little out of fashion just at present on this side of the Loire."

"As they soon also shall be on the other," said Westerman.

"Well, I have told him," and Denot pointed to Santerre, "what it is I propose to do for you, and the terms on which I will do it."

"Terms indeed!" said Barrère. "The Republic is not accustomed to make terms with her servants. Come, tell us at once: are you a republican?"

Denot hesitated; not that he was ashamed to own himself a republican, but his blood was boiling with passion at the language and tone in which he was addressed, and yet he did not dare to shew his anger.

"Of course he is a republican," said Santerre, "or why would he come here? Take a glass of wine, friend Denot, and pluck up your courage," and Santerre passed the wine-bottle to him. "If you are true to us, you need not fear us."

"He must pronounce himself a republican," said Barrère, "or we cannot deal with him. Come, young man, can you put your mouth to so much inconvenience as to give us some slight inkling of your present political principles? All we know of you as yet is, that three weeks since you were a pestilent royalist, and a leader of royalists."

"I am a republican," said Denot.

"The Republic is made happy by your adhesion," said Barrère, bowing to him with mock solemnity across the table.

"What surety do you mean to offer us, citizen Denot," said Westerman, "that you are acting with us in good faith?"

"Do I not give you my life?" said Denot. "What other surety can I give, or can you require? What am I, or what are the royalists to gain by my proving false?"

"You say truly," answered Westerman; "you give us your life as a surety for your good faith to us. You may be assured that we will exact the penalty, if we have the slightest suspicion of foul play."

Denot made no answer, and he was questioned no further. The party soon after broke up, and the young deserter was handed over to the care of one of Santerre's sub-officers, with injunctions that he should be well and civilly treated, but that he should not be allowed to go abroad by himself; in fact, he was to be regarded as a prisoner.

"Do not be disheartened," said Santerre to him. "You can understand that under the circumstances, such precautions must be necessary. The day after tomorrow we start on our march, and you shall ride close to myself. When Clisson and Durbellière are in ashes, you shall be free to take your own course; in the meantime, no indignity shall be offered to you."

On the day named by Santerre, the whole republican army started from Angers, and commenced their march towards the Bocage. They proceeded on their route for several days without finding any enemy to contend with. They kept on the northern shore of the Loire till they reached Saumur, where they remained a couple of days, and employed themselves in punishing the inhabitants in whose houses the leaders of the Vendeans had been entertained. It was in vain that these poor men pleaded that they had not even opened their doors to the royalists till after the republican General had capitulated; that they had given nothing which they had been able to refuse, and, in fact, that they had only sold their goods and let their rooms to the Vendeans, when they could not possibly have declined to do so. Their arguments were of no avail; they were thrown into prison as criminals, and left for trial by the revolutionary tribunal.

Although Saumur had so lately been besieged and taken by the royalists, there was hardly a vestige of the conquerors left in it. Their attempt to place a garrison in the town had proved entirely a failure; the peasants who had undertaken the work had left the place by scores at a time, and before a fortnight was over, the commandant found himself with about twenty-five men, and consequently he marched back into La Vendée after his army. The town was perfectly tranquil when the republicans entered it, but the citizens were afflicted and out of spirits; their shops were closed, and their goods hidden; the bakers had no bread, the butchers no meat, and the grocers had neither oil nor sugar. They knew well what it was to sell their merchandise to the troops of the Convention, and to be paid for them by the government in assignats.

Many of those who had formed the former garrison of Saumur, were now with the army; men whom Chapeau and his assistants had shaven, men still bald, and smarting from the indignity to which they had been subjected. They wreaked their vengeance on the scene of their disgrace, and on all those who had in any way lent, or were suspected to have lent, their aid to its consummation. The furniture of the Town-hall was broken in pieces; the barbers' shops were ransacked, and their razors, brushes, and basins scattered through the street; nor was this the worst; one poor wretch was recognized who had himself wielded a razor on the occasion; he was dragged from his little shop by those on whom he had operated, and was swung up by his neck from a lamp-iron in the sight of his wife and children, who had followed his persecutors through the street. The poor woman pleaded on her knees for the life of her husband, as a wife can plead for the life of him whom she loves better than the whole world. She offered all her little wealth and her prayers; she supplicated them with tears and with blessings; she seized hold of the knees of the wretch who held the rope, and implored him by his remembrance of his father, by his regard for his own wife, his love for his own children, to spare to her the father of her infants; but she asked in vain; the man, feeling that his legs were encumbered, spurned the woman from him with his foot, and kept his hand tight upon the lamp-rope till the dying convulsions of the poor barber had ceased.

No notice was taken by the republican Generals of this murder; at any rate no punishment followed it; the next morning the army resumed its march, and left the town hated, cursed, feared, and yet obeyed. The people were now royalists in their hearts, but they did not dare to express their feelings even in whispers to each other, so frightful to them was the vengeance of the Republic. There was much policy in the fearful cruelty of the Jacobins; it was the only means by which they could have retained their power for a month.

The republicans marched on from Saumur to Montreuil, and from Montreuil to Thouars, and still found no one in arms to oppose them. Here they separated; a small party, headed by Santerre and Denot, penetrated at once from Thouars into the Bocage, and made for the château of Durbellière. It was believed that both de Lescure and Larochejaquelin were there, and Santerre expected that by hurrying across the country with a small force, he would be able to take them both and burn the château, and afterwards rejoin Westerman at Chatillon. Barrère, whose duties were not strictly those of a soldier, had not accompanied the army beyond Saumur. Westerman and the main body of the army still continued southward till they reached Parthenay, from which place it was his intention to proceed through the revolted district, burning every village; utterly destroying the towns which had not proved themselves devoted to the Republic, and slaughtering the peasants, their wives, and children wherever he could find them.

The Vendeans had not yet sufficiently matured their plans to enable them to encounter successfully the republican army. The death of Cathelineau had

had a great effect upon the peasants: those who were with him had returned home in sorrow and despair, and this feeling was general, even among those who had not been at Nantes. De Lescure and Henri, however, had not despaired; after having seen the body of his General consigned to the dust, Henri had returned to Clisson, and he and his cousin were again busy in raising recruits, or rather in collecting their men, when they heard that Westerman, with an enormous army, was marching into Parthenay, and that it was his intention to proceed from thence into the Bocage, by way of Amaillou and Bressuire.

They had hardly heard this report, when the little village of Amaillou was on fire; it was the first place that was utterly burnt down, and laid in ashes by the republicans; not a house was left standing, or hardly the ruined wall of a house. The church itself was set on fire and burnt, with its pictures, its altars, and all its sacred treasures; the peasants ran from the ruins, carrying with them their wives and children, the old, the crippled, and infirm: hundreds were left dead and dying among the smoking ashes. This feat having been accomplished, Westerman continued on towards Bressuire, intending to burn the château at Clisson, as he passed it on his way.

The district between Amaillou and Bressuire is thickly studded with trees. The roads, or rather lanes, are all lined by avenues of limes and beeches. The fields are small, and surrounded by lofty hedges, which are also, in a great measure, composed of large trees, and the whole country in July, when the foliage is at the thickest, has almost the aspect of one continued forest.

Westerman had obtained guides to show him the road to Clisson. It was about six o'clock in the evening when the advanced portion of his army, consisting of three thousand men, had proceeded about a league from Amaillou. He was himself riding nearly at the front of the column, talking to his aide-de-camp and one of the guides, when he was startled by hearing a noise as of disturbed branches in the hedge, only a few feet in advance of the spot in which he was standing; he had not, however, time to give an order, or speak a word on the subject, before a long sudden gleam of fire flashed before his eyes; it was so near to him that it almost blinded him: a cannon had been fired off close to his face, and it was easy to track the fatal course of the ball; it had been directed right along the road, and was glutted with carnage before its strength was spent.

Nor did the cannon shot come alone: a fearful fire from about five hundred muskets was poured from the hedge on either side, directly into the road: the assailants were within a few feet of their enemy at the moment they were firing, and every shot took effect. Out of the four hundred men who headed the column, above half were killed, or so badly wounded as to be incapable of motion. The narrow lane, for it was no more than a lane, was nearly blocked up with carcases. Westerman, who was possessed of a courage that was never shaken, was nevertheless so thunderstruck, that he knew not what orders to give. The republicans at the head of the column, who had not themselves been struck, fired their fusils into the hedges, but their fire did no injury; it was all lost among the leaves, for the men who had attacked them were kneeling on their knees or lying on their bellies, and in the confusion which they had occasioned, were reloading their muskets.

The guide and the aide-de-camp to whom Westerman was speaking, had both fallen, and the horse upon which he himself was riding was so badly wounded, as to be unmanageable. He got off, and ran along under the hedge till he met an officer. "Give me your horse, Gerard," said he; "but no, stay where you are, gallop back, and tell Bourbotte to bring up the men. Quick, mind—so quick, that they can neither see nor hear what has happened. Bid him force his way through the hedge to the right, when he gets to the corner."

The young officer turned quickly to obey the command of his General, and had already put his spur to the horse's flank, when another broad flash of light streamed through the hedge on the left, and the horseman and horse fell to the ground, and were mingled with a heap of wounded and dying. Young Gerard did not live long enough to be conscious of the blow which killed him. Another volley of musketry followed the cannon shot, and hardly left a man standing of those who had been the foremost. The attack had taken place so quickly, that the Vendeans had not yet had time to load again; but one of two cannons had been kept as a reserve, and about a hundred muskets had not been fired till de Lescure gave the word of command. The first attack was made under the direction of Henri Larochejaquelin.

Westerman was standing between the hedge and the mounted officer, when the latter fell with his horse, and the blood from the poor animal nearly covered him from head to foot. "Into the field, my men," said he to those who were near enough to hear him; "follow me through the hedge," and with a considerable effort he forced his way through the underwood, and he was followed and accompanied by all those who were still standing near him; but when he got there, not one of the Vendeans was to be seen; there were traces enough of them in the grass, and among the broken boughs, but the men had retreated after the first fire, and were now again lying in ambush behind the next hedge.

In about five minutes, there were two or three hundred republicans in the fields to the right of the road, for the army was still advancing; but they did not know where to go or what to do. They were looking about for an enemy, and in dread of being fired on, not only from the hedges, but even out of the trees. Westerman, however, got the men formed into some kind of order, and bid them advance; they did so, and on coming near to the second hedge, received another murderous fire, for every royalist had now had time to reload.

The combat continued for some time, for the republicans contrived to make their way into the second field; but the royalists again sheltered themselves behind the further hedge, and repeated their fire from their lurking-place. It was in vain that the republicans fired into the hedges; their shot either passed over the heads of the Vendeans, or were lost among the roots and trunks of the trees. Every one of the royalists, on the other hand fired, with a clear aim, and almost invariably with deadly effect. Westerman felt that it would be useless to pursue them; his soldiers, moreover, were already flying without orders. He had not the least idea what was the number of the enemy with whom he was engaged, what was their means of carrying on the battle, or on what side of him the greater number of them were situated; he therefore determined to retreat, and led back the whole of his army over the still burning ashes of the miserable village which he had destroyed that morning. The greater portion of the men were forced to go back as far as Parthenay, but he himself remained with a small detachment in the neighbourhood of Amaillou. He was determined, if possible, to be revenged that same night for the defeat which he had experienced.

The two cousins were at Clisson when they first heard that Westerman was actually on his road towards Bressuire, and they had lost no time in taking the best measures in their power to stop his progress, but they had not even hoped that their effort would have been so successful as it proved. The tocsin had been rung in the three neighbouring parishes, and about seven hundred men had been collected. These men all possessed muskets, but they themselves had no ammunition, and the whole supply which could be found in the district, including the little depot at Clisson, only sufficed to give the men some three and some four rounds each. When Westerman, with his ten thousand men, retreated from about seven hundred, the royalists had not one charge of powder to three muskets among them.

About ten in the evening Henri and de Lescure returned on foot from the battle to the château of Clisson. Henri still had the red scarf round his neck and waist, and stuck in the latter he had three or four pistols, of various sizes, all of which had been used in the recent engagement. On his shoulder he held a rifle, which he carried like a fowling-piece, and he walked home with the air and look of a man returning from a day's sport, well contented with the execution he had done.

Not so de Lescure: he was thoughtful, if not sad; and though he would not, either by a tone or a look, rebuke the gaiety of his companion, it was very evident that he did not share it. The peasants returned along the road, hurrying to their homes, shouting with glee and full of triumph. As they passed their leaders, they cheered the darling heroes who had led them to another victory, and would, had they been allowed to do so, have carried them home upon their shoulders. They had no thoughts of any further battle, or of future bloodshed and misery. They had been victorious over the blues, and that was sufficient for the present evening. They were able to return home and tell their wives and sweethearts of their triumph, and that without any drawback from friends lost or wounded. In all their contests, the Vendeans had never been victorious with so few calamities to themselves.

"I saw Westerman himself," said Henri to his friend. "I am sure I did, and what's more I was within pistol shot of him, but I hadn't a pistol loaded at the moment, or I would have put an end to his career. I wonder how he likes his reception in the Bocage."

"He is not the man to be easily daunted," said de Lescure. "You'll find it will not be long before he advances again. If he were to march to Bressuire tomorrow, what is to stop him?"

"Why not stop him tomorrow as we have done today?" said Henri.

"The men are all gone home," said the other.

"They will all assemble again tomorrow," said Henri; "we have only to have the bells rung at seven o'clock, or six, or five, or when you will, and you will find that every man will be ready for another day's work, and that without a murmur."

"And will they bring powder with them, Henri?"

"Why, we are rather short off for powder," said he. "Our affair tonight was all very well, for the enemy lost an immense number, and we lost none; but yet it was unsatisfactory, for the fellows have left nothing behind them. I'll tell you what, Charles, we ought to follow them to Parthenay."

"Impossible," said de Lescure.

"Why impossible, Charles? Why is Parthenay, which is not better fortified than Clisson, be more unassailable than Saumur, where everything appeared to be against us?"

"We were all together then, and now we are scattered. I'll tell you what, Henri," he continued, after walking on silent for a few steps. "I'll tell you what we must do: we must leave this district altogether; we must leave it to be ravaged by fire and sword; we must leave it to Westerman, to wreak his vengeance on it, and go to Chatillon, taking with us every armed man that will follow us. We cannot stand an invasion here in the south."

"Heavens, Charles! what do you mean? Will you not stay to protect the poor wretches who are so ready to fight for us?"

"We can protect no one by staying here. We cannot hope to contend single-handed with such an army as that which was but just now advancing to Bressuire. We can have given them a check, but you know we cannot repeat the effort of this evening. D'Elbée and Stofflet are at Chatillon; your own followers are all in that vicinity. When there, we can communicate with Bonchamps and Charette. We must go to Chatillon."

"And your wife, Charles, and Marie! you will not leave them in the château?"

"If your father and Agatha will receive them, they shall go to Durbellière."

"There you are right," said Henri. "Whatever may be the danger, let us have them together; we shall then at any rate be able to feel that we know the point which is to be defended most closely."

"We will start tomorrow, Henri; tomorrow evening. May God grant that that may be time enough. Westerman cannot collect his men so as to force a march as far as Clisson tomorrow; but before a week is over, I know that the château will be a ruin."

"Will you leave the furniture?" said Henri.

"Yes," answered de Lescure; "furniture, horses, cattle, corn—everything but my wife and child. Let everything go: am I not giving it to my King?"

CHAPTER VIII.
CLISSON.

De Lescure had calculated wrongly with regard to Westerman's return. It was true that he could not have again put his ten thousand men in marching order, and have returned with his whole force the next day from Bressuire as far as Clisson, but Westerman himself did not go back beyond Amaillou, and he detained there with him a small detachment of mounted men, whom he had commanded at Valmy, and whom he well knew. He kept no officers but one cornet and two sergeants, and with this small force he determined, if possible, to effect that night what his army of ten thousand men had so signally failed in accomplishing.

About half a mile from Amaillou there was a large château, the owner of which had emigrated; it had been left to the care of two or three servants, who had deserted it on the approach of the republican army, and when Westerman and his small troop rode up to the front gate, they found no one either to admit them or to dispute their entrance. Here he bivouacked for an hour or two, and matured his project, which, as yet, he had communicated to no one.

He had entrusted the retreat of the army to General Bourbotte, who, in spite of their quarrel at Angers, was serving with him; and without staying even to ascertain what was the amount of loss he had sustained, or to see whether the enemy would harass the army as it retreated, he had separated from it at Amaillou, and reached the château about ten o'clock in the evening. He had with him a couple of guides, who knew the country well, and accompanied by these, he resolved to attack Clisson that night, to burn the château of M. de Lescure, and, if possible, to carry back with him to Bressuire the next morning the two Vendean chiefs, whom he knew were staying there.

Westerman understood enough of the tactics of the Vendeans to know that this was practicable, and he had the quick wit and ready hand to conceive the plan, and put it in practice: he knew that the peasants would not remain in barracks, or even assembled together during the night, if they were near enough to their own homes to reach them; he knew that they would spend the remainder of their long summer evening in drinking, dancing, and rejoicing, and that they would then sleep as though no enemy were within a hundred miles of them; he knew that nothing could induce them to take on themselves the duties of sentinels, and that there would, in all probability, be but little to oppose him in attacking Clisson that night.

Westerman first had the horses fed, and having then refreshed his men with meat, wine, and brandy, he started at two o'clock. He was distant from Clisson about three leagues, according to the measurement of the country, or a little better than seven miles. There had hardly been any darkness during the night, and as he and his troopers sallied out of the château-yard, the dawn was just breaking in the East.

"Never mind," said he to the young cornet who rode by his side; "the light will not hurt us, for we will make them hear us before they see us. We will be back as far as this before thirty men in the parish are awake. It will be best for them who sleep soundest."

"Except for those in the château, General," said the cornet: "those who sleep there will wake to a warm breakfast."

"They will never eat breakfast more, I believe and trust," said Westerman; "for I do not think that we shall be able to take the brigands alive. Their women, however, may receive some of our rough republican hospitality at Bressuire. You had better prepare your prettiest bow and your softest words, for this sister of de Lescure is, they say, a real beauty. She shall ride to Bressuire before you on your saddle-cloth, if you choose to load your arms with such a burden; but don't grow too fond of her kisses, for though she were a second Venus, the guillotine must have the disposal of her."

The cornet made no answer, but his young heart turned sick at the brutality of his companion. His breast had glowed with republican zeal at the prospect of a night attack on the two most distinguished of the royalist chiefs. The excitement of the quick ride through the night-air, the smallness of the party, the importance of the undertaking, the probable danger, and the uncertainty, had all seemed to him delightful; and the idea of rescuing a beautiful girl from the flames was more delightful than all; but the coarseness and cruelty of his General had destroyed the romance, and dissipated the illusion. He felt that he could not offer a woman his protection, that he might carry her to a scaffold.

At about two, Westerman started on his expedition. His men carried their sabres, still sheathed, in their hands, to prevent the noise which they would have made rattling against their saddles; but still their journey through the country was anything but quiet. They only rode two abreast, as the roads were too narrow to admit of more. Westerman himself and one of the guides headed the column, and the young cornet and veteran sergeant closed the rear. They went at a fast trot, and the noise of their horses' hoofs sounded loudly on the hard parched ground. In spite of their precautions, their sabres rattled, and the curbs on their bridles jingled; and the absence of all other noises made Westerman fear that their approach must be audible, even through the soundness of a peasant's sleep.

On they rode, and as they drew near to the château, Westerman put spurs to his horse, and changed his trot into a gallop; his troop of course followed his example, and as they came to the end of their journey they abandoned all precautions; each man dropped his scabbard to his side, and drew the blade; each man put his hand to his holster, and transferred his pistol to his belt, for he did not know how soon he might have to leave his saddle; each man drew the brazen clasps of his helmet tight beneath his chin, and prepared himself for action.

"These are the Clisson woods," said the guide, almost out of breath with the quickness of his motion.

"How infernally dark they make it," said Westerman, speaking to himself. "We had light enough till we got here."

"And there are the gates," said the guide. "That first entrance which is open, goes to the back of the house; a little beyond, there is another, which leads to the front; there you will find a gate, but it is merely closed with a latch."

"Craucher," said Westerman, speaking to the second sergeant, who was riding immediately behind him, "stand at the corner, and bid the men follow me at a quick trot—all of them, mind; tell Cornet Leroy that I have changed my mind," and Westerman, followed by his troop, dashed up the narrow avenue which led through the wood to the back of the house.

The château of Clisson was surrounded by large woods, through which countless paths and little roads were made in every direction for the convenience of the woodmen, and the small tumbrils which were used for bringing out the timber and faggots. These woods came close up to the farm-yard of the château, which was again divided from the house by large walled gardens, into which the back windows opened. The road up which Westerman had ridden led under the garden-wall to the farm-yard, but another road from the front, running along the gable-end of the house, communicated with it. The door used by the servants was at the side of the château, and consequently the readiest way from the public road to the servants' door, was that by which Westerman had, at the last moment, determined to force an entrance into the château.

He trotted up till he faced the garden-wall, and then turned short round to the house, and as he rode close up under the gable-end, he gave Sergeant Craucher directions to take three men and force the door; but he and the sergeant soon saw that this trouble was spared them, for the door stood wide open before them.

We will now go back to the inhabitants of the château. De Lescure and Henri had returned thither about eleven o'clock, and although their safe return, and account of the evening's victorious engagement for a while quieted the anxious fears of Marie and Madame de Lescure, those ladies by no means felt inclined to rest quietly as though all danger were removed from their pillows. They were in a dreadful alarm at the nearness of the republicans; they knew well that their ruthless enemies spared none that fell into their hands. I should belie these heroines if I said that they feared more for themselves than for those they loved so dearly, but they were not accustomed yet to the close vicinity of danger; and when they learned that a battle had been lost and won that evening, within a mile or two, in the very next parish to that in which they lived, they looked at each other, and trembling asked what next was to be done.

"You must not leave us, Charles, you must not leave us again," said Madame de Lescure to her husband; "indeed you must not leave us here." She paused a moment, and then added, with an accent of horror which she could not control, "What would become of us if these men came upon us when you were away?"

"Wherever you go, let us go with you," said Marie, forgetting in her excitement her usual maidenly reserve, and laying her little hand as she spoke upon her lover's arm; then blushing, she withdrew it, and turned to her brother.

"Do not turn from him, Marie," said her sister-in-law. "You will soon want his strong arm, and his kind, loving heart."

"Charles will not desert me, Victorine," said Marie, blushing now more beautifully than ever, for though she knew that Henri loved her, he had never absolutely told her so. "Though you are his dearest care, he will always have a hand to stretch to his poor Marie."

Before she had finished speaking, Henri held her close in his embrace. It was perhaps hardly a fitting time for him to make an avowal of his love; but lovers cannot always choose the most proper season for their confessions. He was still hot from the battle which he had fought; his hands were still black with powder; the well-known red scarf was still twisted round his belt, and held within its folds his armament of pistols. His fair, long hair was uncombed, and even entangled with his exertions. His large boots were covered with dust, and all his clothes were stained and soiled with the grass and weeds through which he had that night dragged himself more than once, in order to place himself within pistol-shot of his enemies; and yet, soiled and hot as he was, fatigued with one battle, and meditating preparations for another, there, in the presence of de Lescure and his wife, he clasped Marie to his manly heart, and swore to her that his chief anxiety as long as the war lasted, should be to screen her from all harm, and that his fondest care through his whole life should be to protect her and make her happy.

Unusual circumstances and extraordinary excitement often cause the customary rules and practices of life to be abandoned; and so it was now.

Marie received the love that was offered her, frankly, affectionately, and with her whole heart. She owned to her lover how well and truly she had loved him, and there, before her brother and his wife, plighted to him her troth, and promised to him then the obedience and love, which she soon hoped to owe him as his wife. Such declarations are usually made in private, but the friends now assembled had no secrets from each other, and they all felt that strange times made strange scenes necessary.

They then arranged their plans for the morrow. The day had already been an eventful one, but they little dreamed how much more was to be done before the morrow's sun was in the heavens; and yet even then they did not separate for the night: luckily for them all, they determined that too much was to be done to allow them yet to retire to rest.

It was resolved that on the following day they should leave Clisson for Durbellière, and hand over the château and all it contained—the farm and all its well-filled granaries, the cattle and agricultural wealth of the estate, to the fire and plunder of the republicans. The plate, however, they thought they could save, as well as the ladies' jewels and clothes, and other precious things which might be quickly packed and easily moved. They went to work at once to fill their trunks and baskets; and as the means of conveyance were then slow, de Lescure went out into the stables, and had the waggon prepared at once, and ordered that the oxen which were to draw it should be ready to start at three o'clock, in order that the load, if possible, might reach Durbellière the same night.

Master and mistress, servants and guests, worked hard, and at about two o'clock, the hour at which Westerman and his troop were starting for their quick ride, they had completed their task.

"You have killed yourself, dearest love," said Henri, pressing his arm round Marie's waist.

"Oh, no!" said she, smiling, but still so weary that she could hardly have stood unless he had held her; "I have not fought and conquered ten thousand republicans; but I don't know how you must feel."

Henri, however, insisted that she should go to bed and she, delighted to show her first act of obedience to his will, did as he desired her. She was soon undressed; she offered her prayers to heaven for her brother and sister-in-law, but with a stronger fervour for the dear companion and protector to whom she had sworn to devote her life, and then she laid her head upon her pillow, intending to think over her happiness; a few moments, however, were sufficient to change her half fearful thoughts of love and danger into blessed dreams of love and happiness. Poor girl! she did not long enjoy her happy rest.

De Lescure and Henri determined to remain up till the departure of the waggon. Madame de Lescure went up to her room, and the two gentlemen went down towards the farmyard. The waggon stood at the kitchen-door already packed, and the two servants were bringing the oxen down the road to yoke them to it.

"Go out at the front gate, François, and by the church at Terves; it is the better road. You will remain a couple of hours in Bressuire. We shall overtake you before you reach Beaulieu."

The servant acknowledged his master's commands, and fastened the last rope which bound the oxen to their burden. He spoke to his beasts, and accompanied his word with a goad from a pointed stick he held in his hand, when his farther progress was stopped by Henri's calling from a little distance down the road.

"Stop, François, stop!" said he. "Charles, come here; some one is coming hither at the top of his speed. Don't you hear the noise of hoofs upon the road?"

De Lescure ran to him, and kneeling down, put his ear to the ground. "It's a donkey or a mule," said he; "it is not a horse's foot."

"Come down the avenue," said Henri, "and let us see who it is. Whether mule or horse, the beast is going at his full speed."

"Better stay where we are," said de Lescure. "If he be coming to us, his news will reach the house quicker than by our going to meet him."

The rider grew nearer and nearer, and in a few moments turned up the road leading to the back of the house. The steps of the tired brute became slower as he trotted up the avenue, although the sound of a cudgel on his ribs were plainly audible. Henri and de Lescure were standing under the garden wall, and as the animal drew near them, they saw it was a jaded donkey, ridden by a peasant girl.

"Fly, for the sake of God!" said the girl, even before she dismounted from the donkey; "fly for the sake of the blessed Virgin. Take the ladies from the château, or they will be burnt—be burnt—be burnt!"

As she screamed the last words she slipped from the donkey, and almost fainted with the exertion she had undergone. She was the daughter of one of M. de Lescure's servants, and had been sent from Clisson into service at the château, from whence Westerman started on his expedition. When the republicans made their appearance there, she had fled with the other servants, but she had hung about the house, and about an hour and a half before Westerman left the place she learnt, through some of the soldiers, his intention of attacking Clisson that night.

"Who is coming to burn us, Marian?" said de Lescure, endeavouring by his own assumed coolness to enable her to collect her thoughts and power of speech.

"The blues—the blues!" screamed the girl. "They had all but overtaken me when I got to the short cut through the wood. There they are, there they are," and the noise of the advancing troop was distinctly audible through the stillness of the night.

The poor girl was quite exhausted, and fell to the ground fainting. De Lescure and Henri had both stood still for a moment, after having been made to comprehend that an immediate attack was about to be made on the château, but it was only for a moment.

"We must carry them through the wood, Charles," said Henri, whispering. "It is our only chance."

"True—true," said de Lescure. "Turn the oxen, Francois, turn them back through the yard into the farm-road, and then keep to the left into the wood. We will meet you at the seven limes."

"Take Victorine out through the garden," said Henri to his cousin, who was now hurrying into the house, "and through the iron gate. I saw the other day that the key was in it, and we can turn it. I tried it myself. I will bring Marie after you."

Henri stayed a moment to assist in turning the cumbrous waggon, and ran back to open the farm gates.

"Close the gates after you, Francois," said he, "and put the tressels close against them. If you lose a minute in doing it, you will gain five in delaying these devils. If you hear them following you in the wood-road, draw the waggon across the track and leave it."

He was only delayed two minutes by going back to the yard gates, but those two minutes were nearly fatal to him and Marie. Marian also delayed him again as he returned to the house.

"Where am I to go, M. Henri," said she; "what am I to do? they will be sure to kill me, for they saw me at Amaillou, and will know that I gave the warning."

"Hide yourself, my girl," said Henri: "hide yourself, but not in the house, for that will soon be a mass of ruins. Hide yourself in the woods; there cannot be many of these devils here, and they will not remain long."

He hurried into the house as he ceased speaking, and at the moment he did so Westerman and his thirty men turned the corner of the avenue. He rushed from the back door through the passages of the château into the hall, where he seized hold of a large cloak belonging to de Lescure, which he threw over his shoulder as he ran up stairs. On the stairs he met his cousin, with Madame de Lescure and the nurse and child.

"Haste, Henri, for God's sake, haste," said she; "I heard the tramp of their horses through my open window."

De Lescure had opened the summer door leading into the garden as he came up stairs, to have it ready for his exit, and he, and those under his care, escaped through it into the garden.

"Shut the garden door," roared Henri to him from the top of the staircase. "Shut the door, whatever you do." De Lescure could not understand his object, but he trusted his cousin, and closed the door as he passed through it. Henri had perceived that it would be impossible for him to regain the hall, and had resolved to jump from the window of the staircase into the garden, with his precious burden in his arms. He foresaw that if the door were left open, pursuit through it would be both inevitable and fatal.

Marie's room was close to the top of the stairs, and her lover did not use much ceremony in opening the door. In going to and from his wife's chamber, de Lescure had not passed it, and therefore the innocent girl slept soundly till Henri's sudden entrance roused her from her dreams.

"Who's that—who's that," said she, raising her head upon her pillow. The window curtains of the room were hardly closed, and she recognised immediately Henri's tall figure, and singular costume. "Oh! Henri, what has happened? what brings you here?"

"Rise, dearest, we must fly," said he: "we have not a moment—we fear the blues are coming." He dreaded that she would have lost all power of motion, had he told her that they were already beneath the windows.

"Haven't I time to dress?" said she; "I won't be a moment—not one minute."

"No, darling," answered he, raising her from the bed, as though she were an infant, and folding her in her brother's cloak. "We haven't one instant to throw away. Remember who has you in his arms: remember that it is I, your own Henri, who am pressing you to my heart." He took her up from the bed in his left arm, and with his right hand arraigned the cloak around her person, and carrying her out into the passage, hurried to the window which he had left open.

This window looked from the opposite end of the house to that at which Westerman found the open door. It was on the first landing of the staircase, and was therefore distant from the ground but little more than half the height of the ground floor, but a hard gravel path ran immediately under it; and though the leap was one which few young men might much hesitate to take with empty arms, it was perilous with such a burden as Henri had to carry. He however did not think twice about it, and would have considered himself and his charge nearly safe could he have reached the window unmolested, but that he was not allowed to do.

As he began to descend the stairs the loud noise of the troopers' boots, and the quick voice of Westerman giving his commands in the hall, told him at once that the house was already occupied by the blues. Even then, at that awful moment, he rejoiced at his precaution in having desired de Lescure to close the garden door. He took a large horse pistol from his belt, and holding it by the barrel, jumped down three stairs at a time, and already had his foot on the sill of the open window, when serjeant Craucher, who had been the first of the blues to enter the house, rushing up the stairs, succeeded in getting hold of the cloak which covered Marie. He pulled it from off her neck and shoulders, and her beautiful dark clustering curls fell down over Henri's shoulder. Her pale face, and white neck and bosom were exposed: her eyes were fast closed, as though she expected instant death, but both her arms were tightly fastened round her lover.

Craucher stumbled in his hurry in rushing up the stairs, but he still held fast to the collar of the cloak.

"I must stop your further journey, my pretty dear," said he: "the night air is not good for you—by heavens it's the red—"

He never finished his speech, or attempted to make another. On entering the back door he had struck his brazen head-piece against the lintel; the shock had broken the clasp, and his head was consequently bare. As he pulled at the cloak, Henri raised his right arm powerfully, and drove the butt-end of the pistol which he held, right through his skull, and scattered his brains upon the staircase. The grasp of the dying man was so firm that he could not extricate the cloak from his fingers. He saw that his only chance of escape was to relinquish it; he did so, and as he leapt from the window to the ground, poor Marie had nothing round her but her slight night dress.

Henri stumbled as he came to the hard gravel, but still he allowed no portion of Marie's body to touch the ground. He recovered himself in a moment, and made for the iron gate leading from the garden to the wood, through which de Lescure and his wife had escaped.

As Henri leapt from the window Westerman's eye had caught sight of the red scarf, and he knew that it was Larochejaquelin who was escaping. He rushed himself to the window, though, had he known it, he might have gone into the garden through the door, which was close at his hand. He leapt on the path, and was immediately on Henri's track. It was about three hundred yards from the house to the iron gate, and when Westerman was again on his feet, Henri had covered two thirds of the distance.

Run now, Henri, run your best, for the load you carry is heavy, and the German is strong and light of foot; his pistols, too, are loaded, and he well knows how to use them; but yours are empty, and you will not find another bare skull opposed to your heavy right hand; run, dear friend, and loving cousin; run faster with that precious trembling burden of yours, or all you have yet done, will have been done in vain.

But what avails his running: he did run fast and well, laden as he was, and fatigued with no ordinary day's work: he gained the gate, while as yet his pursuer was above a hundred yards behind him; but of what avail would that be, if he were obliged to leave the passage free for his enemy: it was impossible that he should continue to hold his ground, while he carried the fainting girl in his arms. It was then that that wonderful presence of mind, in the midst of the most urgent danger, of which Henri Larochejaquelin showed so many instances during war, stood him in stead, and saved two lives, when salvation seemed impossible.

In wandering about the place some days before, he had passed through this gate, and observing that the key stood in the lock, he had idly turned it backwards and forwards, locking and relocking the gate without an object; he had then observed that though the key worked easily, there was something wrong about the wards which prevented him from drawing it out after the lock was turned. The gate was made of iron bars, which were far enough asunder to allow of his hand and arm being passed through, so that when outside the gate he could then turn the key which was on the inside.

All these particulars he remembered in that moment of agony, and resolved what he would do to overcome the difficulties which they threw in his way. Having passed through the gate, he dropped his now senseless companion beneath the shelter of the wall, and passing his hands through the bars, turned the key and locked it. He then took out a short hunting-knife which he wore, and passing that also through the bars of the gate, he inserted it in the handle of the key, and then wrenching it round with all his force, broke the key in the wards: all the smiths in Poitou could not have locked the gate closer, or made it more impossible to open it.

Though the feat is tedious to explain, it did not take half a minute in performance; but still it allowed Westerman to come within pistol shot of him before he could get beneath the shelter of the wall. The German, however, in his anxiety to get through the gate, omitted to fire, though he had the pistol in his hand; he seized hold of the iron bars and shook them impotently: strong as he was, the gate was much too firm to be moved by his strength; the wall was twelve feet high, and utterly beyond his power to scale without a ladder.

He felt that he was foiled, and returned to the château to wreak his vengeance upon the inhabitants who might be left there, and on the furniture and walls of the house itself.

Henri pursued his way unopposed, and at the appointed spot, a little greensward surrounded by seven lime trees, he found his cousin and the rest of the party waiting for him, as well as François with the waggon.

"Is she safe—is she alive?" asked Madame de Lescure, almost frantic with grief and fear.

"She is alive, and I believe unhurt," said Henri; "but I fear she is senseless. She is quite undressed, too, as I was obliged to leave the cloak in which I had covered her, in the dying grasp of a trooper whom I killed." He gently laid her down, with her head in the lap of her kind sister, and then turned his back upon the party, that he might not gaze on the fair bosom, which was all exposed, and the naked limbs, which her dishevelled night dress did not suffice to cover.

Madame de Lescure and her nurse hastened to strip themselves of a portion of their clothes; it had been lucky that neither of them were undressed at the time of the attack, and though they were ill-prepared for a long journey, having neither caps nor strong shoes, nor shawls of any kind, yet they contrived between them to dress poor Marie decently. The nurse gave her shoes and stockings, declaring that going barefoot would not trouble her the least, and before many minutes had been wasted, they were again ready to proceed.

De Lescure and Henri had not lost these precious moments: the waggon was again put into motion: the three men carefully armed themselves: they loaded their pistols, for among the goods they were taking away, was the little remnant of gunpowder which was left among them: they decided that on hearing the first sound of pursuit, they would leave the waggon, and betake themselves to the thickest part of the woods; but both de Lescure and Henri were of opinion that they would not be followed.

"There cannot be many of them," said Henri, "and what there are, are all mounted. They are the German hussars; I know them by their brazen helmets. They won't attempt to follow us through the woods."

"They would have been after us before now had they intended doing so," said de Lescure. "The way was clear for them through the farm-yard, François, was it not?"

"No, Monseigneur," said François. "It was anything but clear. I turned the big bull out of his stall into the yard as I came out, and closed the gate behind me: he would gore a dozen of them before they could make their way through."

Whether the pursuit was arrested by the bull, or prevented by any other cause, the fugitives were not interrupted. They walked wearily and painfully, but yet patiently, and without a complaint above a league, before the women ventured to get upon the waggon. They then got out upon the road to Bressuire, at no great distance from that town, and on reaching Bressuire they got refreshment and proper clothes, and hired a voiture for the remainder of their journey.

Marie had hardly spoken from the moment when Henri dragged her from her bed, to that in which he helped her in the waggon; but after she had been sitting for a while, she indulged in a flood of tears, which she had restrained as long as she felt that her life depended on her exertions, and then calling Henri to her side, she thanked him, as she so well knew how to do, for all he had done for her.

"You have saved my life, dearest, now," said she, "and ten times more than my life; but I will not say that I love you better than I did before. Had I not known that it was your arms which were around me, I must have died when that horrid countenance glared over me on the stairs. Have I dreamt since, or was I really looking upon that face, when the agony of death came across it?" And as she asked the question, she closed her eyes, and her whole body trembled violently.

"I will tell you all that happened another time, love," said he; "we will not talk of these things now. A day or two at Durbellière will restore you to your spirits, and then we will rejoice over our escape."

They got into a voiture at Bressuire, and from thence continued their journey in something more like comfort, while Francois with the waggon followed them; but the two ladies were not destined to reach Durbellière that night. When they were about half-way between Bressuire and the château, they were met by a man on horseback, who was already on his way to Clisson. It was Jean Stein, who was hurrying as fast as his beast could carry him from Durbellière to M. Larochejaquelin; but instead of explaining now what was the purport of his errand, we will return to Clisson, and see how Westerman finished there the task he had undertaken.

When he found himself foiled at the gate, he returned as quickly as possible to the house. His men had already ransacked every room, and in their anxiety to find the more distinguished inhabitants of the château, allowed the domestics to escape; but few of them had been in bed, and even they were overlooked in the anxiety of the troopers to find M. de Lescure. They did not dream that any warning could have been given to the château, nor could they conceive it possible that at three o'clock in the morning the royalists should have been up, and ready for instant flight. It was not till nearly five that they satisfied themselves that neither de Lescure nor his wife, nor any of his family were in the house; and then, at the command of their General, they commenced the work of destruction.

The troopers got hay and straw from the farm-yard (not without some opposition from the loose bull,) and piled them in every room in the château; they then took the furniture, beds, curtains, wearing apparel, and every article of value they could find, and placed them in heaps, in such a way as to render them an immediate prey to the flames. They did the same to the barns and granaries, in which there were large stores of corn, and also to the stables, in which stood the horses and cattle; the bull, which François had loosened, was the only animal about the place that did not perish. Having systematically prepared the château and out-houses for a huge bonfire, they put a light to the straw in various places, and re-mounting their horses, stood around it till they saw that no efforts which the peasants might use could extinguish the flames. Westerman then gave the word of command for their return; they started at a sharp trot, and he did not allow them to slacken their pace till he had again passed the ruins of the little village of Amaillou.

While the troopers were thus preparing to set the château in a blaze, the General himself was not idle; he seated himself in the salon, and having had pen, ink, and paper brought to him, he wrote the following despatch to the President of the Convention, in which, it will be observed, he studiously omitted all mention of the defeat which he had incurred between Amaillou and Clisson, and the retreat which his army had been forced to make. The date is given in the denomination which will be intelligible to the reader, as the Fructidors and the Messidors, Brumaires and Nivoses, which had then been adopted by the republicans, now convey no very defined idea to people, who have not yet scrupled to call the months by their old aristocratic names, or to count the year from their Saviour's birth.

"Château of Clisson, July 1798.

"Citizen President,

"I have the honour to acquaint you that I have already succeeded in carrying the arms of the Convention as far as the residence of the most powerful of the rebel leaders. As I am writing, my men are preparing to set fire to this den of aristocratic infamy, and within an hour the stronghold of the redoubted de Lescure will be level with the ground.

"This wretched country is so crowded with ravines and rocks, and the roads are so narrow, so deep, and so bad, that I have been forced to make my way hither with a small detachment of thirty men only, but I have found that sufficient to drive the tiger from his lair. He, and the other rebel leader, Larochejaquelin, have fled into the woods, without either money, arms, or even clothing; and I doubt not soon to be able to inform the Convention that, at any rate, they can never again put themselves at the head of a rebellious army.

"Citizen President, deign to receive from my hands the only trophies which I have deemed myself justified in rescuing from the flames which are about to consume this accursed château. I enclose the will and a miniature portrait of the aristocrat, de Lescure.

"I pray you to receive, and to make acceptable to the Convention, the most distinguished,

"&c. &c. &c.

"WESTERMAN."

CHAPTER IX.
SANTERRE.

Santerre and Adolphe Denot left the main army at Thouars, and made their way to Argenton with about four thousand men. From thence, Durbellière was distant about four leagues; and Santerre lost no time in making his preparations for destroying that château, as Westerman was at the same moment doing at Clisson. Generally speaking, the people of the towns, even in La Vendée sided with the republicans; but the people of Argenton were supposed to be royalists, and Santerre therefore gave positive orders that every house in it should be destroyed. He did not, however, himself want to see the horrid work done, but hurried on to Durbellière, that he might, if possible, surprise the Vendean chiefs, whom he believed to be staying there. About one hundred and fifty men followed him, and the remainder of the army was to march on to Bressuire, as soon as Argenton was in ashes.

Santerre, since he had left the company of the other Generals at Thouars, had become more familiar and confidential with Denot, and rode side by side with him from Argenton, talking freely about the manners of the country, and the hopes of the royalists, till he succeeded in getting the traitor into good humour, and obtaining from him something like a correct idea of the state of the country.

"And this is the parish of St. Aubin?" said Santerre, as they drew near to Durbellière.

"Yes," said Denot, "this is the parish of St. Aubin; and the estate of the Larochejaquelins."

"And they are popular with the people?" said Santerre. "They must have been well loved, or they would not have been so truly followed."

Denot blushed at the heavy accusation against himself which these words conveyed; but he made no answer.

"And this old man, my friend?" said Santerre, "this ancient cripple that you tell me of? he is too old, too infirm, I suppose, to care much about this revolt?"

"Not at all," said Denot; "no one in the country is more anxious for success than the old Marquis."

"There you are again, friend," said Santerre, "I know you'll get your neck into danger. Have I not told you that the Republic knows nothing of Marquises?"

"I only called him by the name he goes by, as you'd call a man Peter, if his name were Peter. I didn't mean to say he was a Marquis," said Denot, excusing himself.

"But you mustn't say so at all, unless you speak of him as a criminal, as you would speak of a perjurer, or a parricide. But as to this foolish old man; is he not doting? If I thought that, I might perhaps be excused in sparing him."

"Doting!" said Denot; "not at all; he has all his faculties as much as you or I."

Santerre gave a look of disgust at the wretch, who would not even follow his hint by giving such an account as might spare the life of the old man, who had been his host, his guardian, and his friend. He said nothing further, however, but trotted on quickly, till the cherry groves of Durbellière were in sight, and then he halted to give his final orders to his men, and make arrangements that the house should be surrounded.

"You remember our bargain, citizen General?" said Denot.

"What bargain?" asked the brewer.

"Why, about the young lady; the girl, you know," replied the other. "No one is to interfere between me and Agatha Larochejaquelin. She is to be my prize and my reward."

"I will be as good as my word," said Santerre, "as long as you are true to yours; but I own I pity the young lady the treatment she is likely to receive from her lover," and as he spoke, he rode up to the front door of the house, accompanied by Denot and a company of men on horseback.

The immediate arrival of republican soldiers in the neighbourhood of Durbellière was neither expected, or even feared by the inhabitants of the château, or it would not have been left by Henri, as it had been, perfectly undefended. The truth was this: the royalists had hitherto been so very generally successful against the republicans; and that, when every odds of number, arms, and position had been in favour of their enemies, that they had learnt to look with contempt upon the blues, as they called them. Hitherto the royalists had always been the attacking party; the republicans had contented themselves with endeavouring to keep their position within the towns; and when driven from thence, had retreated altogether out of the revolted district. Except lately at Nantes, the Vendeans had as yet incurred no great reverse; they had not, therefore, learnt to fear that their houses would be attacked and burnt; their corn and cattle destroyed; and even their wives and children massacred. The troops which had now been dispatched by the Convention for the subjection of the country, were of a very different character from those with whom the Vendeans had as yet contended, and the royalists were not long before they experienced all the horrors of a civil war, in which quarter was refused them by their enemies, and mercy even to children was considered as a crime.

When Santerre rode up to the door of the château, ten men might have taken possession of Durbellière. It was a fine July evening, about seven o'clock. The old Marquis had been wheeled in his easy chair out of the house, to the top of the broad steps which led from the back of the château into the garden. Agatha was sitting at his feet on the top step, reading to him, and the little Chevalier Mondyon, who retained no semblance of the soldier about his person, except the red scarf round his waist, was seated straddle-legged atop of one of the huge white lions which guarded the entrance.

"Agatha, I hear horsemen," said the boy, jumping off his seat. "There— there—quite plain!"

"It is Henri and Charles coming from Clisson," said Agatha.

"If it be, they have a troop of cavalry with them," said the Chevalier. "Perhaps it's the Prince de Talmont, for I think they have not so many horsemen with them in the south," and the little Chevalier ran out to greet, as he thought, his gallant friends.

"Whoever they be, Agatha," said the old Marquis, "give them a warm welcome if they come in the King's name. They will know that I cannot rise to meet them, but make them welcome to everything in and about the château."

Agatha had closed her book, and was rising to execute her father's wishes, when Momont, the grey-haired butler, hurrying round from the kitchen-door as fast his old legs would carry him, screamed out: "The blues! the blues!"

Agatha, who was in the act of entering the house as she heard the fearful cry, turned instantly back to her father's side. She was deadly pale, but she spoke not a word. She grasped her father's hand, and fixed herself close to his chair, determined in that position to await the worst that her enemies could do her.

"Run, Agatha, run," said the Marquis, "into the garden, my dear love. The gate will be open at the back. Run, Agatha, for your life!" Agatha, however, did not stir.

"Do you hear me, Agatha?" continued the old man, wildly supplicating her to go from him. "Do you hear me, my daughter? If you would have my blessing before I die, do as I bid you now. What are my grey hairs to your young life, that you should sacrifice yourself for me?"

It was of no avail, for the daughter stood fast by her disabled father's side, grasping his right hand so that nothing should tear her from him, and turning her beautiful face towards the house, watching for the approach of her enemies. Nor had she to watch long; before the Chevalier had been gone five minutes, Santerre, with his sword drawn, tramped heavily through the house, followed by Denot, and a score of his men. The door from the salon to the garden steps was open, and without waiting a moment in the house, he marched through and confronted Agatha and her father.

"Here is your damsel safe, at any rate, friend Denot," said Santerre, "and a pretty girl she is too, but a bitter royalist, no doubt, by the proud turn of her white neck."

Denot did not immediately follow Santerre on to the steps. He had firmly resolved to thrust himself upon Agatha as a conqueror; to rush upon her as an eagle upon its prey, and to carry her off with a strong hand, disregarding her cries, as the eagle disregards the bleating of the lamb; but the first glance he had got of his victim somehow startled his resolve, and scared the blood from his cheek, and almost from his heart. When Santerre, however, called to him, he was obliged to follow; and then, making fearful grimaces with his lips, and scowling with his eyes, he stalked out before the astonished father and daughter.

"Yes, Agatha," he said, looking full upon her, but not daring to turn an eye upon the countenance of her much more indignant father, "yes, Agatha, I have come, as I told you I would come—I have come to claim you, and no power shall now gainsay me. I have come to seize you as my own; to take you with a strong hand, and an out-stretched arm. My prayers were of no avail; you shall find that my sword is more powerful. When last I sought you, it was as a suppliant, I now come for you as a conqueror. Come, Agatha, you are now mine. All the powers of earth shall not rescue you from my arms."

"You appear to me, Sir, to come as a traitor," said Agatha.

"A good republican, my dear," said Santerre: "he comes as a good republican."

Agatha did not deign to make any further reply, but as Santerre and the men had now left the steps and gone into the house, Denot put his hand on her arm to lead her away from her father's side.

"Leave her alone," shouted the old man, now speaking for the first time since his eyes had rested on the republican soldiers. "Leave her alone, thou false wretch, thou basest of all miscreants. Touch her not, or—or—," and the poor Marquis strove in vain to rise from his chair to his daughter's help. "Momont, Chapeau, Arthur—Arthur," he halloed. "My daughter—my daughter, oh! my daughter!"

No one, however, came to his aid, and Agatha, finding resistance to be in vain, suffered Denot to lead her into the house, without uttering another word.

Not the slightest resistance was made to Santerre and his men; he took possession of the château without a word even being said to stop him. The servant girls hid themselves in the garrets, but were soon brought down again, and bade to set quiet in the hall, till their fate should have been decided on. Momont attempted to conceal himself in the garden, but he was soon found and brought back again, and stationed among the women. Chapeau was not seen at all, and even the little Chevalier was missing for a time, though he returned of his own accord before Santerre had been long in possession of the place.

Santerre seated himself with two of his officers in the largest of the salons, and ordered that the old Marquis should be brought before him. He was rather perplexed as to what he should next do; his orders were to destroy everything—houses, property, and life; to spare neither age, sex, nor imbecility; and Santerre, undertaking the commission, had thought, in his republican zeal, that he would find no weakness in himself to militate against the execution of such orders. He was mistaken in himself, however. He had led the fierce mobs of Paris to acts of bloodshed and violence, but in doing so he had only assisted with an eager hand in the overthrow of those who he thought were tyrannizing over the people. He had stood by at the execution of a King, and ordered the drums to beat to drown the last words of the dying monarch; but the King had been condemned by those whom Santerre looked on as the wisest and best of the nation; and in acting as he had done, he had been carried on as well by ideas of duty as excitement. He found his present a much more difficult task. Indeed, after sitting still for some few minutes in that easy chair, meditating what he would do next, he found that the work which he had undertaken was one which he literally could not go through with.

"Is the old gentleman there?" said he; and as he asked, the Marquis, with his eyes closed, and his hands crossed on his breast, was wheeled into the room. Agatha was seated, or rather was crouching, on a sofa in the corner, for Adolphe Denot was standing over her uttering threats and words of love alternately, the latter of which, however, sounded by far the most horrible in poor Agatha's ears.

"Give me a pen and paper," said Santerre, and having got them, he continued writing for a minute or two. "Now, my old friend," said he, addressing the Marquis, "I am given to understand that you yourself, personally, have never lent a hand to this iniquitous revolt. Is it so?"

"I am too old and too infirm to carry a sword," said the Marquis, "but what little I could do for my King, I—."

"Exactly—exactly," said Santerre, interrupting him, "you are a cripple I see. There is no evidence wanting to show that you haven't taken up arms. It is this pestilent son of yours has brought you into trouble."

"He would have been no son of mine had he not acted as he has done," said the old man indignantly.

"Will you hold your silly tongue, my friend," said Santerre. "He is doting, quite doting, I see," and he turned round to his brother officers, as though appealing to them to corroborate his opinion.

"Either that, or else he must be very fond of Mademoiselle Guillotine," said one of them.

"Well, now, old gentleman, answer me this question," said Santerre, "do you want to die this evening?"

"If I could but think that my daughter was safe, and out of the power of that viper, whom I have warmed in my bosom, death would not be unwelcome to me."

"Viper!" said Denot, curling his lips, and speaking through his closed teeth. "Warmed in your bosom! I have yet to learn, old man, that I owe you ought; but if it be a comfort to you to know it, know that no worse evil awaits your daughter than to become the wife of a true Frenchman."

"True!" said the Marquis. "Yes, as true as the Prince of Darkness."

"Come, old man," said Santerre, "we know nothing about Princes, nor yet about Marquises. You must be content now to call the devil by his plain name, though I rather believe it has already been decided in Paris, that the gentleman is nothing but a foul fiction of the aristocrats. Come, if you wish to save your neck, put your signature to this little document."

"I will sign nothing that is put before me in such a manner," said the Marquis.

"Why you have not even read it. Take the pen in your hand, I tell you; it is only a proclamation of the truth, that you have not taken up arms against the republic."

Agatha understood the object of the republican General, though her father did not. She sprang from the corner in which Denot had placed her, and coming close to her father, whispered to him.

"The gentleman means well to you, father, though his words are rough. He wishes to save us. He will save both of us, father, if he can. Read the paper, and if there be nothing absolutely untrue in it, put your name to it."

"Read it yourself, Agatha," said he, "and if you then tell me to sign it, I will do so."

Agatha took up the paper which Santerre had written, and read, but not aloud, the following words:

"I hereby proclaim myself a true son of the Republic, and a citizen brother of all free Frenchmen. I declare that I have never carried arms against the Convention myself, and demand that I may not be accounted responsible for any misguided members of my family, who may have done so."

Twice Agatha read the words, and as she did so, her father's eyes rested anxiously on her face. "Well, my child," said he, "your father's honour is in your hands; tell me what I am to do," and he mechanically held the pen within his fingers, which Santerre had thrust into his hand.

"We will die, father," said she, "if these men please it," and she put down the document on the table on which it had been written. "I cannot ask you to denounce our dear, our gallant Henri. I cannot bid you to deny your King. Death at any rate will not dishonour us. We will only beg of this gentleman that in his mercy he will not separate us," and putting her arm round her father's neck, she fastened her hand upon the folds of his coat, as though determined that nothing should again separate her from his side.

"Denounce Henri!" said the old man; "denounce my own dear, gallant son, the most loyal of those who love their King—the bravest of the brave! No, Sir! I give you no thanks for your mercy, if you intended any. I, and my daughter, Sir, cannot bear arms for our King; she by reason of her sex, and I from my infirmities; but, Sir, we can die for him; we can die for him as readily as the bravest who falls in the first ranks of the battle. Had I still so much power in my own house as to command a cup of wine, I would drink my last pledge to my royal master—but it matters not; the heart and the will are still the same," and taking off the tasselled velvet cap which he wore, he waved it above his head, exclaiming, "Vive le Roi! vive le Roi!"

"The accursed, pestilent old fanatic!" said Santerre, spurning the table as he rose in his passion, and upsetting it into the middle of the room; and then he walked up and down the salon with rapid strides, trying to induce himself to give orders for the immediate execution of the staunch old royalist.

"What is to be done next, General?" said one of his officers, who did not quite admire the evident clemency of the brewer.

"The accursed, pestilent old fanatic!" he repeated between his teeth; and then he said, after drawing a long breath: "they must go to Paris, and let Fouquier Tinville deal with them. There may be secrets that I know not of. I think it better that they should go to Paris." And he felt relieved of a heavy load in having devised a scheme by which he could avoid having himself to give the order for the execution. "Let him be locked up, and well treated, mind you. He shall go to Saumur in his own carriage, and Barrère may send him to Paris how he pleases, or to the devil if he chooses."

"And the servants, General?"

"Oh! ah, yes, the servants!" said Santerre, walking out into the hall to inspect them; "women, an't they? What, five, six, seven, nine women, one old man, and a boy; well, I suppose we must have them out in a row, and shoot them."

Down on their knees went the nine women and the boy, imploring that their innocent lives might be spared to them. Momont, like his master, had still some spirit in his bosom, and kept his seat, saying to himself, but out loud, "I told him so—I told him so. I told him that we who remained here needed as much courage as those who went to the wars; but now, he that talked so much, he's the only one to run away." The poor butler alluded to Chapeau, who had certainly been in the house a few minutes before the arrival of the republicans, and who as certainly had not been seen since.

"I suppose we must have them out before the house, and fire upon them?"

And he turned to the officer who was next to him, as though asking his advice.

"If you ask my advice, General, I would make no difference between the lot; ten minutes should see the last of the whole set of them—the old man, his daughter, and the rest. If we are to send every master of a family with his children up to Paris, or even to Saumur, the tribunals can never do their work, nor can the guillotines fall half fast enough for them."

"When I ask your advice on one subject, Captain, I do not expect you to give it me on another," said Santerre. "Sergeant, take those women out, and the old man, and the boy, stand them in a line upon the gravel plot there, and bring a file of musketeers." And the republican General again began pacing up and down the room, as though he did not at all like the position in which his patriotic zeal had placed him.

The poor women were dragged by their limbs out before the door, screeching as they went, and filling the air with their loud, agonizing cries. Momont walked after them, with his head hanging down, his knees shaking, and his back bent double; but still he was walking himself; he was still able to save himself the disgrace of being dragged out like the women. When he got to the front door, he attempted to totter back, but a republican soldier stopped him.

"My master! my dear master!" said Momont, "let me but kiss his hand, and I will come back."

The soldier let him pass in, and the old man in a moment was at his master's feet. "God bless you, Monseigneur!" said he, "God bless you! Say one word of kindness to your servant, before he is shot for loving his master and his King."

The Marquis put his hand on the grey hairs of the old butler, and moved his lips, but he said nothing: the power of speech for the time failed him; the energy he had displayed, and the excitement he had felt, had been too much for him, and he was unable to reply aloud to the blessing of his faithful servant.

"God bless you, Momont," said Agatha, calmly, as she stood close to her father, still holding to his coat, and supporting his head against her body. "Let your last thoughts be of the Saviour who died for you, and so shall your death be only the end of all your troubles."

He was not allowed to remain longer on his knees, but was hurried back to the spot where the women were awaiting their doom. The soldiers could not get them to stand; they were crouching down on the ground in all positions, one or two with their heads almost buried in the earth, one or two kneeling, and still screaming for mercy. The old housekeeper had fallen on her haunches, and was looking up to heaven, while she wildly struck the ground with her hands; the poor page had made a last, but futile effort to escape with the aid of his heels, but he had been at once caught, and was now bound by his waist to a tree, which grew close to the road on which the wretched party were huddled; the poor boy had quite forgotten his attempt at manhood and mingled his loud screams with those of the women.

"General," said the sergeant, stepping up to him, "the men are ready; will you give the word to fire?"

Two salons, one looking to the front of the house, and the other to the back, communicated with each other by folding-doors, which were now wide open. Santerre, the Marquis, Denot, Agatha, and the other republican officer, were in the back room; the unfortunate wretches doomed to die were collected on the gravel before the windows of the front room; the carabineers who were to fire on them stood in a double file on the broad area before the front door, and above the steps. Santerre, on being addressed by the sergeant, stalked into the front room to give the order; his altered face plainly shewed the strong passion which was at work within his heart. As he passed from one room to the other, he threw his cap upon the ground, and trampled on it; then clenched his fist, and bit his lip till the blood ran. The fatal word "Fire" was on his tongue; but, without intending it, he looked through the window, and his eyes fell on the wretched creatures who were expecting death, and he was unable to give the command. He sank back upon a chair, and hiding his face in both his hands, he said to the sergeant, in a low voice:

"They must get some one else for this work, I am not the man I thought I was." He then rose and said, in a voice he vainly attempted should appear calm and dignified, "Sergeant, keep the prisoners in custody this night: I have changed my mind. Be ready to march at four tomorrow morning. We will have a bonfire to light us on our journey: see that there are plenty of faggots ready before you let the men sleep."

The poor women were unable to raise themselves and walk away, when they were made to understand that they were not to die that night. Some prayed, others screamed almost louder than before: one or two of them fainted, and continued fainting the greater part of the night: they were all of them taken into the house, and kept together in the kitchen surrounded by a guard.

"Citizen General!" said Denot to Santerre, stepping up to him after this scene was over; "I have performed my part of my engagement I believe."

"Well, man, supposing you have; what do you want? Are you going to grumble because I have not slaughtered the wretches you have betrayed to me?"

"Not at all, General; you know your own duty, doubtless. I am going to return to Saumur, to which place I desire an escort for myself and this young lady."

"By heaven I pity her!" said Santerre. "I don't know what has come to me tonight, that I should trouble myself with the cares of a swarm of aristocrats." And then he said, addressing Agatha, "Are you ready and willing, young woman, for a midnight ride with this hot young lover, who seems so fond of you?"

"She must be ready, General Santerre," said Denot, taking hold of Agatha's hand: "it is now my turn to command her: she must be ready, whether she be willing or no."

"You will not force me to leave my father?" said Agatha, appealing to Santerre. "You will not deliver a poor unprotected girl into the hands of such a maniac as that."

"Maniac!" said Denot. "But I care not; your words are to me like the empty wind: the time had gone by for words between you and me, when you refused to listen to those I addressed to you upon my knees. Come, Agatha, come; my heart's treasure—for still you are so; come, my love, my captive, and my bride!" And Denot essayed to go, as though he expected Agatha to follow him through the world like a tame dog.

"Oh, Sir, protect me from him!" said Agatha, still appealing to Santerre. "He is mad—you see and hear he is mad! I have not asked you for my life, nor do I so now; but I pray you, I beseech you, by the remembrance of the females who are dear to yourself save me from the power of that frantic man. Had he not been mad, had he not utterly lost his senses, he would have been the last to have brought you hither."

"I have thought something like that myself pretty one," said Santerre. "Come, Denot, you shall talk to the lady tomorrow; we will leave her with her father tonight." "Your word, General!" said Denot, assuming his furious look, "your plighted word and honour. Was she not to be my prize, my captive, my reward. You dare not go back from the promise you have made me."

"Nonsense, man alive," said Santerre. "You can't carry her off tonight. I believe in my heart she's right, and that you're as mad a man as ever roared in a hospital. Let go her arm, I tell you; you shall not drag her about in that way."

The Marquis, during this scene, was endeavouring to throw his arms round his daughter, so as to protect her; but his efforts were but of little avail. Agatha herself still held to her father by one hand, but the other she was unable to extricate from her persecutor's grasp. She did not scream or cry, for there was something within her—a memory of Cathelineau's last moments, of her brother's gallantry, and her father's loyalty, which strongly urged her to repress her tears before a republican; but her strength was almost gone, her nerves were all but over strung, when she heard a sudden noise behind her of some one rushing into the room, and Adolphe Denot quickly dropped her hand, and gave a yell of pain. He had received a sharp blow of a cherry switch across his face, and the blood was running from both his cheeks.

Santerre, and the other republican officers in the room, put their hands to their pistols, and prepared to defend themselves, but the only person who appeared was a young boy: to be sure he had the dreadful red scarf round his waist; but he had no weapon but his cherry stick, after having given Denot the blow across his face, he made no farther use of that. It was the little Chevalier who had arrived so opportunely; he took Agatha's hand in his, and pressed it closely, and took his place beside her without speaking a word.

"And who the deuce is this young bantam cock?" said Santerre.

"I am the little Chevalier Mondyon," said Arthur; "a true royalist, and sworn knight to Agatha Larochejaquelin. And that man there is a traitor and a false knave; he is not fit to be punished with a sword like a gentleman."

"Well crowed, my bantam," said Santerre; "and be good enough to tell me where you come from. No, friend Denot, no, we'll have no dagger work just at present." And putting his huge hand on the other's shoulder, he dragged him back as he was about to plunge his knife into the little Chevalier.

"I came from the cherry wood there," said Arthur. "Maybe you think I ought not to have run away, and deserted my lady love. Maybe I'm rather ashamed of my own self, but at any rate when you speak of it, say that I came back of my own accord. I'm not a bit afraid to die now," and as he spoke he squeezed Agatha's hand. His heart was full of apprehension, lest she should suspect for a moment that he had really fled from her through fear, but Agatha understood well his ready wit, and appreciated his more than boyish courage.

Santerre now made his arrangements for the night. All the inhabitants of the château were kept under strict surveillance. The Marquis, his daughter, and the Chevalier were allowed to remain together, and Denot was prevented from annoying them. At day-break the following morning Durbellière was to be burnt, and Santerre, with his prisoners, would then proceed to join Westerman at Bressuire.

"Let him slaughter them, if he likes," said he to himself, "I don't care what he says of me. I am at any rate too well known to be suspected. I don't know what came over me today, but had the Republic depended on it, I could not have done it," and he flung himself down on one of Agatha's sofas, and slept not the less soundly for having began his career of extermination in so vacillating a manner.

CHAPTER X.
THE RESCUE.

The little Chevalier had no intention of saving himself, and deserting his friends, when, on Santerre's approach, he ran off, leaving Agatha and the Marquis at the garden door of the château. He knew that Chapeau was at the smith's forge, with his own pony. He had himself sent him there; and as soon as he perceived, on running round the side of the house, that the whole front was occupied by the blues, his first idea was to go after his pony, and ride as fast as the animal could carry him to Echanbroignes, and bring the royalists from thence to the rescue of their friends at Durbellière. With this object he clambered over the garden-wall, and well knowing every foot of the ground, reached the forge in a few minutes. Chapeau and the smith were there, as was also the pony, and a breathless countryman was already telling them that the château was surrounded by the whole army of blues.

"Here's the Chevalier," said Chapeau, stopping the peasant in his story. "In the name of Heaven, M. Arthur, what is all this?"

"That traitor, Denot, has brought a parcel of blues down upon the château," said the Chevalier. "The Marquis and Mademoiselle Agatha are already in their hands; they will be murdered before morning. What is to be done? Oh! Chapeau, what are we to do to save them?"

"M. Denot!" said Chapeau. "You don't mean to say M. Denot has turned blue—"

"I saw him with my own eyes," said the boy; "he was one of the officers commanding the men; but there was another over him, a big, clumsy, noisy man; he it was I saw first of all, and Denot was behind him; and then there was a crowd of horsemen following them. Both drawing-rooms were full before we knew they were in the house at all."

"And how did you get through them, M. Arthur?" said Chapeau.

"I got over the wall behind the stables. I never went into the house at all. But what on earth are we to do, Chapeau? Can't we get the men from Echanbroignes to come to the rescue?"

The matter was then discussed between them, and it was decided that Chapeau should take the pony, and collect the men at Echanbroignes and on the road thither, and that he should return with them, if possible, during the night; that the smith should go off to St. Laud, and get Father Jerome to bring with him the men from thence, and that Arthur should return to the château.

"No," said he, when Chapeau pressed him to undertake the mission to Echanbroignes, "I will not leave Mademoiselle Agatha and the Marquis any longer. They will think I have run away. Besides, maybe, I can be of some service to them there. At any rate, I will go and see what is going on; but, Chapeau, our lives depend on you. Don't lose one single minute now, even though you should ride poor Bayard to death," and he put his hand on the neck of the pony, whom he had named after the flower of chivalry.

Chapeau and the smith started on their important missions, and the Chevalier slowly, but manfully, walked back to the château. No one stopped him as he walked through the open gates, and in at the back door. On getting into the hall, he heard the sound of the Marquis's voice, as he was praying Santerre to preserve his daughter from Denot, and then, hurrying into the room, he made use of the little cherry stick which he carried, in the manner which has been described.

None of the inhabitants of the château went to bed that night; indeed, the beds were all occupied by the troopers, who threw themselves down to sleep, without taking off their boots, wherever they could find any convenient place to lie down. To do Santerre justice, he repeatedly pressed the Marquis to go to his own room, assuring him that he should not be further disturbed than by the presence of a sentinel; but the old man insisted on remaining in the salon, and Agatha and the Chevalier sat with him. Santerre, and Denot, and a cavalry sergeant, remained in the same room, and a couple of sentinels were stationed on the top of the steps at the back of the house, and four at the front. None of the party in the salon slept, excepting Santerre; but they all sat silent; neither Arthur nor Agatha dared to speak to each other on the subject which at that time filled their thoughts. The night seemed dreadfully long to Arthur, and yet hardly long enough. He discovered soon after his return, that it was Santerre's purpose to burn the château early in the morning, and then to take the inhabitants away with him as prisoners; and he greatly feared that Chapeau would not be able to return in time to prevent the conflagration. He anxiously watched the first break of day, and listened intently, but for a long time in vain, for the noise of coming feet. About half-past two, a soldier came and whispered to the sergeant, who then woke Santerre, and whispered to him, but the General was sleepy, and did not wish his dreams should be disturbed. He muttered something to the sergeant, who again left him, and resumed the seat in which he had sat since he first entered the room. Denot had risen two or three times during the night, and paced rapidly and uneasily about. Whenever he had done so, Agatha had firmly grasped both her father's chair and the Chevalier's hand, as though she feared he was about to renew his attempts to drag her away, but he did not either touch her or speak to her. He was probably aware that the sergeant, who sat there without once closing his eyes through the long hours, had orders to prevent him from doing so.

The Chevalier had no watch, and could not see how the hours were going, but it seemed to him as though it were broad day. He thought it must be five, six, nay seven o'clock; and he could not understand why the lazy republicans remained so passive and so quiet, nor could he imagine why Chapeau was so long in coming. The whole affair seemed to him so strange that he could hardly help fancying that he was dreaming. There sat close to him his dear friend Agatha, with her eyes wide open, fixed on Denot, and she had been gazing in this way for hours after hours, without speaking a word. There was the Marquis close to her, equally silent, but also wide awake, though his eyes were closed. Arthur was sure that he was awake. There was Denot marching to and fro. Adolphe Denot, who but the other day was in the house, not only as a friend, but as a comrade, eager in the cause in which they were all embarked, as much at home in the château as Henri Larochejaquelin himself: and now he was the worst of traitors, and the most cruel of enemies—there was the sergeant of the republican army, sitting as quiet and composed as though he were merely idling his time away in his own barracks; and there was Santerre—the much talked of republican brewer and General; the sanguinary, remorseless, fanatic democrat; the sworn enemy of all that was noble, loyal and gentle, the dreaded Santerre; for the Chevalier had now learned the name of the big, clumsy, noisy man, whom he had seen leading his troops into the salon where he was now sleeping—there he was, sleeping fast: while care, anxiety, or a sense of duty banished sleep from all the others, he, who had so much more need than others to be watchful, was snoring loud, and dreaming of the denizens of the faubourgs, who used to love him so well. All this seemed to Arthur like a dream from which he could not awake—there were his enemies, his deadly enemies, before and around him. He knew that it was the practice of the republican soldiers to massacre all whom they took bearing arms against the Republic he had even heard that it was now their horrid purpose to go further than this, and to slaughter the inhabitants of the whole district which had revolted; at any rate his own doom would be death; he was certain that he had not many days, probably many hours, to live, unless Chapeau should arrive in time, and with sufficient force, to rescue the whole party. Yet he felt no fear; he could not sufficiently realize the position in which he found himself, to feel the full effects of its danger. The republican sergeant sat immediately in front of him, and each kept his eye fixed on the other's face; not that either of them had any object in doing so, any particular motive for watching the other's countenance, but soon after day-break the gaze of each had become fixed, and it seemed as though neither of them were able to turn away his eyes.

Arthur occupied his mind in speculating on the character of the soldier, in trying to guess from his features whether he were a cruel or a kind-hearted man; whether he were a ferocious democrat, eager for the blood of all who had been born in a rank above him, or merely a well-trained soldier, obeying the behests of those under whose orders it was his duty to act. The Chevalier had no idea that his own or his friends' fate depended in any way on the man's disposition; but such thoughts came across his brain unwittingly, and he could not restrain them. At last, he felt that he had a kind of intimacy with the sergeant; that if he should chance to meet him after three or four years had passed, he should greet him as an old acquaintance, whom he had well known, and he was sure that the sergeant had the same feeling respecting him.

The day dawned soon after two o'clock, and as by degrees the clear sun-light streamed in at the uncurtained windows, Arthur, in his impatience, thought that the day was advancing; but in reality it was not yet five o'clock, when Santerre, waking with a tremendous yawn, stretched his huge limbs, and then jumped up from the sofa on which he had been lying.

"Now for a bonfire," said he, "and then for breakfast; or perhaps we had better get our breakfast first, and have our bonfire afterwards. Old gentleman, I have no doubt my men took strange liberties with your cellar and larder last night. I hope they have left enough about the place to furnish you with the last meal you will ever eat in this château."

"I know, Sir, what soldiers are in a house," said the old man. "I will not say that your men are welcome here, for that would be falsehood; but I begrudge them nothing that they eat and drink."

"Well, that's kind of you; but, considering that all which is not now eaten and drunk, will be immediately wasted and spoilt, you would certainly be foolish to allow the consumption of your provisions to make you uneasy. Here, sergeant," and then Santerre spoke aside to the sergeant, and gave him various orders, which the man departed to obey.

"And now, General Santerre," said Denot, marching close up to him, "are you prepared to make good your promise to me? Are you prepared to give me an escort for myself and this lady, and to allow us to commence our journey from hence to Saumur?"

Denot's personal appearance had not been at all improved by the blow which Arthur had given him across his face. Both his cheeks were much swollen immediately beneath the eyes, and one of them was severely cut. He felt that his looks were against him, and he endeavoured to make up for the injury his countenance had sustained by the sternness of his voice, and the determined rigour of his eye. "I presume, General Santerre," added he, "that your plighted word is sufficient warrant to me for your good faith."

"There is the lady," said Santerre, pointing to Agatha. "I did not undertake to protect you from the wrath of any rivals you might have in her affections. It seems to me that at present she prefers that young dare-devil slip of aristocracy to your patriotic ardour. If she won't go to Saumur with you, I can't make her."

"By all the powers of heaven and hell, she shall go with me!" said Denot, advancing towards her.

"Beware the switch—beware the switch again, thou false knave!" said the little Chevalier, jumping up, and standing immediately before Agatha, with his cherry stick in his hand. Denot had no other arms about him but his dagger, and that he drew, as he advanced towards the boy.

"No daggers—I will have no daggers," shouted Santerre. "Sergeant, take the dagger from him, unless he puts it up."

"Beware the switch, thou traitor! beware the switch, thou knave!" continued the Chevalier, shaking the stick at Denot, upon whose arm the strong hand of the sergeant, who had returned to the room, was now laid heavily.

"I will choke the brat as I would an adder," said Denot, attempting to shake off the sergeant's hand. "There, take the dagger," and he dropped it on the ground, and rushing at the boy, got inside the swing of his stick, and made a grasp at his throat. Arthur, however, was too quick for him, and pushing away his hand, fastened his own arms round his adversary. They were now close locked in each other's embrace, and kicking, plunging, and striving, each did his best to throw the other to the ground.

"Oh! Sir, kind Sir, for mercy's sake separate them!" said Agatha, appealing to Santerre; "he is but a boy, a child, and that wretched man is mad. He'll murder the boy before your eyes, if you do not separate them."

"He won't find it so easy though," said the Chevalier, panting, and out of breath; but still holding his own, and, indeed, more than his own; for he had fixed his left hand in Denot's hair, and was pulling his head backwards with such force, that he nearly broke his neck.

"I think the young one has the best of it," said Santerre; "but come, citizen Denot, your loves and your quarrels are troublesome to us; we have other work to attend to. Get up, man, get up, I tell you."

Denot, by his superior weight and strength, had succeeded in getting the Chevalier to the ground, but Arthur still kept his hold in his hair, and though Adolphe was on the top of his foe, he did not find it very easy to get up.

"Get up, I say," said Santerre. "You'll gain nothing by wrestling with that fellow; he's more than a match for you. Well, Captain, what's the matter?"

The room in which the party had passed the night looked out into the garden at the back of the house. The front room communicated with this by folding-doors, which during the night had been closed. These doors were now violently thrown open, and one of the officers, followed by about a dozen men, rushed into the room.

"The road is crowded with men," said the officer; "thousands of these brigands are on us. The château will be surrounded in five minutes."

"H—— and the d——," said Santerre between his teeth. "This comes of playing the fool here," and he hurried out of the room in company with the officer.

"Hurrah!" said the Chevalier, jumping to his feet. "I knew they'd be here soon—I knew they'd be here soon," and running to Agatha's side he caught hold of her hand, and covered it with kisses.

Denot also arose. He had also heard the officer say that the peasants were coming on them, and he felt that if he were taken, he could expect no mercy from those who had so lately been his friends. He did not, however, attempt to fly, but he stood still on the spot where he got up, and after wiping his hot brow with his handkerchief, he said slowly and mournfully—"Agatha Larochejaquelin, you now see to what your conduct has reduced me; and with my last breath I tell you that I owe my disgrace, my misery, and my death—ay, and the loss of my eternal soul, to you, and to you only. Ay, shudder and shake, thou lovely monster of cruelty. Shake and grieve with remorse and fear. You may well do so. My living form shall trouble you no more, but dead and dying I will be with you till the last trump sounds on the fearful day of judgment."

Agatha did not answer him. She felt assured that he was mad, and she only pitied him. She had now too reason to hope that she and her father, and their whole household, would be relieved from their horrible position, and she no longer felt anything like anger against the unfortunate wretch whom uncontrolled passions had absolutely maddened. Arthur, in his anxiety to see what was going forward, was about to leave the room, but Agatha laid her hand upon his arm to detain him, merely looking towards Denot as she did so.

"And do you think," said Denot, "that puny boy could really stop my way, if I chose to put out my right hand against him. Boy, I despise and disregard you! would before I die that it might be allowed me to measure arms with any man, who would dare to say that he would advocate your cause!"

"Beware the switch, traitor—beware the switch!" repeated the Chevalier.

"Be quiet, Arthur, do not anger him," whispered Agatha. "It is not generous, you know, to insult a fallen foe."

"There are no terms to be kept with a traitor, Agatha. If we get the better of this, Santerre, as I am sure we shall now, you shall see that I know how to treat a generous foe generously."

When Santerre reached the front of the house, he at once saw that any attempt on his part to oppose the crowd of armed peasants who were now close upon him, would be futile. The only mode of escape which appeared to him at all practicable, was to attempt to ride through them. He gave the command "to horse," and got so far himself as to mount into his saddle; but it was of no use, he was surrounded by a crowd of peasants before he got to the gate, and he soon found himself on foot again, and unarmed. Some ten or twenty of his men, who were ready to jump into the saddle at the moment when they were first aware of the approach of the royalists, escaped, but the remainder in a few minutes found themselves prisoners in the château.

The peasants were headed by Father Jerome, the priest of St. Laud, and it was he who first mounted the steps leading up to the front door of the house. "Thank God," said he, speaking more to himself than to those around him. "Thank God!" and he stood up against the pedestal of one of the lions, the heavy wooden crucifix which he had carried in his hand as he marched, or rather ran, to the succour of his friends at Durbellière; and then he took off his cap, and with the sleeve of his dusty grey coat he wiped the perspiration from off his brow. "And the Marquis and Mademoiselle are unhurt? Thank God—thank God! we were just in time, but we had a smart run for it."

Chapeau had already dived into the kitchen through the window, and had learnt that at any rate the republicans had as yet shed no blood.

"And how did the Marquis bear it, Momont?" said he. "It was enough to kill the old gentleman."

"Why, yes," said Momont. "We had to bear a good deal, but we did bear it manfully and well. We were all led out to be shot, you know."

"What, the Marquis and Mademoiselle and all?" said Chapeau.

"No, not the Marquis and Mademoiselle; they were to be beheaded after us, but the rest of us were all taken out—the muskets loaded—the men to shoot us all in a line."

"Oh! Chapeau, it was so awfully dreadful," said the cook. "If I live a thousand years I shall never get over this night."

"Oh, yes! most dreadfully awful," said the laundress. "I was carried in from the spot, and have not been able to move a limb since. I doubt I never shall put a foot to the ground again."

"The muskets were to their shoulders," continued Momont. "We heard them cocked: each man took deliberate aim; the women here were screeching and screaming."

"Of course we were," said the confidential maid. "Hadn't we good cause to scream, waiting to be killed every minute. I'm sure I wonder I ever came to my senses again. I declare when they came to pick me up, I thought it was all over, and that I'd been shot already."

"Well, I don't think anybody heard me scream," said Momont: "but there's a difference I know between a man and a woman. 'It's all for my King and my master,' said I to myself. Besides a man can die but once, and it's a great thing to die honourably." The old man turned round to receive the approbation, which he considered was due to the sentiment he had expressed, and found that Chapeau was gone. The kitchen, however, was filled with peasants, and in them Momont found ready listeners and warm admirers.

Both Chapeau and the priest had spent the greater portion of the night in collecting what they considered would be a sufficient number of men to enable them to attack, with any chance of success, the republican soldiers who had taken possession of Durbellière. They had neither of them the slightest idea what amount of force had been brought against the château, and, consequently, wasted much time in procuring many more men than were necessary for the purpose. The three hundred, who were immediately got together on the sounding of the tocsin in the village of Echanbroignes, would have been sufficient to have done the work without further assistance, for they were all well armed, and, by this time, tolerably well trained in the use of their arms.

There was ten times more confusion now in the château, than there had been during the night: every room and passage was crowded with peasants, who took up their positions there under the plea of guarding their prisoners, and with the girls and women of the neighbourhood who flocked to that place, as soon as they heard that the horrible blues were all prisoners, and that the Marquis and Mademoiselle were once more at liberty. Agatha's troubles were by no means ended. Provisions of some kind were to be procured for the friends who had come so far and done so much to relieve them; and she had no one on whom she could depend to assist her in procuring them: the servants all considered themselves utterly unfitted for anything, except talking of the events of the evening; and though every one was burning with affection and zeal for Monseigneur and Mademoiselle, no one appeared willing to make himself useful.

The reaction on his feelings was too much for the poor Marquis. During the long evening and night, in which he had been a prisoner and looking forward to nothing but death; in which he had sat beside his fondly-loved daughter, whose fate he feared would be so much more horrible than death itself, he had patiently and manfully born his sufferings; he had even displayed a spirit for which few gave him credit, who were accustomed to his gentle temper and mild manners; but the unexpected recovery of his own and his daughter's liberty upset him entirely. As soon as he had pressed Father Jerome's hand, and thanked Chapeau fur what he had done, he begged that he might be carried off to his bed, and left there quietly till the return of his son, for whom, he was told, a messenger had been sent.

Santerre and Denot were both kept under a strong guard in the saloon in which they had passed the night; and there the priest, Chapeau, and the young Chevalier passed the greater part of the day, anxiously waiting the arrival of Henri Larochejaquelin.

"I never liked that man," said the priest, whispering to Arthur and Chapeau, for the latter, from his exertion and zeal was looked upon rather as an officer in the royalist army, than as a servant. "I never liked Adolphe Denot, but I could never say why. The tone of his voice was disagreeable to me, and the expression of his features aroused in me both dislike and distrust. It is not long since M. Henri rebuked me for being hard on him, and judging him harshly; and I was angry with myself for having done so. I knew, however, there was something wrong within him. He has turned out to be as base a creature as ever trod the earth."

"It will be a desperate blow to M. Henri," said Chapeau, "for he loved him as though he were his brother."

"I will be his brother now," said Arthur; "he shall love me in his place."

"Ah! M. Arthur," said Chapeau, "his heart is large enough to love us both; but when he hears how nobly you behaved last night, how you stood by Mademoiselle Agatha, and protected her, you will be his real brother indeed."

The little Chevalier's heart rose high within him, as he attempted to speak slightingly of his own services. "Oh!" said he, "I couldn't do much, you know, for I had only a stick; but of course we red scarfs will always stick to each other. Denot, you know, never was a red scarf Well, thank heaven for that; but I tell you what, Father Jerome, that Santerre is not such a bad fellow; and so I shall tell Henri; he is not a bad fellow at all, and he scorns Denot as he deserves to be scorned."

CHAPTER XI.
ANNOT STEIN.

It will be remembered that the party escaping from the Château of Clisson met Jean Stein, when they had come within four or five leagues of Durbellière. He had been sent from Echanbroignes, by Chapeau, to tell Henri what had happened, to assure him that every possible effort would be made to rescue his father and sister from the republicans, and if possible to save the château, and to beg him to return home as speedily as he possibly could. Jean was spared the greatest portion of his journey, and having told his tale, added that perhaps "Messieurs would not think it prudent to take the ladies with them to Durbellière just at present."

"Oh heavens! what are we to do?" said Madame de Lescure; "we are running from one hostile army into the middle of another. Poor Agatha! my poor Agatha! what will become of her?"

"Had we not better send them to Chatillon?" said Henri, speaking to de Lescure. "They will, at any rate, be safe there for a time."

"We won't be sent any where—indeed we won't—will we, Marie?" said Madame de Lescure. "Pray, Charles, pray do not send us away. Let us go where you go. It cannot be worse for us than it is for you."

"You cannot go to the château, dearest, when we have every reason to suppose it is in the hands of the republicans, and more than probably burnt to the ground by this time."

"Oh! don't send me back to Chatillon," said Marie; "it would be hours and hours before we should hear what happens to you, and what has happened to Agatha."

"If the ladies wouldn't think ill of going to Echanbroignes," said Jean Stein, "they would be safe there, and near at hand to learn all as it goes on at Durbellière. I am sure father and Annot would do their best to make the ladies comfortable, as long as they might be pleased to stay there."

After considerable discussion this plan was adopted. The party travelled on together, till the roads to Durbellière and Echanbroignes separated; and then, with many charges, the two ladies were entrusted to the care of the smith's son.

"We will come to you, or send to you the moment we are able," said de Lescure, "whether our news be good or bad. I trust we shall find them safe, and that we shall all be together tomorrow at Durbellière."

Marie and Madame de Lescure reached the village safely late in the evening, and found no one in the smith's house but Annot. Even Michael Stein himself had been moved by hearing that the republicans were absolutely in possession of the château, and, old as he was, he had made his way over to Durbellière, and had not yet returned. Annot, however, received them with good news; she had heard different messages from the château during the day, and was able to tell them not only that the Marquis, Agatha, and the house were safe, but that the republican soldiers were all prisoners, and that Santerre—that object of horror to many Vendean royalists, had himself been captured by the strong hand and bold heart of Jacques Chapeau.

Neither of the ladies knew Annot Stein, or had even heard of her; but Annot, though at present she was rather doleful, was not long in making herself known to them, and explaining to them her own particular connexion with the château.

She made up her own bed for one of them, and her father's for the other. They were not, she said, such as ladies like them were accustomed to sleep on, but the sheets were clean, and perhaps for one night they would excuse the want of better accommodation. Madame de Lescure and Marie declared that they were only too happy in being able to rest quietly, with the knowledge that their friends were in safety. Poor ladies! they were destined before long to encounter worse hardships than Annot Stein's little bed, and frugal supper.

"But, Madame," said Annot, as she sat demurely on the corner of her chair, "this Santerre is not the sort of man at all we all took him to be. Peter was over here, though he has gone back again now, and Peter says he is quite a good fellow in his way."

"What, Santerre!" said Marie, shuddering. "Oh! he is a most horrid monster! It was he that led out our dear sainted King to be murdered; it was he that urged on the furious mob to spill so much blood. They say that in all Paris there is not a greater wretch than this Santerre."

"I don't know, Mademoiselle," said Annot, "but he certainly wasn't so bad last night, for he might have killed them all had he chosen: and instead of that he didn't kill any one, or let any of his party kill them either, only he frightened poor old Momont nearly to death."

"God may have softened his heart," said Madame de Lescure; "if he has really spared our friends, we will not speak ill of him."

"If he has done so," said Marie, "he will have his reward; for I am sure Charles and Henri will spare him now that he is in their power."

"That's just what the people say," said Annot; "they say that it's M. Henri's turn to be generous now, and that they're sure he won't hurt a hair of this Santerre. Only they're determined on one thing—and it was all Chapeau and Father Jerome could do to stop them till M. Henri came home—they are determined to hang that horrid wretch Denot, the monster! I shouldn't wonder if he were swinging by this time."

"And is it really true," said Madame de Lescure, "that it was M. Denot who led the republicans to Durbellière?"

"Oh! that's a positive fact," said Annot, "there's no doubt on earth about that; and behaved most brutally to Mademoiselle Agatha. He would have killed her with his own hand, before her father, only M. Santerre wouldn't let him. He had his dagger out and all, and M. Santerre took it from him with his own hand, and wouldn't let him speak another word. Oh! indeed, ladies, M. Santerre is not half so bad as he looks to be."

"People say that the father of evil himself is painted blacker than he really is," said Marie.

"I don't know about that, Mademoiselle, and I didn't hear that this Santerre was painted black at all; and if he were so, I think Peter would have told me. But then, ladies, the little Chevalier Mondyon came in in the middle. It was he that sent Chapeau over here to bring the red scarfs to the rescue. He is a little darling, is the Chevalier. I suppose you know him, Mademoiselle?"

"Indeed I do, Annot, and love him dearly; he is an old sweetheart of mine."

"He's too young to have a sweetheart yet, Mademoiselle; but you'll see some of the ladies will be quarrelling for him yet, when he's a year or two older. Well, after sending Jacques over here, he went back as bold as possible into the middle of the republicans, before Santerre and all. M. Denot was at his worst then. He had hold of Mademoiselle Agatha, and was dragging her away from the Marquis, in spite of Santerre and the whole of them, when the Chevalier raises his stick, and strikes him across the face. I warrant you he let go Mademoiselle's hand when he felt the sharp stick come across his eyes."

"It must have been a horrid sight for Agatha," said Madame de Lescure.

"Oh! indeed it was, Madame. Only fancy that traitor Denot going on in that way, right before her eyes all night, and no one to protect her but the little Chevalier; for when it got late M. Santerre threw himself on the floor, and slept and snored like a hog. They say it was all for love, Mademoiselle. They say this Denot was greatly in love with Mademoiselle Agatha, and that she wouldn't look at him. Is it true, she was so very scornful to him?"

"She was never scornful to any one," said Marie; "but if he ever asked her for her love, I have no doubt she told him that she could not give it to him."

"That's just what they say; and that then he asked her more and more, and went down on his knees to her, and prayed her just as much as to look at him; and kissed her feet, and cried dreadfully; and that all she did was to turn aside her face, and bid him rise and leave her."

"What would you have had her say, Annot, if she felt that she could not love him?"

"Oh! I'm not presuming to find fault with her, Mademoiselle; heaven forbid! Of course, if she couldn't love him, she could do nothing but refuse him. But, heigho! it's a very dreadful thing to think of that a nice young man like him—for I'm told that this Denot was a very nice young man—should be so bewildered by love as he has been."

"Love couldn't make a man a traitor," said Marie, "nor yet a coward."

"I don't know, Mademoiselle, love is a very fearful thing when it doesn't go right. Perhaps love never made you feel so angry that you'd like to eat your lover's heart?"

"Gracious goodness, no," said Marie; "why, Annot, where did you get such a horrid idea as that?"

"Ah! Mademoiselle, your lover's one in a hundred! So handsome, so noble, so good, so grand, so amiable, so everything that a young lady could wish to dream about: one, too, that never has vagaries and jealousies, and nasty little aggravating ways. Oh! Mademoiselle, I look upon you as the happiest young lady in the world.

"What on earth, Annot, do you know about my lover, or how on earth can you know that I have a lover at all? Why, child, I and my cousin Agatha are both going to be nuns at St. Laurent."

"The blessed Virgin forbid it," said Annot. "Not but what Mademoiselle Agatha would look beautiful as a nun. She has the pale face, and the long straight nose, and the calm melancholy eyes, just as a nun ought to have; but then she should join the Carmelite ladies at the rich convent of our Blessed Lady at St. Maxent, where they all wear beautiful white dresses and white hoods, and have borders to their veils, and look so beautiful that there need hardly be any change in them when they go to heaven; and not become one of those dusty-musty black sisters of mercy at St. Laurent."

"That's your idea of a nun, is it?" said Madame de Lescure.

"I'm sure, Madame, I don't know why any girl should try to make herself look ugly, if God has made her as beautiful as Mademoiselle Agatha."

"And you think then Mademoiselle de Lescure is not fit for a nun at all?"

"Oh, Madame, we all know she is going to be married immediately to the finest, handsomest, most noble young nobleman in all Poitou. Oh! I'd give all the world to have such a lover as M. Henri just for ten minutes, to see him once kneeling at my feet."

"For ten minutes," said Marie. "What good would that do you? that would only make you unhappy when the ten minutes were gone and past."

"Besides, what would you say to him in that short time?" said Madame de Lescure.

"Say to him! I don't know what I'd say to him. I don't think I'd say one word, but I'd give him such a look, so full of affection and gratitude, and admiration, and—and—and downright real true love; that, if he had any heart in him at all, I don't think he'd be so base as to go away from me when the ten minutes were over."

"That's what you call borrowing a lover for ten minutes, is it?" said Marie; "and if, as you say, this young gentleman is my property, what am I to do for a lover the while?"

"I was only wishing, Mademoiselle, and you know there's no harm in wishing. Besides, the finest lady in the world couldn't rob you of your lover, let alone a poor girl like me. He is so true, and so noble, and so good."

"And have not you a lover of your own, Annot?"

"Oh, indeed I have, and a very good one. For all my talking in that way, I was never badly off for lovers, and now I've chosen one for good and all; and I love him dearly, Madame; dote on him, and so does he on me, but for all that there was a time when I really would have eaten his heart, if I could have got at it."

"But that was before you had accepted each other."

"Not at all, Mademoiselle; not long since. I loved then as dearly as I do now, but he let me walk home by myself three long leagues without speaking a word to me, and all because I said that a man in a picture had fine whiskers."

"A man in a picture! why this lover of yours must be a very jealous man, or else he must be very badly off for whiskers himself?"

"No he's not, Mademoiselle; he's as nice a pair as you'd wish to see; that is, begging your pardon, as nice a pair as I'd wish to see; and he's not a jealous man either about other things."

"And when do you mean to marry him, Annot?"

"Oh, Mademoiselle, we are only waiting for you."

"Waiting for me, child! What on earth do you mean? who told you I was going to be married at all?"

It was no wonder that Marie should be astonished at finding her wedding so confidently spoken of by a stranger in Echanbroignes, considering that it was not yet twenty-four hours since Henri had declared his love for her at Clisson.

"But you are going to be married to M. Henri, are you not, Mademoiselle?"

"Who told you all this? how is it you come to know so much about this young lady and M. Henri?" said Madame de Lescure.

"Why, Jacques Chapeau told me. My own husband, that is, as is to be."

"Oh! that explains the mystery," said Marie; "and so Chapeau is your lover is he? Chapeau is the man who couldn't bear the mention of the fine pair of whiskers you saw in the picture? and did he tell you that his master was going to be married immediately?" and Marie blushed as she asked the question.

"Indeed he did, Mademoiselle, and he said besides—"

"Well, what did he say besides?"

"Why, I hardly like to say now, Mademoiselle; it will look like asking a favour when I thought you could not well refuse it; and perhaps Jacques was wrong to say anything at all about it."

Marie, however, was not long in inducing Annot to reveal to her Chapeau's little plan of taking his own wife over to Durbellière to wait upon his master's wife, and she, moreover, promised that, as far as she herself was concerned, she would consent to the arrangement, if, which she expressly inserted, she should ever marry M. Larochejaquelin.

"But an't you engaged to him, Mademoiselle?"

"Well, Annot," answered she, "as you have told me so much, I don't mind telling you that I am. But it will be long, probably, before I am married, if ever I am. Men have other things to think of now than marriage, and, alas! women too. We must wait till the wars are over, Annot."

"But I thought the wars were over now, Mademoiselle. Haven't they got that Santerre prisoner up at Durbellière?"

"There's much, very much, I fear to do yet, and to suffer, before the wars will be really over," said Madame de Lescure. "Heaven help us, and guide us, and protect us! Come, Marie, let us go to rest, for I trust Charles will send for us early in the morning."

Annot gave such assistance to her two guests as they required, and was within her power, and then seating herself in her father's large arm chair in the kitchen, pondered over the misery of living in times when men were so busy fighting with their enemies, that they had not even leisure to get married.

"And what, after all, is the use of these wars?" said she to herself "What do they get by taking so many towns, and getting so many guns, and killing so many men? I don't know who's the better for it, but I know very well who's the worse. Why can't they let the blues alone; and the blues let them alone? I worked my poor fingers to the bone making a white flag before they went to Saumur, and all they did was to leave it in the streets of Nantes. There's not so much as a bottle of beer, and hardly a bushel of flour left in Echanbroignes. There's the poor dear lovely Cathelineau dead and gone. There's M. Henri engaged to the girl of his heart, and he can't so much as stay a day from fighting to get himself married; and there's Jacques just as bad. If Jacques cares a bit for me, he must take himself off, and me with him, to some place where there's not quite so much fighting, or else I'll be quit of him and go without him. I've no idea of living in a place where girls are not, to be married till the wars are over. Wars, wars, wars; I'm sick of the wars with all my heart."

CHAPTER XII.
SENTENCE OF DEATH.

After parting with their companion, de Lescure and Henri were not long in reaching Durbellière; and on the road thither they also learnt that Santerre, and upwards of a hundred blue horsemen, were prisoners in the château, or in the barns, out-houses, or stables belonging to it; and that the whole place was crowded with peasants, guarding their captives. As they entered the château gates, they met Chapeau, who was at the bottom of the steps, waiting for them; and Henri immediately asked after his father.

"Monseigneur is much fatigued," said Chapeau, "but apparently well; he is, however, still in bed."

"And my sister?" said Henri.

"Mademoiselle has of course been much fatigued, but she is well; she is with your father, M. Henri."

"And tell me, Chapeau, is it true, is it really true that M. Denot brought the blues here, and that since he has been here he has treated my sister in the manner they describe?"

"It is true as gospel, M. Henri. I knew that this would be the worst of the whole affair to you. I knew you would sooner the château should have been burnt than have heard this. We are only waiting for you and M. de Lescure, to hang him as a traitor from the big chestnut out on the road-side. You might have seen as you came in, that they have the ropes and everything ready."

Henri shuddered as he followed his cousin into the house. The steps were crowded with his own followers, who warmly welcomed him, and congratulated him on the safety of his father, his sister, and his property; but he said very little to them; he was thinking of the friend whom he had loved so well, who had so vilely disgraced himself, and whose life he now feared he should be unable to save.

"Where is he?" said he to Chapeau.

"Who—Monseigneur?"

"No—M. Denot."

"He is in the great salon, with Santerre, and Father Jerome, and the Chevalier, and three or four of the lads from Echanbroignes."

"Charles," said he, as he reached the door of the salon, "do you go in. You are better able to say what should be said, and to do what must be done, than

I am. I will go up to my father. But, Charles," and he spoke into his ear, so that no one else should hear him, "save his life—for my sake, save his life. He is mad, and does not know what he has been doing." De Lescure pressed his cousin's hand, and as Henri ran up stairs to his father, he entered the room, where the party abovementioned were sitting.

The occupants of the room certainly formed a very remarkable group. The first person whom de Lescure saw was Adolphe Denot; he was seated in a large arm-chair, placed against the wall immediately opposite the door, and between the stove and the folding-doors which opened into the other room. His legs were stretched out to their full length before him his hands were clasped together between his legs; his head was bent down, so that his chin rested on his breast; he was scowling awfully, his eyebrows nearly met above his eyes, and he continued constantly curling and twisting his lips, sometimes shewing his teeth, and sometimes completely covering his under with his upper lip. He had sat twelve hours, since Agatha had left the room in the morning, without speaking a word, or once changing his position. He had refused food when it had been brought to him, with an indignant shake of the head; and when Santerre had once half jocularly told him to keep up his spirits, and prove himself a man, he had uttered a horrible sound, which he had meant for a laugh of derision, such as is sometimes heard to proceed from dark-haired, diabolical, provincial tragedians.

There were three men from Echanbroignes in the room, distinguished by the notable red scarf, acting as guards, to prevent the escape of the prisoners; but as the two objects of their care during the whole day had made no attempt at escaping, the guards had by degrees laid aside the eager watchfulness with which they had at first expressed their readiness to pounce upon their captives, should they by any motion have betrayed an intention to leave their seats, and were now resting on three chairs in a row, each man having his musket between his legs, and looking as though they were peculiarly tired of their long inactive services. Santerre and Father Jerome were seated together on a sofa, and the Chevalier occupied a chair on the other side of a table on which the prisoner and the priest were leaning. When Santerre found that he and his men were in the hands of the royalist peasants, he at first rather lost both his temper and his presence of mind. He saw at once that resistance was out of the question, and that there was very little chance that he would be able to escape; he began to accuse himself of rashness in having accepted from the Convention the very disagreeable commission which had brought him into his present plight, and to wish that he was once more among his legitimate adherents in the Quartier St. Antoine. He soon, however, regained his equanimity. Those whom he had in his rough manner treated well, returned the compliment; and he perceived that, though he would probably be kept a prisoner, his life would not be in danger, and that the royalists were not inclined to treat him either with insult or severity.

He by degrees got into conversation with the Chevalier; and before the day was over, even Father Jerome, much as he abhorred a republican, and especially a leader of republicans, and an infidel, as he presumed Santerre to be, forgot his disgust, and chatted freely with the captive Commissioner. The three dined together in the afternoon, and when de Lescure entered the room, wine and glasses were still on the table. A crowd of the royalist peasants followed de Lescure to the door of the salon, and would have entered it with him, had not Chapeau, with much difficulty, restrained them. They were most anxious to hear sentence pronounced on the traitor, who had betrayed their cause, and insulted the sister of their favourite leader; and could not understand why the punishment, which he had so richly merited, should be delayed. All that Chapeau and Father Jerome had ventured to ask of them was to wait till Henri himself should arrive; and now, that he had come, they conceived that judgment should at once be passed, and sentence of death immediately executed.

When de Lescure entered the room, they all, except Denot, rose from their chairs; the three guards stood up, and shouldered their muskets, the Chevalier ran up to him to shake hands with him, and Father Jerome also came out into the middle of the room to meet him. He looked first at Denot, who kept his eyes steadily fixed on the ground; and then at Santerre, whom he had never, to his knowledge, seen before. Santerre, however, knew him, for he immediately called him by his name.

"My soldiers have met with a reverse, General de Lescure," said he, "which has thrown me and them into the power of your friends. I take the earliest opportunity of thanking you for the kind treatment we have received."

"If, at some future time, when our soldiers may be in your power, you will remember it; the Marquis de Larochejaquelin will feel himself amply repaid for such attention as he has been able to shew you," said de Lescure.

"You know we were in General Santerre's power last night," said the Chevalier; "and he could have shot us all had he pleased it; indeed we all expected it, when the blues came upon us."

"They shall not find that we will be less merciful, Arthur," said de Lescure. "General Santerre knows that the Vendean royalists have never disgraced themselves by shedding the blood of the prisoners whom the chance of war may have thrown into their hands. He knows that they can be brave without being cruel. I grieve to say that the republicans have hitherto not often allowed us to repay mercy with mercy. We shall now be glad to take advantage of the opportunity of doing so."

"What will you do with him, M. de Lescure," said Father Jerome in a whisper, pointing to Denot. "I never before saw the people greedy for blood; but now they declare that no mercy should be shown to a traitor."

"We must teach them, Father Jerome, that it is God's will that those who wish to be pardoned themselves must pardon others. You have taught them lessons more difficult to learn than this; and I do not doubt that in this, as in other things, they will obey their priest." And as he spoke de Lescure laid his hand on the Curé's shoulder.

"You won't hang him then?" whispered the Chevalier.

"You wouldn't have me do so, would you, Arthur?"

"Who—I?" said the boy. "No—that is, I don't know. I wouldn't like to have to say that anybody should be hung; but if anybody ever did deserve it, he does."

"And you, Father Jerome?" said de Lescure, "you agree with me? You would not have us sully our pure cause with a cold-blooded execution?"

The three were now standing at an open window, looking into the garden. Their backs were turned to Santerre and Denot, and they were speaking in low whispers; but nevertheless Denot either guessed or overheard that he was the subject of their conversation. The priest did not immediately answer de Lescure's appeal. In his heart he thought that the circumstances not only justified, but demanded the traitor's death; but, remembering his profession, and the lessons of mercy it was his chief business to teach, he hesitated to be the first to say that he thought the young man should be doomed.

"Well, Father Jerome," said de Lescure, looking into the priest's face, "surely you have no difficulty in answering me?"

The Curé was saved the necessity of answering the appeal; for while he was still balancing between what he thought to be his duty, and that which was certainly his inclination, Denot himself interrupted the whisperers.

"M. de Lescure," said he, in the deep, hoarse, would-be solemn voice, which he now always affected to use. De Lescure turned quickly round, and so did his companions. The words of a man who thinks that he is almost immediately about to die are always interesting.

"If you are talking about me," said the unfortunate wretch, "pray spare yourself the trouble. I neither ask, nor wish for any mercy at your hands. I am ready to die."

As de Lescure looked at him, and observed the alteration which a few weeks had made in his appearance—his sunken, sallow cheeks; his wild and bloodshot eyes; his ragged, uncombed hair, and soiled garments—as he thought of his own recent intimacy with him—as he remembered how often he had played with him as a child, and associated with him as a man—that till a few days since he had been the bosom friend of his own more than brother, Henri Larochejaquelin, the tears rushed to his eyes and down his cheeks. In that moment the scene in the council-room at Saumur came to his mind, and he remembered that there he had rebuked Adolphe Denot for his false ambition, and had probably been the means of driving him to the horrid crime which he had committed. Though he knew that the traitor's iniquity admitted of no excuse, he sympathized with the sufferings which had brought him to his present condition. He turned away his head, as the tears rolled down his cheeks, and felt that he was unable to speak to the miserable man.

Had de Lescure upbraided him, Denot's spirit, affected and unreal as it was, would have enabled him to endure it without flinching. He would have answered the anger of his former friend with bombast, and might very probably have mustered courage enough to support the same character till they led him out to death. But de Lescure's tears affected him. He felt that he was pitied; and though his pride revolted against the commiseration of those whom he had injured, his heart was touched, and his voice faltered, as he again declared that he desired no mercy, and that he was ready to die.

"Ready to die!" said the Curé, "and with such a weight of sin upon your conscience; ready to be hurried before the eternal judgment seat, without having acknowledged, even in your own heart, the iniquity of your transgressions!"

"That, Sir, is my concern," said Denot. "I knew the dangers of the task before I undertook it, and I can bear the penalties of failure without flinching. I fear them not, either in this world or in any other world to come."

De Lescure, overcome with distress, paced up and down the room till Chapeau entered it, and whispered to him, that the peasants outside were anxious to know what next they were to do, and that they were clamorous for Denot's execution. "They are determined to hang him," continued Chapeau, who had induced de Lescure to leave the room, and was now speaking to him in the hall. "They say that you and M. Henri may do what you please about Santerre and the soldiers, but that Adolphe Denot has betrayed the cause, insulted Mademoiselle, and proved himself unfit to live; and that they will not leave the château as long as a breath of life remains in his body."

"And you, Chapeau, what did you say to them in reply?"

"Oh, M. de Lescure, of course I said that that must be as you and M. Henri pleased."

"Well, Chapeau, now go and tell them this," said de Lescure: "tell them that we will not consent that this poor wretch shall be killed, and that his miserable life has already been granted to him. Tell them also, that if they choose to forget their duty, their obedience, and their oaths, and attempt to seize Denot's person, neither I nor M. Henri will ever again accompany them to battle, and that they shall not lay a hand upon him till they have passed over our bodies. Do you understand?"

Chapeau said that he did understand, and with a somewhat melancholy face, he returned to the noisy crowd, who were waiting for their victim in the front of the house. "Well, Jacques," said one of them, an elderly man, who had for the time taken upon himself the duties of a leader among them, and who was most loud in demanding that sentence should be passed upon Denot. "We are ready, and the rope is ready, and the gallows is ready, and we are only waiting for the traitor. We don't want to hurry M. Henri or M. de Lescure, but we hope they will not keep us waiting much longer."

"You need not wait any longer," said Chapeau, "for Adolphe Denot is not to be hung at all. M. de Lescure has pardoned him. Yes, my friends, you will be spared an unpleasant job, and the rope and the tree will not be contaminated."

"Pardoned him—pardoned Adolphe Denot—pardoned the traitor who brought Santerre and the republicans to Durbellière—pardoned the wretch who so grossly insulted Mademoiselle Agatha, and nearly killed M. le Marquis," cried one after another immediately round the door. "If we pardon him, there will be an end of honesty and good faith. We will pardon our enemies, because M. de Lescure asks us. We will willingly pardon this Santerre and all his men. We will pardon everything and anybody, if M. Henri or M de Lescure asks it, except treason, and except a traitor. Go in, Jacques, and say that we will never consent to forgive the wretch who insulted Mademoiselle Larochejaquelin. By all that is sacred we will hang him!"

"If you do, my friends," answered Chapeau, "you must kill M. de Lescure first, for he will defend him with his own body and his own sword."

Chapeau again returned to the house, and left the peasants outside, loudly murmuring. Hitherto they had passively obeyed their leaders. They had gone from one scene of action to another. They had taken towns and conquered armies, and abstained not only from slaughter, but even from plunder, at the mere request of those whom they had selected as their own Generals; now, for the first time they shewed a determination to disobey. The offence of which their victim had been guilty, was in their eyes unpardonable. They were freely giving all—their little property, their children, their blood, for their church and King. They knew that they were themselves faithful and obedient to their leaders, and they could not bring themselves to forgive one whom they had trusted, and who had deceived them.

Chapeau returned to the house, but he did not go back to M. de Lescure. He went upstairs to his master, and found him alone with his sister, and explained to them what was going on before the front-door.

"They will never go away, Mademoiselle, as long as the breath is in the man's body. They are angry now, and they care for no one, not even for M. Henri himself; and it's no wonder for them to be angry. He that was so trusted, and so loved; one of the family as much as yourself, M. Henri. Why, if I were to turn traitor, and go over to the republicans, it could hardly be worse. If ever I did, I should expect them to pinch me to pieces with hot tweezers, let alone hanging."

"I will go down to them," said M. Henri.

"It will be no use," said Chapeau, "they will not listen to you."

"I will try them at any rate, for they have never yet disobeyed me. I know they love me, and I will ask for Adolphe's life as a favour to myself: if they persist in their cruelty, if they do kill him, I will lay down my sword, and never again raise it in La Vendée."

"If it were put off for a week, or a day, M. Henri, so that they could get cool; if you could just consent to his being hung, but say that he was to have four-and-twenty hours to prepare himself, and then at the end of that time they wouldn't care about it: mightn't that do? Wouldn't that be the best plan, Mademoiselle?"

"No," said Henri. "I will not stoop to tell them a falsehood; nor if I did so, would they ever believe me again." And he walked towards the passage, intending to go down to the front-door.

"Stop, Henri, stop a moment!" said Agatha, "I will go down to them. I will speak to them. They are not accustomed to hear me speak to them in numbers, as they are to you, and that of itself will make them inclined to listen to me. I will beg them to spare the unfortunate man, and I think they will not refuse me."

She got up and walked to the door, and her brother did not attempt to stop her.

"Let me go alone, Henri," said she. "You may, at any rate, be sure that they will not hurt me." And, without waiting for his reply, she descended the stairs, and walked into the hall. When Chapeau left them, the crowd were collected immediately in the front of the house and on the steps, but none of them had yet forced their way into the château; since he had gone upstairs, however, they had pushed open the door, and now filled the hall; although their accustomed respect for the persons and property of those above them, had still kept them from breaking into the room, in which they knew were M. de Lescure and Adolphe Denot. The foremost of them drew back when they saw Agatha come among them, and as she made her way to the front-door, they retreated before her, till she found herself standing on the top of the steps, and surrounded by what seemed to her a countless crowd of heads. There was a buzz of many voices among them, and she stood there silent before them a moment or two, till there should be such silence as would enable them to hear her.

Agatha Larochejaquelin had never looked more beautiful than she did at this time. Her face was more than ordinarily pale, for her life had lately been one of constant watching and deep anxiety; but hers was a countenance which looked even more lovely without than with its usual slight tinge of colour. Her beautiful dark-brown hair was braided close to her face, and fastened in a knot behind her head. She was dressed in a long white morning wrapper, which fell quite down over her feet, and added in appearance to her natural high stature. She seemed to the noisy peasants, as she stood there before them, sad-looking and sorrowful, but so supremely beautiful, to be like some goddess who had come direct from heaven to give them warning and encouragement. The hum of their voices soon dropped, and they stood as silent before her, as though no strong passion, no revenge and thirst for blood had induced them, but a moment before, all but to mutiny against the leaders who had led them so truly, and loved them so well.

"Friends, dear friends," she began in her sweet voice, low, but yet plainly audible to those whom she addressed; and then she paused a moment to think of the words she would use to them, and as she did so they cheered her loudly, and blessed her, and assured her, in their rough way, how delighted they were to have saved her and the Marquis from their enemies.

"Dear friends," she continued, "I have come to thank you for the readiness and kindness with which you have hurried to my protection—to tell you how grateful I and mine are for your affection, and at the same time to ask a favour from your hands."

"God bless you, Mademoiselle. We will do anything for Mademoiselle Agatha. We all know that Mademoiselle is an angel. We will do anything for her," said different voices in the crowd. "Anything but pardon the traitor who has insulted her," said the man who had been most prominent in demanding Denot's death. "Anything at all—anything, without exception. We will do anything we are asked, whatever it is, for Mademoiselle Agatha," said some of the younger men among the crowd, whom her beauty made more than ordinarily enthusiastic in her favour. "Mademoiselle will not sully her beautiful lips to ask the life of a traitor," said another. "We will do anything else; but Denot must die." "Yes, Denot must die," exclaimed others. "He shall die; he is not fit to live. When the traitor is hung, we will do anything, go anywhere, for Mademoiselle."

"Ah! friends," said she, "the favour I would ask of you is to spare the life of this miserable young man. Hear me, at any rate," she continued, for there was a murmur among the more resolute of Denot's enemies. "You will not refuse to hear what I say to you. You demand vengeance, you say, because he has betrayed your cause, and insulted me. If I can forgive the insult, if my brother can, surely you should do so too. Think, dear friends, what my misery must be, if on my account you shed the blood of this poor creature. You say he has betrayed the cause for which you are fighting. It is true, he has done so; but it is not only your cause which he has betrayed. Is it not my cause also? Is it not my brother's? Is it not M. de Lescure's? And if we can forgive him, should not you also do so too? He has lived in this house as though he were a child of my father's. You know that my brother has treated him as a brother. Supposing that you, any of you, had had a brother who has done as he has done, would you not still pray, in spite of his crimes, that he might be forgiven? I know you all love my brother. He deserves from you that you should love him well, for he has proved to you that he loves you. He—Henri Larochejaquelin—your own leader, begs you to forgive the crime of his adopted brother. Have we not sufficient weight with you—are we not near enough to your hearts, to obtain from you this boon?"

"We will, we will," shouted they; "we will forgive—no, we won't forgive him, but we'll let him go; only, Mademoiselle, let him go from this—let him not show himself here any more. There, lads, there's an end of it. Give Momont back the rope. We will do nothing to displease M. Henri and Mademoiselle Agatha," and then they gave three cheers for the inhabitants of Durbellière; and Agatha, after thanking them for their kindness and their courtesy, returned into the house.

For some days after the attack and rescue, there was great confusion in the château of Durbellière. The peasants by degrees returned to their own homes, or went to Chatillon, at which place it was now intended to muster the whole armed royalist force which could be collected in La Vendée. Chatillon was in the very centre of the revolted district, and not above three leagues from Durbellière; and at this place the Vendean leaders had now determined to assemble, that they might come to some fixed plan, and organize their resistance to the Convention.

De Lescure and Henri together agreed to give Santerre his unconditional liberty. In the first place, they conceived it to be good policy to abandon the custody of a man whom, if kept a prisoner, they were sure the Republic would make a great effort to liberate; and who, if he ever again served against them at all, would, as they thought, be less inclined to exercise barbarity than any other man whom the Convention would be likely to send on the duty. Besides, Agatha and the Marquis really felt grateful to Santerre, for having shown a want of that demoniac cruelty with which they supposed him to have been imbued; and it was, therefore, resolved to escort him personally to the northern frontier of La Vendée, and there set him at liberty, but to detain his soldiers prisoners at Chatillon; and this was accordingly done.

They had much more difficulty in disposing of Denot. Had he been turned loose from the château, to go where he pleased, and do what he pleased, he would to a certainty have been killed by the peasantry. De Lescure asked Santerre to take charge of him, but this he refused to do, saying that he considered the young man was a disgrace to any party, or any person, who had aught to do with him, and that he would not undertake to be responsible for his safety.

Denot himself would neither say or do anything. Henri never saw him; but de Lescure had different interviews with him, and did all in his power to rouse him to some feeling as to the future; but all in vain. He usually refused to make any answer whatever, and when he did speak, he merely persisted in his declaration that he was willing to die, and that if he were left alive, he had no wish at all as to what should become of him. It was at last decided to send him to his own house at Fleury, with a strong caution to the servants there that their master was temporarily insane; and there to leave him to his chance. "When he finds himself alone, and disregarded," said de Lescure, "he will come to his senses, and probably emigrate: it is impossible for us now to do more for him. May God send that he may live to repent the great crime which he has attempted."

Now again everything was bustle and confusion at Durbellière. Arms and gunpowder were again collected. The men again used all their efforts in assembling the royalist troops, the women in preparing the different necessaries for the army. The united families were at Durbellière, and there was no longer any danger of their separation, for at Clisson not one stone was left standing upon another.

VOLUME III.

CHAPTER I.
ROBESPIERRE'S CHARACTER.

We will now jump over a space of nearly three months, and leaving the châteaux of royalist La Vendée, plunge for a short while into the heart of republican Paris. In the Rue St. Honoré lived a cabinet-maker, named Duplay, and in his house lodged Maximilian Robespierre, the leading spirit in the latter and more terrible days of the Revolution. The time now spoken of was the beginning of October, 1793; and at no period did the popularity and power of that remarkable man stand higher.

The whole government was then vested in the Committee of Public Safety— a committee consisting of twelve persons, members of the Convention, all of course ultra-democrats, over the majority of whom Robespierre exercised a direct control. No despot ever endured ruled with so absolute and stringent a dominion as that under which this body of men held the French nation. The revolutionary tribunal was now established in all its horror and all its force. A law was passed by the Convention, in September, which decreed that all suspected people should be arrested and brought before this tribunal; that nobles, lawyers, bankers, priests, men of property, and strangers in the land, should be suspected unless known to be acting friends and adherents of the ultra-revolutionary party; that the punishment of such persons should be death; and that the members of any revolutionary tribunal which had omitted to condemn any suspected person, should themselves be tried, and punished by death. Such was the law by which the Reign of Terror was organized and rendered possible.

At this time the Girondists were lying in prison, awaiting their trial and their certain doom. Marie Antoinette had been removed from the Temple to the Conciergerie, and her trial was in a day or two about to commence. Her fate was already fixed, and had only to be pronounced. Danton had retired from Paris to his own province, sick with the shedding of so much blood, jealous of the pre-eminence which Robespierre had assumed; watching his opportunity to return, that he might sell the republic to the royalists; equally eager, let us believe, to save his country as to make his fortune, but destined to return, only that he also might bend his neck beneath the monster guillotine. Marat, the foulest birth of the revolution, whose licentious heat generated venom and rascality, as a dunghill out of its own filth produces adders' eggs—Marat was no more. Carnot, whose genius for war enabled the French nation, amidst all its poverty and intestine contests, even in the pangs and throes of that labour in which it strove to bring forth a constitution, to repulse the forces of the allied nations, and prepare the way for future conquests, was a member of the all-powerful Committee, and we cannot suppose that he acted under the dictation of Robespierre; but if he did not do so, at any rate he did not interfere with him. The operations of a campaign, in which the untaught and ill-fed army of republican France had to meet the troops of England, Flanders, Prussia, Austria, Sardinia, and Spain, besides those of royalist France, were sufficient to occupy even the energies of Carnot.

Robespierre, in the Convention and in the Committee, was omnipotent; but he also had his master, and he knew it. He knew that he could only act, command, and be obeyed, in union with, and dependence on, the will of the populace of Paris; and the higher he rose in that path of life which he marked out for himself with so much precision, and followed with so much constancy, the more bitterly his spirit chafed at the dependence. He knew it was of no avail to complain of the people to the people, and he seldom ventured to risk his position by opposing the wishes of the fearful masters whom he served, but at length he was driven to do so, and at length he fell.

Half a century has passed since Robespierre died, and history has become peculiarly conversant with his name. Is there any one whose character suffers under a more wide-spread infamy? The abomination of whose deeds has become more notorious? The tale of whose death has been oftener told; whose end, horrid, fearful, agonized, as was that of this man, has met with less sympathy? For fifty years the world has talked of, condemned, and executed Robespierre. Men and women, who have barely heard the names of Pitt and Fox, who know not whether Metternich is a man or a river, or one of the United States, speak of Robespierre as of a thing accursed. They know, at any rate, what he was—the demon of the revolution; the source of the fountain of blood with which Paris was deluged; the murderer of the thousands whose bodies choked the course of the Loire and the Rhone. Who knows not enough of Robespierre to condemn him? Who abstains from adding another malediction to those which already load the name of the King of the Reign of Terror.

Yet it is not impossible that some apologist may be found for the blood which this man shed; that some quaint historian, delighting to show the world how wrong has been its most assured opinions, may attempt to vindicate the fame of Robespierre, and strive to wash the blackamoor white. Are not our old historical assurances everywhere asserted? Has it not been proved to us that crooked-backed Richard was a good and politic King; and that the iniquities of Henry VIII are fabulous? whereas the agreeable predilections of our early youth are disturbed by our hearing that glorious Queen Bess, and learned King James, were mean, bloodthirsty, and selfish.

I am not the bold man who will dare to face the opinion of the world, and attempt to prove that Robespierre has become infamous through prejudice. He must be held responsible for the effects of the words which he spoke, and the things which he did, as other men are. He made himself a scourge and a pestilence to his country; therefore, beyond all other men, he has become odious, and therefore, historian after historian, as they mention his name, hardly dare, in the service of truth, to say one word to lessen his infamy.

Yet Robespierre began his public life with aspirations of humanity, which never deserted him; and resolutions as to conduct, to which he adhered with a constancy never surpassed. What shall we say are the qualifications for a great and good man?—Honesty. In spite of his infamy, Robespierre's honesty has become proverbial. Moral conduct—the life he led even during the zenith of his power, and at a time when licentiousness was general, and morality ridiculous, was characterized by the simplicity of the early Quakers. Industry—without payment from the State, beyond that which he received as a member of the Convention, and which was hardly sufficient for the wants of his simple existence, he worked nearly night and day in the service of the State. Constancy of purpose—from the commencement of his career, in opposition at first to ridicule and obscurity, then to public opinion, and lastly to the combined efforts of the greatest of his countrymen, he pursued one only idea; convinced of its truth, sure of its progress, and longing for its success. Temperance in power—though in reality governing all France, Robespierre assumed to himself none of the attributes or privileges of political power. He took to himself no high place, no public situation of profit or grandeur. He was neither haughty in his language, nor imperious in his demeanour. Love of country—who ever showed a more devoted love? For his country he laboured, and suffered a life which surely in itself could have had nothing attractive; the hope of the future felicity of France alone fed his energies, and sustained his courage. His only selfish ambition was to be able to retire into private life and contemplate from thence the general happiness which he had given to his country. Courage—those who have carefully studied his private life, and have learnt what he endured, and dared to do in overcoming the enemies Of his system, can hardly doubt his courage. Calumny or error has thrown an unmerited disgrace over his last wretched days. He has been supposed to have wounded himself in an impotent attempt to put an end to his life. It has been ascertained that such was not the fact, the pistol by which he was wounded having been fired by one of the soldiers by whom he was arrested. He is stated also to have wanted that firmness in death which so many of his victims displayed. They triumphed even in their death. Louis and Vergniaud, Marie Antoinette, and Madame Roland, felt that they were stepping from life into glory, and their step was light and elastic. Robespierre was sinking from existence into infamy. During those fearful hours, in which nothing in life was left him but to suffer, how wretched must have been the reminiscences of his career! He, who had so constantly pursued one idea, must then have felt that that idea had been an error; that he had all in all been wrong; that he had waded through the blood of his countrymen to reach a goal, which, bright and luminous as it had appeared, he now found to be an ignis fatuus. Nothing was then left to him. His life had been a failure, and for the future he had no hope. His body was wounded and in tortures; his spirit was dismayed by the insults of those around him, and his soul had owned no haven to which death would give it an escape. Could his eye have been lit with animation as he ascended the scaffold! Could his foot have then stepped with confidence! Could he have gloried in his death! Poor mutilated worm, agonised in body and in soul. Can it be ascribed to want of courage in him, that his last moments were passed in silent agony and despair?

Honesty, moral conduct, industry, constancy of purpose, temperance in power, courage, and love of country: these virtues all belonged to Robespierre; history confesses it, and to what favoured hero does history assign a fairer catalogue? Whose name does a brighter galaxy adorn? With such qualities, such attributes, why was he not the Washington of France? Why, instead of the Messiah of freedom, which he believed himself to be, has his name become a bye-word, a reproach, and an enormity? Because he wanted faith! He believed in nothing but himself, and the reasoning faculty with which he felt himself to be endowed. He thought himself perfect in his own human nature, and wishing to make others perfect as he was, he fell into the lowest abyss of crime and misery in which a poor human creature ever wallowed. He seems almost to have been sent into the world to prove the inefficacy of human reason to effect human happiness. He was gifted with a power over common temptation, which belongs to but few. His blood was cool and temperate, and yet his heart was open to all the softer emotions. He had no appetite for luxury; no desire for pomp; no craving for wealth. Among thousands who were revelling in sensuality, he kept himself pure and immaculate. If any man could have said, I will be virtuous; I, of myself, unaided, trusting to my own power, guarding myself by the light of my own reason; I will walk uprightly through the world, and will shed light from my path upon my brethren, he might have said so. He attempted it, and history shows us the result. He attempted, unassisted, to be perfect among men, and his memory is regarded as that of a loathsome plague, defiling even the unclean age in which he lived.

At about five o'clock in the afternoon on an October day, in 1793, Robespierre was sitting alone in a small room in the house of his friend, Simon Duplay, the cabinet-maker. This room, which was the bed-chamber, reception-room, and study of the arbitrary Dictator, was a garret in the roof of Duplay's humble dwelling. One small window, opening upon the tiles, looked into the court-yard in which were stored the planks or blocks necessary to the cabinet-maker's trade. A small wooden bedstead, a long deal table, and four or five rush-bottomed chairs, constituted the whole furniture of the apartment.

A deal shelf ran along the wail beneath the slanting roof, and held his small treasure of books; and more than half of this humble row were manuscripts of his own, which he had numbered, arranged, and bound with that methodical exactness, which was a part of his strange character. He was sitting at a table covered with papers, on which he had now been laboriously preparing instructions for those who, under him, carried on the rule of terror; and arranging the measured words with which, at the Jacobins, he was to encourage his allies to uphold him in the bloody despotism which he had seized.

The weight upon his mind must have been immense, for Robespierre was not a thoughtless, wild fanatic, carried by the multitude whether they pleased: he led the people of Paris, and led them with a fixed object. He was progressing by one measure deeply calculated to the age of reason, which he was assured was coming; and that one measure was the extermination of all who would be likely to oppose him. The extent of his power, the multiplicity of his cares, the importance of his every word and act, and the personal danger in which he lived, might have ruffled the equanimity of a higher-spirited man than he is supposed to have been; but yet, to judge from his countenance, his mind was calm; the traces of thought were plain on his brow, but there was none of the impatience of a tyrant about his mouth, nor of the cruelty of an habitual blood-shedder in his eyes. His forehead showed symptoms of deep thought, and partially redeemed the somewhat mean effect of his other features. The sharp nose, the thin lips, the cold grey eyes, the sallow sunken cheeks, were those of a precise, passionless, self-confident man, little likely to be led into any excess of love or hatred, but little likely also to be shaken in his resolve either for good or evil. His face probably was a true index to his character. Robespierre was not a cruel man; but he had none of that humanity, which makes the shedding of blood abominable to mankind, and which, had he possessed it, would have made his career impossible.

His hair was close curled in rolls upon his temples, and elaborately powdered. The front and cuffs of his shirt were not only scrupulously clean, but starched and ironed with the most exact care. He wore a blue coat, a white waistcoat, and knee-breeches. His stockings, like his shirt, were snow-white, and the silver buckles shone brightly in his shoes. No one could have looked less like a French republican of 1793 than did Robespierre.

He had just completed a letter addressed jointly to Thurreau and Lechelle, the commissioners whom he had newly appointed to the horrid task of exterminating the royalists of La Vendée. Santerre had undertaken this work, and had failed in it, and it was now said that he was a friend and creature of Danton's; that he was not to be trusted as a republican; that he had a royalist bias; that it would be a good thing that his head should roll, as the heads of so many false men had rolled, under the avenging guillotine. Poor Santerre, who, in the service of the Republic, had not shunned the infamy of presiding at the death of Louis. He, however, contrived to keep his burly head on his strong shoulders, and to brew beer for the Directory, the Consulate, and the Empire.

Thurreau and Lechelle, it was correctly thought, would be surer hands at performing the work to be done. They had accepted the commission with alacrity, and were now on the road to commence their duties. That duty was to leave neither life nor property in the proscribed district. "Let La Vendée become a wilderness, and we will re-populate it with patriots, to whom the fertility of fields, rich with the blood of traitors, shall be a deserved reward." Thus had Robespierre now written; and as he calmly read over, and slowly copied, his own despatch, he saw nothing in it of which he could disapprove, as a reasoning being animated with a true love of his country. "Experience has too clearly proved to us that the offspring of slaves, who willingly kiss the rod of tyrants, will have no higher aspiration than their parents. In allowing them to escape, we should only create difficulties for our own patriot children. Hitherto the servants of the Convention have scotched the snake, but have not killed it; and the wounded viper has thus become more furiously venomous than before. It is for you, citizens, to strike a death-blow to the infamy of La Vendée. It will be your glory to assure the Convention that no royalist remains in the western provinces to disturb the equanimity of the Republic." Such were the sentiments he had just expressed, such the instructions he had given, calmly meditating on his duty as a ruler of his country; and when he had finished his task, and seen that no expression had escaped him of which reason or patriotism could disapprove, he again placed the paper before him, to write words of affection to the brother of his heart.

Robespierre's brother was much younger than himself; but there was no one whom he more thoroughly trusted with State secrets, and State services of importance; and no one who regarded him with so entire a devotion. Robespierre the elder believed only in himself; Robespierre the younger believed in his brother, and his belief was fervid and assured, as is always that of an enthusiast. To him, Maximilian appeared to be the personification of every virtue necessary to mankind. Could he have been made to understand the opinion which the world would form of his brother's character, he would have thought that it was about to be smitten with a curse of general insanity. Robespierre's vanity was flattered by the adoration of his brother, and he loved his worshipper sincerely. The young man was now at Lyons, propagating the doctrines of his party; and in his letters to him, Robespierre mingled the confidential greetings of an affectionate brother with those furious demands for republican energy, which flooded the streets of the towns of France with blood, and choked the rivers of France with the bodies of the French.

"I still hope," he wrote, slowly considering the words as they fell from his pen, "for the day when this work will have been done—for the happy day when we shall feel that we have prevailed not only against our enemies, but over our own vices; but my heart nearly fails me, when I think how little we have yet effected. I feel that among the friends whom we most trust, those who are actuated by patriotism alone are lukewarm. Lust, avarice, plunder, and personal revenge, are the motives of those who are really energetic . . . It is very difficult for me to know my friends; this also preys heavily on my spirits. The gold of the royalists is as plentiful as when the wretched woman, who is now about to die, was revelling in her voluptuous pride at Versailles. I know that the hands of many, who call themselves patriots, are even now grasping at the wages for which they are to betray the people. A day of reckoning shall come for all of them, though the list of their names is a long one. Were I to write the names of those whom I know to be true, I should be unable to insert in it above five or six. . . . I look for your return to Paris with more than my usual impatience. Eleanor's quiet zeal, and propriety of demeanour, is a great comfort to me; but even with her, I feel that I have some reserve. I blame myself that it is so, for she is most trustworthy; but, as yet, I cannot throw it off. With you alone I have none. Do not, however, leave the work undone; remember that those who will not toil for us, will assuredly toil against us. There can be none neutral in the battle we are now waging. A man can have committed no greater crime against the Republic than having done nothing to add to its strength. I know your tender heart grieves at the death of every traitor, though your patriotism owns the necessity of his fall. Remember that the prosperity of every aristocrat has been purchased by the infamy of above a hundred slaves! How much better is it that one man should die, than that a hundred men should suffer worse than death!"

When he had finished his letter, he read it accurately over, and then having carefully wiped his pen, and laid it near his inkstand, he leant back in his chair, and with his hand resting on the table, turned over in his mind the names and deeds of those who were accounted as his friends, but whom he suspected to be his enemies. He had close to his hand slips of paper, on which were written notes of the most trivial doings of those by whom he was generally surrounded; and the very spies who gave him the information were themselves the unfortunate subjects of similar notices from others. The wretched man was tortured by distrust; as he had told his brother, there were not among the whole body of those associates, by whose aid he had made himself the ruling power in France, half-a-dozen whom he did not believe to be eager for his downfall and his death. Thrice, whilst thus meditating, he stopped, and with his pencil put a dot against the name of a republican. Unfortunate men! their patriotism did not avail them; within a few weeks, the three had been added to the list of victims who perished under the judicial proceedings of Fouquier Tinville.

It had now become nearly dark, and Robespierre was unable longer to read the unfriendly notices which lay beneath his hand, and he therefore gave himself up entirely to reflection. He began to dream of nobler subjects—to look forward to happier days, when torrents of blood would be no longer necessary, when traitors should no longer find a market for their treason, when the age of reason should have prevailed, and France, happy, free, illustrious, and intellectual, should universally own how much she owed to her one incorruptible patriot. He thought to himself of living on his small paternal domain in Artois, receiving nothing from the country he had blessed but adoration; triumphant in the success of his theory; honoured as more than mortal; evincing the grandeur of his soul by rejecting those worldly rewards, which to his disposition offered no temptation. But before he had long indulged in this happy train of thought, he was called back to the realities of his troubled life by a low knock at his door, and on his answering it, a young woman, decently, but very plainly dressed, entered the garret with a candle in her hand; this was Eleanor Duplay; and when Robespierre allowed himself to dream of a future home, she was the wife of his bosom, and the mother of his children.

CHAPTER II.
ROBESPIERRE'S LOVE.

Eleanor Duplay was not a beautiful young woman, nor was there anything about her which marked her as being superior to those of her own station of life; but her countenance was modest and intelligent, and her heart was sincere; such as she was she had won the affection of him, who was, certainly, at this time the most powerful man in France. She was about five-and-twenty years of age; was the eldest of four sisters, and had passed her quiet existence in assisting her mother in her household, and in doing for her father so much of his work as was fitting for a woman's hand. Till Robespierre had become an inmate of her father's house, she had not paid more than ordinary attention to the politics of the troubled days in which she lived; but she had caught the infection from him, as the whole family had done. She had listened to his words as though they fell from inspired lips: the pseudo-philosophical dogmas, which are to us both repulsive and ridiculous, were to her invaluable truths, begotten by reason, and capable of regenerating her fellow-creatures. Robespierre was to her, what her Saviour should have been; and he rewarded her devotion, by choosing her as the partner of his greatness.

Robespierre's affection was not that of an impassioned lover; he did not show it by warm caresses or fervid vows; but yet he made her, whom he had chosen, understand that she was to him dearer than any other woman; and Eleanor was prouder of her affianced husband, than though the handsomest youth of Paris was at her feet.

As she entered his chamber, he was thinking partly of her, and he was not sorry to be thus interrupted. She carried a candle in one hand, and in the other a bouquet of fresh flowers, which she quietly laid among his papers. Robespierre either had, or affected a taste for flowers, and, as long as they were to be gotten, he was seldom seen without them, either in his hand or on his coat.

"I thought you would want a light, M. Robespierre," said she, for though she hoped to be closely connected with him, she seldom ventured on the familiarity of calling him by his Christian name. Had she been a man, her democratic principle would have taught her to discontinue the aristocratic Monsieur; but, even in 1793, the accustomed courtesy of that obnoxious word was allowed to woman's lips. "I thought you would want a light, or I would not have interrupted you at your work."

"Thanks, Eleanor: I was not at work, though; my brain, my eyes, and hands were all tired. I have been sitting idle for, I believe, this half hour."

"Your eyes and hands may have been at rest," said she, sitting down at the end of the table, "but it is seldom that your thoughts are not at work."

"It is one of the high privileges of man, that though his body needs repose, the faculties of his mind need never be entirely dormant. I know that I have reasoned in my sleep as lucidly as I have ever done awake; and though, when awake, I have forgotten what has passed through my mind, the work of my brain has not been lost: the same ideas have recurred to me again, and though in the recurrence, I cannot remember when I have before employed myself with arranging them, still they come to me as old friends, with whom I am well acquainted. The mind will seldom complain of too much labour, if the body be not injured by indulgence or disease."

"But too much labour will bring on disease," said Eleanor, in a tone which plainly showed the sincerity of the anxiety which she expressed. "We never get a walk with you now; do you know that it is months since we were in the Champs Elysées together; it was in May, and this is October now."

"Affairs must be greatly altered, Eleanor; many things which are now undone must be completed, before we walk again for our pleasure: a true patriot can no longer walk the streets of Paris in safety, while traitors can come and go in security, with their treason blazoned on their foreheads."

"And yet do not many traitors expiate their crimes daily?"

"Many are condemned and die; but I fear not always those who have most deserved death. Much blood has been shed, and it has partly been in compliance with my counsel. I would that the vengeance of the Republic might now stay its hand, if it could be so, with safety to the people. I am sick of the unchanging sentences of the judges, and the verdicts of juries who are determined to convict. I doubt not that those who are brought before them are traitors or aristocrats—at any rate, they are not at heart republicans, and if so, they have deserved death; but I should be better pleased, if now and then a victim was spared." He paused for a while, and then added, "The blood of traitors is very sickening; but there are those Eleanor, in whose nostrils it has a sweet savour: there are butchers of the human kind, who revel in the horrid shambles, in which they are of necessity employed. Such men are to me accursed—their breath reeks of human blood."

Eleanor shuddered as she listened to him: but it was not the thought of all the blood, which he whom she loved had shed, which made her shudder: she had no idea that Robespierre was a sanguinary man: she sympathized with the weakness of humanity which he confessed, and loved him for the kindness of his heart—and he was not a hypocrite in his protestation; he believed that there was nothing in common between himself and the wretches who crowded round the last sufferings of the victims whom he had caused to ascend the scaffold. He little thought that, in a few years, he would be looked upon as the sole author of the barbarities of which he now complained.

It was seldom that Robespierre had spoken so openly to Eleanor Duplay of his inmost thoughts. She was flattered and gratified to think he had thought her worthy of his confidence, that he had chosen her to listen to the secrets of his heart, and she felt that, if she had influence with him, it would become her as a woman to use it on behalf of those whom it might be in his power to save from a fearful death.

"And are there many more who must die?" said she. "When I hear the wheels of that horrid cart, as it carries the poor creatures who have been condemned, on their last journey, my heart, too, sickens within me. Will these horrid executions go on much longer?"

"There are still thousands upon thousands of men in France, who would sooner be the slaves of a King, than draw the breath of liberty," answered he.

"But they can be taught the duties and feelings of men, cannot they? They think, and feel now only as they have been brought up to think and feel."

"Had they not been too stubborn to learn, they have had a lesson written in letters of blood, which would have long since convinced them—if it be necessary, it must be repeated I for one will not shrink from my duty. No though I should sink beneath the horrid task which it imposes on me."

They both then sat silent for a while; though Robespierre had ventured to express to the girl, whom he knew to be so entirely devoted to him, a feeling somewhat akin to that of pity for his victims, he could not bear that even she should appear to throw a shadow of an imputation on the propriety and justness of his measures, although she only did so by repeating and appealing to the kindly expressions which had fallen from himself. He had become so used to the unmeasured praise of those among whom he lived, so painfully suspicious of those who, in the remotest degree, disapproved of any of his words or deeds, so confident of himself, so distrustful of all others, that even what she had said was painful to him, and though he himself hardly knew why, yet he felt that he was displeased with her. Eleanor, however, was altogether unconscious of having irritated his sore feelings; and relying on the kind tone of what he had said, and the confident manner in which he had spoken to her, she determined to obey the dictates of her heart, and intercede for mercy for her fellow-creatures. Poor girl! she did not know the danger of coming near the lion's prey.

She had heard much of the Vendeans, and though those who had spoken in her hearing of the doings of the royalist rebels were not likely to say much to excite sympathy on their behalf still she had learnt that they were true to each other, faithful to their leaders, generous to their enemies, and brave in battle. The awful punishment to be inflicted on the doomed district had also been partially discussed in her hearing; and though the Republic had no more enthusiastic daughter than herself, her woman's heart could not endure the idea that even the innocent children of a large province should be condemned to slaughter for their fathers' want of patriotism. What work so fitting for the woman whom a ruler of the people had chosen for a wife, as to implore the stern magistrate to temper justice with mercy? In what way could she use her influence so sweetly as to ask for the lives of women and children?

And yet she felt afraid to make her innocent request. Robespierre had never yet been offended with her. Though he had given her counsel on almost every subject, he had never yet spoken to her one word of disapprobation still she knew that he had inspired her with fear. She made some attempts to begin the subject, which he did not notice, for he was still brooding over the unpleasant sensation which her words had occasioned; but at last she gathered courage, and said:

"The soldiers of the Republic have at last overcome the rebels of La Vendée—have they not, M. Robespierre?"

"It is not enough to conquer traitors," answered he, "they must be crushed, before the country can be safe from their treachery."

"Their treason must be crushed, I know."

"Crimes between man and man can be atoned for by minor punishments: crimes between citizens and their country can only be properly avenged by death. You may teach the murderer or the thief the iniquity of his fault; and when he has learnt to hate the deed he has committed, he may be pardoned. It is not so with traitors. Though the truest child of France should spend his life in the attempt, he would not be able to inspire one aristocrat with a spark of patriotism."

"Must every royalist in La Vendée perish then?" said Eleanor.

Robespierre did not answer her immediately, but leaning his elbow on the table, he rested his forehead on his hand, so as nearly to conceal his face. Eleanor thought that he was meditating on her question; and remembering that he had declared that he should be pleased if now and then a victim might be spared, again commenced her difficult task of urging him to mercy.

"They talk of shedding the blood of innocent children—of destroying peasant women, who can only think and feel as their husbands bid them. You will not allow that this should be done, will you?"

"Is the life of a woman more precious to her than that of a man? It is a false sentiment which teaches us to spare the iniquities of women because of their sex. Their weakness entitles them to our protection, their beauty begets our love; but neither their weakness or their beauty should be accepted as an excuse for their crimes."

"But poor innocent babes—it is not possible that they should have committed crimes."

"In the religion of Christ it is declared, that the sins of the fathers shall be visited on the children, to the third and fourth generation. The priests who made these laws, and handed them down to their flocks, as the very words of their God, had closely studied human nature. I do not believe that an Almighty Creator condescended to engrave on stone, with his own finger, these words, as they would feign that he did do; but the law is not the less true; the children must expatiate, to the third and fourth generation, the sins of their fathers. Nature, which is all benignant, wills that it should be so."

"If this be so, will not nature work out her own law. Will it not be punishment enough that so many women should lose their husbands; so many children their fathers? You, I know, are averse to shedding blood; you would spare life whenever your sense of duty would allow you to do so. Try what clemency will do in La Vendée. Try whether kindness will not put a stop to the bitterness of their enmity. Do, dearest, for my sake."

It is possible that Eleanor had never before spoken to her lover in language so tender; it is also probable that she had never before asked of him any request, in which ought of a political nature was concerned. Be that as it may, as soon as she had finished speaking, her face became suffused with scarlet, as though she had said something of which she was ashamed. One would think that there was nothing in the term of endearment which she had used which could have displeased a betrothed husband; nothing in the petition she, had made which could have angered a political friend. Robespierre, however, soon showed that he was displeased and angered; nay, worse still, that his black, unmanly suspicion was aroused. To his disordered brain it seemed that Eleanor was practising on him her woman's wiles for some unworthy purpose, and that treason lurked in her show of humanity and affection. He believed that she, who had always believed in him, loved him, almost worshipped him, had become in an instant false and designing.

He looked her steadily in the face a moment or two before he answered, and she did not bear calmly the fierce glance of his eye; she saw at once that she had angered him, and, in spite of her love, she could not but know how dark and terrible was his anger.

"Who has set you on to talk to me of this?" he said slowly, still keeping his eyes fixed on hers.

"Set me on, M. Robespierre! what do you mean? Who should have set me on?"

"There are hundreds, I grieve to say, ready to do so. Some of them are daily near you. I should have thought, though, that with you I might have been safe."

"Safe with me! And do you doubt it now—do you doubt that you are safe with me?" and as she spoke, she laid her hand upon his arm, and attempted to appeal to his affection. He gently withdrew his arm from her grasp, and again concealed his face with his hand. "As I stand here alive before you," continued she, speaking with a more assured voice than she had hitherto used, "I have not whispered a word to man or woman upon this subject, but yourself."

Eleanor had risen from her chair when her companion first expressed his suspicion, and she was now standing; but Robespierre remained seated, still shading his eyes with his hand, as though he had nothing further to say to her, and would wish to be alone. She, however, felt that she could not leave him without some further explanation on her part, some retraction on his; but she knew not how to set about it. The most eloquent men in France had found it difficult to explain anything to Robespierre's satisfaction. No one had yet been able to make him retract the word which he had spoken.

"Say that you believe me, M. Robespierre," said she; "for mercy's sake, say that you do not doubt me! Do you not know that I would always obey you, that your words are always to me the words of truth? I have done wrong, I doubt not, in speaking to you of public matters. I beg your pardon, and promise that I will not so transgress again; but before I leave you, tell me that you do not distrust my fidelity."

"I would still wish to hope, Eleanor, that you are truly anxious for the welfare of your country, and the safety of your friend," said he, still, however, without looking up.

"Indeed I am, most anxious; anxious above all things for your welfare and safety. I should think little of my life, could I give it to promote the one, or secure the other."

"Tell me then, I conjure you, who are they who have desired you to beg for the lives of these Vendean rebels," and as he spoke, he leapt from his chair, and putting his hand upon her shoulder, looked sternly into her face.

"As God is my judge—"

"Bah! if neither love of your country or of me, nor yet fear of the punishment due to traitors, will keep you true," (and he slightly shook her with his hand, as he slowly uttered the last fearful words), "the judgment of God will not have much effect upon you."

"True!" said the poor girl, almost confounded with her horror at the charge against her, amid the violence of the man. "True! Oh! Sir, for mercy's sake, tell me what it is of which you accuse me—tell me what it is that I have done. No man has spoken of you behind your back words which you might not yourself have heard. No man has desired me to ask you to spare the rebels. No man has even dared to hint to me, that I should do or say ought in opposition to you."

"Some woman has done it then," said he.

"My God! that you should think so foully of me! No, Sir, neither man, nor woman, nor child. You said that, were it possible, you would wish that the hand of the executioner might be stayed. It was your own words that set me on to say what I did. I did not dream that I should displease you. Tell me, M. Robespierre, tell me that you are not angry with me, and I will forget it all."

"Forget it all. Yes, things trivial and of no concern are long remembered, but matters on which depend the life and death of those we ought to love, are soon forgotten if they are unpleasant. No, Eleanor, do not forget it all. Do not forget this—remember that I never have, and never will, allow my feelings as a private man to influence my conduct as a public functionary. I have many duties to perform; duties which are arduous, disagreeable, and dangerous, but difficult as they are, I believe that I am able to perform them. I do not wish for advice, and I will not permit interference. Now go down, Eleanor; our friends are below, I heard their steps a while since, as they came in. I have but a few words to write, and I will join you."

"But you will tell me before I go that we are friends again," said the poor girl, now weeping. "You will say that you do not distrust me."

"I do not believe that you meant evil to me, but you were indiscreet. Let that be sufficient now, and bear this in mind, Eleanor—you know the place you hold in my affections, but were you still nearer to me than you are; were you already my wife, and the mother of my children, I would not stand between you and the punishment you would deserve, if you were untrue to your country."

After hearing this energetic warning, Eleanor Duplay left her lover's room, firmly believing that she had greatly sinned in speaking as she had done, but conscious, at any rate, of having intended no evil, either to him or to the unfortunate country respecting which he expressed so constant a solicitude.

As soon as she was gone, he again took up the papers which he had written, and re-read them with great care. In the letter to the two Commissioners he underscored the passages which most forcibly urged them to energy in their work of destruction, and added a word here and there which showed more clearly his intention that mercy should be shown to none. He then turned to his letter to his brother. In that he said that Eleanor's conduct had been a source of great comfort to him, and that he blamed himself for still feeling any reserve with her. He now erased the passage, and wrote in its stead, "even with Eleanor Duplay I have some reserve, and I feel that I cannot throw it off with safety!" and having done this, he, laboriously copied, for the second time, the long letter which he had written.

When he had finished his task, he left his own chamber, and went down into a room below, in which the family were in the habit of assembling in the evening, and meeting such of Robespierre's friends as he wished to have admitted. The cabinet-maker, and his wife and daughters, together with his son and nephew, who assisted him in his workshop, were always there; and few evenings passed without the attendance of some of his more intimate friends. They were, at first, merely in the habit of returning with him from the Jacobins' club, but after a while their private meetings became so necessary to them, that they assembled at Duplay's on those nights also on which the Jacobins did not meet.

When Robespierre entered the humble salon, Lebas, St. Just, and Couthon were there; three men who were constant to him to the last, and died with him when he died. As far as we can judge of their characters, they were none of them naturally bad men. They were not men prone to lust or plunder; they betrayed no friends; they sought in their political views no private ends; they even frequently used the power with which they were invested to save the lives of multitudes for whose blood the infuriate mob were eager. Lebas and St. Just were constant to the girls they loved, and Couthon, who was an object of pity as a cripple, was happy in the affection of a young wife whom he adored; and yet these were the men who assisted Robespierre in organizing the Reign of Terror, and with him share the infamy of the deeds which were then committed. They were all of them young when they died. They were men of education, and a certain elevation, of spirit. Men who were able to sacrifice the pleasures of youth to the hard work of high political duties. Blood could not have been, was not, acceptable to them; yet under how great a load of infamy do their names now lie buried!

"We thought you were going to seclude yourself tonight," said Lebas, "and we were regretting it."

"What have you done with Eleanor," said Madame Duplay, "that she does not come down to us?"

"I thought to have found her here," answered he; "she left me some minutes since. She was not in good spirits, and has probably retired for the night. Tell me, St. Just, do they talk much of tomorrow's trial?"

Robespierre alluded to the trial of Marie Antoinette, as the cruel farce, which was so called, was then to commence. The people were now thirsty after her blood, and thought themselves wronged in that she had been so long held back from their wrath.

"They speak of her execution as of a thing of course," said St. Just; "and they are right; her sand has well nigh run itself out. I wish she were now at her nephew's court."

"Wish rather that she had never come from thence," said Couthon. "She has brought great misfortunes on France. Could she die a thousand deaths, she could not atone for what she has done. Not that I would have her die, if it were possible that she could be allowed to live."

"It is not possible," said Robespierre. "To have been Queen of France, is in itself a crime which it would have been necessary that she should expiate, even had she shown herself mistress of all the virtues which could adorn a woman."

"And she is not possessed of one," said Lebas. "She was beautiful, but her beauty was a stain upon her, for she was voluptuous. She was talented, but her talents were all turned to evil, for they only enabled her to intrigue against her adopted country. She had the disposal of wealth, with which she might have commanded the blessings of the poor, and she wasted it in vain frivolities. She was gracious in demeanour, but she kept her smiles for those only who deserved her frowns. She had unbounded influence over her husband, and she persuaded him to falsehood, dishonesty, and treachery."

"Do not deny that she has courage," said St. Just. "She has borne her adversity well, though she could not bear her prosperity."

"She has courage," said Lebas, "and how has she used it? in fighting an ineffectual battle against the country who had received her with open arms. We must all be judged by posterity, but no historian will dare to say that Marie Antoinette did not deserve the doom which now awaits her."

How little are men able to conceive what award posterity will make in judging of their actions, even when they act with pure motives, and on what they consider to be high principles; and posterity is often as much in error in its indiscriminate condemnation of actions, as are the actors in presuming themselves entitled to its praise.

When years have rolled by, and passions have cooled, the different motives and feelings of the persons concerned become known to all, and mankind is enabled to look upon public acts from every side. Not so the actors; they are not only in ignorance of facts, the knowledge of which is necessary to their judging rightly, but falsehoods dressed in the garb of facts are studiously brought forward to deceive them, and men thus groping in darkness are forced to form opinions, and to act upon them.

Public men are like soldiers fighting in a narrow valley: they see nothing but what is close around them, and that imperfectly, as everything is in motion. The historian is as the general, who stands elevated on the high ground, and, with telescope in hand, sees plainly all the different movements of the troops. He would be an inconsiderate general, who would expect that his officers in action should have had as clear an idea of what was going on, as he himself had been able to obtain.

There was no murder perpetrated during the French Revolution, under the pretext of a judicial sentence, which has created more general disgust than has that of Marie Antoinette. She came as a stranger to the country, which on that account owed to her its special protection. She had been called to France to be a Queen, and her greatest crime was that she would not give up the high station she had been invited to fill. She had been a faithful wife to a husband who did not love her till he knew her well, and who was slow in learning anything. She had been a good mother to the children, who were born, as she believed, to rule the destinies of France.

She had clung to a falling cause, with a sense of duty which was as admirable as her courage, and at last she died with the devoted heroism which so well became her mother's daughter. But what we now look on as virtues, were vices in the eyes of the republicans, who were her judges. Her constancy was stubbornness, and her courage was insolence. Her innocent mirth was called licentiousness, and the royal splendour which she had been taught to maintain, was looked upon as iniquitous extravagance. Nor was this, even in those bloody days, enough to condemn her. Lies of the basest kind were, with care and difficulty, contrived to debase her character—lies which have now been proved to be so, but which were then not only credible, but sure to receive credit from those who already believed that all royal blood was, from its nature, capable of every abomination.

When Lebas so confidently predicated the sentence which posterity would pass on the fall of Marie Antoinette, none of his auditors doubted the correctness of his prophecy. Posterity, however, more partial to the frivolities of courts than to the fury of revolutions, has acquitted the Queen, and passed, perhaps, too heavy a sentence on the judges who condemned her. Till the power of Satan over the world has been destroyed, and man is able to walk uprightly before his Maker, the virtues of one generation will be the vices of another.

CHAPTER III.
THE LAST DAY AT DURBELLIÈRE.

After the re-capture of Durbellière, and the liberation of Santerre, the Vendeans again assembled in arms in different portions of the revolted district, and fought their battles always with valour, and not unfrequently with success. They did not, however, again form themselves into one body, till the beginning of October, when news having reached them that a large army, under fiercer leaders, was to be sent by the Republic for their extermination, it became necessary to take some decided step for their own protection. The Vendean Generals then decided to call together all the men they could collect at Chatillon, a town in the very centre of their country, and there also to prepare such a quantity of military stores and ammunition, as would make the place a useful and secure basis for their movements.

Some jealousy had arisen among the Generals; and on the death of Cathelineau, d'Elbée had been chosen Commander-in-Chief, through the influence of those who were envious of the popularity of M. de Lescure. On the latter, however, the management of the war depended; and though his exertions were greatly impeded by the factious spirit which unfortunately prevailed among the royalists, he nevertheless succeeded in collecting, equipping, and maintaining a considerable army. The republican troops of Lechelle and Thurreau were not long in making their way to the devoted district, and tidings soon reached Chatillon that they were devastating the country round Doué and Vihiers, and that parties of them had advanced to the neighbourhood of Cholet.

It was then determined at Chatillon that the royalist army should advance towards the republicans: that they should fight them on the first field of battle on which they could meet them, and that if beaten, they should cross the Loire into Britanny, and make their way to the coast, to meet the succour which had been promised them from England. Every day that the battle was delayed, hundreds of children and women perished in cold blood, numberless humble dwellings were reduced to ashes. The commands of Robespierre were being executed; the land was being saturated with the blood of its inhabitants.

De Lescure and Larochejaquelin were both staying at Chatillon. But Chatillon is but a league or two from Durbellière, and one or the other of them was almost daily at the château. They had many cares upon them besides those of the army; cares which, though not productive of so much actual labour, sat, if possible, heavier on their hearts. What were they to do with those dear but weak friends who were still at the château? three loving and beloved women, and an infirm old man, more helpless even than the women! They could not be left at Durbellière, for the château would doubtless, before long, be again taken by some marauding party of their enemies, and any death would be preferable to the fate which would there await them.

Henri now felt the weight of those miseries which his father had foretold; when he, flushed with the victory at Saumur, returned home after the campaign in which he had first drawn his sword so gloriously. He felt that he had done his duty, and therefore he regretted nothing; but he also felt that he might probably soon be without the power of protecting those who were so much dearer to him than his life, and the suffering arising from such thoughts was almost more than he could bear.

It was at last determined that the whole party should leave the château, and go over to Chatillon—there would be at any rate a better chance of security there than at Durbellière, and also better means of escape, should the town fall into the hands of their enemies.

It was a grievous thing to tell that old man that he must leave the house, where he had spent his quiet life, and go to strange places, to finish the short remainder of his days amid the turmoil of battles, and the continual troubles and dangers of a moving army. Nevertheless he bore it well. At first he beseeched them to leave him and old Momont, among his birds and cherry trees, declaring that nothing that the blues could do to him would be to him so calamitous as his removal from the spot in which he had so long taken root. But his children soon made him understand that it was impossible that they could abandon him, a cripple as he was, unattended, and exposed to the certain fury of the republicans. He yielded, therefore, and when the sad day came, he blamed no one, as they lifted him into the huge carriage, in which he was removed to Chatillon. To the last he was proudly loyal to the King; and, as he was carried over the threshold of his door, he said, that if God would grant him another favour in this world, it would be, that he might return once more to his own home, to welcome there some scion of his royal master's house.

Henri, de Lescure, and the little Chevalier, all came over to spend the last day at Durbellière, and a melancholy day it was. Madame de Lescure, Marie, and Agatha were also there, and all the servants, most of whom had been born in the family, and all of whom, excepting Chapeau and one maid, were now to be sent abroad to look for their living in a country in which the life itself of every native was in hourly danger. Hard they begged to be allowed to link their fate to that of their young mistress, declaring that they would never more complain, even though they were again called out to die, as they had been on that fearful evening when Santerre had found himself unable to give the fatal order. It was impossible—the safety of four women, who would probably have to be carried backwards and forwards through a country bristling with hostile troops, was a fearful burden to the young leaders; it would have been madness for them to increase it. The wretched girls, therefore, prepared to make their way to the homes of their relatives, knowing that those homes would soon be turned into heaps of ashes. It was a bright warm autumn day this, the last which the Larochejaquelins were to pass together in the mansion in which they had all been born. The men came over early, and breakfasted at the château, and both Henri and Arthur worked hard to relieve the sadness of the party with some sparks of their accustomed gaiety; the attempt, however, was futile; they each felt that their hours of gaiety were gone by, and before the meal was over, they had both resolved that any attempt at mirth that day, would be a stretch of hypocrisy beyond their power.

When breakfast was over, the Marquis begged that, for the last time, he might be wheeled round the garden-walks, which he loved so well, and accordingly he was put into his chair, and, accompanied by his children and friends, was dragged through every alley, and every little meandering path. He would not spare himself a single turn—he had a tear to give to every well-known tree, an adieu to make to every painted figure. To de Lescure and the others, the comic attitudes of these uncouth ornaments was, at the present moment, any thing but interesting; but to the Marquis, each of them was an old and well-loved friend, whom even in his extremity he could hardly bring himself to desert. On their return into the house from the garden, they began to employ themselves with arranging and packing the little articles which they intended to take with them. They had all counted on having much to do during the short hours of this one last day; on being hurried and pressed, so as to be hardly able to get through their task; but instead of this their work was soon done, and the minutes hung heavy on their hands. They would not talk of the things which were near their hearts, for they feared to add to each other's misery; they strove therefore to talk on indifferent subjects, and soon broke down in every attempt they made at conversation.

Agatha never left her father's side for a moment, and though she seldom spoke to him, she did a thousand little acts of sedulous attention, which showed him that she was near to him. Her gentle touch was almost as precious to him as her voice. De Lescure sat near his wife the whole day, speaking to her from time to time in a whisper, and feeling the weight upon his spirits so great that even with her he could hardly talk freely. He was already without a roof which he could call his own, and he was aware his friends would soon be equally desolate; such hitherto had been the result of their gallant enterprise.

Henri had much to say—much that he had made up his mind to say to Marie before he left Durbellière, but he put off the moment of saying it from hour to hour, and it was not till near midnight that it was said. Marie herself, bore herself more manfully, if I may say so, than any of them; she really employed herself, and thought of a thousand things conducive to their future comfort, which would have been forgotten or neglected had she not been there. The little Chevalier tried hard to assist her, but the pale sad face of Agatha, and the silent tears which from time to time moistened the cheeks of the Marquis, and told how acute were the sufferings which he tried in vain to hide, were too much for the poor boy; he soon betook himself alone into the cherry grove, where he wandered about unseen, and if the truth must be told, more than once threw himself on the ground, and wept bitterly and aloud.

They sat down to dinner about three o'clock; but their dinner was, if possible, a worse affair than their breakfast. They were not only sad, but worn out and jaded with sorrow. The very servants, as they moved the dishes, sobbed aloud; and at last, Momont, who had vainly attempted to carry himself with propriety before the others, utterly gave way, and throwing himself on to a chair in the salon, declared that nothing but violence should separate him from his master.

"It is five-and-fifty years," said he, sobbing, "since I first waited on Monseigneur. We were boys then, and now we are old men together It is not natural that we should part. Where he goes, I will go. I will cling to his carriage, unless they cut me down with swords."

No one could rebuke the old man—certainly not the master whom he loved so well; and though they knew that it would be impossible to provide for him, none of them at the moment had the heart to tell him so.

By degrees the daylight faded away, and for the last time, they watched the sun sink down among the cherry trees of Durbellière, and the Marquis, seated by the window, gazed into the West till not a streak of light was any longer visible; then he felt that the sun of this world had set for him for good and all. Even though he might live out a few more weary years, even though the cause to which he was attached should be victorious, yet he knew that Durbellière would be destroyed, and it never could be anything to him how the sun set or rose in any other place. His warm heart yearned towards his house; the very chair on which he sat, the stool on which rested his crippled legs, were objects of an affection which he had before felt, but never till now acknowledged. Every object on which his eye rested gave him a new pang; every article within his reach was a dear friend, whom he had long loved, and was now to leave for ever.

Still he did not utter one word of complaint; he did not once murmur at his fate; he never reminded his son that he had, by his impetuosity, hurried on his old father to destruction. He never repined at the sacrifice he had made—I will not say for his King, for King at present he had none; the throne had been laid low, and the precious blood of him who should have filled it had been shed. No; his sacrifices had been to an abstract feeling of loyalty, which made fealty to the Crown, whether worn or in abeyance, only second in his bosom to obedience to his God.

The day faded away, and they still sat together in the room in which they had dined, each wrapped in his own thoughts, till the darkness of night was upon them, and still no one felt inclined to rise and ask for candles.

After a long pause, Arthur made a bold attempt to break through the heaviness of the evening. "We are not so badly off, at any rate," said he, "as we were on that night when Santerre and his men were here; are we, Agatha?"

"We are not badly off at all," said Henri. "We have now what we never had before—a fine army collected together in one spot, a promise of succour from faithful England, and a strong probability of ultimate success. After all, what are we giving up but an old barrack? Let the rascal blues burn it; cannot we build a better Durbellière when the King shall have his own again?"

"Ah, Henri!" said the Marquis. It was the only reproach he uttered, though the words of his son, intended as they were to excite hope, and to give comfort, had been to him most distasteful.

Henri was in a moment at his father's feet. "Pardon me, father!" said he; "you know that I did not mean to give you pain. We all love the old house—none of us so well as you perhaps; but we all love it; yet what can we do? Were we to remain here, we should only be smothered beneath its ashes."

"God's will be done, my son. He knows that I do not begrudge my house in his service, and in that of my royal master. It is not likely that I should do so, when I have not begrudged the blood of my children."

They were all to start on the following morning by break of day, and, therefore, the necessity of early rising gave them an excuse desired by all, for retiring early for the night. They could not talk together, for every word that was spoken begot fresh sources of sorrow; they could not employ themselves, for their minds were unhinged and unfitted for employment; so they agreed that they would go to bed, and before nine o'clock, the family separated for the night.

They did not, however, all go to rest. Henri, as he handed a light to his cousin, told her that he wanted to speak two words to her in his sister's room, and as she did not dissent, he followed the two girls thither. Two words! It took nearly the whole long night to say those two words.

Henri Larochejaquelin had thought long and deeply on the position in which he and his betrothed were now placed, before he made the request to which he asked her to listen that night, and it was from no selfish passion that he made it. In the presence of his sister, he asked her to marry him as soon as they reached Chatillon, so that when next the army separated, he might deem himself her natural protector. He had already asked and obtained de Lescure's permission. The brother gave it, not absolutely unwillingly, but with strong advice to Henri to take no new cares upon himself during the present crisis, and declaring that he would use no influence with his sister, either one way or the other.

Marie, with a woman's instinct, anticipated the nature of Henri's two words, and in a moment resolved on the answer she would give him: if her lover was generous, so would she be; she would never consent to link herself to him at a moment when the union could only be to him a source of additional cares and new sorrow.

Henri soon made his request: he did not do it, as he would have done in happier times; kneeling at her feet, and looking into her eyes for that love, which he might well know he should find there: he had not come to talk of the pleasures and endearments of affection, and to ask for her hand as the accomplishment of all his wishes; but he spoke of their marriage as a providential measure, called for by the calamitous necessities of the moment, and in every argument which he used, he appealed to Agatha to support him.

"No, Henri," said Marie, after she had already answered him with a faint, but what she intended to be a firm denial. "No, it must not, cannot, ought not be so. I am, I know, somewhat de trop in this tragedy we are playing. There are you and Charles, two good knights and true, and each of you has a lady whom it is his duty to protect. I am a poor forlorn young damsel, and though both of you are so gallant as to offer me a hand to help me over the perilous path we are treading, I know that I am grievously in the way."

"You are joking now, love," said Henri, "and I am not only speaking, but thinking, in most true and sober earnest."

"No, Henri, I am not joking; am I, Agatha? One need not be joking because one does not use harsh, grim words. What I say is true. I must be an additional burden either to you or Charles. You are already the heaviest laden, for you have your father to care for. Besides, I have a claim upon Charles; I have for eighteen years been to him an obedient sister."

"And have you no claim on me, Marie?"

"A slight one, as a cousin; but only in default of Charles. Don't look so unhappy," and she held out her little hand to him as she spoke. "The day may come when I shall have a still stronger claim upon you; when I have been to you for eighteen years an obedient wife."

"These are times when stern truths must be spoken," said Henri. "The lives of us all must now be in constant jeopardy—that is, of us who must go out to battle."

"Ay, and of us women too. Don't be afraid of our lacking courage. Do not be afraid that the truth will frighten us. Agatha, and Victorine, and I, have schooled ourselves to think of death without flinching."

"To think without flinching of the death of others, is the difficulty," said Agatha. "I fear we have none of us as yet brought ourselves to that."

"But we must think of the death of others," said Henri. "Should de Lescure fall—"

"May God Almighty in His mercy protect and guard him!" said the sister.

"But should he fall—and in battle there is none, I will not say so rash, but so forward as him—should he fall, will it not be a comfort to him to know that his sister has a husband to protect her; that his widow has a brother to whom she can turn. Should I fall, will it not be better for Agatha that you should be more closely knit together even than you are?"

"That can never be, can it, Agatha? We can never be more entirely sisters than we are."

"You talk like a child, Marie. You perhaps may never have a warmer love for each other than you now have, but that is not the question. You must see how great would be the advantage to us all of our union being at once completed You should not now allow a phantasy of misplaced generosity to stand in the way of an arrangement which is so desirable."

"Nay, Henri, now you are neither fair nor courteous. You are presuming a little on the affection which I have owned in arguing that I am prevented only by what you call generosity from so immediate a marriage; that is as much as to say, that if I consulted my own wishes only, I should marry you at once."

"It is you that are now unfair," said Agatha. "You know that he did not mean to draw such a conclusion. You almost tempt me to say that he might do so, without being far wrong. You are flirting now, Marie."

"Heaven help me then; but if so, I have committed that sin most unconsciously, and, I believe, for the first time in my life. I have had but one lover, and I accepted him, the very moment that he spoke to me. I can, at any rate, have but little flirtation to answer for."

"Alas! dearest love," said Henri, "we are both driven to think and talk of these things in a different tone from that which is usual in the world. If I was merely seeking to transplant you in days of peace from your own comfortable home, to be the pride and ornament of mine, I would not curtail by one iota the privilege of your sex. I wouldn't presume to think that you could wish yourself to give up your girlish liberty. If you allowed me any hope, I would ascribe it all to the kindness of your disposition; your word should be my law, and though I might pray for mercy, I would submissively take my fate from your lips. I would write odes to you, if I were able, and would swear in every town in Poitou that you were the prettiest girl, and sweetest angel in all France, Italy, or Spain."

"Thanks, Henri, thanks; but now you have too much to do to trouble yourself with such tedious gallantries. Is not that to be the end of your fine speech?"

"Trouble myself, Marie!"

"Yes, trouble yourself, Henri, and it would trouble me too. It is not that I regret such nonsense. I accept your manly love as it has been offered, and tell you that you have my whole heart. It is from no girlish squeamishness, from no wish to exercise my short-lived power, that I refuse to do what you now ask me. I would marry you tomorrow, were you to ask me, did I not think that I should be wrong to do so. Am I now not frank and honest?"

Henri put his arms round her waist, and clasped her to his bosom before he answered her:

"You are, you are, my own, own love. You were always true, and honest, and reasonable—so reasonable that—"

"Ah! now you are going to encroach."

"I am going to ask you once again to think of what I have said. It is not to your love, but to your reason, that I now appeal."

"Well, Henri, we will leave love aside, and both of us appeal to reason. Here she sits, always calm, passionless, and wise," and Marie put her hand upon Agatha's arm. "We will appeal to Reason personified, and if Reason says that, were she situated as I am, she would do as you now wish me to do, I will be guided by Reason, and comply." Henri now turned round to his sister, but Marie stopped him from speaking, and continued: "I have pledged myself, and do you do likewise. If Reason gives her judgment against you, you will yield without a word."

"Well, I will do so," said Henri. "I'm sure, however, she will not; Agatha must see the importance of our being joined as closely together as is possible."

"You are attempting to influence Dame Reason, but it will be useless. And now, Reason, you are to remember, as of course you do, for Reason forgets nothing, that you are to think neither of brothers or of sisters. You are entirely to drop your feelings as Agatha, and to be pure Reason undefiled by mortal taint. You are to say, whether, were you, Reason, placed as I am now, you would marry this unreasonable young man as soon as he gets to Chatillon, which means tomorrow, or the day after, or the day after that at the very latest. Now, Reason, speak, and speak wisely."

"You have given me a thankless task between you. I cannot decide without giving pain to one of you."

"Reason always has a thankless task," said Marie. "Reason is her own reward—and a very unpleasant reward she usually has."

"Do you think," said Henri, "it will give so much pain to Marie to be told that she is to marry the man whom she owns she loves?"

"Ah, Henri," said Agatha, "you are prejudiced. I do not mean as to Marie's love, but as to my award. I might, perhaps, not pain her so much by advising her to marry you at once, as I fear I shall pain you by telling her, that in her place, I should not do so."

They both sat in breathless silence to hear their fate from Agatha's lips. Though Marie had appealed to her with a degree of playfulness, which gave to her an air of indifference on the subject, she was anything but indifferent; and yet it would have been difficult to analyse her wishes; she was quite decided that it was becoming in her to refuse Henri's prayer, nay, that it would be selfish in her to grant it; and yet, though she appealed to Reason so confidently to confirm her refusal, there was a wish, almost a hope, near her heart, that Agatha might take her brother's part. They were, neither of them, perhaps, gratified by the decision.

"Reason has said it," said Marie, after a short pause, "and Reason shall be rewarded with a kiss;" and she put her arms round her cousin's neck and kissed her.

"But why, Agatha, tell me why?" said Henri. He, at any rate, was not ashamed to show that he was disappointed.

"Do not be so inconsiderate as to ask Reason for reasons," said Marie.

"I will tell you why, Henri. I would never consent to make myself a burden to a man at a moment when I could not make myself a comfort to him; besides, the time of marriage should be a time of joy, and this is no time for joy. Again, there is a stronger and sadder reason still. Did you ever see a young widow, who had not reached her twentieth year? if so, did you ever see a sadder sight? Would you unnecessarily doom our dear Marie to that fate! I know you so well, my dear brother, that I do not fear to speak to you of the too probable lot of a brave soldier!"

"That is enough!" said Henri, "I am convinced."

"Do not say that, Agatha, do not say that," said Marie, springing up and throwing herself into her lover's arms. "Indeed, indeed, it was not of that I thought. Though we should never marry, yet were you to fall, your memory should be the same to me as that of a husband. I could never forget your love—your disinterested love—there is no treasure on this side the grave which I so value. It is the pride of my solitary hours, and the happiness of the few happy thoughts I have. The world would be nothing to me without you. When you are away, I pray to God to bring you back to me. When you are with us I am dreading the moment that you will go. Oh, Agatha, Agatha! why did you say those last fearful words!"

"You asked me for the truth, Marie, and it was right that I should tell it you; it was on my tongue to say the same to Henri, before you appealed to me at all."

"You were right, dearest Agatha," said Henri; "and now, God bless you, Marie. I value such love as yours highly as it is worth. I trust the day may come when I can again ask you for your hand."

"I will never refuse it again. You shall have it now, tomorrow, next day, any day that you will ask it. Oh, Agatha! my brain is so turned by what you have said, that I could almost go on my knees to beg him to accept it."

"Come, Henri, leave us," said Agatha, "and prevent such a scandal as that would be; there are but a few hours for us to be in bed."

Henri kissed his sister, and when he gave his hand to Marie, she did not turn her lips away from him; and as he threw himself on his bed, he hardly knew whether, if he could have his own way, he would marry her at once or not.

———————————————————

CHAPTER IV.
THE CHAPEL OF GENET.

About ten days after the departure of the Larochejaquelins from Durbellière, three persons were making the best of their way, on horseback, through one of the deepest and dirtiest of the byeways, which in those days, served the inhabitants of Poitou for roads, and along which the farmers of the country contrived with infinite pains and delay, to drag the produce of their fields to the market towns. The lane, through which they were endeavouring to hurry the jaded animals on which they were mounted, did not lead from one town to another, and was not therefore paved; it was merely a narrow track between continual rows of high trees, and appeared to wind hither and thither almost in circles, and the mud at every step covered the fetlocks of the three horses. The party consisted of two ladies and a man, who, though he rode rather in advance of, than behind his companions, and spoke to them from time to time, was their servant: a boy travelled on foot to show them the different turns which their road made necessary to them; and though, when chosen for the duty, he had received numerous injunctions as to the speed with which he should travel, the urchin on foot had hitherto found no difficulty in keeping up with the equestrians. The two ladies were Madame de Lescure and her sister-in-law, and the servant was our trusty friend Chapeau. And we must go back a little to recount as quickly as we can, the misfortunes which brought them into their present situation.

No rest was allowed to the Vendean chiefs after reaching Chatillon from Durbellière. The rapid advance of the republican troops made them think it expedient to try the chance of battle with them at once. They had consequently led out their patriot bands as far as Cholet, and had there, after a murderous conflict, been grievously worsted. No men could have fought better than did the Vendean peasants, for now they had joined some degree of discipline and method to their accustomed valour; but the number of their enemies was too great for them, and they consisted of the best soldiers of whom France could boast. The Vendeans, moreover, could not choose their own battle-field. They could not fight as they had been accustomed to do, from behind hedges, and with every advantage of locality on their side. They had thrown themselves on the veteran troops, who had signalized themselves at Valmy and Mayence, with a courage that amounted to desperation, but which, as it had not purchased victory, exposed them to fearful carnage. D'Elbe, who acted as Commander-in-Chief, fell early in the day. Bonchamps, whose military skill was superior to that of any of the Vendeans; was mortally wounded, and before the battle was lost, de Lescure—the brave de Lescure, whom they all so loved, so nearly worshipped—was struck down and carried from the field.

There was an immense degree of superstition mixed up with the religious fervour of the singular people who were now fighting for their liberty; and many of them sincerely believed that de Lescure was invulnerable, and that they were secure from any fatal reverse as long as he was with them. This faith was now destroyed; and when the rumour spread along their lines that he had been killed, they threw down their arms, and refused to return to the charge. It was in vain that Henri Larochejaquelin and the young Chevalier tried to encourage them; that they assured them that de Lescure was still living, and exposed their own persons in the thickest of the enemy's fire. It was soon too evident that the battle was lost, and that all that valour and skill could do, was to change the flight into a retreat.

Many personal reasons would have made Henri prefer returning towards Chatillon, but it had been decided that, in the event of such a disaster as that which had now befallen them, the cause in which they were engaged would be best furthered by a general retreat of all the troops across the Loire into Brittany; and consequently Henri, collecting together what he could of his shattered army, made the best of his way to St. Florent. The men did not now hurry to their homes, as they did after every battle, when the war first began; but their constancy to their arms arose neither from increased courage nor better discipline. They knew that their homes were now, or would soon be, but heaps of ruins, and that their only hope of safety consisted in their remaining with the army. This feeling, which prevented the dispersion of the men, had another effect, which added greatly to the difficulty of the officers. The wives, children, and sisters of the Vendean peasants, also flocked to the army in such numbers, that by the time the disordered multitude reached St. Florent, Henri found himself surrounded by 80,000 human, creatures, flying from the wrath of the blues, though not above a quarter of that number were men capable of bearing arms.

De Lescure, in a litter, accompanied them to St. Florent, and Chapeau was sent back to Chatillon to bid the ladies and the old Marquis join the army at that place. Chapeau was sent direct from the field of battle before it was known whether or no M. de Lescure's wound was mortal, and at a moment when Henri could give him nothing but a general direction as to the route which the army was about to take. Chapeau reached Chatillon without accident; but having reached it, he found that his difficulties were only about to commence. What was he to tell Madame de Lescure of her husband? How was he to convey the three ladies and the Marquis from Chatillon to St. Florent, through a country, the greater portion of which would then be in the hands of the blues?

Make the best he could of it, the news was fearfully bad. He told Madame de Lescure that her husband was certainly wounded, but that as certainly he was not killed; and that he had every reason, though he could not say what reason, to believe that the wound was not likely to be fatal. The doubt conveyed in these tidings was, if possible, more fearful than any certainty; added to this was the great probability that Chatillon would, in a day or two, be in the hands of the republicans. They decided, or rather Chapeau decided for them, that they should start immediately for St. Florent; and that, instead of attempting to go by the direct road, they should make their way thither by bye-lanes, and through small villages, in which they possibly might escape the ferocity of their enemies.

A huge waggon was procured, and in it a bed was laid, on which the unfortunate old man could sit, and with the two horses which they had brought with them from Durbellière, they started on their journey. They rested the first night at St. Laurent, the place where Agatha had established an hospital, and where Cathelineau had died. The Sisters of Mercy who had tended it were still there, but the wards were now deserted. Not that the wars afforded no occupants for them, but the approach of the republicans had frightened away even the maimed and sick. On the following morning Madame de Lescure declared that she could no longer endure the slow progress of the waggon, and consequently, Chapeau having with difficulty succeeded in procuring three horses, she started, accompanied by him and her sister-in-law, to make her way as best she could to her husband, while the Marquis and his daughter, with a guide, followed in the cumbrous waggon.

On the second day the equestrians crossed the Sevre, at Mortaigne, and reached Torfou in safety. On the third day they passed Montfaucon, and were struggling to get on to a village called Chaudron, not far from St. Florent, when we overtook them at the beginning of the chapter.

They had already, however, began to doubt that they could possibly succeed in doing so. The shades of evening were coming on them. The poor brutes which carried them were barely able to lift their legs, and, Madame de Lescure was so overpowered with fatigue and anxiety, that she could hardly sustain herself in the pillion on which she sat.

The peasants whom they met from time to time asked them hundreds of questions about the war. Many of the men of the district were already gone, and their wives and children were anxious to follow them, but the poor creatures did not know which way to turn. They did not know where the army was, or in what quarter they would be most secure. They had an undefined fear that the blues were coming upon them with fire and slaughter, and that they would be no longer safe, even in their own humble cottages.

One person told them that Chaudron was distant only two leagues, and hearing this they plucked up their courage, and made an effort to rouse that of their steeds. Another, however, soon assured them that it was at the very least a long five leagues to Chaudron, and again their spirits sank in despair. A third had never heard the name of the place, and at last a fourth informed them, that whatever the distance might be, they were increasing it every moment, and that their horses' heads were turned exactly in the wrong direction. Then at length their young guide confessed that he must have lost his way, and excused himself by declaring that the turnings were so like one another that it was impossible for any one in that country really to remember his way at a distance of more than two leagues from his own home.

"And what village are we nearest to, my friend?" said Chapeau, inquiring of the man who had given the above unwelcome information.

"Why the chapel of Genet," said he, "is but a short quarter of a league from you, and the Curé's house is close by, but the village and the château are a long way beyond that, and not on the straight road either."

"Ask him the Curé's name, Chapeau," said Marie: "we will go there and tell him, who we are.'

"If he lives in his own house quietly now, Mademoiselle," answered Chapeau, "it would be dangerous to do so; he must be one of the constitutional priests." He asked the man, however, what was the name of the Curé.

"Why the regular old Curé went away long since, and another was here a while in his place—"

"Well, and he has gone away now, I suppose?" said Chapeau.

"Why, yes; he went away too a while since, when Cathelineau turned the soldiers out of St. Florent."

"God bless him," said Chapeau, meaning Cathelineau, and not the priest. "And is there no one in the house now, my friend? for you see these two ladies are unable to travel further. If there be a friend living there, I am sure he will procure them some accommodation."

"And where did the ladies come from?" asked the man.

"You need not be afraid," replied Chapeau, "they, and all belonging to them, are friends to the good cause;" and then, after considering within himself for a while, he added, "I will tell you who they are, they are the wife and sister of M. de Lescure."

Had he told the man that they were angels from heaven, and had the man believed him, he could neither have been more surprised, or expressed a stronger feeling of adoration.

The poor man implored a multitude of blessings on the two ladies, whose names were so dear to every peasant of La Vendée, and then told them that after the new priest had ran away, the old Curé had come back to his own house again, but that Father Bernard was a very old man, hardly strong enough even to perform mass, though, as there was no one else to it, he did go through it every Sabbath morning; that for these two days past there had been another priest staying with Father Bernard; he did not, however, know what his name was, but he knew that he had been with the army, and that no priest through all La Vendée had been more active than he had been to encourage the royalists. The man then offered to show them to the Curé's house, and they all turned thither together.

The little chapel was on one side of the road, and the humble house of the parish priest was immediately opposite to it, ensconced among a few trees, at a little distance from the road. The door of the chapel was open, and the murmuring sound of low voices within told the party that vespers were being sung. Madame de Lescure did not like calling at the priest's house without being announced, and she therefore desired Chapeau to go down and explain who she was, and the circumstances under which she begged for the Curé's hospitality, and proposed that she and Marie should get off their horses, and remain in the chapel till Chapeau returned.

They entered the little chapel, and found in it about a dozen peasants on their knees, while a priest was chaunting the vespers from a small side altar, built in a niche in the wall. It was now late, and the light, which even abroad was growing dimmer every moment, was still less strong within the building. They could not, therefore, see the face of the priest as he knelt at the side of the altar, but the voice seemed familiar to both of them.

Madame de Lescure, perhaps as much from fatigue as from devotion, sank down at once upon her knees against a little stone seat which projected from the wall near the door, but Marie remained standing, straining her eyes to try to catch the features of the Curé. After a moment or two she also knelt down, and said in a whisper to her sister, "It is the Curé of St. Laud—it is our own Father Jerome."

They had hardly been a minute or two in their position near the door, when the service for the evening was over, and the priest, rising from the altar, gave his blessing to the little congregation. Some of them rose from their knees and left the chapel, but a portion of them still remained kneeling, with their heads in their hands, trying to make up, by the length and perseverance of their devotion, for any deficiency there might be in its fervour. The two ladies also rose, and though they doubted for a moment what to do, they both advanced to the rude steps of the little altar, at which Father Jerome was again kneeling. He had not seen them as yet, nor had he noticed the entrance of any one, but the ordinary congregation of the chapel; and so absorbed was he, either in his thoughts or his devotions, that he did not even observe them till they were standing close to his elbow.

"Father Jerome," said Madame de Lescure in a low voice, laying her hand on the threadbare sleeve of the old grey coat, which he still wore. "If you could guess the comfort I have in finding you here!"

The priest sprang from his knees at hearing her voice, and gazed at her as though she had been a ghost.

"Is it possible," said he, "Madame de Lescure and Mademoiselle here in the chapel of Genet!" and then turning to the gaping peasants, he said, "go home, my children, go home! I have business to speak of to these ladies."

"Oh, Father Jerome," said Madame de Lescure, as soon as they were alone, "for heaven's sake tell me something of M. de Lescure. You have heard of what happened at Cholet?"

"Yes, Madame, I was there," said the priest.

"You were there! then you can tell me of my husband. For God's sake, speak, Father Jerome! Tell me the worst at once. I can bear it, for it can't be worse than I expect. Is he—is he alive?"

Father Jerome had been in the midst of the hottest part of the battle at Cholet, sometimes encouraging the troops by his words, and at others leading them on by his example, charging at their head, with his huge crucifix lifted high in the air. He had been close to de Lescure when he fell, and had seen him in his litter after he was carried from the field of battle. He could, therefore, have said at once that he had seen him alive after the battle was over, but he had no wish to deceive Madame de Lescure; and at the moment of which we are speaking, he most undoubtedly believed that the wound had been fatal, and that her husband was no more.

A musket-ball had entered just below the eye, and making its way downwards, had lodged itself in the back of his neck. A surgeon had examined the wound before Father Jerome left the army; and though he had not positively said that it would prove mortal, he had spoken so unfavourably of the case, as to make all those who heard him believe that it would be so.

Had Father Jerome expected to see the two nearest and dearest relations of the man whom he thought to be now no more, he would have prepared himself for the difficult task which he would have had to undertake, and no one would have been better able to go through it with feeling, delicacy, and firmness; but such was not the case. The sudden apparition of the wife and sister of his friend seemed to him to be supernatural; and though he at once made up his mind to give no false hope, he could not so quickly decide in what way he should impart the sad news which he had to tell.

Madame de Lescure was trembling so violently as she asked the question, on the answer to which her fate depended, that the priest observed it, and he turned to the altar at the end of the chapel, to fetch a rude chair which stood there for the use of the officiating clergyman, and which was the only moveable seat in the chapel; and whilst doing so, he was enabled to collect his thoughts, so as to answer not quite so much at random as he otherwise must have done.

"Sit down, Madame de Lescure," said he, "sit down, Mademoiselle," and he made the latter sit down on the altar step. "You are fatigued, and you have agitated yourself too intensely."

"Why don't you speak, Father Jerome? Why don't you tell me at once—is he alive?" And then she added, almost screaming in her agitation, "For God's sake, Sir, don't keep a wretched, miserable woman in suspense!"

The priest gazed for a moment at the unfortunate lady. She had, at his bidding sunk upon the chair, but she could hardly be said to be seated, as, with her knees bent under her, and her hands clasped, she gazed up into his face. She felt that her husband was dead but still, till the fatal word was spoken, there was hope enough within her heart to feed the agony of doubt which was tormenting her. Marie had hitherto said nothing; she had made her own grief subservient to that of her brother's wife, and, though hardly less anxious, she was less agitated than the other.

"I cannot tell you anything with certainty, Madame," said the priest at last. "I cannot—"

"Then you do not know that he is dead! Then there is, at any rate, some room for hope!" said she, not allowing him to finish what he was about to say; and she sank back in the chair, and relieved her overwrought mind with a flood of tears.

The priest was firmly convinced that de Lescure was at this moment numbered among the dead, and his conscience forbad him to relieve himself of his dreadful task, by allowing her to entertain a false hope; he had still, therefore, to say the words which he found it so difficult to utter.

He sat down beside Marie on the low step of the altar, immediately opposite to Madame de Lescure; he still had on him the vestments of his holy office, though they were much worn, shabby, and soiled, and the cap, which formed a part of the priest's dress when officiating, was on his head; his shoes were so worn and tattered, that they were nearly falling from his feet, and the stockings, which displayed the shape of his huge legs, were so patched and darned with worsteds of different colours, as to have made them more fitting for a mountebank than a priest. At the present moment, there was no one likely to notice his costume; but had there been an observer there, it would have told him a tale, easy to be read, of the sufferings which had been endured by this brave and faithful servant of the King.

"When God, Madame de Lescure," said he, speaking in a kind, peculiarly solemn tone of voice, "when God called upon you to be the wife of him who has been to you so affectionate a husband, He vouchsafed to you higher blessings, but at the same time imposed on you sterner duties than those which women in general are called upon to bear. You have enjoyed the blessings, and if I know your character, you will not shrink from the duties."

"I will shrink from nothing, Father Jerome," said she. "God's will be done! I will endeavour to bear the burden which His Providence lays on me; but I have all a woman's weakness, and all a woman's fears."

"He who has given strength and courage to so many of His people in these afflicted days, will also give it to you; He will enable you to bear the weight of His hand, which in chastising, blesses us, which in punishing us here, will render us fit for unutterable joys hereafter." He paused a moment; but as neither of the women could now speak through their tears, he went on: "I was close to your husband when he fell, and as his eyes closed on the battlefield, they rested on the blessed emblem of his redemption."

"He is dead then!" said she, jumping from her chair, and struggling with the sobs which nearly choked her. "Oh Sir, if you have the mercy which a man should feel for a wretched woman, tell me at least the truth," and as she spoke, she threw herself on her knees before him.

Father Jerome certainly lacked no mercy, and usually speaking, he lacked no firmness; but now he nearly felt himself overcome. "You must compose yourself before I can speak calmly to you, my daughter—before you can even understand what I shall say to you. I will not even speak to you till you are again seated, and then I will tell you everything. There—remember now, I will tell you everything as it happened, and, as far as I know, all that did happen. You must summon up your courage, my children, and show yourself worthy to have been the wife and sister of that great man whom you loved so well."

"He is dead!" said Marie, speaking for the first time, and almost in a whisper. "I know now that it is so," and she threw herself into her sister's lap, and embraced her knees.

The priest did not contradict her, but commenced a narrative, which he intended to convey to his listeners exactly the same impressions which were on his own mind. In this, however, he failed. He told them that de Lescure had been carried senseless from the field, and had been taken by Henri in a litter on the road towards St. Florent; that he himself had been present when the surgeon expressed an almost fatal opinion respecting the wound, but that the wounded man was still alive when he last saw him, and that, since then, he had heard no certain news respecting him. Even this statement, which the priest was unable to make without many interruptions, acted rather as a relief than otherwise to Madame de Lescure. She might, at any rate, see her husband again; and it was still possible that both the surgeon and Father Jerome might be wrong. As soon as he had told his tale, she, forgetting her fatigue, and the difficulties which surrounded her, wanted immediately to resume her journey, and Father Jerome was equally anxious to learn how she and Marie had come so far, and how they intended to proceed.

Chapeau had in the mean time called on the old priest, and though he had found it almost impossible to make him understand what he wanted, or who the ladies were of whom he spoke, he had learnt that Father Jerome was in the chapel, and was as much gratified as he was surprised to hear it. He had then hurried back, and though he had not put himself forward during the scene which has been just described, he had heard what had passed.

He now explained to Father Jerome the way in which they had left Chatillon, and journeyed on horseback from St. Laurent, and declared, at the same time with much truth, that it was quite impossible for them to proceed farther on their way that night.

"The poor brutes are dead beat," said he. "All the spurs in Poitou wouldn't get them on a league. The night will be pitch dark, too, and, above all, Madame and Mademoiselle would be killed. They have already been on horseback all day—and so they were yesterday: it is quite clear they must rest here tonight."

Chapeau's arguments against their farther progress were conclusive, and as there was no better shelter to which to take them, Father Jerome led them into the little glebe. "There is but one bed left in the place," said he, as he entered the gate, "but you will be very welcome to that; you will find it poor enough; Father Bernard has shared it with me for the last two nights. We poor Curés have not many luxuries to offer to our friends now."

Madame de Lescure tried to utter some kind of protest that she would not turn the poor old man out of his only bed, but she succeeded badly in the attempt, for her heart was sad within her, and she hardly knew what she was saying. They all followed Father Jerome out of the chapel, of which he locked the door, and putting the key into his pocket, strode into the humble dwelling opposite.

They found Father Bernard seated over a low wood fire, in a small sitting-room, in which the smell arising from the burning of damp sticks was very prevalent. There was one small rickety table in the middle of the room, and one other chair besides that occupied by the host, and with these articles alone the room was furnished. That there was no carpet in a clergyman's house in Poitou was not remarkable; indeed it would have been very remarkable if there had been one; but the total want of any of the usual comforts of civilized life struck even Madame de Lescure, unsuited as she was at the present moment to take notice of such things.

The old man did not rise, but stared at them somewhat wildly: he was nearly doting from age; and fear, poverty, and sorrow, added to his many years, had now weighed him down almost to idiotcy. Father Jerome did the honours of the house; he made Madame de Lescure sit down on the chair, and then bustling into the kitchen, brought out a three legged stool, which he wiped with the sleeve of his coat, and offered to Marie. Then he took Chapeau to the door, and whispered to him some secret communication with reference to supper; in fact, he had to confess that there was nothing in the house but bread, and but little of that. That neither he or Father Bernard had a sou piece between them, and that unless Chapeau had money, and could go as far as the village and purchase eggs, they would all have to go supperless to bed. Chapeau luckily was provided, and started at once to forage for the party, and Father Jerome returned into the room relieved from a heavy weight.

"My dear old friend here," said he, laying his hand on the old man's arm, "has not much to offer you; but I am sure you are welcome to what -he has. There is not a heart in all La Vendée beats truer to his sovereign than his. Old age, misfortune, and persecution, have lain a heavy hand on him lately, but his heart still warms to the cause. Does it not my old friend?" And Father Jerome looked kindly into his face, striving to encourage him into some little share of interest in what was going on.

"I don't think I'll ever be warm again," said the old man, drawing his chair still nearer to the dull smoky fire, and shivering as he did so. "Everything is cold now. I don't understand why these ladies are come here, or what they're to do; but they're very welcome, Jerome, very welcome. A strange man came in just now, and said they must have my bed."

"Oh no, Sir," said Madame de Lescure, inexpressibly shocked at the dreadful misery of the poor old man; "indeed, indeed, we will not. It is only for one night, and we shall do very well. Indeed, we would not turn you out of your bed."

"You are welcome, Madame, welcome to it all—welcome as the flowers in May. I know who you are, though I forget your name; it is a name dear to all

La Vendée. Your husband is a great and good man; indeed, you shall have my bed, though you'll find it very cold. Your husband—but, oh dear! I beg your pardon, Madame, I forgot."

I need not say that the evening which they spent at Genet, was melancholy enough, and the privations which they suffered were dreadful. During the early part of the night both Madame de Lescure and Marie lay down for a few hours, but nothing, which could be said, would induce them to keep the old priest longer from his bed. About midnight they got up and spent the remainder of the night seated on the two chairs near the fire, while Father Jerome squatted on the stool, and with his elbows on his knees, and his face upon his hands, sat out the long night, meditating upon the fortunes of La Vendée.

They started early on the next morning, and the priest of St. Laud's went with them, leaving Father Bernard in perfect solitude, for he had neither friend or relative to reside beneath his roof.

"Some of them will come down from time to time," said Father Jerome, "and do what little can be done for him, poor old man! His sufferings, it is to be hoped, will not last many days."

"And will he perform mass next Sunday?" said Marie.

"Indeed he will, if able to walk across the road into the chapel, and will forget no word of the service, and make no blunder in the ceremony. To you he seems to be an idiot, but he is not so, though long suffering has made his mind to wander strangely, when he sees strange faces. There are many who have been called to a more active sphere of duty for their King and country than that poor Curé, but none who have suffered more acutely for the cause, and have born their sufferings with greater patience."

CHAPTER V.
THE VENDEANS AT ST. FLORENT.

The reader, it is hoped, will remember St. Florent; it was here that the first scene of this tale opened; it was here that Cathelineau first opposed the exactions of the democratic government and that the Vendeans, not then rejoicing in that now illustrious name, felt the first flush of victory. It was here that 'Marie Jeanne' was taken from the troops of the Republic by the valour of the townsmen, and, adorned with garlands by their sisters and daughters, was dragged in triumph through the streets, with such bright presentiments of future success and glory.

The men of St. Florent had ever since that day borne a prominent part in the contest; they felt that the people of Poitou had risen in a mass to promote the cause, which they had been the first to take up; and they had considered themselves bound in honour to support the character for loyalty which they had assumed: the consequence was that many of the bravest of its sons had fallen, and that very few of its daughters had not to lament a lover, a husband, or a father.

St. Florent was now a melancholy careworn place. The people no longer met together in enthusiastic groups to animate each other's courage, and to anticipate the glorious day when their sovereign should come among them in person, to thank them for having been the first in Poitou to unfurl the white flag. It is true that they did not go back from their high resolves, or shrink from the bloody effects of their brave enterprise, but their talk now was of suffering and death; they whispered together in twos and threes, at their own door-sills, instead of shouting in the market-place. Cathelineau was dead, and Foret was dead, and they were the gallantest of their townsmen. They had now also heard that everything had been staked on a great battle, and that that battle had been lost at Cholet—that Bonchamps and d'Elbée had fallen, and that de Lescure had been wounded and was like to die. They knew that the whole army was retreating to St. Florent, and that the Republican troops would soon follow them, headed by Lechelle, whose name already drove the colour from the cheeks of every woman in La Vendée. They knew that a crowd of starving wretches would fall, like a swarm of locusts, on their already nearly empty granaries; and that all the horrors attendant on a civil war were crowding round their hearths.

It was late in the evening that the news of the battle reached the town, and early on the next morning the landlord of the auberge was standing at his door waiting the arrival of Henri Larochejaquelin and de Lescure. The town was all up and in a tumult; from time to time small parties of men flocked in from Cholet, some armed, and some of whom had lost their arms; some slightly wounded, and some fainting with fatigue, as they begged admission into the houses of the town's-people. The aubergiste was resolute in refusing admittance to all; for tidings had reached him of guests who would more than fill his house, on whom he looked as entitled to more than all he could give them. It was at his hall door that the first blow had been struck, it was in rescuing his servant that the first blood had been shed; and though the war had utterly ruined him, he still felt that it would ill become him to begrudge anything that remained to him to those who had suffered so much in the cause.

Peter Berrier, his ostler, stood behind him, teterrima belli causa! This man had at different times been with the army, but had managed to bring himself safe out of the dangers of the wars back to the little inn, and now considered himself an hero. He looked on himself in the light in which classic readers look on Helen, and felt sure that the whole struggle had been commenced, and was continued on his account. He was amazed to find how little deference was paid to him, not only by the Vendeans in general, but even by his own town's-people.

"I shall never be made to understand this business of Cholet," said he to his master, "never. There must have been sad want there of a good head; aye, and of a good heart too, I fear. Well, well, to turn and run! Vendean soldiers to turn and run before those beggarly blues!"

"You'd have been the first, Peter, to show a clean pair of heels yourself, if you'd been there," said the landlord.

"Me show a clean pair of heels! I didn't run away at Saumur, nor yet at Fontenay, nor yet at many another pitched battle I saw. I didn't run away here at St. Florent, I believe, when a few of us took the barracks against a full regiment of soldiers."

"You couldn't well run then, for you were tied by the leg in the stable there."

"No, I was not; it was only for a minute or two I was in the stable. Would Cathelineau or Foret have turned their backs, think ye? When I was alongside of those two men, I used to feel that the three of us were a match for the world in arms; and they had the same feeling too exactly. Well, two of the three are gone, but I would sooner have followed them than have turned my back upon a blue."

"You're a great warrior, Peter, and it's a pity you didn't stay with the army."

"Perhaps it is, perhaps it is. Perhaps I shouldn't have left it; but I was driven away by little jealousies. Even great men have their failings. But they certainly made some queer selections when they chose the twelve captains at Saumur.

There's not one of them left with the army now but M. Henri, and what's he but a boy?"

"He has done a man's work at any rate!"

"He's brave, there's no denying that. He's very brave, but what then; there's that impudent puppy of a valet of his, Chapeau; he's brave too: at least they say so. But what's bravery? Can they lead an army? is there anything of the General about them? Can they beat the blues?

"Didn't he manage to beat the blues at Amaillou and at Coron, and at Durbellière? Faith, I think he has done nothing but beat them these three months."

"There's nothing of the General in him, I tell you. Haven't I seen him in battle now; he's quite at home at a charge, I grant you; and he's not bad in a breach; but Lord bless you, he can't command troops."

The landlord and his servant were still standing at the door of the inn, when the party for whom they were waiting made its appearance in the square of the town. It consisted of a waggon, in which the wounded man was lying, of three or four men on horseback, among whom were Henri Larochejaquelin and the little Chevalier, and a crowd of men on foot, soldiers of the Vendean army, who had not left the side of their General since he had fallen at Cholet.

During the latter part of his journey, de Lescure had been sensible, and had suffered dreadfully both in mind and body. He had never felt so confident of success as Henri and others had done, and had carried on the war more from a sense of duty than from a hope of restoring the power of the crown. He now gave way to that despondency which so often accompanies bodily suffering. He felt certain that his own dissolution was near, and on that subject his only anxiety was that he might see his wife before he died. He had, since the power of speech had been restored to him, more than once asserted that the cause of the royalists was desperate, and had, by doing so, greatly added to the difficulties by which Henri was now surrounded. He did not, however, despair; nothing could make him despondent, or rob him of that elastic courage which, in spite of all the sufferings he had endured, gave him a strange feeling of delight in the war which he was waging.

An immense concourse of people gathered round the waggon, as de Lescure was lifted from it and carried up to the bedroom, which had been prepared for him; and they showed their grief at his sufferings, and their admiration of his character as a soldier, by tears and prayers for his recovery. The extreme popularity of M. de Lescure through the whole war, and the love which was felt for him by all the peasants concerned in it, proved their just appreciation of real merit; for he had not those qualities which most tend to ingratiate an officer with his men. He could not unbend among them, and talk to them familiarly of their prowess, and of the good cause, as Henri did. He had the manners of an austere, sombre man; and though always most anxious for the security and good treatment of the prisoners, had more than once severely punished men among his own followers for some breach of discipline. He had, on one occasion, threatened to leave the army entirely if he was not obeyed with the same exactness, as though he actually bore the King's commission; and the general feeling that he would most certainly keep his word, and that the army could not succeed without him, had greatly tended to repress any inclination towards mutiny.

"God bless him, and preserve him, and restore him to us all!" said a woman who had pushed her way through the crowd, so as to catch a glance at his pale wasted face, one side of which was swathed in bandages, which greatly added to the ghastliness of his appearance. "We have lost our husbands, and our sons, and our sweethearts; but what matters, we do not begrudge them to our King. The life of Monseigneur is more precious than them all. La Vendée cannot afford to lose her great General."

De Lescure heard and understood, but could not acknowledge, the sympathy of the people; but Henri, as he tenderly raised his cousin's head, and bore him in his arms from the waggon, spoke a word or two to the crowd which satisfied them; and Arthur Mondyon remained among them a while to tell them how bravely their countrymen had fought at Cholet, against numbers more than double their own, before they would consent to own themselves beaten.

There was an immense deal for Henri Larochejaquelin to do. In the first place he had to collect together the fragments of the disbanded army; to separate the men who were armed from those who had lost their arms, and to divide the comparatively speaking small number of the former, into such bands or regiments as would make them serviceable in case of need.

De Lescure was unable to give him any actual assistance in his work; but his thoughtful brain, reflecting on all the difficulties of Henri's situation, conceived how much they would be increased by the want of any absolute title to authority; he therefore determined, ill as he was, to invest him with the command-in-chief of the shattered army.

Early on the morning after their arrival he begged that all such men as had acted as chief officers among the Vendeans, and who were now in St. Florent, would form themselves into a council in his room, and that it might be proclaimed to the army that they were about to nominate a General-in-Chief. The council was not so numerously attended as that which on a former occasion was held at Saumur. As Peter Berrier had said, most of those who then sat around that council table were now dead, or were, at any rate, hors-de-combat. Only four of the number were now present. De Lescure was lying on his bed, and was a spectacle dreadful to look upon. The hair had been all cut from his head. His face was not only pale, but livid. The greater portion of it had been enveloped in bandages, which he had partly removed with his own hand, that his mouth might be free, so that he could use his weak voice to address his comrades, perhaps for the last time. He uttered neither complaint or groan, but the compressed lips, careworn cheeks, and sunken eyes, gave too certain signs of the agony which he suffered. Henri was there, but he knew the proposal which his cousin was about to make, and he felt, not only that he was unequal to the heavy task which was about to be put on his shoulders, but also that there were still some among their number who were superior to him in skill, rank, and age, and who were to be excluded from the dangerous dignity by the partial admiration which was felt for himself He sat apart in a corner of the room, with his face buried in his handkerchief; his manly heart was overcome; and while de Lescure named him as the only person possessed of sufficient nerve and authority to give the Vendeans a chance of an escape from utter ruin, he was shedding tears like a child.

D'Autachamps and the Prince de Talmont were there also; men, who throughout the war had lent every energy to its furtherance. At another time, and under other circumstances, they might have expressed indignation at being called on to serve under a man so much their junior; but de Lescure's position checked, not only the expression of any such feeling, but the feeling itself. They could not differ from a man who had lost so much in the cause, and was now sealing his devotion with his life. There were five or six others in the room; officers who were now well known in the army, whose courage history has not forgotten to record, but whose names are unnecessary to our tale.

"Gentlemen," said de Lescure to them, as soon as he saw them seated round his bed, and had contrived to get himself so propped up with pillows as to be able to address them, "you all know why I have wished to see you here; you all know the paramount importance of that duty which requires us to provide, as far as may be possible, for the security of the unfortunate peasants who have followed us with such courage, who have shown so much generous loyalty, so much true patriotism. Our first step must be to name some one whom we can all obey. We all know that the army cannot act in unison without one absolute Commander. He who was lately our Commander has fallen in the performance of his duty. Our dear friend Bonchamps is no more. Had I escaped from that awful battle unwounded, it is not improbable that you might have chosen me to undertake the now unenviable duty of guiding a broken army. You will not accuse a dying man of vanity in saying so; but, gentlemen, you all see that such a chance is now impossible. My wound is mortal. A few days, perhaps a few hours, and I shall be removed from this anxious, painful, all but hopeless conflict, in which you, my friends, must still engage; in which some of you will probably fall. I cannot suffer with you future reverses, or lead you to future triumphs; but, if you will allow me, I will use my last breath in naming to you one, whom, I believe, every peasant in La Vendée, and every gentleman engaged in the cause, will follow, if it be necessary, to death. Henri Larochejaquelin is the only man whom all the peasants, all the soldiers, all the officers, know intimately; and the last duty I can perform in the service of my King is to implore you to put him at the head of your troops. He is young, and you will assist his youth with your counsel. He is diffident of himself, and you will encourage him with your assurance and obedience; but he is brave, he is beloved, he is trusted; and above all, he possesses that innate aptitude for war, that power of infusing courage into the timid and lending strength to the weak, which is the gift of God alone, and without which no General can command an army."

Henri had promised his cousin that he would neither interrupt him, or raise any objection to the proposition about to be made. He kept his word as long as de Lescure was speaking, but when he had finished he could not restrain himself from expressing his own sense of his unfitness for the duties they were calling on him to perform. He came forward, and leaning against the head of the wounded man's bed, put his hand upon his shoulder, and speaking almost in a whisper, like a young girl pleading for delay before her lover, he said, "Charles, you forget, I am but one-and-twenty."

No one, however, seconded his objection. No other voice was raised to counteract the wishes of the man who had suffered so much in the cause, and who, had he been spared, would have been at once chosen to guide their future movements.

"With this exception," said the Prince de Talmont; "your case we know is doubtful, but should you recover, should you again be able to come among us before the war be over, Larochejaquelin shall then give place to you."

"There is little chance of that, Prince," said de Lescure, smiling sadly; "but should it occur, there will be no quarrel between me and Henri. I will serve with him as his aide-de-camp."

Henri Larochejaquelin now found himself General-in-Chief of the Vendean army. As he himself had said, he was but one-and-twenty, and yet never was greater energy, firmness, and moral courage required from a General, than was required from him at this moment. Eighty thousand people were on that day told to look to him as the man who was to save them from famine and from the enemy's sword, to protect their lives and the lives of all whom they loved, and eventually to turn their present utter misery and despair into victory and triumph.

Eighty thousand people were there collected in and around St. Florent, men, women, and children; the old and infirm, the maimed and sick, the mutilated and the dying. Poor wretches who had gotten themselves dragged thither from the hospitals, in which they feared to remain, were lying in every ditch, and under every wall, filling the air with their groans. Everything was in confusion; no staff existed competent to arrange their affairs, and to husband the poor means at their disposal. Food was wasted by some, while hundreds were starving. Some houses in the town were nearly empty, while others were crowded almost to suffocation. There was very much to be done, yet every one was idle.

The great work to be accomplished was to transport the Vendean multitude over to the other side of the Loire. It had been at first feared by some that the men of Brittany would be unwilling to receive the beaten royalist army, flying from the bloody vengeance of the republicans, but their neighbours did not prove so unhospitable. A thousand welcomes were sent over to them, and many a happy messenger of good tidings came, assuring Henri that the people of Poitou should find arms, food, clothing, and shelter on the other side of the water.

Henri sat himself to work in earnest. His first difficulty was to get vessels or rafts sufficient to carry the people over. All he could obtain was seven or eight little boats, each capable of holding about six persons, besides the two men who rowed. Timber there was none of size sufficient to make a raft; and though he sent messengers for leagues, both up and down the river, he could not get a barge. He put the small boats to work, but the passage of the river was so tedious that it seemed to him that it would be impossible for him to take over all those who crowded on the banks. The river is broad at St. Florent, and between the marshes which lie on the southern side and the northern bank there is a long island. Between St. Florent and the island the water is broad and the stream slow, but between the island and the other shore the narrow river runs rapidly. Henri at first contented himself with sending the women and children, together with the sick and aged, into the island, thinking that there they would be at any rate for a time safe from the blues, and that some effort might probably be made from the other shore to convey them across the narrow passage. Gradually, however, the island became full, and he was obliged to send his boats round to take the people from thence to the main land.

All day the work continued, and when the dark night came on, the boats did not for a moment cease to ply. Immediately after sunset, the rain began to fall in torrents, and as the anxious wretches did not like to leave the close vicinity of the river, which they had spent the whole day in struggling to attain, thousands of them remained there wet and shivering until the morning. Mothers during the darkness were parted from their children, and wives from their husbands. Those who, worn out with fatigue and weakness, were forced to lie down upon the ground, were trodden upon by others, who pressed on, to reach the river. Some were pushed into the water and screamed aloud that they were about to drown, and when the dawn of the morning came, misery, wretchedness, and fear were to be seen on every face.

During the whole day and night, Henri was either on the bank, or passing between it and the town. He had, early in the day, stripped himself of his coat, and when the evening came, he could not find it. Wet through, in his shirt sleeves, this young generalissimo passed the first night of his command, guarding the entrance into his little vessels; prohibiting more than eight from embarking at a time; striving to his uttermost that none but the weak and aged should be taken over; solacing the sufferings of those near him; bidding the wretched not to despair, and pointing to the opposite shore as the land of hope, where they would soon again find plenty, comfort, and triumph.

He was still at the same duty on the following morning, reckoning up, with something like despair, the small number of those who had as yet passed over, and the multitude who were yet to pass, when the young Chevalier came down to him with the news that Madame de Lescure, and her sister-in-law were in St. Florent. Even the work, on which he was so intent, could not keep him from those respecting whom he was so anxious, and he hurried into town for an hour or two, leaving the Chevalier in his place.

CHAPTER VI.
THE PASSAGE OF THE LOIRE.

M. de Lescure had been two days in St. Florent, when his wife and sister arrived there on horseback, attended by Chapeau. None of the party had ever been in the town before, but it was not long before they were recognized, and the two ladies soon found themselves standing in the inn yard. Madame de Lescure had as yet asked no question about her husband; indeed she had not had opportunity to do so, for she had been hurried through a dense throng of people, none of whom she knew, and when she was lifted from her horse by a strange hand, she had no idea that the window immediately above her head looked from the room in which her husband lay. Chapeau, however, with considerate tact, did not lose a moment in finding the aubergiste, and learning from him enough to enable him to whisper a word of comfort to her.

"He is here, Madame," said he, standing close behind her, "in the room above there. He is somewhat better than he has been, and as strong in his mind as ever. He has been most anxious for your arrival," and then he led the way into the hotel, pushing aside the crowd to the right and to the left; and within five minutes from the time of their entering the town, the two ladies found themselves on the stairs immediately outside the chamber in which was lying the object of all their present anxiety.

For the last four days and four nights, it had been the first and only desire of Madame de Lescure to be with her husband; and now that she was so near him she dreaded to open the door. "Who is with him?" said she, speaking in a whisper, and trembling from head to foot, so that she could hardly stand.

"The little Chevalier is with him always," said the aubergiste, who had followed them up the stairs: "he never leaves him, now that M. Henri is obliged to be away."

"Hadn't I better go in, perhaps," said Chapeau, "and send the Chevalier out? I can tell M. de Lescure that Madame is here; it might be too much for Monsieur to see her all at once."

Without waiting for an answer, Chapeau knocked at the door and went in, while the two ladies sat down on the nearest step, dreading almost to breathe in their intense anxiety; in a few seconds Arthur Mondyon came out, and taking a hand of each of his two friends, pressed them to his lips.

"He knows you are here," said he to Madame de Lescure, "and you are to go into him alone. Marie and I will go down stairs until he sends for us. Be tranquil as you can, while you are with him; you will find him as calm as ever."

She rose, and entered the room on tiptoe, as Chapeau left it; her face was as pale as marble, and her heart beat so violently that she felt that she would hardly be able to reach the chair at the bed-side. De Lescure was lying on a decent but very humble bed, at the farthest end of a large room, in which there were three or four other bedsteads, and an enormous number of common deal chairs and tables piled one a-top of another. He was propped up in the bed on pillows, and as he turned his eyes towards the door, the full light of the sun shone upon his face, and gave an especial ghastliness to its pallor.

Madame de Lescure tried to control herself; but in such moments the feelings of the heart overcome the reason, and the motions of the body are governed by passion alone. In an instant her face was on his bosom, and her arms were locked closely round his body.

"Victorine—my own Victorine," said he, "my greatest grief is over now. I feared that we were not to meet again, and that thought alone was almost too much for my courage."

She was for a time unable to articulate a word. He felt her warm tears as she convulsively pressed her cheek against his breast; he felt the violent throbs of her loving heart, and allowed her a few minutes before he asked her to speak to him. She had thrown off the hat which she had worn before entering the room, and he now gently smoothed her ruffled hair with his hand, and collected together the loose tresses which had escaped down her neck.

"Look up, love," he said; "I haven't seen your face yet, or heard your voice. Come, Victorine, you were not used to be so weak. We must all string our nerves now, dearest: we must all be brave now. We used to praise you for your courage; now is the time for you to show it."

"Oh, Charles! oh, my poor stricken love!" and then she raised her face and gazed into his, till the tears made her eyes so dim that she could hardly see him. "I knew it would come at last," she said; "I knew this fearful blow would come at last. Oh, that we had gone when others went! at any rate I should not have lived to see you thus."

"Do no say that, Victorine; do not speak so—do not allow yourself to think so—or you will rob both of us of our dearest comfort. No, my love; were it to do again, I again would stand by the throne, and you again would counsel me to do so. A doubt on that point would be calamity, indeed; but, thank God, there is no doubt."

"But the misery to see you thus—torn, and mangled, and tortured. And for what? What good have we done with our hot patriotism? Is the King nearer his throne? Are the murders of the Republic less frequent?"

"I fear you are selfish now, love. Did we not know, when we first took up our arms, that many happy wives would be widowed—that numberless children would be made fatherless—that hundreds of mothers would have to weep for their sons. We must not ourselves complain of that fate, to which we have knowingly, and thoughtfully, consigned so many others."

Madame de. Lescure had no answer to make to her husband's remonstrance. She sat herself upon the bed, so that she could support his head upon her bosom; and pressing her lips to his clammy brow, she said in a low voice: "God's will be done, Charles: with all my heart I pity those who have suffered as I now suffer."

She remained sitting there in silence for a considerable time; weeping, indeed, but stifling her sobs, that the sound of her grief might not agitate him, while he enjoyed the inexpressible comfort of having her close to him. He closed his eyes as he leant against the sweet support which she afforded him, but not in sleep; he was thinking over all it might be most necessary for him to say to her, before the power of speech had left him, and taking counsel with himself as to the advice which he would give her.

"Victorine," he said, and then paused a moment for a reply, but, as she did not answer him, he went on. "Victorine, I want you to be all yourself now, while I speak to you. Can you listen to me calmly, love, while I speak to you seriously?"

She said that she would, but the tone in which she said it, hardly gave confirmation to her promise.

"I hardly know what account you have yet heard of that unfortunate battle."

"Oh! I have heard that it was most unfortunate: unfortunate to all, but most unfortunate to us."

"It was unfortunate. I hope those who spoke to you of it, deceived you with no false hopes, for that would have been mere cruelty. Give me your hand, my love; I hope they told you the truth. You know, dearest, do you not, that—that—that my wound is mortal?"

She strove hard to control her feelings. She bit her under lip between her teeth; she pressed her feet against the bed, and grasped the loose clothes with the hand which was disengaged. The virtue on which her husband most prided himself was calmness and self-possession in affliction. She knew that he now expected that virtue from her, and that nothing would so grieve him as to see her render herself weakly up to her sorrow, and she strove hard to control it; but all her exertion did not enable her to answer him. It seemed almost miraculous to herself that she could sit there, and retain her consciousness, and hear him utter such words. Had she attempted to speak, the effort would have overcome her.

"For heaven's sake, Victorine, let nothing, let nobody deceive you; know the worst, and look to Christ for power to bear it, and you will find the burden not too heavy to be borne. You and I, love, must part in this world. We have passed our lives together without one shadow to darken the joy of our union: we have been greatly blessed beyond others. Can we complain because our happiness on earth is not eternal? Is it not a great comfort that we can thus speak together before we part; that I have been allowed to live to see your dear face, to feel your breath on my cheek, and to hear your voice? to tell you, with the assurance which the approach of death gives me, that these sorrows are but for a time, and that our future joys shall be everlasting? And I must thank you, Victorine, for your tender care, your constant love. You have made me happy here; you have helped to fit me for happiness hereafter. It is owing to you that even this hour has but little bitterness for me. Are we not happy, dearest; are we not happy even now in each other's love?"

Madame de Lescure had, while her husband was speaking, sunk upon her knees beside his bed, and was now bathing his hand with her tears.

"I cannot blame you for your tears," he said, "for human nature must have her way; but my Victorine will remember that she must not give way to her sorrow, as other women may do. Rise, dearest, and let me see your face. I feel that I have strength now to tell you all that I have to say. I may probably never have that strength again."

She rose at his bidding, and sat upon the bed where he could look full upon her face; and then he began to pour out to her all the wishes of his heart, all the thoughts which had run through his brain since consciousness returned to him after his wound. After a little while she conquered her emotion, and listened to him, and answered him with attention. He first spoke of their daughter, who was now in safety, with relatives who had fled to England, and then of herself, and the probable result of the Vendean war. He told her that he would not say a word to discourage Henri: that had his life been spared, he should have considered it his own most paramount and sacred duty to further the war with every energy which he possessed; but that he did not expect that it would ever terminate favourably to their hopes. "The King will reign again," he said, "in France; I do not doubt it for a moment; but years upon years of bloodshed will have to be borne; the blood of France will be drained from every province, aye, from every parish, before the guilt which she has committed can be atoned for—before she can have expiated the murder of her King." He desired her to continue with Henri till an opportunity should occur for her to cross over into England, but to let no such opportunity pass. He said that if Henri could maintain his ground for a while in Brittany—if the people would support him, and if English succour should arrive—it was still probable that they might be able to come to such terms with the republicans as would enable them to live after their own fashion, in their own country; to keep their own priests among them, and to maintain their exemption from service in the republican armies. "But should this not be so," he said, "should all the valour of the Vendeans not be able to secure even thus much, then remember that God will temper the wind to the shorn lamb. With a people as with an individual, he will not make the burden too heavy for the back which has to bear it."

He spoke also of Marie, and declared his wish that she should not delay her marriage with Henri. He even said, that should his life be so far prolonged, as to enable him to be carried over into Brittany, and should the army there find a moment's rest, he would wish to see their hands joined together at his bed-side.

"My poor dear Marie!" said Madame de Lescure, almost unconsciously. She was thinking of her sister's future fate; that she also might have soon to bewail a husband, torn from her by these savage wars. De Lescure understood what was passing through her mind, and said:

"I know, love, that there are reasons why they had better remain as they now are. Why they should not indissolubly bind themselves to each other at such a time as this; but we must choose the least of evils. You will both now be a burden—no, I will not say a burden, but a charge—upon Henri; and he has a right to expect that a girl, who will depend for everything on him, shall not shrink from the danger of marrying him. She has been happy to accept his love, and when she may be a comfort to him, she should not hesitate to give him her hand. Besides, dearest, think what a comfort it will be to me to know that they are married before I die."

There was one other subject on which he had made up his mind to speak, but on which even he, calm and collected as he was, found it difficult to express himself; he had, however, determined that it was his duty to do so, and though the words almost refused to come at his bidding, still he went through his task.

"You will be desolate for a time, Victorine, when I shall have left you," said he.

She answered him only by a look, but that look was so full of misery—of misery, blended with inexpressible love—that no one seeing her, could have doubted that she would indeed be desolate when he was gone.

"We have loved each other too well to part easily," he continued, "and, for a time, the world will all be a weary blank to you. May God, who knows how to pour a balm into every wound, which in his mercy He inflicts, grant that

that time may not be long! Listen to me patiently, love. It is a strong sense of duty which makes me pain you; my memory will always be dear to you; but do not let a vain, a foolish, a wicked regret counteract the purpose for which God has placed you here. You are very young, dearest, you have, probably, yet many years to live; and it would multiply my grief at leaving you tenfold, if I thought that your hopes of happiness in this world were to be buried in the grave with me. No, love, bear with me," he said, for she tried to stop him. "The pain which I give you now, may prevent much grief to you hereafter. Remember, Victorine, that should these evil days pass by—should you ever again be restored to peace and tranquil life, my earnest, my last, my solemn prayer to you is, that my memory may not prevent your future marriage."

She was still kneeling by his side, and with her face upturned and her hands clasped together, she now implored him to stop. She uttered no dissent, she made no protestations; but she beseeched him, by their long and tender love, by all the common ties which bound them together, to cease to speak on a subject which was so agonising.

"I have done, love," he said; "and I know that you will not think lightly of a prayer which I have made to you in so serious a manner."

De Lescure had expressed the same wish to his wife on former occasions, which, however, had, of course, been less solemn; and then his wife had answered him with a full, but not grieving heart. "Had our lot," he once said, "been cast in an Indian village, the prejudices of the country would have required you to submit to a horrid, torturing death upon my tomb. The prejudices of Christian lands, which attribute blame to the wife who does not yield herself a living sacrifice to a life of desolation from a false regard to her husband's memory, are, if not so horrid, every whit as unreasonable; such a sentiment is an attempt to counteract God's beneficence, who cures the wounds which he inflicts."

Henri's first care, after having seen Marie and Madame de Lescure, was to provide for their transit, and that of his wounded friend, to the other side of the water; for he felt that if the blues came upon St. Florent before that was done, nothing could prevent the three from being made prisoners. No tidings had yet been received of the advance of the republicans from Cholet towards St. Florent, and the precautions which Henri had taken were such as to ensure him some few hours' notice of their approach. He knew, however, that those hours would be hours of boundless confusion; that the whole crowd of unfortunate wretches who might then still be on the southern side of the river, would crowd into the small boats, hurrying themselves and each other to destruction; that discipline would be at an end, and that all his authority would probably be insufficient to secure a passage for his party. About three o'clock he sent word to Arthur to have the strongest of the boats kept in readiness a little lower down the river than the usual point of embarkation; so that they might, if possible, escape being carried through the throng. He then procured a waggon into which de Lescure was lifted on his bed; his wife sat behind him, supporting his head on her lap, and Henri and his sister walked beside the vehicle down to the water's edge.

The little Chevalier was there with the boat, and he had with him two men, neither of whom were young, and who had been at work the whole day ferrying over the Vendeans to the island. Arthur's figure was hardly that of an aide-de-camp. His head was bare and his face begrimed with mud. He was stripped to his shirt sleeves, and they were tucked up nearly to his shoulders. He still had round his waist the red scarf, of which he was so proud; but it was so soiled and dragged, as hardly to be recognized as the badge of the honourable corps to which he belonged, for he had, constantly since the morning, been up to his breast in the water, dragging women and children out of the river, heaving the boats ashore, or helping to push them off through the mud and rushes.

It was settled on the bank that Arthur should go over with them into Brittany, as Henri felt that he could not conscientiously leave the St. Florent side of the river, while so many thousands were looking to him for directions; and, consequently, as soon as de Lescure and the two ladies had, with much labour and delay, been placed in the boat, he swung himself out of the water into the bow, and the frail bark with its precious load was pushed off into the stream.

The point from which it started was somewhat lower down the stream than that from which the boats had been hitherto put off, and, consequently, as they got into the middle of the river, they found themselves carried down towards the lower part of the island, on which they had intended to land. Had the men who were rowing worked vigorously, this would not have occurred to any great extent; but they pulled slowly and feebly, and every foot which the boat made across, it descended as much down the river. Arthur had been desired to land de Lescure on the island, and another boat had been sent round to be ready to take him at once from thence to the other shore; but when he found that they were unintentionally so near the lower end of the island, it occurred to him that it would save them all much pain and trouble, if he were to run round it, and land them at once on the opposite shore; they would in this way have to make a considerably longer journey, but then de Lescure would be spared the pain of so many different movements.

Madame de Lescure immediately jumped at the proposal. "For heaven's sake, Arthur, do so, if it be possible," said she; "it will be the greatest relief. I do not think we should ever get across to the other boat, if we once leave this."

Arthur was behind the two men at the oars, who had listened to what had been said, without making any observation, or attempting to alter the destination of the boat; rudder there was none, and the steering, therefore, depended entirely on the rowers.

"Do you hear?" said Arthur, stretching forward and laying his hand on the shoulder of the man who was in front. "Never mind the island at all; go a little more down the stream, and then we can cross over at once without landing at all. Do you hear me, friend?" added he, speaking rather hastily, for the boatman took no apparent notice of his instructions.

"We hear you, Monsieur," said the man, "but it is impossible; we could not do it."

"Ah, nonsense!" answered the Chevalier: "not do it—I say you must do it. I wonder you should hesitate for a moment, when you know how M. de Lescure is suffering, and how much those ladies have to go through. Turn the boat down the stream at once, I tell you."

"It is quite impossible," said the old man doggedly, and still holding on to his course; "we should only upset the boat and drown you all. We could never push her through the current on the other side, could we Jean?"

"Quite impossible," said the other. "We should only be carried down into the rushes, or else be upset in the stream."

"Nonsense!" said Arthur. "What's to upset you? At any rate you shall try." And he laid his hand on the oar of the man who was nearest to him, but this, instead of having the effect which he desired, turned the nose of the boat the other way.

"For God's sake, my dear friends, do this favour for us if you can!" said Madame de Lescure. "It may save the life of my husband, and indeed we will reward you richly for your labour. Stop, Arthur, don't use violence; I am sure they will do this kindness for us, if they are able."

"If they won't do it for kindness, they shall do it because they cannot help it," said Arthur, when he saw that the men still showed no disposition to go down the stream; and as he spoke he pulled his pistol out of his belt, and prepared to cock it. The pistol, in truth, was perfectly harmless, for it had been over and over again immersed in the water, and the powder was saturated with wet; but this did not occur to the boatmen, nor, very possibly, to Arthur either; and when he, stepping across the thwart, on which the hinder man was sitting, held the pistol close to the ear of the other, threatening that if he did not at once do as he was bid, he would blow out his brains and take his place on the seat, the poor old man dropped his oar from his hand into the water, and falling on his knees on the bottom of the boat, implored for mercy.

"Spare me, Monsieur! oh, spare me!" said he. "Ladies, pray speak for me: I am not used to this work—indeed I am not—and I and my comrade are nearly dead with fatigue."

Arthur put the pistol back into his belt when the poor man begged for mercy, and pulling the fallen oar out of the water, declared that he would himself row round the island, and that the two old men might take the other oar in turns. They agreed to this, and then he who had been so frightened, and who was plainly the master of the two, told his tale to them, as he filled Arthur's place in the bow of the boat.

"When they had heard," he said, "what his former occupation had been, they would not wonder that the hard work at which they found him was almost too much for him. He was," he said, "a priest, and had been employed above twenty years as Curé in a small parish on the river side, between St. Florent and Chaudron. The other man, who was working with him, had been his sexton. He had, like other Curés, been turned out of his little house by the Republic, but had returned to his parish when he heard that the success of the Vendean arms seemed to promise tranquillity to the old inhabitants of the country. He had, however, soon been again disturbed. The rumour of Lechelle's army had driven him from his home, and he had fled with many others to St. Florent. He had been advised that those who were taken in a priest's garb, would be more subject even than others to the wrath of the republicans, and he had therefore disguised himself; and as from having lived so long near the river he had become somewhat used to the management of boats, he had, for charity's sake, leant his hand to the poor Vendeans, willing," as he said, "to use what little skill and strength he had for those who lost their all in fighting for him, his country, and his religion. But now," he added, "he found himself almost knocked up; and although, when he had been chosen to take over Monsieur and the two ladies, he had not had the heart to decline, still he had found that his strength would fail him. He knew that he and his companion could not, unaided, reach the opposite shore; but if the young gentleman would assist, they would still do their best, and perhaps they might cross over in safety."

This piteous tale soon turned their anger into admiration and friendship. They thanked the kind old man for all that he had done for them, and Arthur once, and over again, turned round to beg his pardon for the violence he had offered him.

"Indeed, then, I picked you out for this job," said he, "because you always worked so hard, and seemed so skilful and anxious, and because I observed that your boat always made the passage quicker than the others. You must not be angry when I tell you that I thought you had been a boatman all your life."

He said he was not angry at all, but flattered; indeed he had spent much of his leisure time in rowing, and was heartily glad that his little skill was now useful to his friends. He soon offered to take his place again at the oar, and when neither his old servant or Arthur would allow him to do so, he declared that he was quite himself again, and that those few minutes' rest had wonderfully recruited him. The ladies both thanked him kindly, but begged him to remain a while where he was, and Marie, from time to time, asked him questions about the past, and tried to hold out hopes to him for the future. The tears came into his eyes, and rolled down his cheeks, and after a while he took the sexton's oar, literally to relieve himself from having to speak.

"It is not he work alone that has upset me," said he after a while, "but the poor people seem so callous. We have worked hard these two days, as the young gentleman knows, and all for charity, and yet till this moment we have not had a kind word. They urge us on to the work, and when we land them at the shore, they do not even thank us as they go away; then we turn back with a heavy heart for another load."

They reached the shore of Brittany in safety, and when de Lescure was placed in the carriage which had been provided for him, he desired that the poor priest might be begged to accompany them on their journey. He declined, however, saying that he had found a sphere in which he could be useful, and that he would stick to the work till it was all done, or till his strength failed him. De Lescure pressed his hand, and begged his blessing, and told him that if there were many such as him in the country, La Vendée might still carry her head high, in spite of all that the Republic could do against her. This praise made the old man's heart light once again, and he returned to his boat, and passed back to St. Florent with his comrade and Arthur, ready to recommence his labours. In the meantime de Lescure and his wife and sister were warmly welcomed on the Breton side of the river, and before night he, for the first time since the battle of Cholet, found himself in comparative security and peace.

When Arthur got back he found that another plan had been started for carrying over the Vendeans, which, if it did not drown them altogether, would be certainly much more expeditious than that of the boats. It had originated with Chapeau, under whose guidance the operations were about to commence.

He had come down to the water-side with his master, and on seeing the way in which the men were working, had calculated that it would yet take above a week to carry over all who remained, and as it was probable that they would be attacked before twenty-four hours were over, he had observed that they might as well give themselves up for lost if they could devise no other scheme of passing over.

"We will do the best we can," said Henri. "If we can get over the women, and children, and wounded, the rest of us can fight our way to the bridge of Ancenis."

"Why not make a raft?" said Chapeau.

"Make one if you can," said Henri, "but it will only go down the stream. Besides, you have neither timber nor iron ready to do it."

Chapeau, however, determined to try, and he employed the men from Durbellière, who knew him, and would work for him, to get together every piece of timber they could collect. They brought down to the bank of the river the green trunks of small trees, the bodies of old waggons, the small beams which they were able to pull down out of the deserted cottages near the river-side, pieces of bedsteads, and broken fragments of barn doors. All these Chapeau, with endless care, joined together by numberless bits of ropes, and at last succeeded in getting afloat a raft on which some forty or fifty men might stand, but which seemed to be anything but a safe or commodious means of transit. In the first place, though it supported the men on it, it did not bear them high and dry above the water, which came over the ankles of most of them. Then there was no possible means of steering the unwieldy bark; and there could be no doubt that if the Argonauts did succeed in getting their vessels out into the river, it would immediately descend the stream, and that it, and those upon it, would either be upset altogether, or taken to whichever bank and whatever part of it, the river in its caprice might please.

In this dilemma a brilliant idea occurred to Chapeau. He still had plenty of rope in his possession, and having fastened one end of a long coil with weights and blocks on the riverside, he passed over with the other end into the island, and fastened it there. The rope, therefore, traversed the river, and by holding on to this, and passing it slowly through their hands, while they strained against the raft with their feet, the enterprising crew who had first embarked reached the island in safety. Ten of the number had to return with the raft, but still from thirty to forty had been taken over, and that without any great delay.

After this first success the boats were sent round to work between the island and the other shore, and the raft was kept passing to and fro over the river the whole night. Nobody got over with dry feet, but still no one was drowned, and upon the whole Chapeau was considered to be entitled to the thanks of the whole army for the success of his invention. He had certainly accelerated their passage fivefold.

CHAPTER VII.
CATHELINEAU'S MOTHER.

The old motto, attributing disrespect to every prophet in his own country, had not been proved true with reference to Cathelineau in St. Florent. His deeds, during the short period of his triumph, had been celebrated there with general admiration, and since his death, his memory had been almost adored. The people of the town had had no public means of showing their appreciation of his valour; they had not as yet had time to erect monuments to his honour, or to establish other chronicles of his virtues, than those which were written in the hearts of his townsmen. He had left an aged mother behind him, who had long been dependent on his exertions for support, and they had endeavoured to express their feeling of his services, by offering to place her beyond the reach of poverty; but, unaccountably enough, she was the only person in St. Florent, who was dissatisfied with her son's career, and angry with the town which had induced him to adopt it.

She still lived in a small cottage near the extremity of St. Florent, which had been the residence of Cathelineau as long as he supported himself by his humble calling. It was now wrecked and shattered, and showed those certain signs of ruin which quickly fall on the dwellings of the aged poor, who have no young relatives round them. Here she would sit and spin, seldom now interrupted by any; though at first her neighbours used to flock thither to celebrate the praises of her son. She had loved her son, as warmly as other mothers love their children; but she had loved him as a hard-working labourer, earning for herself and for him their daily pittance; not as a mighty General, courted and complimented by the rich and great of the land. She had begged him not to go out into the town on the morning when he had been so instrumental in saving his townsmen from the ignominy of being pressed into the service of the Republic; and when he returned in the evening, crowned with laurels, she had not congratulated him. She had uttered nothing but evil bodings to him on the day when he first went to Durbellière; and when he returned from Saumur, chief General of all the forces of then victorious La Vendée, she had refused to participate in the glories which awaited him in his native town. On his departure to Nantes she had prophesied to him his death, and when the tidings of his fall were first brought to her, she merely said that she had expected it. The whole town mourned openly for Cathelineau, except his mother. She wept for him in silence and alone; but she wept for the honest, sturdy, hard-working labourer whom she had reared beneath her roof, and who had been beguiled away by vain people, to vain pursuits, which had ended in his death; while others bewailed the fall of a great captain, who had conferred honour on their town, and who, had he been spared, might have heaped glory on his country. Since that time, she had not ceased to rail on those who had seduced her son into celebrity and danger; and, after a while, had been left to rail alone.

When nearly all the inhabitants of the town flocked down to the river-side, anxious to escape from the wrath of the republicans, she resolutely refused to move, declaring that if it were God's will that she should perish under the ashes of her little cottage, she would do so, and that nothing should induce her, in her extreme old age, to leave the spot on which she had been born, and had always lived. During the whole confusion, attending the passage of the river, she sat there undisturbed; and though she saw all her poor neighbours leave their humble dwellings, and all their little property, to look for safety in Brittany, she did not move.

On the day after that on which de Lescure had passed over, she was sitting alone in her cabin, and the unceasing whirl of her spinning-wheel proved that the distractions of the time had not made her idle. By this time all those who had lived immediately near her, were gone. It is not to be supposed that absolutely every inhabitant of the town left his home; there were some who had taken no prominent part in the war, and who could not believe that the republicans would destroy those whom they found quietly living in their own houses; but all the poorer part of the population were gone, and not a living soul but herself remained in the row of cabins, of which Cathelineau's mother occupied one.

Her wheel was turning fast round, obedient to the quick motion of her foot, and her two hands were employed in preparing the flax before it was caught by the wheel; but her mind was far away from her ordinary pursuit. She had been thinking how true were the prophetic warnings with which she had implored her son to submit to the republicans, and how surely she had foreseen the desolation which his resistance had brought on all around her. And yet there was more of affection than bitterness in her thoughts of her son. She acknowledged to herself his high qualities; she knew well how good, how noble, how generous, had been his disposition. She was, even in her own way, proud of his fame; but she hated, with an unmixed hatred, those whom she thought had urged him on to his ruin—those friends of noble blood, who would have spurned the postillion from their doors had he presumed to enter them in former days; but who had thrust him into the van of danger in the hour of need, and had persuaded him, fond and foolish as he had been, to use his courage, his energy, and his genius, in fighting for them a battle, in which he should have had no personal interest.

As she sat there spinning, and thinking thus bitterly of the causes of all her woe, a figure darkened the door of her cottage, and looking up she saw a young lady dressed in black. She was tall, and of a noble mien; her face was very beautiful, but pale and sad, as were the faces of most in these sad times.

Her dress was simple, and she was unattended; but yet there was that about her, which assured the old woman that she was not of simple blood, and which prepared her to look upon her as an enemy.

It was Agatha Larochejaquelin. She and her father had, by slow stages, reached St. Florent in safety; and, after having seen him at rest, and spoken a word to her brother, her first care had been to inquire after the mother of Cathelineau. She had been told of her solitary state, and of her stubborn resolution to remain at St. Florent, and she determined to offer her any aid in her power, as a duty due to the memory of him, with whom she had been, for a short time, so strangely connected.

The old woman rose mechanically, and made a slight obeisance as she saw Agatha's commanding figure, and then reseating herself, hastily recommenced her work, as though she had forgotten herself, in having been thus far courteous to her guest.

"I have come to express my esteem and respect to the mother of Cathelineau," said Agatha, as soon as she found herself inside the cottage. "I knew and valued your son, and I shall be glad to know his mother. Was not the brave Cathelineau your son, my friend?" she added, seeing that the old woman stared at her, as though she did not as yet comprehend the object of her visit.

"My name is Françoise Cathelineau," said the sybil, "and Jacques Cathelineau was my son."

"And proud you may be to have been his mother. He was a great and good man: he was trusted and loved by all La Vendée. No one was so beloved by the poor as he was; no one was so entirely trusted by the rich and great."

"I wish that the rich and great had left him as they found him. It would be well for him and me this morning, if he had not so entirely trusted them."

"His death was a noble death. He died for the throne which he honoured, and loved so loyally; and his name will be honoured in Poitou, aye, and in all France, as long as the names of the great and the good are remembered. It must be a bitter thing to lose an only son, but his dearest friends should not regret him in such a cause."

"Dearest friends! What do you know of his dearest friends? How can you tell what his dearest friends may feel about it?"

"I know what I feel myself. Perhaps I cannot judge of all a mother's agony in losing her son; but I may truly say, that of those who knew Cathelineau, none valued him more than I did."

"Valued him! Yes, you valued him as you would a war-horse, or a strong tower, but you did not love him. He was not of your race, or breed. His hands were hard with toil, his hair was rough, and his voice was harsh with the night air. The breath of the labouring poor is noisome in the nostrils of the rich. His garments smelt of industry, and his awkward gait told tales of his humble trade. You did not love him: such as you could not have loved a man like him. You have come here to bid me to forget my son, and you think it easy for me to do so, because you and his noble friends have forgotten him. You are welcome, Mademoiselle, but you might have saved yourself the trouble."

"God forbid that I should ask you to forget him. I can never forget him myself."

"Would that I could—would that I could! He left me that morning when I bade him to stay, though I went down on my knees to ask it as a favour. He was a stubborn self-willed man, and he went his own way. He never passed another night under his mother's roof; he never again heard his mother's blessing. I wish I could forget him. Indeed, indeed, I wish I could!" and the old woman swayed herself backwards and forwards in her chair, repeating the wish, as though she did not know that any one was with her in the cottage.

Agatha hardly knew what to say to the strange woman before her, or how to soften her bitterness of spirit. She had felt an unaccountable attraction to Cathelineau's mother. She had imagined that she could speak to her of her son with affection and warmth, though she could not do so to any other living soul She had flattered herself that she should have a melancholy pleasure in talking of his death, and in assuring his aged mother that she had soothed her son's last hours, and given him, in his dying moments, that care which can only be given by the hands of a woman. She now felt herself repulsed, and learnt that the short career of glory which had united her with Cathelineau, had severed him from his mother. Nevertheless her heart yearned to the old woman; she still hoped that, if she could touch the right cord, she might find her way to the mother's heart.

"I thought, perhaps," she said, "you would be glad to hear some tidings of his last moments; and as I was with him when he died, I have come to tell you that his death was that of a Christian, who hoped everything from the merits of his Saviour."

"May his soul rest in peace," said the mother, crossing herself, and mechanically putting her hands to her beads. "May his soul rest in peace. And you were with him when he died, Mademoiselle, were you?"

"I knelt at his bed-side as the breath passed from his body."

"It would have been better for him had one of his own degree been there: not that I doubt you did the duty of a good neighbour, as well as it might be done by one like you. Might I ask you your name, lady?"

"My name is Agatha Larochejaquelin."

"Larochejaquelin! I'm sorry for it. It was that name that first led Jacques into trouble: it was young Larochejaquelin that first made my son a soldier. I will not blame you, for you say you were kind to him at a time when men most want kindness; but, I wish that neither I nor he had ever heard your name."

"You are wrong there, my friend. It was Cathelineau made a soldier of my brother, not my brother who made a soldier of him. Henri Larochejaquelin was only a follower of Cathelineau."

"A Marquis obey a poor postillion! Yes, you stuffed him full with such nonsense as that! You made him fancy himself a General! You cannot fool me so easily. My son was not a companion for noble men and noble ladies. A wise man will never consort with those who are above him in degree."

"We all looked on Cathelineau as equal to the best among us," answered Agatha. "We all strove to see who should show him most honour."

The old woman sat silent for a while, turning her wheel with great violence, and then she moved abruptly round, and facing Agatha, said:

"Will you answer me one question truly, Mademoiselle?"

Agatha said she would.

"Are you betrothed as yet to your lover?"

"No, indeed," answered she; "I am not betrothed."

"And now answer me another question. Suppose this son of mine, who, as you say, was as great as the greatest among you, and as noble as the noblest; suppose he had admired your beauty, and had offered to take you home to his mother as the wife of his bosom, how would you then have answered him? What would you then have thought of the postillion? Would he then have been the equal of gay young counts, and high-blooded marquises?"

Agatha at first made no reply, and a ruby blush suffused her whole face. She was not at all unwilling that Cathelineau's mother should know the feeling which she had entertained for her son, but the abruptness, and the tone of the question, took her by surprise, and for a moment scattered her thoughts.

"Now I have made you angry, Mademoiselle," said the other, chuckling at the success of her scheme. "Now you are wrath that I should have dared to suppose that the daughter of a Marquis could have looked, in the way of love, on a poor labourer who had been born and bred in a hovel like this."

"You mistake me, my friend; I am not angry—I am anything but angry."

"You would have scorned him as a loathsome reptile, which to touch would be an abomination," continued the old woman, not noticing, in her eagerness, Agatha's denial. "You would have run from him in disgust, and the servants would have let loose the dogs at him, or have chained him as a madman. Yes, your delicate frame shakes with horror at the idea, that a filthy stable boy could have looked on your beauty, and have dared to wish to possess it: and yet you presume to tell me that Cathelineau was among you as an equal: he was with you as a Jew is among Christians, as a slobbering drunkard among sober men, as one stricken with fever among the healthy. My son should have been too proud to have eaten bread at a table where his hand was thought unclean, or to have accepted favours, where he dared not look for love."

"You are unjust to Cathelineau," replied Agatha. "You are in every way unjust, both to your son and to me. He accepted no favour from us, but he did—but he did look—" and she paused, as though she still lacked courage to speak the words which were on her tongue, but after a moment she went on and said, "he did look for love, and he did not look in vain."

"He did love, do you say, and not in vain! He did love, and made his love acceptable to one of those fine flaunting ladies who sit at ease all day, twirling a few bits of silk with their small white hands. Do you say such a one as that loved Cathelineau! Who was she? What is her name? Where is she?"

"She is close to you now," said Agatha, sitting down on a low stool at the old woman's feet. "I told you her name a while since. It is I who loved your son: I, Agatha Larochejaquelin."

Françoise Cathelineau dropped from her hand the flax, which she had hitherto employed herself in preparing for the wheel, and pushing from her forehead her loose grey locks, and resting on her knees her two elbows, she gazed long and intently into Agatha's face.

"It is just the face he would have loved," said she aloud, yet speaking to herself. "Yes, it is the face of which he used to dream and talk—pale and sad, but very fair: and though I used to bid him mind his work, and bring down his heart to love some poor honest labouring girl, I did not the less often think over his strange fancies. And Jacques told you that he loved you, did he, Mademoiselle? I wonder at that—I wonder at that; it would have been more like himself to have carried his love a secret to the grave."

"He was dying when he told me that he regarded me above other women; and I am prouder of the dying hero's love, than I could have been had a Prince knelt at my feet."

"He was dying when he confessed his love! Yes, I understand it now: death will open the lips and bring forth the truth, when the dearest hopes of life, when the sharpest pang of the heart fail to do so. Had he not been sure that life with him was gone, he never would have spoken of his love. He was a weak, foolish man. Very weak in spite of all his courage; very weak and very foolish—very weak and very foolish."

She was talking more to herself than to Agatha, as she thus spoke of her son's character, and for a minute or two she continued in the same strain, speaking of him in a way that showed that every little action, every wish of his, had been to her a subject of thought and anxiety; and that she took a strange pride in those very qualities for which she blamed him.

"And did you come to me on purpose to tell me this, Mademoiselle?" she said after a while.

"I came to talk to you about your son, and to offer you, for his sake, the affection of a daughter."

"And when he told you that he loved you, what answer did you make him? tell me: did you comfort him; did you say one word to make him happy? I know, from your face, that you had not the heart to rebuke a dying man."

"Rebuke him! How could I have rebuked him? though I had never owned it to myself I now feel that I had loved him before he had ever spoken to me of love."

"But what did you say to him? tell me what you said to him. He was my own son, my only son. He was stubborn, and self-willed, but still he was my son; and his words were sweeter to me than music, and his face was brighter to me than the light of heaven. If you made him happy before he died, I will kneel down and worship you," and joining her skinny hands together, she laid them upon Agatha's knees. "Come, sweetest, tell me what answer you made my poor boy when he told you that he loved you."

"It is a fearful thing, you know, to speak to a dying man," answered Agatha. "You must not suppose that we were talking as though he were still in the prime of health and strength—"

"But what did you say to him? you said something. You did not, at any rate, bid him remember that he was a poor labouring man, and that you were a lady of high rank."

"We neither of us thought of those things then. I do not know what it was I said, but I strove to say the truth. I strove to make him understand how much I valued, esteemed—and loved him."

"You told him that you loved him; you are sure you told him that. I wish he had lived now. I wish he had lived and won more battles, and beat the blues for good and all, and then he would have married you, and brought you home as his wife to St. Florent, wouldn't he, love? There would have been something in that. There would have been something really grand in that. Such a beautiful bride! such a noble bride! so very, very beautiful!" and the old woman continued gazing at the face of her whom she was fancying to herself a daughter-in-law. "Real noble blood of the very highest. Had he married you, he would have been a Marquis, wouldn't he? I wish he had lived now, in spite of all I said. Why did he die when there was such fortune before him I Why did he die when there was such great fortune before him!"

"He was happy in his death," said Agatha. "I do not think he even wished to live. As it is, he has been spared much sorrow which we must all endure. Though I loved your son, I do not regret his death."

"But I do—but I do," said the old woman. "Had he only lived to call you his wife, there would have been honour in that—there would have been real glory in that. People would then not have dared to say that after all Cathelineau was only a postillion."

"Do not regard what people say. Had a Princess given him her hand, his fame could not be brighter than it was. There was no thought of marriage between us, since we first knew each other. There has been no time for such thoughts; but his memory to me is that of a dear—dear friend."

From the time when Cathelineau first went to Durbellière, after the battle of St. Florent, his mother had expressed the greatest dislike at his attempting to associate with those who were so much above himself in rank; with those who would, as she said, use him and scorn him. She had affected to feel, or perhaps really felt, a horror of the insolence of the great, and had quarrelled with her son for throwing himself among them. This feeling, however, arose, not from contempt, but from admiration and envy. In her secret soul the high and mighty seemed so infinitely superior to those in her own rank, that she had felt sure that her son could not be admitted among them as an equal, and she was too proud to wish that he should be admitted into their company as a humble hanger-on. What Agatha had now confessed to her had surprised and delighted her. There could be no doubt now; there was the daughter of one of the noblest houses in Poitou sitting at her feet in her own cabin, owning her love for the poor postillion. Agatha Larochejaquelin, young, noble, beautiful, grandly beautiful as she was, had come to her to confess that she had given her heart to her son. There was, however, much pain mixed with her gratification. Cathelineau had gone, without enjoying the high honours which might have been his. Had he lived, Agatha Larochejaquelin would have been her daughter-in-law; but now the splendid vision could never be more than a vision. She could solace herself with thinking of the high position her son had won for himself, but she could never enjoy the palpable reality of his honours.

She sat, repeating to herself the same words, "Sad and pale, but very beautiful—sad and pale, but very beautiful; just as he used to dream. Why did he die, when such fortune was before him! Why did he die, when such noble fortune was before him!"

Agatha suffered her to go on for a while before she interrupted her, and then she came to the real purport of her visit. She offered the old woman her assistance and protection, and begged her to pass over with the others into Brittany, assuring her that she should want for nothing as long as Henri or her father had the means of subsistence, and that she should live among them as an honoured guest, loved and revered as the mother of Cathelineau.

On this point, however, she remained obstinate. Whether she still fancied that she would be despised by her new friends, or whether, as she said, she was indifferent to life, and felt herself too old to move from the spot where she had passed so many years, she resolutely held her purpose to await the coming of the republicans. "They will hardly put forth their strength to crush such a worm as me," she said; "and if they do, it will be for the better."

Agatha then offered her money, but this she refused, assuring her that she did not want it.

"You shall give me one thing though, if you will, sweet lady, that I may think of you often, and have something to remind me of you; nay, you shall give me two things—one is a lock of your soft brown hair, the other is a kiss."

Agatha undid the braid which held up her rich tresses, and severing from her head a lock of the full length to which her hair grew, tied it in a portion of the braid, and put it into the old woman's hand; then she stooped down and kissed her skinny lips, and having blessed her, and bid her cherish the memory of her son with a holy love, as she herself did and always would, Agatha. Larochejaquelin left the cabin, and returned to her father.

CHAPTER VIII.
"WHAT GOOD HAS THE WAR DONE?"

The raft which Chapeau had made was by degrees enlarged and improved, and the great mass of the Vendeans passed the river slowly, but safely. As soon as the bulk of the people was over, Henri Larochejaquelin left the southern shore, and crossed over to marshal the heterogeneous troops on their route towards Laval, leaving Chapeau and Arthur Mondyon to superintend and complete the transit of those who remained.

It was a beautiful October evening, and as the sun was setting, the two were standing close to the edge of the water, congratulating themselves that their dirty and disagreeable toil was well nigh over. From time to time stragglers were still coming down to the river-side, begging for a passage, and imploring that they might not be abandoned to the cruelty of the blues, and as they came they were shipped off on the raft. There were now, however, no more than would make one fair load, and Chapeau and Arthur were determined that it was full time for them both to leave the Anjou side of the river, and follow the main body of the army towards Laval.

"We might remain here for ever, Chapeau, if we stayed for the very last of all," said the Chevalier, as he jumped on the raft. "Come, man, get on, we've our number now, and we couldn't take more, if they come. There's some one hallooing up there, and we'll leave the little boat for them. Come, I want to get over and have a run on dry land, for I'm as cold as a stone. This living like a duck, half in the water and half out, don't suit me at all. The next river we cross over, I'll make Henri get another ferryman."

Chapeau still lingered on the shore, and putting his hand up to his ear, listened to the voice of some one who was calling from a distance. It was too dark for him to distinguish any one, but the voice of a woman hallooing loudly, but with difficulty, as though she were out of breath with running, was plainly audible.

"If you mean to wait here all night, I don't," said the Chevalier, "so good night to you, and if you don't get on, I'll push off without you."

"Stop a moment, M. Arthur, there's a woman there."

"I've no doubt there is—there are fifty women there—fifty hundred women, I dare say; but we can't wait while they all drop in one by one. Don't be a fool, Jacques; is not there the small boat left for them?"

Chapeau still listened. "Stop a moment, M. Arthur, for heaven's sake stop one moment," and then jumping on to the raft, he clung hold of the rope, and moored it fast to the shore. "They're friends of my own, M. Arthur;

most particular friends, or I wouldn't ask to keep you. Don't go now; after all we've gone through together, you won't leave my friends behind, if I go on shore, will you, M. Arthur?"

"Oh, I'm a good comrade; if they're private friends, I'll wait all night. Only I hope there ain't a great many of them."

"Only two; I think there are only two," and Chapeau once more jumped on shore, and ran to meet his friends. He had not far to go, for the party was now close to the water's edge. As he had supposed, it consisted only of two, an old man and a girl: Michael Stein and his daughter Annot. Annot had been running; and dragging her father by the hand, had hallooed with all her breath, for she had heard from some of those who still dared to trust themselves to the blues, that the last boat was on the point of leaving the shore. The old man had disdained to halloo, and had almost disdained to run; but he had suffered himself to be hurried into a shambling kind of gait, and when he was met by Chapeau, he was almost as much out of breath as his daughter.

"Oh, oh! for mercy's sake—for heaven's sake—kind Sir, dear Sir," sobbed Annot, as she saw a man approaching her; and then when he was near enough to her to be distinguished through the evening gloom, she exclaimed:

"Mercy on us, mercy on us, its Jacques Chapeau!" and sank to the ground, as though she had no further power to take care of herself now that she had found one who was bound to take care of her.

"You're just in time, Michael Stein; thank God, you're just in time! Annot, come on, its only a dozen yards to the raft, and we'll be off at once. Well, this is the luckiest chance: come on, before a whole crowd are down upon us, and swamp us all."

"Oh me! oh me!" sobbed Annot, still sitting on the ground, as though she had not the slightest intention of stirring another step that night: "to be left and deserted in this way by one's friends—and one's brothers—and—and—one's—" she didn't finish the list, for she felt sure that she had said enough to cut Chapeau to the inmost heart, if he still had a heart.

"Come, dearest girl, come; I'll explain it all by-and-bye. We have not a moment to spare. Come, I'll lift you," and he stooped to raise her from the ground.

"Thank you, M. Chapeau, thank you, Sir; but pray leave me. I shall be better tomorrow morning; that is, if I'm not dead, or killed, or worse. The blues are close behind us; ain't they, father?"

"Get up, Annot; get up, thou little fool, and don't trouble the man to carry thee," said Michael. "If there be still a boat to take us, in God's name let us cross the river; for the blues are truly in St. Florent, and after flying from them so far, it would be sore ill luck to be taken now."

Chapeau, however, would not leave her to herself, but took her up bodily in his arms, and carrying her down to the water's edge, put her on the raft. He and Michael soon followed, and the frail vessel was hauled for the last time over into the island. The news that the enemy was already in St. Florent soon passed from month to mouth, and each wretched emigrant congratulated himself in silence that he had so far escaped from republican revenge. Many of them had still to sojourn on the island for the night, but there they were comparatively safe; and Arthur, Chapeau, and his friends, succeeded in gaining the opposite shore.

Poor Annot was truly in a bad state. When they heard that the ladies had left Chatillon, she and her father, and, indeed, all the inhabitants of Echanbroignes, felt that they could no longer be safe in the village; and they had started off to follow the royalist army on foot through the country. From place to place they had heard tidings, sometimes of one party, and sometimes of another. The old man had borne the fatigue and dangers of the journey well; for, though now old, he had been a hard-working man all his life, and was tough and seasoned in his old age; but poor Annot had suffered dreadfully. The clothes she had brought with her were nearly falling off her back; her feet were all but bare, and were cut and blistered with walking. Grief and despair had taken the colour and roundness from her cheek, and she had lacked time on her mournful journey to comb the pretty locks of which she was generally so proud.

"Oh, Jacques, Jacques, how could you leave us! how could you go away and leave us, after all that's been between us," she said, as he bustled about to make some kind of bed for her in the little hut, in which they were to rest for the night.

"Leave you," said Chapeau, who had listened for some time in silence to her upbraidings; "leave you, how could I help leaving you? Has not everybody left everybody? Did not M. Henri leave his sister, and M. de Lescure leave his wife? And though they are now here all together, it's by chance that they came here, the same as you have come yourself. As long as these wars last, Annot dear, no man can answer as to where he will go, or what he will do."

"Oh, these weary wars, these weary wars!" said she, "will they never be done with? Will the people never be tired of killing, and slaying, and burning each other? And what is the King the better of it? Ain't they all dead: the King, and the Queen, and the young Princes, and all of them?"

"You wouldn't have us give up now, Annot, would you? You wouldn't have us lay down our arms, and call ourselves republicans, after all we have done and suffered?"

Annot didn't answer. She wouldn't call herself a republican; but her sufferings and sorrows had greatly damped the loyal zeal she had shown when she worked her little fingers to the bone in embroidering a white flag for her native village. She was now tired and cold, wet and hungry; for Chapeau had been able to get no provisions but a few potatoes: so she laid herself down on the hard bed which he had prepared for her; and as he spread his own coat over her shoulders, she felt that it was, at any rate, some comfort to have her own lover once more near her.

Jacques and the old smith had no bed, so they were fain to content themselves with sitting opposite to each other on two low stools; the best seats which the hut afforded. Jacques felt that it was incumbent on him to do the honours of the place, and that some apology was necessary for the poor accommodation which he had procured for his friends.

"This is a poor place for you, Michael Stein," he commenced, "a very poor place for both of you, after your own warm cottage at Echanbroignes."

"It's a poor place, truly, M. Chapeau," said the smith, looking round on the bare walls of the little hut.

"Indeed it is, my friend, and sorry am I to see you and Annot so badly lodged. But what then; we shall be in Laval tomorrow, and have the best of everything—that is, if not tomorrow, the day after."

"I don't much care about the best of everything, M. Chapeau. I've not used myself to the best, but I would it had pleased God to have allowed me to labour out the rest of my days in the little smithy at Echanbroignes. I never wanted more than the bread which I could earn."

"You never did, Michael, you never did," said Chapeau, trying to flatter the old man; "and, like an honest man, you endure without flinching what you suffer for your King. Give us your hand, my friend, we've no wine to drink his health, but as long as our voices are left, let us cry: Vive le Roi!"

The old man silently rejected Chapeau's proposal that he should evince his loyalty just at present by shouting out the Vendean war-cry. "I take no credit, M. Chapeau," said he, "for suffering for my King, though, while he lived, he always had my poor prayers for his safety. It wasn't to fight the blues that I left my little home. It was because I couldn't stay any without fearing to see that girl there in the rude hands of Lechelle's soldiers, and my own roof in a blaze. It's all gone now, forge and tools; the old woman's chair, the children's cradle; it's all gone, now and for ever. I don't wish to curse any one, M. Chapeau, but I am not in the humour to cry Vive le Roi!"

"But Michael Stein, my dear friend," urged Chapeau, "look what others have lost too. Have not others suffered as much? Look at the old Marquis, turned out of his house and everything lost; and yet you won't hear a word of complaint fall from his mouth. Look at Madame de Lescure, her husband dying; her house burnt to the ground; without a bed to lie on, or a change of dress and yet she does not complain."

"They have brought it on themselves by their own doings," answered the smith; "and they have brought it on me also, who have done nothing."

"Done nothing! but, indeed, you have, Michael. Have you not made pikes for us, and have not your sons fought for us like brave soldiers?"

"I have done the work for which I was paid, as a good smith should; and as for the boys, they took their own way. No, Jacques Chapeau, I have taken no part in your battles. I have neither been for nor against you. As for King or Republic, it was all one to me; let them who understand such things settle that. For fifty years I have earned my bread, and paid what I owed; and now I am driven out from my home like a fox from its hole. Why should I say Vive le Roi! Look at that girl there, with her bare feet bleeding from the sharp stones, and tell me, why should I say Vive le Roi!"

Chapeau was flabbergasted, for all this was rank treason to him; and yet he didn't want to quarrel with the smith; so he sat still and gazed into his face, as though he were struck dumb with astonishment.

"I remember when you came to my cottage," continued the old man, "and told me that the wars were all over, that the King was coming to Durbellière, and that you would marry Annot, and make a fine lady of her. I told you then what I thought of your soldiering, and your fine ladies. I told you then what it would come to, and I told you true. I don't throw this in your teeth to blame you, M. Chapeau, for you have only served those you were bound to serve; but surely they who first put guns and swords into the hands of the poor people, and bade them go out for soldiers, will have much to answer for. All this blood will be upon their heads."

"You don't mean to blame M. Henri and M. de Lescure, and the good Cathelineau, for all that they've done?" said Chapeau, awe-struck at the language used by his companion.

"It's not for me to blame them; but look at that girl there, and then tell me, mustn't there be some great blame somewhere?"

Chapeau did look at the girl, and all the tenderness of his heart rose into his eyes, as the flickering light of the fire showed him her tattered and draggled dress.

"Thank God! the worst of it is over now, Michael. You're safe now, at any rate, from those blood-hounds; and when we reach Laval, we shall all have plenty."

"And where's this Laval, M. Chapeau?"

"We're close to it—it's just a league or so; or, perhaps, seven or eight leagues to the north of us."

"And how is it, that in times like these, such a crowd of strangers will find plenty there?"

"Why, the whole town is with us. There's a blue garrison in it; but they're very weak, and the town itself is for the King to the backbone. They've sent a deputation to our Generals, and invited us there; and there are gentlemen there, who have come from England, with sure promises of money and troops. The truth is, Michael, we never were really in a position to beat the blues as they ought to be beat till we. got to this side of the river. We never could have done anything great in Poitou."

"I'm sorry they ever tried, M. Chapeau; but I remember when you came back, after taking Saumur, you told me the war was over then. You used to think that a great thing."

"So it was, Michael; it was well done. The taking of Saumur was very well done; but it was only a detail. We've found out now that it won't do to beat them in detail; it's too slow. The Generals have a plan now, one great comprehensive plan, for finishing the war in a stroke, and they're only waiting until they reach Laval."

"It's a great pity they didn't hit on that plan before," said Michael Stein.

The two men laid themselves down on the ground before the fire, and attempted to sleep; but they had hardly composed themselves when they were interrupted by a loud rumour, that there was a vast fire, close down on the opposite side of the river. They both jumped up and went out, and saw that the whole heavens were alight with the conflagration of St. Florent— the blues had burnt the town. The northern bank of the river was covered with the crowd of men and women, gazing at the flames, which were consuming their own houses; and yet, so rejoiced were they to have escaped themselves from destruction, that they hardly remembered to bewail the loss of their property. The town of St. Florent was between three or four miles from the place where they were congregated, and yet they could plainly see the huge sparks as they flew upwards, and they fancied they felt the heat of the flames on their upturned faces.

Early on the following morning, the whole army was on its march towards Laval. The Vendean leaders were well aware that the republicans were now on their track, and they were truly thankful that some unaccountable delay in the movement of the enemy, had enabled them to put a great river between themselves and their pursuers. The garrisons, which the Convention had thrown into the towns of Brittany, were very insufficient, both in numbers and spirit, and the blues abandoned one place after another as the Vendeans approached. They passed through Candé, Segré, and Château-Gonthier without having to fire a shot, and though the gates of the town of Laval were closed against them, it was only done to allow the republican soldiers time to escape from the other side of the town.

The inhabitants of Laval flocked out in numbers to meet the poor Vendeans, and to offer them hospitality, and such comfort as their small town could afford to so huge a crowd. They begrudged them nothing that they possessed, and spared neither their provisions nor their houses. It seemed that Chapeau's promise was this time true; and that, at any rate, for a time, they all found plenty in Laval. Henri established his head-quarters in a stone house, in the centre of the town, and here also he got accommodation for the three ladies and M. de Lescure. Nor did Chapeau forget to include Annot Stein in the same comfortable establishment, under the pretext that her services would be indispensable.

M. de Lescure had suffered grievously through the whole journey, but he seemed to rally when he reached Laval, and the comparative comfort of his quiet chamber gave him ease, and lessened his despondency. The whole party recovered something of their usual buoyancy, and when Henri brought in word, in the evening, that if the worst came to the worst, he could certainly hold out the town against the republican army until assistance reached them from England, they were all willing to hope that the cause in which they were engaged might still prosper.

CHAPTER IX.
LA PETITE VENDÉE.

For four or five days they all remained quiet in Laval, with nothing to disturb their tranquillity, but rumours of what was going on on both sides of the river. The men, with the exception of the old Marquis and de Lescure, were hard at work from morning until night; but they had hardly time or patience to describe accurately what was going on, to those who were left within; and the time passed very heavily with them. Two sofas had been carried to the windows of the sitting-room which they occupied. These windows looked out into the main thoroughfare of the town, and here the Marquis and the wounded man were placed, so that they might see all that was passing in the street. Various reports reached them from time to time, a few of which were confirmed, many proved to be false, and some still remained doubtful; but two facts were positively ascertained. Firstly, that the main army of the republicans had passed the river at Angers, and were advancing towards Laval; and secondly, that there was a considerable number of Breton peasants, already under arms, in the country, who were harassing the blues whenever they could meet them in small parties, and very frequently menacing the garrisons which they found in the small towns.

This last circumstance created a great deal of surprise, not so much from the fact of the Bretons having taken up arms against the Convention, as from a certain degree of mystery which were attached to the men who were roving about the country. It appeared that they were all under the control of one leader, whose name was not known in Laval, but who was supposed to have taken an active part in many of the battles fought on the other side of the river. His tactics, however, were very different from those which had been practised in La Vendée. He never took any prisoners, or showed any quarter; but slaughtered indiscriminately every republican soldier that fell into his hands. He encouraged his men to pillage the towns, where the inhabitants were presumed to be favourable to the Convention; and this licence which he allowed was the means of drawing many after him, who might not have been very willing to fight merely for the honour of defending the throne. After the custom of their country, which was different from that which prevailed in Poitou and Anjou, these peasant-soldiers wore their long flaxen hair hanging down over their shoulders, and were clothed in rough dresses, made of the untanned skins of goats or sheep, with the hair on the outside. The singularity of their appearance at first added a terror to their arms, which was enhanced by the want of experience and cowardice of the republican troops through the country. This wild, roving band of lawless men had assumed to themselves the name of La Petite Vendée, and certainly they did much towards assisting the Vendeans; for they not only cleared the way for them, in many of the towns of Brittany, but they prepared the people to expect them, and created a very general opinion that there would be more danger in siding with the blues than with the royal party.

If the men of La Petite Vendée, had rendered themselves terrible, their Captain had made—not his name, for that was unknown—but his character much more so. He was represented to be a young man, but of a fierce and hideous aspect; the under part of his face was covered with his black beard, and he always wore on his head a huge heavy cap, which covered his brows, shaded his eyes from sight, and concealed his face nearly as effectually as a vizor. He was always on horseback, and alone; for he had neither confidant nor friend. The peasant-soldiers believed him to be invulnerable, for they represented him to be utterly careless as to where he went, or what danger he encountered. The only name they knew him by, was that of the Mad Captain; and, probably, had he been less ugly, less mysterious, and less mad, the people would not have obeyed him so implicitly, or followed him so faithfully.

Such were the tales that were repeated from time to time to Madame de Lescure and her party by the little Chevalier and Chapeau; and according to their accounts, the Mad Captain was an ally who would give them most valuable help in their difficulties. The whole story angered de Lescure, whose temper was acerbated by his own inactivity and suffering, and whose common sense could not endure the seeming folly of putting confidence in so mysterious a warrior.

"You don't really believe the stories you hear of this man, I hope," he said to his wife and sister, one morning; "he is some inhuman ruffian, who is disgracing, by his cruelty, the cause which he has joined, for the sake of plunder and rapine."

"At any rate," said Marie, "he seems to have scared the blues in this country; and if so, he must be a good friend to us."

"If we cannot do well without such friends, we shall never do well with them. Believe me, whoever he may be, this man is no soldier."

De Lescure was, perhaps, right in the character which he attributed to the Captain of La Petite Vendée; but the band of men which that mysterious leader now commanded, held its ground in Brittany long after the Vendean armies were put down in Poitou and Anjou. They then became known by another name, and the Chouan bands for years carried on a fearful war against the government in that part of the province which is called the Morbihan.

About eight o'clock in the evening, Henri and Arthur Mondyon returned to the house, after a long day's work, and were the first to bring new tidings both of the blues and their new ally, the Mad Captain. A portion of the republican army had advanced as far as Antrâmes, within a league or two of Laval; and they had hardly taken up their quarters in the town, before they were attacked, routed, and driven out of it by the men of La Petite Vendée. Many hundreds of the republicans had been slaughtered, and those who had escaped, carried to the main army an exaggerated account of the numbers, daring, and cruelty of the Breton rebels.

"Whoever he is," said Henri, in answer to a question from his sister, "he is a gallant fellow, and I shall be glad to give him my hand. There can be no doubt of it now, Charles, for the blues at Antrâmes certainly numbered more than double the men he had with him; and I am told he drove them helter-skelter out of the town, like a flock of sheep."

"And do you mean to let him have the rest of the war all to himself?" said de Lescure, who was rather annoyed than otherwise at the success of a man whom he had stigmatized as a ruffian.

"I am afraid we shan't find it quite so easy to get the war taken off our hands," said Henri, laughing; "but I believe it's the part of a good General to make the most of any unexpected assistance which may come in his way."

"But, Henri," said Marie, "you must have some idea who this wonderful wild man is. Don't they say he was one of the Vendean chiefs?"

"He says so himself," said Arthur. "He told some of the people here that he was at Fontenay and Saumur; and he talked of knowing Cathelineau and Bonchamps. I was speaking to a man who heard him say so."

"And did the man say what he was like?" said Marie.

"I don't think he saw him at all," answered Arthur. "It seems that he won't let any one see his face, if he can help it; but they all say he is quite a young man."

Chapeau now knocked at the door, and brought farther tidings. The Mad Captain and all his troop had returned from Antrâmes to Laval, and had just now entered the town.

"Our men are shaking the Bretons by the hand," said Chapeau, "and wondering at their long hair and rough skins. Three or four days ago, I feared the Vendeans would never have faced the blues again; but now they are as ready to meet them as ever they were."

"And the Captain, is he actually in Laval at present, Chapeau?"

"Indeed he is, M. Henri. I saw him riding down the street, by the Hôtel de Ville, myself, not ten minutes since."

"Did you see his face, Chapeau?" asked Marie.

"Did he look like any one you knew?" asked Madame de Lescure.

"Did he ride well?" asked the little Chevalier.

"Did he look like a soldier?" asked M. de Lescure.

"Who do you think he is, Chapeau?" asked Henri Larochejaquelin.

Chapeau looked from one to another, as these questions were asked him; and then selecting those of M. de Lescure and his sister, as the two easiest to answer, he said:

"I did not see his face, Mademoiselle. They say that he certainly is a good soldier, M. Charles, but he certainly does not look like any one of our Vendean officers."

"Who can it be?" said Henri. "Can it be Marigny, Charles?"

"Impossible," said de Lescure; "Marigny is a fine, robust fellow, with a handsome open face. They say this man is just the reverse."

"It isn't d'Elbée come to life again, is it?" said Arthur Mondyon. "He's ugly enough, and not very big."

"Nonsense, Arthur, he's an old man; and of all men the most unlikely to countenance such doings as those of these La Petite Vendée. I think, however, I know the man. It must be Charette. He is courageous, but yet cruel; and he has exactly that dash of mad romance in him which seems to belong to this new hero."

"Charette is in the island of Noirmoutier," said de Lescure, "and by all accounts, means to stay there. Had he been really willing to give us his assistance, we never need have crossed the Loire."

"Oh! it certainly was not Charette," said Chapeau. "I saw M. Charette on horseback once, and he carries himself as though he had swallowed a poker; and this gentleman twists himself about like—like—"

"Like a mountebank, I suppose," said de Lescure.

"He rides well, all the same, M. Charles," rejoined Chapeau.

"And who do you think he is, Chapeau?" said Henri.

Chapeau shrugged his shoulders, as no one but a Frenchman can shrug them, intending to signify the impossibility of giving an opinion; immediately afterwards he walked close up to his master, and whispered something in his ear. Henri looked astonished, almost confounded, by what his servant said to him, and then replied, almost in a whisper: "Impossible, Chapeau, quite impossible."

Immediately afterwards, Chapeau left the room, and Henri followed him; and calling him into a chamber in the lower part of the house, began to interrogate him as to what he had whispered upstairs.

"I did not like to speak out before them all, M. Henri," said Jacques, "for I did not know how the ladies might take it; but as sure as we're standing here, the man I saw on horseback just now was M. Adolphe Denot."

"Impossible, Chapeau, quite impossible. How on earth could he have got the means to raise a troop of men in Brittany? Besides, he never would have returned to the side he deserted."

"It does not signify, M. Henri, whether it be likely or unlikely: that man was Adolphe Denot; I'd wager my life on it, without the least hesitation. Why, M. Henri, don't I know him as well as I know yourself?"

"But you didn't see his face?"

"I saw him rise in his saddle, and throw his arms up as he did so, and that was quite enough for me; the Mad Captain of La Petite Vendée is no other than M. Adolphe Denot."

Henri Larochejaquelin was hardly convinced, and yet he knew that Chapeau would not express himself so confidently unless he had good grounds for doing so. He was aware, also, that it was almost impossible for any one who had intimately known Denot to mistake his seat on horseback; and, therefore, though not quite convinced, he was much inclined to suspect that, in spite of improbabilities, his unfortunate friend was the mysterious leader of the Breton army. He determined that he would, at any rate, seek out the man, whoever he might be; and that if he found that Adolphe Denot was really in Laval, he would welcome him back, with all a brother's love, to the cause from which, for so Henri had always protested, nothing but insanity had separated him.

"At any rate, Chapeau, we must go and find the truth of all this. Moreover, whoever this man be, it is necessary that I should know him: so come along."

They both sallied out into the street, which was quite dark, but which was still crowded with strangers of every description. The wine-shops were all open, and densely filled with men who were rejoicing over the victory which had been gained that morning; and the Breton soldiers were boasting of what they had done, while the Vendeans talked equally loudly of what they would do when their Generals would once more lead them out against the blues.

From these little shops, and from the house-windows, an uncertain flicker of light was thrown into the street, by the aid of which Henri and Chapeau made their way to the market-place, in which there was a guard-house and small barrack, at present the position of the Vendean military head-quarters. In this spot a kind of martial discipline was maintained. Sentinels were regularly posted and exchanged; and some few junior officers remained on duty, ready for any exigence for which they might be required. Here they learnt that the Bretons, after returning from Antrâmes, had dispersed themselves through the town, among the houses of the citizens, who were willing to welcome their victorious neighbours, but that nothing had been seen of their Captain since he disbanded his men on the little square. They learnt, however, that he had been observed to give his horse in charge to a man who acted as his Lieutenant, and who was known to be a journeyman baker, usually employed in Laval.

After many inquiries, Henri learnt the name and residence of the master baker for whom this man worked, and thither he sent Chapeau, while he himself remained in the guard-house, talking to two of the Breton soldiers, who had been induced to come in to him.

"We none of us know his name, Monsieur," said one of them, "and it is because he has no name, we call him the Mad Captain; and it is true enough, he has many mad ways with him."

"For all his madness though, he is a desperate fine soldier; and he cares no more for a troop of blues than I would for a flock of geese," said the other.

"I think its love must make him go on as he does," continued the first.

"There's something more besides that," said the second, "for he's always fearful that people should take him for a coward. He's always asking us whether we ever saw him turn his back to the enemy; and bidding us be sure, whenever he falls in battle, to tell the Vendeans how well he fought. That's what makes us all so sure that he came from the other side of the water."

"Then, when he's in the middle of the hottest of the fight," said the first, "he halloos out 'Now for Saumur—here's for Saumur—now for the bridge of Saumur!' To be sure he talks a deal about Saumur, and I think myself he must have been wounded there badly, somewhere near the brain."

Though Henri did not quite understand why Denot should especially allude to Saumur in his mad moments, yet he understood enough of what the men told him about their Captain, to be sure that Adolphe was the man; and though he could not but be shocked to hear him spoken of as a madman, yet he rejoiced in his heart to find that he had done something to redeem his character as a loyal soldier. He learnt that Denot had been above two months in Brittany; that he had first appeared in the neighbourhood of Laval with about two hundred men, who had followed him thither out of that province, and that he had there been joined by as many more belonging to Maine, and that since that time he had been backwards and forwards from one town to another, chiefly in the Morbihan; and that he had succeeded in almost every case in driving the republican garrison from the towns which he attacked.

After Henri had remained a couple of hours in the guard-house, and when it was near midnight, Chapeau returned. He had found out the lodgings of the journeyman baker, had gone thither, and had learnt, after many inquiries, which were very nearly proving ineffectual, that the Mad Captain, whoever he was, occupied a little bed-room at the top of the same house, and that he was, at the very moment at which these inquiries were being made, fast asleep in his bed, having given his Lieutenant, the journeyman baker, strict orders to call him at three o'clock in the morning.

Henri and Chapeau again started on their search; and making their way, for the second time, through the dark, crowded streets, reached a small miserable looking house, in a narrow lane, at one of the lower windows of which Chapeau knocked with his knuckles.

'I told M. Plume that I should call again tonight,' said he, "and he'll know its me."

"And is M. Plume the baker?" asked Henri.

"He was a baker till two months since," answered Chapeau, "but now he's a soldier and an officer; and I can assure you, M. Henri, he doesn't think a little of himself. He's fully able to take the command-in-chief of the Breton army, when any accident of war shall have cut off his present Captain; at least, so he told me."

"You must have had a deal of conversation with him in a very short time, Chapeau."

"Oh, he talks very quick, M. Henri; but he wouldn't let himself down to speak a word to me till I told him I was aide-de-camp-in-chief to the generalissimo of the Vendean army; and then he took off the greasy little cap he wears, told me that his name was Auguste Emile Septimus Plume, and said he was most desirous to drink a cup of wine with me in the next estaminet. Then I ran off to you, telling him I would return again as soon as I had seen that all was right at the guard-house."

"Knock again, Chapeau," said Henri, "for I think your military friend must have turned in for the night."

Chapeau did knock, and as he did so, he put his mouth close to the door, and called out "M. Plume—Captain Plume—Captain Auguste Plume, a message—an important message from the Commander-in-Chief of the

Vendean army. You'll get nothing from him, M. Henri, unless you talk about Generals, aide-de-camps, and despatches; advanced guards, flank movements, and light battalions."

M. Plume, or Captain Plume, as he preferred being called, now opened the door, and poking his head out, welcomed Chapeau, and assured him that if he would step round to the wine shop he would be with him in a moment.

"But, my dear friend Captain Plume, stop a moment," said Chapeau, fixing his foot in the open doorway, so as to prevent it being closed, "here is a gentleman—one of our officers—in fact, my friend," and he whispered very confidentially as he gave the important information, "here is the Commander-in-Chief, and he must see your General tonight; to arrange— to arrange the tactics of the united army for tomorrow."

Auguste Emile Septimus Plume, in spite of his own high standing, in what he was pleased to call the army of Brittany, felt himself rather confused at hearing that a General-in-Chief was standing at the door of his humble dwelling; and, as he again took off his cap, and putting his hand to his heart made a very low bow, he hesitated much as to what answer he should make; for he reflected within himself that the present quarters of his General, were hardly fitting for such an interview.

"The General upstairs," said he, "is snatching a short repose after the labours of the day. Would not tomorrow morning—early tomorrow morning—"

"No," said Henri, advancing, and thrusting himself in at the open door, "tomorrow morning will be too late; and I am sure your General is too good a soldier to care for having his rest broken; tell me which is his room, and I'll step up to him. You needn't mind introducing me." And as he spoke he managed to pass by the baker, and ran up a few steps of the creaking, tottering stairs.

The poor baker was very much annoyed at this proceeding; for, in the first place, he had strict orders from his Commander to let no one up into his room; and, in the next place, his own wife and three children were in the opposite garret to that occupied by the Captain, and he was very unwilling that their poverty should be exposed. He could not, however, turn a Commander-in-Chief out of the house, nor could he positively refuse to give him the information required; so he hallooed out, "The top chamber to the right, General; the top chamber to the right. It's a poor place," he added, speaking to Chapeau; "but the truth is, he don't choose to have more comforts about him than what are enjoyed by the poorest soldier in his army."

"We won't think any the worse of him for that," said Chapeau. "We're badly enough off ourselves, sometimes—besides, your Captain is a very old friend of M. Henri."

"An old friend of whose?" said Plume.

"Of M. Henri Larochejaquelin—that gentleman who has now gone upstairs: they have known each other all their lives."

Auguste Plume became the picture of astonishment. "Known each other all their lives!" said he; "and what's his name, then?"

"Why, I told you: M. Henri Larochejaquelin."

"No, but the other," and he pointed with his thumb over his shoulder up the stairs. "My Captain, you know; if he's the friend of your Captain, I suppose you know what his name is?"

"And do you mean to say, you don't know yourself, your own Captain's name."

Plume felt the impropriety, in a military point of view, of the fact. He felt that, as second in command, he ought to have been made acquainted with his General's name, and that it would have been difficult to find, in the history of all past wars, a parallel to his own ignorance. He also reflected, that if Chapeau knew that the two Generals had been friends all their lives, he must probably know both their names, and that therefore the information so very necessary might now be obtained.

"Well then, M. Chapeau," (he had learnt Chapeau's name), "I cannot say that I do exactly know how he was generally called before he joined us in Brittany. You know so many people have different names for different places. What used you to call him now when you knew him?"

"But you have some name for him, haven't you?" said the other, not answering the question.

"We call him General, or Captain, mostly," said Plume. "Those are the sort of names which come readiest to a soldier's mouth. In the same way, they don't call me Plume, or M. Plume, or Captain Plume, but just simply Lieutenant; and, do you know, I like it better."

The Lieutenant was a tall, lanky, bony man, from whose body the heat of the oven, at which he had always worked, seemed to have drawn every ounce of flesh. He was about forty, or forty-five, years of age. He was nearly bald, but a few light, long, straggling locks of hair stood out on each side of his head. He still wore most of the dress in which he had been accustomed to work, for proper military accoutrements had not yet come within his reach. He had, however, over his shoulder an old bawdrick, from which usually hung a huge sabre, with which he gallantly performed the duties of his present profession. It cannot be said the Lieutenant had none of the qualities of a soldier, for he was courageous enough; but, beyond that, his aptitude for military duties was not pre-eminent. He always marched, or rather shuffled along, with a stoop in his back, which made his shoulders as high as his head. He had not the slightest idea of moving in time; but this was of little consequence, for none of his men could have moved with him if he had. When on active duty, he rushed about with the point of his drawn sword on a level with his breast, as though he were searching for "blues" in every corner, with a fixed determination of instantly immolating any that he might find. He had large saucer eyes, with which he glared about him, and which gave him a peculiar look of insane enthusiasm, very fitted for the Lieutenant, first in command, under a mad Captain. Such was Auguste Plume, and such like were the men who so long held their own ground, not only against the military weakness of the Directory, but even against the military strength of Napoleon.

We will leave Chapeau and his new friend still standing in the passage, for Plume could not invite him in, as none of the rooms were his own except the little garret upstairs; and we will follow Henri as he went in search of the Mad Captain, merely premising that all Plume's efforts to find out the name of his superior officer were unavailing. Without any farther invitation, Henri hurried up the stairs, snatching as he went a glimmering rush-light out of the çi-devant baker's hands; and when he got to the top he knocked boldly at the right-hand door. No one answered him, however, and he repeated his knocks over and over again, and even kicked and hallooed at the door, but still without effect. He then tried to open it, but it was fastened on the inside: and then he kicked and hallooed again. He distinctly heard the hard breathing within of some one, as though in a heavy sleep; and be the sleeper who he might, he was determined not to leave the stairs without waking him; and, therefore, diligently sat to work to kick again.

"Is that you, Auguste?" said a hoarse, sickly woman's voice, proceeding from the door of the opposite chamber. "Why don't you bring me the candle?"

"No, Madame," said Henri, "the gentleman is now downstairs. He lent me your candle for a minute or two, while I call upon my friend here. I hope you'll excuse the noise I make, but I find it very difficult to wake him."

"And why should you want to wake him?" said the woman. "It's three nights now since he stretched himself on a bed, and he'll be up again long before daylight. Give me the candle, and go away, and tell that unfortunate poor man below to come to his bed."

There was a tone of utter misery in the poor woman's voice, which touched Henri to the heart. She had uttered no complaint of her own sufferings; but the few words she had spoken made him feel all the wretchedness and the desolation of homes, which he and his friends had brought upon the people by the war; and he almost began to doubt whether even the cause of the King should have been supported at so terrible a cost. He could not, however, now go back, nor was he willing to abandon his present object, so he again shook and kicked the door.

"That'll never rouse him, though you should go on all night," said a little urchin about twelve years old, the eldest hope of M. and Madame Plume, who rushed out on the landing in his ragged shirt. "If Monsieur will give me a sou, I'll wake him." Henri engaged him at the price, and the boy, putting his mouth down to the key-hole, said, or rather whispered loudly, "Captain—Captain—Captain—the blues—the blues."

This shibboleth had the desired effect, for the man within was instantly heard to start from his bed, and to step out upon the floor.

"Yes, yes; I'm ready, I'm up," said he, in the confused voice of a man suddenly awoke from a sound sleep. "Where's Plume? send Plume to me at once."

Henri immediately recognized the voice of Adolphe Denot, and all doubt was at an end. Denot came to the door, and undid the wooden bolt within, to admit, as he thought, the poor zealous creature who had attached himself to him in his new career; and when the door opened, the friend of his youth—the man whom he had so deeply injured—stood before him. Henri, in his anxiety to find out the truth of Chapeau's surmise, had energetically and, as it turned out, successfully pursued the object of his search; but he had not for a moment turned over in his mind, what he would say to Denot if he found him; how he would contrive to tell him that he forgave him all his faults; how he would explain to him that he was willing again to receive him into his arms as a friend and a brother. The moment was now come, when he must find words to say all this; and as the awkward bolt was being drawn, Henri felt that he was hardly equal to the difficulties of his position.

If Henri found it difficult to speak, with Denot the difficulty was much greater. The injuries which he had inflicted on his friend, the insults which he had heaped on his sister, rushed to his mind. He thought of his own deep treachery, his black ingratitude; and his disordered imagination could only conceive that Henri had chosen the present moment to secure a bloody vengeance. He forgot that he had already been forgiven for what he had done: that his life had been in the hands of those he had injured, and had then been spared by them, when their resentment was fresh and hot, and when he had done nothing to redeem his treason. He had, he thought, reconciled himself to the cause of La Vendée; but still he felt that he could not dare to look on Larochejaquelin as other than an enemy.

Denot started back as he recognized his visitor, and Henri's first object was to close and re-bolt the door, so that their interview might not be interrupted. "Adolphe," he said, in a voice intended to express all the tenderness which he felt, "I am delighted to have found you."

Denot had rushed to a miserable deal table which stood near his bed, and seized his sword, which stood upon it; and now stood armed and ready for assault, opposite to the man who loved him so dearly. His figure and appearance had always been singular, but now it was more so than ever. He had been sleeping in his clothes, and he had that peculiar look of discomfort which always accompanies such rest. His black, elfish, uncombed locks, had not been cut since he left Durbellière, and his beard for many days had not been shorn. He was wretchedly thin and gaunt; indeed, his hollow, yellow cheeks, and cadaverous jaws, almost told a tale of utter starvation. Across his face he had an ugly cicatrice, not the relic of any honourable wound, but given him by the Chevalier's stick, when he struck him in the parlour at Durbellière. Nothing could be more wretched than his appearance; but the most lamentable thing of all, was the wild wandering of his eyes, which too plainly told that the mind was not master of itself.

Henri was awe-stricken, and cut to the heart. What was he to say to the poor wretch, who stood there upon his guard, glaring at him with those wild eyes from behind his sword! Besides, how was he to defend himself if he were attacked?

"Adolphe," he said, "why do you raise your sword against your friend? Don't you see that I have come as your friend: don't you see that I have no sword?"

The other hesitated for a moment, with the weapon still raised as though for defence; and then flinging it behind him on the floor, exclaimed: "There, there—you may kill me, if you will," and having said so, he threw himself on the bed, and sobbed aloud, and wailed like an infant.

Henri knelt down on the floor, by the side of the low wooden stretcher, and putting his arm over Adolphe's shoulder, thought for a while what he could say to comfort the crushed spirit of the poor wretch, whose insanity had not the usual effect of protecting him from misery. It occurred to him that his late achievements, as leader of the Breton peasants, in which, at any rate, he had been successful, would be the subject at present most agreeable to him, and he determined, therefore, to question him as to what he had done.

"Come, Adolphe," he said, "get up; we have much to say to each other, my friend. I have heard much of what you have done here, in Laval and in Brittany. You have been of great service to us; but we must act together for the future. Of course you know that there are 80,000 Vendeans on this side of the river: men, women, and children together."

For some minutes Denot still lay with his face buried in the bed, without answering, and Henri knelt beside him in silence, trying to comfort him rather by the pressure of his hand, Than by the sound of his voice; but then he raised himself up, and sitting erect, with his face turned away from his friend, he said:

"It's no use for you to try to speak of what I have done in Brittany, when we both know that your heart is full of what I did in Poitou."

"By the God of heaven, from whom I hope for mercy," said Henri, solemnly, "I have freely, entirely forgiven you all cause of anger I ever had against you."

Denot still sat with his face averted, and he withdrew his hand from Henri's grasp, as he muttered between his teeth: "I have not asked for forgiveness; I do not want forgiveness;" and then starting up on his feet, he exclaimed almost with a shriek: "How dare you to talk to me, Sir, of forgiveness? Forgiveness! I suppose you think I have nothing to forgive! I suppose you think I have no injuries which rankle in my breast! A broken heart is nothing! Shattered ambition is nothing! A tortured, lingering, wretched life is nothing! I suppose you will offer me your pity next; but know, Sir, that I despise both your forgiveness and your pity."

"I will offer you nothing but my friendship, Adolphe," said Henri. "You will not refuse my friendship, will you? We were brothers always, you know; at least in affection."

"Brothers always! No, we were never brothers: we never, never can be brothers," screamed the poor madman through his closed teeth. "Oh! if we could have been brothers; if—if we could be brothers!" and the long cherished idea, which, in his frenzy, he even yet had hardly quite abandoned, flashed across his brain, and softened his temper.

"We can at any rate be friends," said Henri, approaching him, and again taking his hand. "Come, Adolphe, sit down by me, and let us talk quietly of these things."

"There are some things," said he, in a more composed manner, "of which a man can't very well talk quietly. A man can't very well talk quietly of hell-fire, when he's in the middle of it. Now, I'm in the very hottest of hell-fire at this moment. How do you think I can bear to look at you, without sinking into cinders at your feet?"

Henri was again silent for a time, for he did not know what to say to comfort the afflicted man; but, after a while, Denot himself continued speaking.

"I know that I have been a traitor—a base, ignoble, wretched traitor. I know it; you know it; she knows it;" and as he confessed his wretchedness, he put his bony hand to his forehead, and pushing back his long matted hair, showed more clearly than he had yet done the ineffable marks of bitter sadness, which a few months had graven on his face. "All La Vendée knows it," continued he; "but no one knows the grief, the sorrow, the wretched sorrow, which drove me to madness, and made me become the thing I am. I know it though, and feel it here," and he put his hand on his heart, and looked into his companion's face with a melancholy gaze, which would have softened the anger of a sterner man than Henri Larochejaquelin.

"My poor, poor Adolphe," said Henri, moving himself close to Denot's side, and putting his arm round his neck and embracing him. "We all know how you have suffered. We know—we always knew, it wasn't your proper self that turned against the cause you loved so well; but, Adolphe, we won't talk of these things now."

"You just now said we must talk of them, and you were quite right. After what has passed, you and I cannot meet without having much to say," and again the madman jumped to his feet; and as he paced up and down the room, his fiercer humour again came upon him. "Henri," he exclaimed; and as he spoke he stood still, close to the other, "Henri, why don't you avenge your sister's honour? Why don't you punish the dishonour which I brought on your father's hoary head? Henri, I say, why don't you seize by the throat the wretched traitor who brought desolation and destruction into your family?" and he stretched out his long gaunt neck, as though he expected that Larochejaquelin would rise from his bed, and take him at his word.

Henri felt that it was useless to endeavour to reason with him, or to answer the raving of his madness, but he still hoped, that by a mixture of firmness and gentleness, he might yet take him away from his present miserable dwelling, and by degrees bring him back to a happier state of mind. The difficulties in his way, however, were very great; for he knew how serious would be the danger and folly of leading him again into Agatha's presence.

"Nonsense, Adolphe," said he. "Why do you talk to your friend of vengeance? Come, take up your sword, and come away. This is a cold, damp place; and besides, we both want refreshment before our next day's work. Before six hours are gone, the republican army will be near Laval, and you and I must be prepared to meet them," and he picked up Denot's sword, and handed him his cap, and took his arm within his own, as though to lead him at once out of the room.

"And where are you going to?" said Denot, hesitating, but not refusing to go.

"Why, first, we'll go to the guard-house, and I'll show you a few of our picked men, who are there on duty; real dare-devils, who care no more for a blue than they do for a black-beetle; and then we'll go to the Angers gate. It's there that Lechelle will show himself; and then—and then—why, then we'll go home, and get some breakfast, for it will be nearly time for us to go to horse."

"Go home!" said Denot; "where's home?"

"Do you know the big stone house, with the square windows, near the market-house?"

"Yes, I know it: but tell me, Henri: who are there? I mean of your own people, you know—the Durbellière people?"

"Why, we're all there, Adolphe—Marie, and Victorine, and Charles, and Agatha, and my father and all. Poor Charles! You've heard of his state, Adolphe?"

"Yes, yes, I heard. I wish it had been me—I wish, with all my heart, it had been me," and then he paused a while; and again laying down his sword and cap, he said "Henri, you're an angel; I'm sure you are an angel; but all are not like you. I will not go with you now; but if you'll let me, I'll fight close by your side this day."

"You shall, Adolphe, you shall; up or down we'll not leave each other for a moment; but you must come with me, indeed you must. We should be sure to miss each other if we parted."

"I'll meet you at the gate, Henri, but I will not go with you. All men are not like you. Do you think that I could show myself to your father, and to de Lescure? Don't I know how their eyes would look on me? Don't I feel it now?" and again it seemed as though he were about to relapse into his frenzy; and then he continued speaking very gently, almost in a whisper: "Does de Lescure ever talk about the bridge of Saumur?"

Now Henri, to this day, had never heard a word of the want of courage which Denot had shown in the passage of the bridge of Saumur. No one but de Lescure had noticed it; and though he certainly had never forgotten it, he had been too generous to speak of it to any one. Henri merely knew that his two friends, Charles and Adolphe, had been together at the bridge.

He had heard from others of de Lescure's gallant conduct. It had oftentimes been spoken of in the army, and Henri had never remarked that an equal tribute of praise was not given to the two, for their deeds on that occasion. He now answered quite at cross purposes, but merely with the object of flattering the vanity of his friend:

"He will never forget it, Adolphe. No Vendean will ever forget the bridge of Saumur. We will all remember that glorious day, when we have forgotten many things that have happened since."

Poor Denot winced dreadfully under the blow, which Henri so innocently inflicted; but he merely said "No—I will not go with you—you needn't ask me, for my mind is made up. Do you know, Henri, I and de Lescure never loved each other? never—never—never, even when we were seemingly such good friends, we never loved each other. He loved you so well, that, for your sake, he bore with a man he despised. Yes: he always despised me, since the time you and I came home from school together. I do not blame him, for he tried hard to conceal what he felt; and he thought that I did not know it; but from the first day that we passed together I found him out, and I was never happy in his company."

All this was perfectly unintelligible to Henri, and was attributed by him to the frenzy of madness; but, in fact, there was truth in it. Denot's irregular spirit had been cowed by de Lescure's cold reasoning propriety, and he now felt it impossible to submit himself to the pardon of a man who, he thought, would forgive and abhor him. It was to no purpose Henri threatened, implored, and almost strove to drag him from the room. Denot was obstinate in his resolve, and Henri was at last obliged to leave him, with the agreement that they should both meet on horseback an hour before daybreak, at the gate of the town, which led towards Angers.

When Henri returned downstairs he found Chapeau still seated on the lower step, and Plume standing by, discoursing as to the tactics and probable success of the war.

"You found I was right, M. Henri?" said Chapeau, as he followed his master out into the street.

"Yes, Chapeau, you were quite right."

"And is he very bad, M. Henri?" said he, touching his forehead with his finger. "I suppose he cannot be all right there."

"He has suffered dreadfully since we saw him, and his sufferings have certainly told upon him; but there is every reason to hope, that, with kind treatment, he will soon be himself again; but, remember, till after today we will say nothing to any of them about his being here."

It was now three o'clock, and Henri had to be on horseback before six; he had but little time, therefore, either for rest or conversation. Henri and Chapeau hurried home, after having given orders at the guard-house that all the men on whom they could depend should be under arms before daybreak; and, having done so, they laid down and slept for the one short hour which was left to them of the night.

CHAPTER X.
LAVAL.

When Henri arose from his sleep, the whole house was up and stirring, and men and women were moving about through the dark rooms with candles in their hands. They all knew that this would be an eventful day for their cause; that much must depend on the success of that day's battle. If they were beaten now, their only hope would be to run farther from their homes, towards the coast, from which they expected English aid; but if fortune would once more visit their arms, they might hope to hold their position in Laval, and in other towns in the neighbouring and friendly province of Brittany. The gallant and cordial assistance which the Vendeans had received from the strangers among whom they were now thrown, had greatly tended to give them new hopes; and the yesterday's victory, which had been gained by the men called La Petite Vendée, over the advanced troops of the republicans, had made the Poitevins peculiarly anxious to exhibit their own prowess to their gallant friends.

Henri, Arthur, and one or two other Vendean officers, sat down to a hurried breakfast, while Marie and Agatha moved about the room, behind their chairs, attending to their wants. Chapeau had now too many of a soldier's duties to give his time to those of a serving-man, and the sisters and wives of the Vendean officers had long since learnt to wait on the heroes whom they loved and admired. De Lescure was already seated on his sofa, by the window, and his wife was, as usual, close to his side. He had wonderfully improved since he reached Laval; and though it was the firm conviction, both of himself and of his surgeon, that his wound must ultimately prove mortal, he was again alive to all that was done, and heart and soul intent on the interests of the war.

"Oh! what would I give to be but one hour today on horseback!" said he. "To lie pinioned here, and hear the sounds of brave men fighting! To know that the enemy are in the very street beneath me, and yet to be unable to strike a blow! Oh! it is fearfully tormenting."

Henri said something intended to comfort him.

"It is well for you to talk," continued de Lescure. "How would you have borne it yourself? You would have fretted and fumed, and dashed yourself like a bird against its cage, till either your senses or your breath had left you. Henri," he then added, in a calmer tone, "I feel that you will be successful today."

"That's a most glorious omen," said Henri, jumping up; "I look on success as certain when predicted by Charles, for he is the least sanguine among us all."

"But, Henri," said he, "take my advice, and don't attack them till they are close to the town. You may be sure they will be ready enough to give you an opportunity. After having driven us across the Loire like wild geese, Lechelle will not doubt his power to drive us also from the streets of Laval."

It was agreed among them that de Lescure's advice should be taken, and that none of the Vendeans should advance above a league on the road towards Antrâmes. It was already known that General Lechelle, and his whole army, were in the neighbourhood of that town; and it was not likely that, as he had pursued the Vendeans so far, he would remain there long without giving them the opportunity they now desired, of again trying their strength with them.

As Henri prepared to leave the room, the little Chevalier rose to accompany him: "No," said Henri, stopping him. "Do you remain with Chapeau today. Wherever you are, I know you will do well, but today we must not ride together." As the boy looked woefully disappointed, he added, "I will explain to you why, this evening, if we both live through the day to meet again."

He then kissed his sister, and Madame de Lescure and his cousin. They all of them knew that he was going into the midst of the hottest danger, where the visits of death would be thick and frequent; and they felt how probable it was that, before many hours were over, he might be brought back to them dead or dying. He either made some sign to her, or else from a feeling that she was dearer than the others to him, Marie followed him from the room. He said but a few words to her, as he held her in his close embrace, and she answered him with but one; but with that one she promised him, that if he returned safe and victorious from this day's contest, she would no longer object to join her hand and fate to his.

Henri immediately went to the gate, where he had promised to meet Adolphe, and there he found him on horseback, surrounded by his Breton followers, on foot. He had still the same wild, gaunt look about him, which had so startled his friend when he first saw him; but there was more of hope and spirit in his countenance, and he spoke, if he did not look, like a soldier.

We will now leave the warriors of La Vendée to obtain what success they can against the experienced troops of the republican army—the men so well known in many a bloody battle as the soldiers of Mayence, and will return and stay a while with the women and wounded man, who were left to all the horrors of a long day's suspense.

For a considerable time they said nothing to each other as to the probable events of the day, for they knew well that they could hear no news for some few hours to come. By degrees the cold grey dawn of an October morning broke into the room, and the candles were put out. Any ordinary employment at such a time was utterly out of the question, so they clustered together at the window and waited for such news as chance might bring them from time to time. Annot Stein, who was now living with them in the house, came in and joined them, and after a while the old Marquis was brought into the room, and took his station at the opposite window to that occupied by de Lescure.

The noises in the street were incessant. Soldiers on horseback and on foot; cannons and waggons passed on without a moment's pause: the men shouted as they went by, eager for revenge against the enemy who had driven them from their homes; and women mixed themselves in the crowd, shrieking and screaming as they parted from their husbands or their lovers.

The morning air was cold and chill, but still de Lescure insisted on having the windows open, that he might cheer with his voice the men as they passed below him, and that he might call to those by name whom he might chance to know. His wife was astonished to find how many he remembered, and to perceive that every soldier, as he passed, recognized the wan face of his General, and expressed his sincere delight at again seeing his features.

"Well done, Forestier! well done, my gallant friend!" he exclaimed, as a tall, handsome man rode by, who, from his garb and arms, was evidently an officer. He had, however, like many of the officers, belonged to a lowly rank, and still looked up with reverence to those of his fellow-soldiers, whose blood was more noble than his own. "You are never missing when strong arms are wanted."

The man took off his cap, and bowed low to the saddle bow. Had he been born to the manner, he could not have done it with more grace. "God bless you, General," he said, "God grant that we may soon see you here among us again;" and a thousand loud clamorous voices echoed the wish. A tear rose to de Lescure's eye, which none but his wife could mark: he knew that his friend's kind wishes were vain; that he had now, personally, no hope except in death; and he could not entirely repress a vain regret that he might live to witness the success of his party, of which, since his sojourn in Laval, he had taught himself to be sanguine.

It was but a moment before the tear was gone, and his eyes were again on fire with enthusiasm. "Ah, de Bauge—good de Bauge!" he exclaimed, as a friend of his early youth passed by, using at the moment every effort to repress the wild clamouring hurry of his followers. "God prosper thee, dear friend! Oh, that we now had but a score or two such soldiers as thou art!"

"We have many hundreds here as good," said de Bauge, pausing a moment from his work to salute the friends whom he recognized at the window.

"Thousands perhaps as brave, thousands as eager, if they did but know how to use their courage," answered de Lescure.

After this there was a lull for a few moments, and then a troop of cuirassiers trotted down the street, jingling their bridles, swords, and spurs as they moved. This small body of cavalry had been, for some time, the pride and strongest hope of the Vendeans. They had been gradually armed, horsed, and trained during the war, by the greatest exertions of the wealthiest among their officers, and they had certainly proved to be worth all the trouble they had cost. They were now, alas! reduced to half the number, which had ridden out of Chatillon before the battle of Cholet; but the remnant were still full of spirit, and anxious to avenge their fallen brethren. Their bright trappings and complete accoutrements, afforded a strange contrast to the medley appearance of the footmen, who retreated back to the houses, to make way for the horses; and told more plainly than any words could do, the difference between an army of trained soldiers, and a band of brave, but tumultuous peasants.

It was now nine o'clock; and shortly after the horsemen had all passed through the street, the little Chevalier came in with the news, that they were immediately about to attack the blues; the republican army being already within a mile of the town; and that Henri was at that moment leaving the guard-house, and preparing to lead the attack; and when he had told so much aloud to them all, he stooped down to whisper to de Lescure, that Adolphe Denot was riding everywhere through the town at Henri's right hand, and that he was the redoubtable Mad Captain, the leader of La Petite Vendée.

De Lescure had not time to question the Chevalier, or to express his surprise, before Henri was seen coming down the street on horseback, almost at full gallop, and at his right hand rode a man, whom they did not all immediately recognize. Agatha, however, knew at the first glance who the stranger was, and with an instinctive feeling that the sight of her would be painful to him, she retreated behind her father's couch, so that he could not well see her from the street. When Chapeau had first whispered into his master's ear the name of Adolphe Denot as the leader of the Bretons, Agatha had truly guessed the purport of his whisper; and it cannot, therefore, be said that she was startled to see Adolphe once more by her brother's side; but still she could not but shudder as she remembered the circumstances under which she had last seen him, and the inhuman crime of which he had been guilty.

Henri rode a little in advance, and as he passed, he merely turned his laughing face towards his friends, and kissed his hand to the window. Denot, till he was nearly close to the house, had not thought of the neighbourhood he was in; nor had he the least idea that any but the usual inhabitants of the town were looking down on him, till his wandering eyes fell full upon the faces of Marie and Madame de Lescure, who were standing close to the open window. Immediately the blood rushed to his face, and suffused it almost with a purple red: he checked his horse suddenly, and, for a moment, looked full up at the window, where he met the cold gaze of de Lescure fixed full upon him. The pause was but for a moment; he could not bear the ordeal of that look, but fixing his eyes to the ground, he struck his spurs into his horse, and hurried out of the sight of those on whom he did not dare to turn his face.

"Agatha, my love, in the name of the Blessed Virgin, who was that?" said the Marquis, rubbing his eyes, before which an Unearthly apparition seemed to have appeared. "Who was that that rode by with Henri? only that I know it is impossible, I should have said that it was Adolphe Denot."

"It is Adolphe, Sir," said Arthur Mondyon; "it is he that is the Mad Captain, who has been knocking the blues about in such a wonderful manner. I suppose he got tired of Santerre, or Santerre of him. I thought they wouldn't agree long together."

"Arthur!" said Agatha, "you should speak kindly of him now; don't you see that Henri has forgiven him; if he can forgive him, surely you ought to do so."

"And is it really true that Henri and Adolphe Denot are again friends?" said the Marquis, speaking rather to himself than to any one else. "Well, I should have thought that would have been impossible. If Henri can forgive him, we all ought to do so too; but—but—but I do not think that I could feel at ease if he were in the room with me."

"I do not think he will come to us, father," said Agatha. "Did you not observe his face as he passed? the very sight of us seemed to cut him to the heart."

Adolphe had been quite right, when he said that they were not at all like Henri. There was not one of the whole party who did not strive, heartily and truly, to forgive the treason and iniquity of which he had been guilty; but there was not one there who did not, at the same time, feel a secret wish that he or she might never again be under the same roof with the man who had been a traitor, both to his friends and to his King.

Arthur Mondyon soon left them, and hurried out to bear his part in the contest which was just commencing. He was a little jealous to think that his accustomed place near Henri should have been taken from him by one who had proved himself so faithless as Denot, but still he was not inclined to pass such a day as this in-doors, with sick men and trembling women. He promised, however, to come to them himself from time to time, or if that were impossible, to send them news of what was going on; and as it was probable that the thickest of the fight would be either in the town, or immediately on the skirts of it, there was no reason why he should not keep his promise.

For a couple of hours they remained in dreadful suspense, hearing nothing and fearing everything. It seemed to them as though whole days must have passed in those two hours. De Lescure became dreadfully impatient, and even irritable; declaring at one moment that he was quite equal to mount his horse, and that he would go out and see what they were about; and then again almost fainting, with the exhaustion occasioned by his intense excitement. Then he would lament the inexperience of Henri, expressing his dread that his indiscretion this day would ruin all their hopes: and, again, when he saw how painful these surmises were to Agatha and Marie, he would begin to praise his courage and indomitable good spirits, and declare that their strongest safeguard lay in the affection to his person, which was shared by every peasant of La Vendée.

Their suspense was at length broken; not by any visit or message from their own party, but by a most unexpected and unwelcome sight. On a sudden, they again heard the tumultuous noise of troops coming down the street; but, on this occasion, they were entering, instead of leaving the town; and as the rushing body of men turned a corner in the street, it was seen that they all wore the well-known blue uniform of the republican regiments. Yes, there in truth were the blues, now immediately under the house they were occupying: file after file of sturdy, grizzled veteran soldiers, hurried through the streets in quick, but regular time. Men quite unlike their own dear peasant soldiers; men with muskets in their hands, shakos on their heads, and cartouche boxes slung behind their backs. The three ladies, before whose sight this horrid reality of a danger, so long apprehended, suddenly appeared, had never been so near a scene of absolute battle. Agatha, it is true, had had to endure through one long and dreadful night the presence of Santerre and his men in the château of Durbellière; but then she had no active part to play; she had only to sit in quiet, and wait for her doom: now they all felt that something should be done, some means should be tried to escape from the danger which was so close to them.

The women immediately withdrew from the window, and wheeled away the couch on which the Marquis was lying, but nothing would induce de Lescure to allow himself to be stirred; in fixed silence, with his head resting low on the window sill, he gazed on the crowded soldiers, as they poured thick and numerous into the town.

"Oh, where is Henri now?" said Madame de Lescure. "What shall we do—where are we to go? Speak, Charles, for heaven's sake, speak!"

Marie had opened the door, and now stood with it in her hands, wishing to run, and yet not choosing to leave her companions in misfortune; while Agatha vainly endeavoured with her unassisted strength to remove her father from the room.

"Henri is just where he ought to be," said de Lescure. "There—there—now they come—now they come. By heavens, there's Denot leading—and see, there's de Bauge and Arthur—dear boy, gallant boy. Well done, Henri Larochejaquelin: had you been grey it could not have been better done; he has got the blues as it were into a wine-press; poor devils, not one can escape alive."

De Lescure, when he first saw the republicans coming down the street, had for a moment thought that the town was in their hands; but a minute's reflection served to show him, that were such really the case, they would have driven before them hundreds of the retreating Vendeans. The peasants had never yet so utterly forgotten their courage, as to throw down their weapons at the first sight of their enemy, and fly without making an effort for victory, and de Lescure was sure that such could not now have been the case. It immediately occurred to him, that the passage of the gate must have been purposely left free to the devoted blues, and that Henri and his men would fall upon them in the town, where their discipline and superior arms, would be but of comparatively little use to them.

He was right; for while the women were yet trembling, panic-struck at the first sight of their enemies, Henri and his party had entered the long street from the market-place, and with a fierce yell of defiance, the Vendean cavalry rushed upon the astonished blues, meeting them almost beneath the very window from which de Lescure was looking.

The three women crouched round the aged Marquis in the farthest corner of the room, comforted to find that he whom they so trusted still expected victory; but nearly fainting with fear, and deafened with the sounds of the conflict. To de Lescure the sight was pleasure itself; as he could not be in the fight, the next thing was to see the combatants and cheer his friends. The foremost of the republican soldiers soon gave way beneath the weight of the attack; though they fought sturdily, and did their best to keep their ground. They could not, however, retreat far; their own men still advancing behind blocked up the way; and after a while, that which De Lescure had predicted took place: another party of Vendeans had attacked them in the rear, and occupied the only gate through which they could leave the city.

And now the slaughter in the street was dreadful, and the blues hemmed in on every side fought desperately for their lives, like beasts at bay. Every now and again the Vendeans retreated a step or two, driven back by the fury of their foes, and then again regained their ground, advancing over the bodies of the slain. No one in the strange medley on which he was looking, was more conspicuous to de Lescure's eyes than Adolphe Denot; he had lost his cap in the confusion of the fight, and his thin, wan face, disfigured by the wound which the Chevalier had given him, was plainly to be seen; and de Lescure was shocked by the change which he saw there: the only weapon he bore was a huge sabre, which he swung round his head with a strength which could not have been expected from his attenuated frame; he was often the most forward, always among the first of the assailants; and frequently became surrounded by the blues, who were prevented by the closeness of the crowd from using their arms. He had caught de Lescure's eye, and from time to time turned his face up toward the window, as though anxious to discover whether he who had before witnessed his cowardice was now looking upon his prowess.

"By heavens! he fights well," said de Lescure to his wife, who was gradually creeping somewhat nearer to her husband, but still unable to face the horrors of that open window. "He is greatly changed—look—look at him now; well done, Adolphe—well done: there, there; he's down! Poor fellow, I fear he has struck his last blow: gallant Henri, brave Henri—there, they are up again together; but Denot's face is covered with blood. He still has his sword, however—well done, Denot: bravely done Denot: no man of those living or dead, ever struck a better blow than that."

These last words were distinctly heard by him to whom they were addressed, and as he again turned up his face, a ray of triumph illumined his sunken eyes; he did not, however, or he could not speak, for the heat of the battle was carried back again towards the gate, and the tumultuous sea of fighting men was hurried away from the spot where they had been contending.

While this scene was going on in the street, another set of combatants were engaged near the gate; and here two men of very different natures, but of similar station in life, found themselves together during a temporary pause, after a protracted struggle. These were Michael Stein, and Auguste Emile Septimus Plume. In spite of all that he had himself said against the trade, Michael had, in his old age, turned soldier, and had been fighting sturdily with a huge woodman's axe, a weapon which he had chanced to meet with, and the use of which came readily to his hand: he was now sitting on the step of the gate-house, wiping with the sleeve of his coat the perspiration which the unaccustomed work had brought to his forehead, and listening to the praises of M. Plume, who was standing over him, leaning on his sword.

"That axe of yours," said Auguste, "is a singular weapon, and perhaps not entirely fitted for military purposes; but I must own you have used it well— it fell with decided effect this morning on many a poor fellow's head and shoulders. You have probably, my friend, fought many a battle with these fellows of Mayence?"

"Not a battle I ever fought before, Monsieur," said Michael; "nor do I ever wish to fight another; it's horrid weary work, this of knocking men's brains out, not to talk of the chance a man runs of losing his own."

"But ain't you one of the Vendeans, my gallant comrade?" asked Auguste.

"If you mean, did I come over from Poitou with them, I certainly did; but I only came because I could not help it, and because I could not live to see a little girl I have fall into the hands of the butchers; it was not for any love of fighting that I came."

"But yet you take to it kindly, my friend. I am considered to know something of the sword exercise, and I thought you wielded that axe, as though your arm had been used to a sabre this many a year."

"I am a blacksmith," said Michael, shortly; "and I have been fifty years ringing hammers on an anvil: that makes a man's arm lusty."

"Indeed," said the other, "a blacksmith—well, you may be a blacksmith, and yet a good soldier. Now you wouldn't believe it, but I'm a baker—you wouldn't take me to be a baker by my trade, would you now?"

Michael Stein looked at him, and told him he couldn't well give an opinion, as he knew nothing about bakers.

"I knew you wouldn't," said the other; "no one on earth would take me to be a tradesman—that's what they all say; I have that kind of manner about me, that I look like a soldier—I did when I hadn't been at it above a week. Every one used to say, Plume, you were born to be an officer; Plume, you will live to be a General: and if I don't get killed in the wars, I think I shall. Now it's only three months since I joined, and I am already second in command in the whole army."

Michael Stein stared at him, as he repeated his words, "Second in command in the whole army!"

"Indeed I am, my friend, the second in command. You wouldn't believe it, now, but I was sticking loaves of bread into an oven three or four months ago."

"The second in command!" said Michael, still regarding his companion with a look in which incredulous surprise and involuntary reverence were blended. "I suppose you're a great way above Jacques Chapeau, then?"

"Oh, my friend Chapeau—and do you know my friend Chapeau? No, I'm not above him; he's not in our army; he's second in command himself in the Vendean army. You know I belong to La Petite Vendée."

At this moment, the very man of whom they were speaking, the redoubtable Chapeau, came up with a large party of straggling Vendeans, out of breath with running; they were in full pursuit of the blues, who were now said to be flying towards Antrâmes and Château-Gonthier.

"Come, my friends," said Chapeau, "no idling now; come to Antrâmes, and we'll get plenty of arms, if we get nothing else. What, is it you, Captain Plume. I'm told you did as well as the best today; and what—my dear old friend Michael: a soldier at last, eh, Michael Stein! Come, man, don't be ashamed to give us your hand; you've joined us in very good time, for the Vendeans never gained such a victory as they have today. Come on, old friend, we'll get another sight of these running devils at Antrârnes."

"They may run for me, M. Chapeau, and run far enough, before I try to stop them; do you know I'm nearly ashamed of what I've been doing as it is."

"Ashamed!—ashamed of what?" said Chapeau.

"Why look there," said Michael; and as he spoke, he pointed with his foot to the body of a republican soldier, who lay calmly at his ease, in the sleep of death, not three yards from the spot where the old man was now standing.

"Not an hour since, that poor fellow ran this way, and as he passed, he had no thought of hurting me; he was thinking too much of himself, for half-a-dozen hungry devils were after him. Well, I don't know what possessed me, but the smell of blood had made me wild, and I lifted up my axe and struck him to the ground. I wish, with all my heart, the poor man were safe at Antrâmes."

It was in vain that Chapeau tried to persuade the smith that he had only done his duty in killing a republican, who would certainly have lived to have done an injury to the cause, had he been suffered to escape. Michael Stein would not, or could not, understand the arguments he used; and decidedly declared that if he found it possible to avoid fighting for the future he would do so.

"Do you know, M. Chapeau," he said at last, "when I first took this axe in my hand, this morning, I had hardly made up my mind on which side I should use it. It was only when I thought of the boys and of Annot, that I determined to go with the Vendeans. It wasn't possible for a man not to fight on one side or the other—that's the only reason I had for fighting at all."

Chapeau became rather ashamed of his friend's irregular doctrines, and hurried on; explaining to Plume, who accompanied him, that Michael Stein was a queer eccentric old man, but a thorough good royalist at heart. "Why he has two sons among the red scarfs," he added, to settle the point.

"Has he, indeed?" said Plume, who had never heard who the red scarfs were.

CHAPTER XI.
DEATH OF ADOLPHE DENOT.

Nothing could be more complete than the success of the Vendeans, not only in the town of Laval, but also outside the gate; nor could any error be more fatal than that committed by the republican General, Lechelle. Previous to this day he had never been worsted since he had been sent from Paris with orders to exterminate the Vendeans; he had driven them from Chatillon, their own chosen position in the centre of their own territory across the Loire; and he had rashly conceived that he had only to show himself before Laval again, to scare them from their resting-place, and scatter them farther from their own homes. He had marched his army up to Laval early on the morning of the fight; and his best men, the redoubtable Mayençais, indignant at the treatment which a few of their brethren had received from Denot's followers on the previous day, marched boldly into the town, conceiving that they had only to show themselves to take possession of it. The result has been told. One half of these veteran troops fell in the streets of Laval—many of the remainder were taken alive; a few only escaped to consummate their disgrace by flying towards Antrâmes at their quickest speed, spreading panic among the republican troops who had not yet come up close to the town.

The news of defeat soon communicated itself; and the whole army, before long, was flying to Antrâmes. The unfortunate Lechelle himself had been one of the first to leave the town, and had made no attempt to stop his men until he had entered Antrâmes. Nor did he long remain there: as the straggling fugitives came up, they told how close and fast upon their track the victorious brigands were coming; and that the conduct of the peasants now was not what it had been when the war commenced, when they were fighting in their own country, and near their own homes. Then they had spared the conquered, then they had shed no blood, except in the heat of battle; now they spared none; they had learnt a bloody lesson from their enemies, and massacred, without pity, the wretches who fell into their hands. Antrâmes was not a place of any strength; it could not be defended against the Vendeans; and Lechelle had hardly drawn his breath in the town, before he again left it, on the road to Château-Gonthier.

Henri and Denot were among the first of the pursuers; indeed, of so desultory a nature was the battle, that the contest was still continued near the gate of the town, while they were far on their road towards Antrâmes. They passed almost in a gallop through that place, and did not stop until they found themselves, towards evening, close to the bridge, leading into Château-Gonthier. Here they perceived that Lechelle had made some little attempt to defend his position. He had drawn out two cannons to the head of the bridge; had stayed the course of a few fugitives, with whom he attempted to defend the entrance into the town; and had again taken upon himself the duties of a General.

The pursuers now amounted to about three hundred horsemen, the very men who had made the first attack on the blues in the streets of Laval, and Henri knew that so soon after their complete and signal success nothing could daunt them, and that, in all probability, no effort of the beaten republicans could turn them back.

"Come," said he, speaking to those who were nearest to him, "only a few yards farther, and we shall be far enough. It shall never be said that the vanquished slept in the town while their conquerors lay in the fields;" and again he put spurs to his horse, and with a yell of triumph, his men followed him over the bridge.

It would be difficult to say who was first, for Henri, Adolphe, and nearly a dozen others, galloped across the bridge together, and the whole troop followed them pell-mell into the town. The two cannons were soon taken; the irresolute blues, who, with only half a heart, had attempted to defend themselves, were driven from their positions, and Henri at once found himself master of the place.

A few of his gallant followers had fallen on the bridge. It could not be expected but what this should be the case, for they made their attack in the face of two field-pieces and a discharge of musketry, from a body of men quite as numerous as their own; but Henri had not perceived till he reached the square in the middle of the town, that Adolphe Denot was no longer by his side.

"Did you see M. Denot?" said he to a soldier, who was now standing on the ground at his horse's head.

"You mean the gentleman who was riding with you all the day, General—he who had lost his cap?"

"Yes, yes, did you see him? he passed over the bridge with me."

"General," said the man, "he never passed the bridge. He fell on the very centre of it. I saw him fall, and his horse galloped into the town without a rider."

Arthur Mondyon soon brought him confirmation of the news. He had been struck by a musket ball on the breast, while they were crossing the bridge, and the whole troop of horsemen, who were behind, had passed over his body. He had, however, been taken up, and brought into the town; whether or no his life was extinct, Arthur could not say, but he had been told that the wound would certainly prove mortal.

Henri's first duty, even before attending to his friend, was to endeavour to save the lives of such of the blues as were yet in the town, and, if possible, to get the person of Lechelle. It was well known that he had entered the place with the fugitives, and it was believed that he had not since escaped from it. Some few of the republican soldiers had made their way out of the town, on the road towards Ségré, but there was every reason to believe that the General had not been among them. The inhabitants of Château-Gonthier were very favourable to the Vendean cause; Henri received every information which the people could give him, and at last succeeded in tracing Lechelle into a large half-ruined house, in the lower portion of which, a wine shop, for the accommodation of the poorer classes, was kept open. Here they learnt, from the neighbours, that he had been seen to enter the house, and an old woman, who alone kept her position behind the counter, confessed with some hesitation, that a man, answering the description of him they sought, had entered the shop about an hour since; that he had hastily swallowed a large quantity of brandy, and then, instead of leaving the shop, had rushed through the inner door and gone upstairs.

"He wasn't here a minute in all," said she; "and he said nothing about paying for what he took—and, when I saw him going in there, I thought it best to let him have his own way."

"And he is there still," said Chapeau, who had now again joined his master.

"Unless he went out through the window, he is; there is no other way out than what you see there."

"Go up, Chapeau," said Henri, "and take two or three with you; if he be there, he must come down; but remember that he is an officer, and in misfortune."

"I will remember," said Chapeau, "that he sent us word to Chatillon, that he would not leave alive in La Vendée a father or mother to lament their children, or a child to lament its parents: those were bitter words; maybe he will be sorry to have them brought to his memory just at present."

"Remember what I tell you, Chapeau," said his master; "whatever he may have said, it is not now your duty to sit in judgment on him."

"For God's sake, gentlemen, don't do him a harm here," said the old woman; "for mercy's sake, Monsieur," and she turned to Henri, "don't let them take his life; to tell you the truth, when he begged for some hole to hide in, I bid him to go upstairs; I could do no less. I should have done the same if it had been one of you."

Henri said what he could to tranquillize her, assuring her that the man should, at any rate, not be killed before her eyes; and this seemed to be sufficient to reassure her. Chapeau and four others had gone upstairs; and those below were not kept waiting long, before the heavy tread of the men descending was heard on the stairs, as though they were carrying down a weight among them. Such was the case: Henri stepped forward and opened the door; and as he did so, the men staggered into the room with their burden, and then gently dropped upon the floor the dead body of the republican General. The unfortunate man had shot himself.

Henri turned out of the shop without saying a word; and as the others prepared to follow him, one of the men knelt down beside the body, and wrenched from the hand, which still held it fast, the fatal pistol which had so lately done its work. "At any rate," said he, "there is no use in leaving this behind us; I doubt not but I can make a better use of it than General Lechelle has done."

The Chevalier had said but the truth, in declaring that Adolphe Denot's wound was mortal; the musket ball had passed right through his lungs, passing out between his shoulders; and his limbs had been dreadfully torn and bruised by the feet of the horses which had passed over him. Still, however, he had been carried alive into the town, had been laid in a settle-bed in the little inn, and had his wounds dressed with such surgical skill as the town afforded. He had spoken once since he fell, and had then begged, in an almost inarticulate whisper, that Henri Larochejaquelin would come to him, and this message had been delivered, and was attended to.

There were not many to watch and attend his bed-side, for many others beside him in the town were in the same position; and though it was known to a few that the Mad Captain of La Petite Vendée had been seen during the whole day riding by the side of their own General, Denot had not yet been recognized by many of the Vendeans, and most of those around him were indifferent to his fate. When Henri reached the room in which he lay, no one was with him, but the poor baker of Laval, who had entered the town with Chapeau, and having heard that his Captain was mortally wounded, had lost not a moment in tendering him his services. The poor man was sitting on a low stool, close by Denot's head, and in his lap he held a wooden bowl of water, with which, from time to time, he moistened the mouth of the wounded man, dipping his hand into the water, and letting the drops fall from his fingers on to his lips.

"Hush! hush!" he said, as Henri entered the room; "for mercy's sake, don't shake him; the black blood gushes out of his mouth with every move he gets."

The two men did not recognize each other, for they had only met for a moment, and that by the faint light of a rush candle. Plume, therefore, had no idea of giving up his place or his duty to a man whom he conceived was a stranger; and Henri was at a loss to conceive who could be the singular looking creature that seemed to take so tender an interest in his friend.

Henri advanced up to the bed on tiptoe, and gazed into Denot's face; he had been shocked before, but he now thought that never in his life had he seen so sad a sight: the colour of his skin was no longer pale, but livid; his thin, dry lips were partially open, and his teeth, close set together, were distinctly visible; his eyes were at the moment closed, as though he were in a stupor, and his long black matted hair hung back over the folded cloak on which his head rested: his sallow, bony hands lay by his side, firmly clenched, as though he had been struggling, and his neck and breast, which had been opened for the inspection of the surgeon, was merely covered with a ragged bloody towel.

"Is he asleep?" asked Henri, in a whisper, such as seems to come naturally to every one, when speaking by the bed-side of those who are in great danger, but which is generally much more painfully audible to a sick man than the natural voice.

Denot opened his eyes, and showed, by the slight motion of his head, that he had heard his friend's voice, but he was at the moment unable to speak.

Plume made a signal to Henri to be quiet, and he therefore sat himself down at the other side of the bed, to watch till Adolphe should gain strength to speak to him, or till the breath should have passed from his body. Plume, in the meantime, continued his occupation, causing a few drops of water to fall from time to time between those thin shrivelled lips; and in this way a long half-hour passed over them.

At last Henri heard his name scarcely pronounced by the dying man, and the dull eyes opened, though it was evident that the film of death had nearly hidden all objects from their view; still it was evident that he knew who it was that sat by his bed-side, and he faintly returned the pressure of the hand which grasped his own. Henri stooped down his ear to catch the words which might fall from his lips; but for a while he made no farther attempt to speak—an inexpressible look of confused trouble passed across his face and forehead, as he attempted to collect his disordered thoughts, and again he closed his eyes, as though the struggle was useless; at last he again muttered something, and Henri caught the words 'de Lescure,' and 'bridge of Saumur.'

"Yes, yes, he shall," said Henri, trying to comfort him, but still not understanding what it was that weighed so heavily on his breast; he felt, however, that a promise of compliance would give him comfort. "He shall, indeed; I will tell him, and I know he will."

Again the eyes were closed, and the struggle to speak was discontinued. Plume gave over his task, for it was evident that no care of his could any longer be of avail, and he walked away from the bed, that he might not overhear the words which his Captain strove to speak to his friend; but Henri remained, still holding Denot's hand: then a thought struck him, which had not earlier occurred to him, and beckoning to Plume to come to him, he dismissed him, in a whisper, to endeavour to find a priest, without the loss of another moment, and bring him to the aid of the dying man.

Though Denot's sight and speech were almost gone, the sense of hearing was still left to him, and he understood what Henri said. He again moved his head in token of dissent; again pulled his friend towards him by the hand, and again muttered out a word, the last that he ever attempted to utter; that one word Henri heard as plainly as though it had been spoken with the full breath of a strong man—it was his sister's name.

Adolphe Denot survived this last effort of his troubled spirit, but a few moments; the sepulchral rattle in his throat soon told the sad tale of his dissolution; and Plume hurrying up to the bed-head, assisted Henri in composing the limbs of the dead man.

For three months Denot and Plume had consorted together; they had been a strange fantastic pair of comrades, but yet not altogether ill-matched: nothing could be more dissimilar than they had been in age, in birth, and previous habits, but they had met together with the same wishes, the same ambition, the same want of common sense, and above all the same overweening vanity; they had flattered each other from the moment of their first meeting to the present day, and thus these two poor zealous maniacs, for in point of sanity the Lieutenant was but little better than his Captain, had learnt to love each other.

And now Plume, having carefully completed what the exigencies of the moment required, gave way to his sincere grief, and bewailed his friend with no silent sorrow. Henri, who had totally forgotten the little that he had heard of the martial baker, was at a loss to conceive who could be the man, a stranger to himself who found cause for so much sorrow in the death of Adolphe Denot. As for himself, he had tenderly loved Denot as a brother; he had truly forgiven him his gross treachery; and he had determined to watch over him, and if possible protect him from farther sorrow: but after the interview he had had with him, he could not conceal from himself that Adolphe was still insane; and he felt that death had come to him in an honourable way, atoning for past faults, and relieving him from future sufferings. He could not grieve that his friend had fallen in battle, bravely doing his duty in the cause to which he was bound by so many ties.

"He was the bravest man, and the best soldier, and the most honourable gentleman in the whole army," said Plume, sobbing; "and now there's no one left but myself," and then recovering himself he made to the manes of the departed warrior a loyal promise, which he fully determined to keep. "Thou art gone, my brave commander, my gallant commander," he said, standing suddenly upright, and stretching his long arms over the corpse, "thou art gone, and I doubt not I shall follow thee: but till that moment shall come, till a death, as honourable as thine own, shall release me from my promise, I swear that I will not disgrace the high station which thy departure obliges me to fill. It was thou who first tutored my unaccustomed arm to wield the sword; it was thou who badest me hear unmoved the thunder of an enemy's artillery; it was thou who taughtest me all I know of military tactics, and the art of war. Rest in peace, dear friend, dearest of instructors, I will not disgrace thy precepts." And so finishing, he stooped down, kissed the face of the dead body which he apostrophized, made a cross on the bosom, and muttered a fervent prayer for the welfare of the departed soul.

If Henri was surprised before, he was now perfectly astounded; nothing could be less poetical, less imposing, or have less of military grandeur about it than the figure of poor Auguste Plume. What could he mean by saying that he was now called on to fill a high station? Who could it be that confessed to owe so deep a debt of gratitude to the dead man?

"Had you known M. Denot long?" asked Henri, when he conceived that Plume was sufficiently composed to hear and answer a question.

"What's that you say his name was?" said Plume, eagerly, pricking up his ears. "I beg your pardon, Sir, I didn't exactly catch the word."

"And didn't you know the name of the friend, whom you seem to have valued so highly?"

"Indeed, to tell you the truth, Sir, I did not. We two used to have a good deal of talk together: for hours and hours we've sat and talked over this war, and he has told me much of what he used to do in Poitou, when he served with the Vendeans; but I could never get him to tell me his name. It was a question he didn't like to be asked; and yet I am sure he never did anything to disgrace it."

"His name was Adolphe Denot," said Henri.

"Adolphe Denot—Adolphe Denot! well, I am very glad I know at last. One doesn't like not to know the name of the dearest friend one ever had; especially after he's dead. But wasn't he Count Denot, or Baron Denot, or something of that sort?"

"No, he had no title; but yet he was of noble blood."

"I suppose then we must call him General Denot—simple General; it sounds as well as Count or Marquis in these days. Was he a General when you knew him in La Vendée?"

"I have known him all my life," replied Henri.

"Indeed!" said Plume: and then gazing at his companion, from head to foot, he continued, "An't you the gentleman that came with Chapeau to see him last night? An't you the Commander-in-Chief of the Vendeans?"

Henri gave him to understand that he was.

"Then this meeting is very lucky," said Plume, "most exceedingly fortunate! I am now the Commander-in-Chief of La Petite Vendée. We must unite our forces. I am not ambitious—at least not too ambitious; you shall be the chief, I will be next to you. Chapeau, I am sure, will be contented to be third here, over the body of our friend, let us concert our measures for utterly exterminating the republicans. We have now been victorious, proudly, grandly victorious; my voice shall be for a march to Paris. Come, General, give me your hand. Hand in hand, like true comrades, let us march to Paris, and thunder at the doors of the Convention."

As he spoke, Auguste Emile Septimus held out his hand to the young Commander; and Henri could not refuse the proffered grasp. He now remembered Chapeau's description of the martial baker; and as he underwent the merciless squeeze which Plume inflicted on him, the young Marquis meditated, with something like vexation, on the ridiculous figure and language of him who now claimed his friendship and confidence. He had before been on terms of perfect equality with men equally low in station with poor Plume. Cathelineau had been a postillion; Stofflet, a game-keeper; but he had admired the enthusiastic genius of Cathelineau, he had respected the practical iron energy of Stofflet—he could neither admire nor respect Auguste Plume—and yet he could not reject him.

He endeavoured, in as few words as he could, to make his companion understand, that highly as he appreciated his disinterested offer, he could not, at the present moment, accede to it. That many officers, high in the confidence of the whole army, must be consulted before any important step was taken; that, as for himself his duty required him to hurry back to Laval as quick as he could. That, as regarded him, Plume, he advised him to return to his own men, and endeavour to organize them into a regular corps, in doing which he promised him that practical assistance should not be wanting; and that, as regarded the body of their mutual friend, he, Henri, would give orders for its immediate burial; and having said so much as quickly as he could speak, Henri Larochejaquelin hurried from the room, leaving the unfortunate Plume to renew his lamentations over his friend. He had cause to lament; the only man likely to flatter his vanity was gone. He would never again be told that he was born for great achievements—never again promised that bravery, fidelity to his commander, and gallant demeanour among his comrades, would surely lead him to exalted duties.

Such were the precepts with which the insanity of Denot had inflamed the mad ambition of his poor follower. He now felt—not his own unfitness, for that he could not suspect—but the difficulty, the impossibility to get his talents and services acknowledged; and he again sat down to weep, partly for his friend, and partly for himself.

Henri passed the remainder of the night in Château-Gonthier, and early on the next morning he returned towards Laval. The road was covered with swarms of Vendeans, now returning from the pursuit in which they had nearly exterminated the unfortunate army which had followed them across the Loire. They had crossed that river panic-stricken and hopeless; now they were shouting with triumph, and exulting with joy, confident of success. None of those who returned were without some token of success; some carried back with them the muskets of the republican infantry; others, the sabres of the cavalry; and others, more joyful in their success than any, were mounted on their horses. They all loudly greeted Henri as he passed, and declared that nothing should ever conquer them, now that they had the General over them, whom they themselves had chosen.

Henri, though he well knew the difficulties which were before him, could not but be triumphant as he listened to the cheers of his followers; he had certainly been pre-eminently successful in the first attempts which had been made under his own sole command; and it is not surprising that this, joined to the confidence of youth, should have made him feel himself equal almost to any enterprise. Then another subject of joy filled his heart; Marie had promised that if the Vendeans were now successful, if they could look forward to spending one quiet week in Laval, she would no longer refuse to join her hand to his and become bone of his bone, and flesh of his flesh— that promise she would now realize; and therefore as he rode back through the gate of Laval, Henri felt happier than he had done for many a long, weary, tedious day.

CHAPTER XII.
VENDEAN MARRIAGES.

The young General's good news had preceded him, and when he entered the room where his friends were assembled, they were one and all ready to embrace and congratulate their successful soldier; he received the blessing of his father, the praises of de Lescure, the thanks and admiration of Madame de Lescure, and what he valued more than all, Marie's acknowledgments of the promise she gave him, when last he left her side.

During his absence, three unexpected visitors had reached Laval; the first was Father Jerome, who had followed the army, and now brought them news from the side of Nantes, that Charette was still at the head of a large body of royalists, and was ready to join himself with the main army, somewhere to the north of the Loire, if any plan could be struck out for their future proceedings, to which both he and Henri could agree; and the others were perfect strangers. Two gentlemen had called at the guard-house, and asked for M. de Larochejaquelin: on hearing that he was not in Laval, they had desired to see M. de Lescure, and had, when alone with him, declared that they came from England, with offers of assistance, both in men and money; one of these gentlemen had with him a stick, and after having carefully looked round the room to see that no one but de Lescure could observe him, he had broken the stick in two, and taken from the hollow space within it, a letter addressed to the Commander-in-Chief of the Vendean army.

These two gentlemen were both Vendeans, but early in the contest they had passed over into England; they had now returned, habited like peasants, and in this disguise had come over on their dangerous mission, passing first into Jersey and thence to the coast of Normandy; they had walked the whole distance, through the province of Brittany, passing themselves off, in one place as good republicans, and in another as true loyalists; they had, however, through all their dangers, managed to keep the important stick, the promises contained in which could not have arrived at a moment when they would have been more welcome.

Granville was the point at which it was decided that the English troops should land, and de Lescure was strongly of opinion that the Vendean army, relieved of its intolerable load of women and children, should proceed thither to meet their allies; and this plan, though with some dissentient voices, was agreed to. They could not, however, start quite immediately; nor was it necessary for them to do so; and the few days of secure rest which so many of them anxiously desired, was given to the army.

At length Henri found leisure to tell them all the sad, but still pleasing story of Denot's conduct and fate—of the gallantry by which he had redeemed so many sins, and of the death by which he had set a seal to the forgiveness of them all. Each of them had already learnt that Adolphe was the mysterious leader, the Mad Captain of La Petite Vendée, and they listened with deep attention to the story which they now heard of the way in which he had been living, and of the manner of his death.

"Poor fellow," said Henri, "I understand it all, except about the bridge of Saumur; from the time when I found him in his wretched chamber, to the moment of his death, he was talking of that, and connecting your name, Charles, with everything he said; I do not at all know what was in his thoughts, but something connected with the bridge of Saumur was either a great trouble to him, or a great triumph."

And then de Lescure told him what had happened; how the poor fellow's heart had failed him, at the moment when courage was so necessary; how he had feared to advance at the decisive moment, and had shrunk back, appalled, conquered, and disgraced. Henri now understood why de Lescure had not allowed Denot to be chosen at Saumur, as one of the twelve leaders of the army; why he had subsequently so generally distrusted him; and expressed so little surprise of the conduct of which he had been guilty at Durbellière.

"His history," said de Lescure, "gives us a singular insight into the intricacies of a man's character; Adolphe was not naturally a coward, for madness aggravates the foibles of our nature, and no one can have shown himself more capable of gallantry than he did yesterday; but he wanted that sustained courage which is only given by principle, and trust in God. May He forgive his sins, mercifully remembering his infirmities!"

Some time after this, preparations were made for the marriage of Henri and Marie—such preparations as the time and place allowed. There was now neither inclination nor opportunity for a fête, such as would have graced the nuptials of Marie de Lescure at a happier time; she now neither desired, nor could have endured it. Father Jerome had promised to perform the ceremony; Agatha would be her bridesmaid; and her brother and her father-in-law, both on their sick couches, would be her wedding-guests. Still she was happy and cheerful; she loved Henri Larochejaquelin with her whole heart, the more probably on account of the dangers through which they had already passed together, and she had firmly resolved to endure, without complaining, those which were still before them.

Two days before the ceremony was to take place, Chapeau came up to his master, as they were together leaving the quarters of some of the troops, and with a very serious face, begged permission to speak to him. Now, as it usually happened that Chapeau passed a considerable portion of the day talking to his master in a most unconstrained way, on every conceivable subject, Henri felt sure that something very much out of the common way was going to be said; however, he at once gave the desired permission.

"And Monsieur is positively going to be married on Wednesday morning?" commenced Chapeau.

"Why you know as well as myself that I am," said Henri.

"Oh, of course, yes—of course I know it, as Monsieur has been condescending enough to tell me; and will Madame, that is Mademoiselle as she is at present, go with Monsieur to Granville."

"What the deuce are you about, Chapeau, with all this rhodomontade? didn't I tell you that she would go with me."

"And the other ladies, Mademoiselle Agatha and Madame de Lescure, they will remain in Laval?"

"Yes, they will remain in Laval with my father and M. de Lescure: but you know all that already, as well as I do."

"But Madame de Larochejaquelin, that is, when she is Madame, she will want some young woman to attend her. Madame, of course, cannot go to Granville without some decent female to be near her; of course it will be quite impossible, will it not, Monsieur?"

"Now, Chapeau, tell me at once what you are coming to, and don't pretend to be so considerate and modest. You know that it is arranged that your own fiancée, Annot Stein, should accompany my wife."

"Yes—but, M. Henri, Annot Stein has some scruples; or rather—"

"Scruples! Oh, by all means, let her stay behind then. I'll have no one with me who has any scruples; tell her to stay with her father. I'll speak to Mademoiselle de Lescure."

"But Monsieur is in such a hurry," said Chapeau, who had not the slightest intention to have the matter arranged in this way. "I was wrong to say that Annot has scruples; indeed she hasn't got any—not one at all—it is I that have them."

"You! Now, Chapeau, may I ask the particular favour of you, to let me know at once, what you mean to ask of me?"

"Why, you see, M. Henri, Annot is a poor lone girl, quite unprotected as any one may say, though, of course, she will not be unprotected, when she will have the protection of Monsieur and Madame; but still she is a poor lone girl, and as such, she won't have the—the—the what d'ye call it, you know, which she would have as a married woman—the confidence and station, you know: she wouldn't be half so useful to Madame; and, therefore, perhaps,

Monsieur will think that she and I had better be married at the same time as Madame."

Chapeau had it all his own way; his arguments were unanswerable; and as no good reason could be given, why a wife would not be as serviceable to the man as it was to the master, it was agreed that they both should be married on the same day, at the same hour, in the same room, and by the same priest. The honour of this was almost too much for poor Annot, and quite upset her father, Michael Stein, who did not at all like the idea of not having his own way, after his own fashion, at his own only daughter's wedding. However, he was ultimately reconciled to the melancholy grandeur of the ceremony, by arrangements which were made for some substantial evening comfort below stairs; and although no banquet was prepared for the wedding of the master and the mistress, the valet and the lady's maid were as well provided, as though they had been united in peaceful times, and in a quiet church.

And now the sun had risen brightly on the morning which was to add another care to those which already burthened the shoulders of Henri Larochejaquelin. They all sat down together and ate their quiet breakfast in the parlour, to which a fortnight's habitation had now accustomed them. Henri wore no bridal dress. He had on the uniform of a Vendean officer, and round his waist was fastened a white scarf with a black knot, the distinguishing mark which he now bore of his rank in the army as Commander-in-Chief. Marie de Lescure was dressed in white, but her dress was as simple and unadorned as it could be well made; no bride, young, beautiful, and noble was ever prepared for the altar with less costly care, with less attention to the generally acknowledged proprieties of hymeneal decoration. Agatha and Madame de Lescure had in no respect altered their usual attire. It may easily be understood that leaving their homes in the manner they had done, they had not brought with them a full wardrobe; and since their arrival in Laval, they had had more pressing cares than that of supplying it.

De Lescure was daily getting weaker; but still the weaker he got the less he suffered, and the more capable he became of assuming his accustomed benevolent demeanour and anxious care for others. Both he and his wife knew that he was approaching the term of his mortal sufferings; but others, and among them Henri was the most sanguine, still hoped that he would recover; and there certainly was nothing in his cheery manner On the morning of the wedding, to make any one think that such hopes were misplaced. The old Marquis was more sad and melancholy than he had used to be among his beloved birds and cherry trees at Durbellière; and, on this occasion, he was probably the saddest of the party, for he was the one who would have rejoiced the most that the wedding of his son should be an occasion of joy to relatives, servants, tenants, and the numerous neighbours among whom he had always lived with so much mutual affection.

The most singular figure of the whole party was Father Jerome, the Curé of St. Laud's. He still wore the same long grey coat in which he was first introduced to the reader at Durbellière; which had since that time figured at Saumur and many another scene of blood and violence, and which we last saw when he was found by Madame de Lescure in the chapel at Genet. It had now been so patched and darned, that its oldest friends could not have recognized it. But Father Jerome still maintained that it was good enough for the ordinary run of his present daily duties, though he jocosely apologized to Marie for appearing, on such an occasion, in so mean a garment.

As soon as the breakfast was over, the table on which it had been eaten, was converted into a rude altar, and the ceremony was commenced. Jacques Chapeau and Annot, whose turn was immediately to follow, stood close up to the table, opposite to their master and mistress; but Michael Stein and his two sons, who of course were to be present at Annot's marriage, and who had prepared to seat themselves on the stairs till their presence should be required, had also been invited to attend; and they now sat but very ill at their ease, on three chairs, in the very farthest corner of the room. Michael Stein, though chance had thrown him among the loyal Vendeans, had in his heart but little of that love and veneration for his immediate superiors, which was the strong and attractive point in the character of the people of Poitou. Though he had lived all his life in the now famous village of Echanbroignes, he had in his disposition, much of the stubborn self-dependence of the early republicans; and he did not relish his position, sitting in the background as a humble hanger-on in the family of a nobleman and an aristocrat. He was, however, unable to help himself; his sons were Vendeans; his daughter was just going to marry the confidential follower of the Vendean Commander-in-Chief; and he himself had been seen fighting for La Vendée: there he sat, therefore, quiet, though hardly happy, between his two stalwart sons, with his thin hair brushed over his forehead, and his huge swarthy hands crossed on his knees before him.

The marriage ceremonies were soon performed: and then Henri and Chapeau, each in their turn, led their brides from the altar; and all went on as quietly in the one room which they occupied, as though nothing beyond their daily occupations had occurred.

"God bless you, my children!" said the old Marquis, "this is but a sad wedding; but it is useless to regret the happy times which are gone, it seems for ever."

"Not for ever, father," said Marie, kissing the old man's face, "Henri and I still look forward to having our wedding fete; perhaps in Paris—perhaps in dear La Vendée, when we shall once more be able to call our old homes our own; then we will make you, and Agatha, and Victorine, make up fivefold for all that has been omitted now. Will we not, Henri?"

Below stairs, Chapeau and Annot, wisely thinking that no time was like the present, endeavoured to be as gay as they would have been had they enjoyed their marriage-feast in the smith's own cottage; one or two of Chapeau's friends were asked on the occasion, and among them, Plume condescended to regale himself though the cheer was spread in the kitchen instead of in the parlour. Michael, now relieved from the presence of aristocracy, eat and drank himself into good humour; and even received, with grim complacency, the jokes of his Sons, who insisted on drinking to his health as a new recruit to the famous regiment which was drawn from the parish of Echanbroignes.

"Well, my girl, may heaven take care of you!" said he, kissing his daughter, "and of you too, Jacques," and he extended the caress to his son-in-law. "I won't say but what I wish you were a decent shoe-maker, or—"

"Oh, laws, father," said Annot, "I'm sure I should never have had him, if he had been."

"The more fool you, Annot; but I wish it all the same; and that Annot had had a couple of cows to mind, and half-a-dozen pigs to look after; but it's too late to think of that now; they'll soon have neither a cow nor a pig in La Vendée; and they'll want neither smiths nor shoemakers; however, my boy, God bless you! God bless you! ladies and gentlemen, God bless you all!" and then the smith completed the work he had commenced, and got as tipsy as he could have done, had his daughter been married in Poitou.

CHAPTER XIII.
CONCLUSION.

We have told our tale of La Vendée; we have married our hero and our heroine; and, as is usual in such cases, we must now bid them adieu. We cannot congratulate ourselves on leaving them in a state of happy prosperity, as we would have wished to have done; but we leave them with high hopes and glorious aspirations. We cannot follow the Vendeans farther in their gallant struggle, but we part from them, while they still confidently expect that success which they certainly deserved, and are determined to deserve that glory, which has since been so fully accorded to them.

In the foregoing pages much fiction has been blended with history, but still the outline of historical facts has been too closely followed to allow us now to indulge the humanity of our readers by ascribing to the friends we are quitting success which they did not achieve, or a state of happiness which they never were allowed to enjoy. It would be easy to speak of the curly haired darlings, two of course, who blessed the union of Henri Larochejaquelin and Marie de Lescure; and the joy with which they restored their aged father to the rural delights of his château at Durbellière. We might tell of the recovery of that modern Paladine, Charles de Lescure, and of the glorious rebuilding of the house of Clisson, of the ecclesiastical honours of Father Jerome, and of the happy marriage, or with more probability, the happier celibacy of the divine Agatha. But we cannot do so with propriety: facts, stern, untoward, cruel facts, stare us in the face, and would make even the novelist blush, were he, in total disregard of well-thumbed history, to attempt so very false a fiction.

Still it is necessary that something should be said of the subsequent adventures of those with whom we have for a while been so intimate, some short word spoken of the manner in which they adhered to the cause which was so dear to them. We cannot leave them in their temporary sojourn at Laval, as though a residence there was the goal of their wishes, the end of their struggle, the natural and appropriate term of their story; but as, unfortunately, their future career was not a happy one, we will beg the reader to advance with us at once over many years; and then, as he looks back upon La Vendée, through the softening vista of time, the melancholy termination of its glorious history will be less painful.

On the 7th July, 1815, the united English and Prussian armies marched into Paris, after the battle of Waterloo, and took military possession of the city. It was a remarkable but grievous day for Paris; the citizens generally stayed within their houses, and left the streets to the armed multitude, whom they could not regard as friends, and with whom they were no longer able to contend as enemies. In spite of the enthusiasm with which Napoleon was greeted in Paris on his return from Elba, there were very many royalists resident in the city; men, who longed to welcome back to France the family of the Bourbons, and to live again beneath the shelter and shade of an ancient throne. But even these could not greet with a welcome foreigners, who by force had taken possession of their capital. It was a sad and gloomy day in Paris, for no man knew what would be the fate, either of himself or of his country: shops were closed, and trade was silenced; the clanking of arms and the jingling of spurs was heard instead of the busy hum of busy men.

On the evening of this day, a stout, fresh-coloured, good-looking woman, of about forty years of age, was sitting in a perruquier's shop, at the corner of the Rue St. Honoré and the Rue St. Denis, waiting for the return of her husband, who had been called upon to exercise his skill on the person of some of the warriors with whom Paris was now crowded. The shutters of the little shop were up, as were those of all the houses in the street, and the place was therefore dark and triste; and the stout, good-looking woman within was melancholy and somewhat querulous. A daughter, of about twenty years of age, the exact likeness of her mother, only twenty years less stout, and twenty years more pretty, sat with her in the shop, and patiently listened to her complaints.

"Well, Annot," she said, "I wonder at your father. He had a little spirit once, but it has all left him now. Had he been said by me, he wouldn't have raised a bit of steel over an English chin for the best day's hire that ever a man was paid—unless, indeed, it was to cut the fellow's throat!"

"If he didn't, mother, another would; and what's the good of throwing away their money?"

"No matter—it's a coward's work to go and shave one's country's enemies. Do you think he'd have shaved any of the blues' officers in La Vendée twenty years ago, for all the money they could have offered him? He'd have done it with a sword, if he had done it at all. Well, I suppose it's all right! I suppose he's only fit to use a razor now."

"But you always say those were horrid days in La Vendée; that you had nothing to eat, and no bed to sleep in, nor shoes to your feet; and that you and father couldn't get married for ever so long, because of the wars?"

"So they were horrid days. I don't think any one will live to see the like again. But still, one don't like to see a man, who once had a little spirit, become jacky to every one who has a dirty chin to be scraped. Oh, Annot, if you'd seen the men there were in La Vendée, in those days; if you'd seen the great Cathelineau, you would have seen a man."

After having read this conversation, no one will be surprised to hear that on the board over the shop window, the following words, in yellow letters, were decently conspicuous:

JACQUES CHAPEAU,

PERRUQUIER.

Madame Chapeau was now disturbed in her unreasonable grumbling by a knock at the closed door, and on her opening it, an officer in undress uniform, about fifty years of age, politely greeted her, and asked her if that was not the house of M. Jacques Chapeau. From his language, the visitor might at first have been taken for a Frenchman; his dress, however, plainly told that he belonged to the English army.

"Yes, Monsieur, this is the humble shop of Chapeau, perruquier," said our old friend, the elder Annot, who, in spite of her feelings of hostility to the English, was somewhat mollified by the politeness and handsome figure of her visitor: she then informed him that Chapeau was not at home; that she expected him in immediately; and that his assistant, who was, in some respects, almost as talented as his master, was below, and would wait upon Monsieur immediately; and she rang a little bell, which was quickly responded to by some one ascending from a lower region.

The visitor informed Madame Chapeau that he had not called at present as a customer, but that he had taken the liberty to intrude himself upon her for the purpose of learning some facts of which, he was informed, her husband could speak with more accuracy than any other person in Paris.

"It is respecting the battles of La Vendée," said he, "that I wish to speak to him. I believe that he saw more of them than any person now alive."

Madame Chapeau was considering within herself whether there would be any imprudence in confessing to the English officer the important part her husband had played in La Vendée, when the officer's question was answered by another person, whose head and shoulders now dimly appeared upon the scene.

These were the head and shoulders of Chapeau's assistant, who had been summoned from his own region by the sound of his mistress's bell; the stairs from this subterranean recess did not open on to any passage, but ascended at once abruptly into the shop, so that the assistant, when called on, found himself able to answer, and to make even a personal appearance, as far as his head was concerned, without troubling himself to mount the three or four last stairs. From this spot he was in the habit of holding long conversations with his master and mistress; and now perceiving that neither the head nor chin of the strange gentleman were to be submitted to his skill, he arrested his steps, and astonished the visitor by a voice which seemed to come out of the earth.

Indeed he did, Monsieur, more than any one now alive—more even than myself, and that is saying a great deal. Jacques Chapeau was an officer high in command through the whole Vendean war; and I, even I, humble as I am now, I also was thought not unworthy to lead brave men into battle. I, Monsieur, am Auguste Plume; and though now merely a perruquier's poor assistant, I was once the officer second in command in the army of La Petite Vendée.

The gentleman turned round and gazed at the singular apparition, which the obscurity of the shop only just permitted him to distinguish. Auguste Plume was now above sixty years old, and completely bald; his face was thin, lanternjawed, and cadaverous; and his eyes, which were weak with age, were red and bleared; still he had not that ghastly, sick appearance, which want both of food and rest had given him in the glorious days to which he alluded: after the struggle in La Vendée, he had lived for some time a wretched life, more like that of a beast than a man; hiding in woods, living on roots, and hunting with the appetite of a tiger after the blood of stray republicans; his wife and children had perished in Carrier's noyades in the Loire; he himself had existed through two years of continued suffering, with a tenacity of life which almost reached to a miracle. He had joined the Chouans, and had taken an active part in the fiercest of their fierce acts of vengeance. But he had lived through it all; and now, in his old age, he had plenty and comfort; yet he looked back with a fond regret to the days of his imagined glory and power; he spoke with continual rapture of his own brave achievements, and regretted that he had not been allowed to continue a life, the miseries of which it would be impossible to exaggerate.

"Bah, Auguste," said his mistress; "the gentleman does not care to hear of your La Petite Vendée; it is of M. Henri—that is, of the young Marquis de Larochejaquelin, and of Madame and of Mademoiselle Agatha, and of M. de Lescure, and of Charette, and the Prince de Talmont, that Monsieur will want to hear!"

The stranger was in the act of explaining that the hostess was right in her surmise, when the master of the house himself returned. In spite of what he had suffered, years had sat lightly on Chapeau, as they had done on his wife. He was now a fat, good-humoured, middle-aged, comfortable man, who made the most, in his trade, of the éclat which attended him, as having been the faithful servant of the most popular among the Vendean leaders. He never wearied his customers with long tales of his own gallantry; he even had the unusual tact to be able to sink himself, in speaking, as he was often invited to do, of the civil war: he was known to have been brave, faithful, and loyal, and he was accordingly very popular among the royalists of Paris, who generally preferred his scissors and razors to those of any other artist in the city.

The officer, who was now seated in the shop, his wife and daughter, and his assistant, began at once to explain to him the service which he was required to perform; and Chapeau, bowing low to the compliments which the stranger paid to him, declared with his accustomed mixture of politeness and frank good nature, that he would be happy to tell anything that he knew.

The gentleman explained, that in his early years he had known de Lescure intimately; that he had met Larochejaquelin in Paris, and that he had made one of a party of Englishmen, who had done their best to send arms, money, and men from his own country into La Vendée. Chapeau was too well bred to allude to the disappointment which they had all so keenly felt, from the want of that very aid; he merely bowed again, and said that he would tell Monsieur all he knew.

And so he did. From the time when Henri Larochejaquelin left Laval for Granville, nothing prospered with the Vendeans; the army, as it was agreed, had left that place for Granville, and their first misfortune had been the death of de Lescure.

"He died in Laval?" asked the officer.

"No," said Chapeau. "When the moment for starting came, he insisted on being carried with the army; he followed us in a carriage, but the jolting of the road was too much for him—the journey killed him. He died at Fougères, on the third day after we left Laval."

"And Madame?" asked the stranger.

"It is impossible for me now," said Chapeau, "to tell you all the dangers through which she passed, all the disguises which she had to use, and the strange adventures which for a long time threatened almost daily to throw her in the hands of those who would have been delighted to murder her; but of course you know that she escaped at last."

"I am told that she still lives in Poitou, and I think I heard that, some years after M. de Lescure's death, she married M. Louis Larochejaquelin."

"She did so—the younger brother of my own dear lord. He was a boy in England during our hot work in La Vendée."

"Yes; and he served in an English regiment."

"So I had heard, Monsieur; but you know, don't you, that he also has now fallen."

"Indeed no!—for years and years I have heard nothing of the family."

"It was only two months since: he fell last May at the head of the Vendeans, leading them against the troops which the Emperor sent down there. The Vendeans could not endure the thoughts of the Emperor's return from Elba. M. Louis was the first to lift his sword, and Madame is, a second time, a widow. Poor lady, none have suffered as she has done!" He then paused a while in his narrative, but as the stranger did not speak, he continued: "but of M. Henri, of course, Monsieur, you heard the fate of our dear General?"

"I only know that he perished, as did so many hundred others, who were also so true and brave."

"I will tell you then," said Chapeau, "for I was by him when he died; he fell, when he was shot, close at my feet: he never spoke one word, or gave one groan, but his eyes, as they closed for the last time, looked up into the face of one—one who, at any rate, loved him very well," and Chapeau took a handkerchief from a little pocket in his wife's apron, and applied it to his eyes.

"Yes," he continued, "when the bullet struck him, I was as near to him as I am to her," and he put his hand to his wife's head. "It might have been me as well as him, only for the chance. I'll tell you how the manner of it was. You know how we all strove to cross back into La Vendée, first at Angers and afterwards at Ancenis; and how M. Henri got divided from the army at Ancenis. Well, after that, the Vendean army was no more; the army was gone, it had melted away; the most of those who were still alive were left in Brittany, and they joined the Chouans. Here is my friend, Auguste, he was one of them."

"Indeed I was, Monsieur, for a year and eight months."

"Never mind now, Auguste, you can tell the gentleman by and bye; but, as I was saying, M. Henri was left all but alone on the southern bank of the river—there were, perhaps, twenty with him altogether—not more; and there were as many hundreds hunting those twenty from day to day."

"And you were one of them, Chapeau?"

"I was, Monsieur. My wife here remained with her father in Laval; he was a crafty man, and he made the blues believe he was a republican; but, bless you, he was as true a royalist all the time as I was. Well, there we were, hunted, like wolves, from one forest to another, till about the middle of winter, we fixed ourselves for a while in the wood of Vesins, about three leagues to the east of Cholet, a little to the south of the great road from Saumur. From this place M. Henri harassed them most effectually; about fifty of the old Vendeans had joined him, and with these he stopped their provisions, interrupted their posts, and on one occasion, succeeded in getting the despatches from Paris to the republican General. We were at this work for about six weeks; and he, as he always did, exposed himself to every possible danger. One morning we came upon two republican grenadiers; there were M. Henri, two others and myself there, and we wanted immediately to fire upon them; but M. Henri would not have it so; he said that he would save them, and rushed forward to bid them lay down their arms; as he did so, the foremost of them fired, and M. Henri fell dead without a groan."

"And the two men—did they escape?"

"No, neither of them," said Chapeau; and for a moment, a gleam of savage satisfaction flashed across his face; "the man who fired the shot had not one minute spared him for his triumph; I had followed close upon my master, and I avenged him."

"And where was his young wife all this time?"

"She was with Madame de Lescure, in Brittany; and so was Mademoiselle Agatha; they were living disguised almost as peasants, at an old château called Dreneuf; after that they all escaped to Spain; they are both still alive, and now in Poitou; and I am told, that though they have not chosen absolutely to seclude themselves, they both pass the same holy life, as though they were within the walls of a convent."

It was long before Chapeau discontinued his narrative, but it is unnecessary for us to follow farther in the sad details which he had to give of the loss of the brave Vendean leaders. The Prince de Talinont, Charette, Stofflet, Marigny, all of them fell: "And yet," said Chapeau, with a boast, which evidently gave him intense satisfaction, "La Vendée was never conquered. Neither the fear of the Convention, nor the arms of the Directory, nor the strength of the Consul, nor the flattery of the Emperor could conquer La Vendée, or put down the passionate longing for the return of the royal family, which has always burnt in the bosom of the people. Revolt has never been put down in La Vendée, since Cathelineau commenced the war in St. Florent. The people would serve neither the republic nor the empire; the noblesse would not visit the court; their sons have refused commissions in the army, and their daughters have disdained to accept the hands of any, who had forgotten their allegiance to the throne. Through more than twenty years of suffering and bloodshed, La Vendée has been true to its colour, and now it will receive its reward."

Chapeau himself, however, more fortunate, though not less faithful, than his compatriots, had not been obliged to wait twenty years for his reward; he owned, with something like a feeling of disgrace, that he had been carrying on his business in Paris, for the last fifteen years, with considerable success and comfort to himself; and he frankly confessed, that he had by practice inured himself to the disagreeable task of shaving, cutting and curling beards and heads, which were devoted to the empire; "but then, Monsieur," said he apologizing for his conduct, "there was a great difference you know between them and republicans."

Five-and-thirty years have now passed, since Chapeau was talking, and the Vendeans triumphed in the restoration of Louis XVIII to the throne of his ancestors. That throne has been again overturned; and, another dynasty having intervened, France is again a Republic.

How long will it be before some second La Vendée shall successfully, but bloodlessly, struggle for another re-establishment of the monarchy? Surely before the expiration of half a century since the return of Louis, France will congratulate herself on another restoration.